Evita, Inevitably

D1603370

Evita, Inevitably

Performing Argentina's Female Icons
Before and After Eva Perón

Jean Graham-Jones

THE UNIVERSITY OF MICHIGAN PRESS · ANN ARBOR

Copyright © by the University of Michigan 2014
All rights reserved

Published in the United States of America by
The University of Michigan Press
Manufactured in the United States of America
⊗ Printed on acid-free paper

2017   2016   2015   2014   4   3   2   1

A CIP catalog record for this book is available from the British Library.
ISBN 978-0-472-07233-0 (hardcover : alk. paper)
ISBN 978-0-472-05233-2 (pbk. : alk. paper)

ISBN 978-0-472-12055-0 (e-book)

Contents

Acknowledgments   vii

Introduction: Evita at the Intersections of
Argentine Femiconicity, Nation, and Performance   1

One   Camila O'Gorman and the Making of an Argentine Femicon   15

Two   The (Many, Many) Lives of Eva Perón   60

Three   Performing Evita's Afterlives   98

Four   Argentine Madonnas, Pop Stars, and
Performances of Immediacy and Virtuality   132

Conclusion: Toward a Complicated Understanding of
Eva Perón and Argentine Femiconicity in Performance   166

Notes   179

Index   249

Acknowledgments

This book has gestated for so long that my first graduate research assistant is now a tenured associate professor. I have many people to thank for assisting me on the way.

My initial debt of gratitude is to Florida State University and the CUNY Graduate Center for supporting my research trips and writing. My CUNY colleagues warmly received me into their culture of intellectual exchange, for which I thank especially Glenn Burger, Marvin Carlson, Mario DiGangi, José del Valle, Frank Hentschker, Judith Milhous, David Savran, Lía Schwartz, Pamela Sheingorn, and the departed Daniel Gerould and Isaías Lerner. My thanks go as well to my former FSU colleagues, particularly Bill Cloonan, Terry Coonan, Roberto Fernández, Ray Fleming, Donna Nudd, Mark Pietralunga, Delia Poey, Rob Romanchuk, Lisa Wakamiya, and Lori Walters, in addition to Santa Arias, Jean Dangler, Laura Edmondson, Anita Gonzalez, Nancy Powers, and Shonna Trinch, now dispersed across the continent. My graduate students at both institutions played key roles in the development of this project, and I thank especially Noelia Díaz, Andy Goldberg, Gad Guterman, María Hernández Ojeda, Andrew Kircher, Dan Poston, Manuel Simons, Jennifer Thompson, Rosita Villagómez, and Kenn Watt. Former students and now colleagues working on Argentine performance and iconicity have influenced and enriched my thinking; special appreciation goes to Linell Ajello, Karina Carballo, Elisa Legon, Lindsay Livingston, Milton Loayza, Ana Martínez, David Rodríguez-Solás, Ruth Wikler-Luker, and Laura Williams. I am grateful to Lynette Gibson for shouldering the day-to-day during my time as program head.

The Freie Universität's International Research Center "Interweaving Performance Cultures," directed by Erika Fischer-Lichte and Gabriele Brandstetter, provided me that rare luxury of space and time to reflect and write. I am particularly indebted to Christel Weiler and her team (especially Antje, Armin, Claudia, Holger, and Torsten) and to my other fellows for their stimulating observations: Gastón Alzate, Rustom Bharucha, Peter Eckersall, Friederike Felbeck, Helen Gilbert, Katherine Mezur, Margaret Werry, and Phillip Zarrilli. Thanks to Hedda Kage for providing a home away from home.

This book would simply not exist without my extended Buenos Aires community of friends, artists, and scholars, and while I wish I could specify the many contributions of each, space limits me to listing them by name: Daniel Altamiranda, Lola Arias, Cristina Banegas, the entire Silvia Cañaveral-Aníbal Ilguisonis clan, Ana María Casó, Beatriz Catani, Jorge Dubatti, Cristina Escofet, Mempo Giardinelli, Andrew Graham-Yooll, Federico León, Raúl Liberotti and Catalina Mangialavori, Julio López and Roberto Piñeiro, Claudia Mazza, Ricardo Monti, Osvaldo Pellettieri (qepd), Shoshana Polanco, Sandra Ribotta and Ricardo Tagger, Martín Rodríguez, Eduardo Rovner, Beatriz Seibel, Paula Simkin, Rafael Spregelburd and Isol, Claudio Tolcachir and the Timbre 4 gang, Beatriz Trastoy, Luisa Valenzuela, Daniel Veronese, and China Zorrilla. I thank the staff members at the Archivo General de la Nación, the Biblioteca Nacional, and especially Argentores for access to their archives.

I also wish to acknowledge the support and friendship of fellow *latinoamericanistas* scattered throughout the Americas: David W. Foster, Paola Hernández, Jorge Huerta, Jill Lane, Gerardo Luzuriaga, Sirena Pellarolo, Michael Schuessler, Tamara Underiner, Adam Versényi, Brenda Werth, and Patricia Ybarra. My thanks to more than one of you for accompanying me to all those Evita shows!

Many of the ideas here were tested at various meetings of the International Federation for Theatre Research, the American Society for Theatre Research, Performance studies International, and Latin American Theatre Today. I thank particularly Barbara Grossman, James Harding, Brian Herrera, Michal Kobialka, Janelle Reinelt, Nick Salvato, Mike Sell, and Stacy Wolf for vital feedback at critical moments in this process.

LeAnn Fields, senior editor at the University of Michigan Press, has been instrumental in not only seeing the book through production but helping it achieve final shape. I thank her, the entire Michigan team, and the two anonymous readers for their feedback and generous suggestions.

Thank you, Brian, for your unfaltering love and steady support, no matter how challenging that can prove to be. And I send my heartfelt gratitude to anyone who ever said "that sounds like a fascinating project," or "what a fabulous idea for a book," or "I can't wait to read it"—and kept me going over the past long decade. Finally, this book is dedicated to the memory of two individuals who shaped me in ways I cannot come close to expressing: my mentor and dear friend, George Woodyard, and my much-loved father, Dan Graham. I miss you every day.

EARLIER VERSIONS OF a few sections of this book have been published as "'The truth is . . . my soul is still with you': Documenting a Tale of Two Evitas," *Theatre Survey* 46, no. 1 (May 2005): 67–78, and "La Pista 4's *Cadáveres*: Radiophonics and the Argentinean Staging of Disappearance," *Latin American Theatre Review* 42, no. 2 (Spring 2009): 5–13. I thank these publishers for permission to reprint these essays here in altered form.

Introduction

Evita at the Intersections of Argentine
Femiconicity, Nation, and Performance

As I sat in Manhattan's darkened IFC Center theatre on a blustery January afternoon waiting for Steven Soderbergh's bio-epic *Che* to begin its four-hour-plus journey, I reflected on my personal attraction to what were once called "lives." Drawn to historical fiction since a young child, to this day I have a hard time passing up literary and pop-cultural biographies, and they're typically in the mix of books piled beside my bed. I'm obviously not alone: famous and not-so-famous Johnsons continue to seek and find their Boswells; biopics are made and remade (Soderbergh's is only one of some twenty films based on the life of Ernesto Guevara[1]); lives are told and retold in bestselling books; and astounding numbers of fan websites, blogs, and Facebook pages, not to mention the success of reality television and Twitter, perhaps most persuasively attest to our society's ongoing absorption with the lives of the rich and/or famous in a world where seemingly each one of us is an icon in potentia if not in fact. And so I found myself in New York, awaiting yet one more biographical take on the doomed Argentine-Cuban revolutionary.

Like Che, her compatriot and frequent transnational partner in performance, Eva Perón commands, more than sixty years after her death, a popular fascination that exceeds the borders of her native Argentina. As a Brazilian tourist's photo documents, the two are often positioned side by side in effigy even though they never met.

Latin American literature scholar Nina Gerassi-Navarro points out

Figure 1: Evita and Che, greeting tourists in the Buenos Aires neighborhood of La Boca. Photo by "Agua," posted on Flickr (17 April 2008), http://www.flickr.com/photos/maisagua/3702379207/. Courtesy of the photographer.

that both Che and Evita underwent iconographic transformation in the 1990s, as versions of their lives and images exploded onto the transnational scene: "[F]rom England to Japan, everyone felt entitled to reproduce, to appropriate these two legendary figures. At the same time, as a consequence of this transnational appropriation, both Evita and Che have been depoliticized of their political and historical capital in order to be reaffirmed as commercial icons."[2] The actress-turned-second-wife of Argentine president Juan Perón (1895–1974), Eva Perón lived only thirty-three years (1919–1952). Yet notwithstanding Gerassi-Navarro's concerns about Evita's depoliticization in the late twentieth-century transnational marketplace, Evita's capital—commercial, social, symbolic, historical, *and* political—has only increased since her untimely death. Sociologist Javier Auyero provides evidence that, as recently as the 1990s, Peronism's many local female political bosses still "performed" Evita, not simply by dying their hair blonde but by embodying "the way a woman should behave if she is going to be a public, Peronist woman."[3] Just as the so-called Evita effect continues to be ascribed to U.S. and Argentine presidential politics alike,[4] her rags-to-riches-to-ravaging story remains in near-constant circulation in film, theatre, and music. Eva's life has been told in practically every book format, including Perón-approved children's editions and U.S. Scholastic books.[5] An intrinsic component of twenty-first-century Buenos Aires's burgeoning international travel industry are the Evita tours that take the visiting tourist to the train station of her big-city arrival; the presidential palace; the site of the Eva Perón Foundation (and today the National University of Buenos Aires's Engineering School); the church where she married Perón; her only Buenos Aires statue and her newly installed murals; her burial place in the Duarte family's Recoleta Cemetery mausoleum; and the recently created Evita Museum, "where you will really penetrate the heart of the 'mother' of the desperate and abandoned."[6] Long before her resurrection at the hands of Hollywood, Disney, Madonna, the Simpsons, and Lady Gaga,[7] Eva Perón was being performed in Argentina, on balconies, in the theatre, on tour buses, at the movies, in books, and on television. Her images continue to be resuscitated and recycled in a seemingly endless series of attempts at discovering the "essence" of the Evita enigma—often summed up in that impossible question, "Who was the 'real' Eva Perón?"

On all these stages, national and transnational iconography of Eva Perón has tended to alternate between sensationalized images of sanctified martyr and sensationalized images of demonized fraud. We scholars have not remained untouched; critical Evitamania often approaches a politics of personal identification (to which even such respected Perón experts as Julie Taylor have been susceptible, as inferred from her memoir-cultural reflection, *Paper Tangos*[8]), and only rarely does the discussion move beyond questions of "was she or wasn't she?" or "did she or didn't she?" Conjectures and truth-claims quickly consolidate into myths taken as truth, individual lives are rendered legendary, and scholarship sinks back into the quagmire of easy polarizations. This book proposes to use the tools of discursive, visual, and performance analysis as a way out of the polarizing, personalized impasse in which most Evita scholarship and cultural production have so often found themselves stalled.

In order to dislodge this critical and artistic deadlock, I attempt a broader view: while placing Evita artistic iconography at the center of my study, I qualify and question this very centrality by providing a larger context for the performance of female iconicity in and outside Argentina, before and after the historical Eva Perón. This book thus takes into additional consideration the many performances inspired by other Argentine female icons: Camila O'Gorman, the young woman who scandalized mid-nineteenth-century Argentina by eloping with her confessor-priest and was punished by execution, and popular devotional figures such as nineteenth-century legend "Difunta" Correa and recently deceased cumbia-pop performer Gilda, as well as the country's patron saint, the Virgin of Luján. Casting a purposefully broad historical, cultural, and artistic net to include theatrical performances from the late nineteenth, twentieth, and early twenty-first centuries in conjunction with films, novels, poems, (auto)biographies, legends, prayer cards, sculptures, and paintings, as well as blogs, photologs, and social networks, I document the many ways in which these Argentine "femicons" have been and continue to be staged.

WHEN CONSIDERING THE myriad performances of historical entities like Eva Perón, we should bear in mind that the staged historical body is reconstructed during what Freddie Rokem calls a "secondary elaboration" or re-doing.[9] The historical body-as-staged thus easily lends itself to discussions of surrogation and effigy, and in the process provides me an initial theoretical entry-point into the work of iconicity—and its popular cultural relations, myth and celebrity—in the Argentine femiconic performances studied in this book. In referring to the many cultural representations discussed here as "performances," I hold to Joseph Roach's idea of performance as a substitute that attempts both to embody and to replace a preexisting entity.

With these preliminary considerations in mind, allow me to approach the term "femicon" through its root, "icon," a word so overused today that it means practically everything and nothing. In a recent book on icons, Martin Kemp takes pains to define his widely circulating subjects: "An iconic image is one that has achieved wholly exceptional levels of widespread recognizability and has come to carry a rich series of varied associations for very large numbers of people across time and cultures, such that it has to a greater or lesser degree transgressed the parameters of its initial making, function, context, and meaning."[10] Kemp does not stray far from the Greek *eikon* (image or portrait); among his examples are Christ, DNA, Da Vinci's *Mona Lisa*, and Alberto Korda's famous photograph of Che.[11] Yet even the visual image is not so easily categorized as simply iconic (or indexical, the other semiological tag frequently attached to the visual). As W.J.T. Mitchell prompted us decades ago, images themselves are "something like an actor on the historical stage, a presence or character endowed with legendary status, a history that parallels and participates in the stories we tell ourselves."[12] Paralleling and participating histories; images functioning as actors: icon's agentive status is even further complicated in today's usage, where the term is employed to refer both to the historical person or object and to circulating representations of that person or object.[13] Such complexities of application are found in Sarah M. Misemer's extended study of the four Latin American "secular saints" Carlos Gardel, Frida Kahlo, Selena, and Eva Perón. Misemer traces icon's move from orthodox Russian iconography, as a "medium for communicating moral dogma," into later cultural, national, and political symbolic systems, largely through the modern technologies of photography and film.[14] In this examination of what she calls "double performances,"[15] Misemer studies her four historical subjects' own carefully created personae as well as the work of artists who went on to portray them.

Misemer's approach calls to mind Marvin Carlson's ghosting and Jacques Derrida's *hantise*, as well as Roach's embodied *and* replaced "surrogate." All have paved the way for a critical engagement with our contemporary concept of icons and/in performance.[16] Roach reminds us that effigy can be a verb: it bodies forth.[17] As effigying surrogates, icons perform a dual function—they are cultural agents *and* cultural products—and widely circulating, transnational icons create a referential mise en abyme. The Brazilian tourist photo posted on Flickr and reproduced above offers a useful illustration: two effigies, Che and Evita, stand on the balcony of one of many brightly painted buildings in the Buenos Aires working-class neighborhood (and tourist destination) of La Boca.[18] These surrogates themselves reference not only the historical persons they ostensibly represent but also the many photographic and filmic representations contained in our collective and individual documentary archives (Evita's pulled-back hairdo and raised arm, Che's beret and beard), as well as the many artistic portrayals of these two iconic figures. Finally, their reproduced photo in a Flickr tourist album and its possibilities of potentially infinite circulation suggest just how imbricated the two icons have become in Buenos Aires's tourist industry. Iconic images, like Internet memes, seem to take on self-perpetuating, haunting, and seemingly transcendent lives of their own.[19]

Nevertheless, and despite appearances to the contrary, icons are very personally, politically, historically, culturally, and generationally grounded, and that contextual ground is constantly shifting. We tend to be on a "first-name basis" with our icons, and our identification with them tends toward the intensely personal and even autobiographical. In their contribution to an academic essay collection on the Coen Brothers' film *The Big Lebowski*, Dennis Hall and Susan Grove Hall propose several common features of icons (even as they tend to elide individual and image), all of which are contextual:

1) "An icon [like Marilyn Monroe] often generates strong responses; people identify with it, or against it; and the differences often reflect generational differences";

2) "An icon stands for a group of related things and values [e.g., John Wayne as cowboy, representing a traditional masculinity or a politics of conservatism]"; and

3) "An icon [such as the U.S. log cabin] commonly has roots in historical sources . . . , often changing over time and reflecting present events or forces."[20]

I take Hall and Grove Hall's historicizing approach even farther in my study of Argentina's femicons. Icons are subjected to periodic or cyclical resuscitation and re-iconization, often in apparent response to or arising out of specific sociohistorical moments (as Gerassi-Navarro suggests in her earlier-cited statement regarding the 1990s transnationalization of Evita and Che). Such resuscitation and re-iconization, in the Argentine case, are intrinsic to the remarkable transformative ability, fluidity, and longevity of the femicon Eva Perón.

What Hall and Grove Hall qualify as the "culturally fluid" icon stands in uneasy and intersecting company with celebrity and myth.[21] To engage with these related terms, I draw inspiration from sources such as Michael L. Quinn's essay on celebrity and acting[22] and Chris Rojek's concepts of celebrity, celetoid, and celebrification.[23] While discussions of celebrity representation in popular and elite cultures have largely been constrained to film theory and criticism (initiated by Richard Dyer's influential 1979 monograph, *Stars*[24]), many of that discipline's sociological and signifying considerations—such as shifting cultural contexts, the celebrity industry, and the performing body—easily apply to live and other mediated performances.

Roland Barthes's concern over myth's depoliticizing power still holds validity for contemporary considerations of icons and iconicity.[25] Susan Hayward expands Barthes's pioneering work on the mythologizing process to point out three semiological levels at play in our viewing an iconic image of Marilyn Monroe: denotatively a photograph; connotatively associated—depending on the photo's context—with early Marilyn's star qualities or late Marilyn's "depression, drug-taking and untimely death";

and mythically understood "as activating the myth of Hollywood."[26] Undergirding the iconographic processes of Misemer's Latin American secular saints and Hayward's Hollywood diva is the idea that icons are created and thereby mediated; the icon cannot be separated from the technology producing it.

As with mythology, iconography runs the risk of confusing the created icon with its historical referent. Argentine historian Marysa Navarro, building upon Barthesian theory, cautions us about mistaking myth for the historical elements employed in the mythologizing process:

> In some cases, such as Evita's, the falsity of the construction [of the myth] can be demonstrated partially or completely, and nevertheless said construction can achieve such acceptance that it ends up being more powerful than the facts upon which it rests.
>
> Evita is an unquestionable example of how a person can be transformed into myth, and also an example of the power her mythology has had and continues to have.[27]

Icons are collectively made, unmade, and remade. Che's iconographer Michael Casey only slightly overstates (and problematically universalizes) the function of the icon—in his case (and Kemp's), Korda's endlessly reproduced 1960 photograph of the Argentine revolutionary in Havana—when he writes that it is "a repository for the collective pool of dreams, fears, beliefs, doubts, and desires that makes up the human condition."[28] Present in iconic performances and their reception is a shared ambivalent mythopoesis, in which our "historical" need to make the myth flesh runs up against our "critical" desire to demystify the flesh through mediation and appropriation.

Nowhere is that collective ambivalence more evident than in our relationship to celebrity. Chris Rojek terms celebrity "the attribution of glamorous or notorious status to an individual within the public sphere."[29] In Rojek's preliminary definition (which he expands and complicates over the course of his book-length study), we can immediately detect the presence of our own participation in what the author calls the "cultural fabrication" of celebrities, an activity that from the outset seems destined for the polarizing battles over, say, Evita's status as glamorous and/or notorious. Rojek's definition inaugurates another tension: the "split between a private self and a public self."[30] Roach's monographic study of "it"—the charisma, presence, sex appeal, magnetism, and moxie that seem essential to the celebrity-subject—takes this very tension as a point of departure. Indeed, Roach argues for a further requirement of tension within the performing subject: "It is the power of apparently effort-less embodiment of contradictory qualities simultaneously: strength *and* vulnerability, innocence *and* experience, and singularity *and* typicality among them."[31] Recent "democratization" of media has even more radi-cally altered how we engage with our icons. With digitalized information now produced by consumers and audiences (and not just the celebrity industry), a "user-subjectivity" has emerged to transform the relation-ship between icon and observer. In today's world, where anyone with a camera and a computer can become a YouTube star, what P. David Mar-shall calls a "new narcissism with the production of the self at the centre" has modified the "sources of our celebrity."[32] The iconizing process sus-tains its own contradictions.

Regina Janes invokes Peircean semiotics to express her own concerns regarding iconic celebrityhood: "When iconicity becomes celebrity, the principal casualty is Peirce's notion of an icon. An icon, Peirce tells us, signifies because of what it is in itself; it partakes of the character of its own dynamic image."[33] Whereas Peircean iconicity might suggest a sub-stitution approaching such completion that the distinction between "the real and the copy" falls away, I, like most of the other performance schol-ars I've cited, hold that iconic performances both resemble and paral-lel their objects. Iconic performances are, as Roach might say, "double-bodied."[34] Even more importantly, in today's world such embodiment and replacement operate often synchronously. Icon has become synony-mous with a sort of über-celebrity in what Janes terms seemingly infinite "versionings."

Janes titled her 2002 essay "Femicons." The portmanteau word en-joys multiple contemporary valences: as Japanese PlayStation game, manga-like graphic image, oral contraceptive brand, and shorthand for feminist—and sometimes simply female—icon, which is how Janes em-ploys the term. I understand femicon as referencing both female and feminist iconicity as well as participating in the larger cultural collective imaginary suggested in the other contemporary popular usages of the term. Gendering plays a determinant role in the iconic and iconographic performances of my subjects, and accordingly I build upon recent dis-cussions of representation and reconstruction of the female body as the site of national myth-making and iconography and of the performed construction of memory.[35] This book attempts to account for the many ways Argentine femicons have historically been and continue to be per-formed, often in service to a long-held idea of national and increasingly transnational mythology and/or celebrity but just as frequently reduced to the single iconic figure of Eva Perón.

OVER A DECADE AGO Argentine theatre historian Beatriz Seibel presented me with a list of "Eva Perón versions." Included in that initial roster were seven plays, three films, and two television programs, all of which (with one Uruguayan exception) were created in Argentina.[36] Today the list of plays has more than doubled in length and includes an invented encounter between Eva and South American Independence hero José de San Martín[37]; a live performance of a purported radio-play by 1990s troupe Pista 4; Evita's coffin carried onstage during post-dictatorship experimental cabaret group Gambas al Ajillo's final show; and even the fusion of Eva Perón with the Virgin Mary in Jaime Kogan's 1993 staging of Ricardo Monti's play *La oscuridad de la razón* [The Obscurity of Reason]. As recently as 2011, two new Argentine films were released—one, *Juan y Eva* [Juan and Eva], focuses on the Peróns' "love story"[38]; the other, *Eva de la Argentina* [Eva of Argentina, or Argentina's Eva],[39] the country's first animated "political" film, combines original graphics with historical photos and Evita's own recorded voice, all narrated by a character clearly based upon Rodolfo Walsh, the disappeared author of one of the best-known Eva-centered texts (though she is never mentioned by name in the short story).[40] Eva Perón's iconic images continue to reflect an apparently never-ending collective desire to know the historic woman, even as she is just as often employed—like the tango—as iconic shorthand for the "real Argentina," both within and outside the country.

While there is an enormous and easily overwhelming body of scholarship on Eva Perón, very few critics and historians have focused on the performative elements operating in artistic reconstructions of her life and death, and the limited existing performance analysis has been restricted to either Evita's own self-portrayals[41] or individual play and film criticism.[42] Book-length studies, in general, have ignored the wealth of stage performances. One case in point is Susana Rosano's 2006 *Rostros y máscaras de Eva Perón* [Eva Perón's Faces and Masks], which examines the literature and film produced about Evita from 1951 to 2003 but includes only one play (Copi's infamous *Eva Perón*, discussed at length in chapter three here). And while Misemer wisely dedicates her iconographic analysis to the above-named four "secular saints" of Latin America, only one of the four chapters focuses on Eva Perón and thus understandably cannot discuss in depth what the author terms "Evita's performing

body"—in life and in death—as holy relic and site for Argentina's continued political struggles. *Evita, Inevitably* is a necessary contribution to the
"new cultural history" of Peronism heralded in Matthew B. Karush's and
Oscar Chamosa's recent essay collection.[43] Albeit less abundant, scholarship about cultural representations of Camila O'Gorman's short life
has followed similar paths in overlooking the history of theatrical performance; and most scholarly work on Argentina's popular devotional
figures is sociological or hagiographical, with little or no metacritical reflection on the national mythologizing operating within these localized
venerations in a country where apparently, as one anonymous but presumably Argentine newspaper critic wrote, "anyone can be transmuted
into a messiah."[44] Simply put, there has not been a study—in either English or Spanish—that approaches this book's scope in bringing together
various Argentine female icons to examine how their multiple representations respond to and perpetuate often conflicting ideas of nation and
(trans) national identity.

I contend that the vacillation observed in cultural representations
of Eva Perón—typically, but not always, between Santa Evita and "that
woman"—points to a larger national (and, indeed, transnational) ambivalence and at times uncertainty regarding Evita and Argentina's
other femicons. While Eva Perón occupies this project's center as the
Argentine femicon with the greatest global cultural currency, she is by
no means the country's only femicon, and our understanding of the ambivalence that forms part of her lasting femiconic status is deepened by a
longer view. Thus this project moves chronologically through Argentine
cultural history, from the nineteenth century's earliest representations of
Camila O'Gorman's story and twentieth- and twenty-first-century reconstructions of Eva Perón's living body and cadaver, to recent Internet performances. Different and distinctive periods frame each chapter: chapter one refers to Argentina's history of dictatorship, which can be seen as
extending from the colonial period to the late twentieth century; chapter two engages with the historical weight of twentieth-century Peronism;
and chapters three and four grapple with recent crises—the 1990s, when
post-dictatorship Argentina embraced neoliberal globalized economics
and culture, with the disastrous result of 2001's socioeconomic crash and
the growing role of technology in what has euphemistically been called
the country's "Latin-Americanization." The book possesses an additional
logic of the iconographic process: it first looks at how an earlier historical figure is rendered mythological, then examines how conflicting national identity scripts are constructed during the life of a historical figure

only to see them deconstructed through posthumous effigy, and finally explores how iconicity is constructed and disseminated through virtual media.

Chapter one's subject is Camila O'Gorman, the mid-nineteenth-century bourgeoise executed for her rebellious behavior by orders from then-dictator Juan Manuel Rosas. O'Gorman's romantic elopement with her confessor-priest, Uladislao Gutiérrez, has frequently been reinterpreted as symbolic of youthful resistance in the face of authoritarian repression. After an initial, largely narratological examination of early Camila-inspired historiographic practices, observed in memoirs, historical accounts, and the first theatrical and film versions of her life, this chapter traces her impact on the Argentine national consciousness and her creation as a national femiconic figure by pairing different versions of her story, all created within the last forty years, some of the most difficult and violent in Argentina's history: Avant-garde poet Enrique Molina's 1973 novel, *Una sombra donde sueña Camila O'Gorman* [A Shadow where Camila O'Gorman is Dreaming]; Griselda Gambaro's 1982 play, *La malasangre* [Bad Blood]; María Luisa Bemberg's 1984 Oscar-nominated film, *Camila*; and Ricardo Monti's 1989 play, *Una pasión sudamericana* [A South American Passion-Play], restaged in the early twenty-first century together with an abbreviated version, *Finlandia* [Finland]. All these artistic versions of Camila O'Gorman's "tragic romance" (or, as I argue in the majority of cases, romantic tragedy) challenge easy distinctions between mythologizing and historiography, between fact and fiction. This initial chapter concludes with a reflection on Camila's problematic status as an icon still in the making.

It would appear that only unquestionably established "femicons" like Eva Perón can be transgressed or pluralized in wildly divergent representations and accounts. There, too, even Evita's myriad representations have not been without their controversies. Located at the core of my project, chapters two and three function as companion studies in which the mythologizing of Eva Perón and her many artistic reconstructions and deconstructions are examined. Chapter two, "The (Many, Many) Lives of Eva Perón," begins with a proposed alternative genealogy of Evita performances through the various national and international reconstructions of her lives as exemplified in two rock operas: Tim Rice and Andrew Lloyd Webber's 1978 *Evita* and Nacha Guevara's 1986 *Eva, el gran musical argentino* [Eva, the Great Argentine Musical]. This comparison introduces chapter two's discussion of the construction, rehearsal, and critique of the Evita "myths" through biographical narrative, film, and theatre. I first turn to four biographies (with Perón's own ghost-written autobiography, *La razón de mi vida* [My Mission in Life], hovering nearby) to examine how two key moments in Eva Perón's story are recounted and thus demonstrate how each published "life" contributes in its own way to an overarching historiographic construction and reification of a certain Evita "myth" (or multiple competing myths). The chapter continues its extended analysis by considering two recent films and three plays—all created after Argentina's return to democracy—that attempt to reconstruct Perón's life from five different generic vantage points: as quasi-documentary (Eduardo Mignogna's 1984 *Evita; quien quiera oír, que oiga* [Evita: listen if you want to]); as cautiously political feature film (Juan Desanzo's 1996 *Eva Perón*); as an overtly politicized Latin American play (Osvaldo Guglielmino's *Eva de América* [Eva of America], published in 1983 and staged in 1987); as a 1994 staging of Leónidas Lamborghini's Eva-dedicated poems, themselves a rewriting of her attributed autobiography (*Eva Perón en la hoguera* [Eva Perón on the Bonfire]); and as an imagined encounter between Eva Perón and her generally regarded political, cultural, and class enemy, Victoria Ocampo (Mónica Ottino's hugely popular play, *Eva y Victoria* [Eva and Victoria], premiering in 1992). The chapter concludes with a return to Nacha Guevara, the 2008 revival of *Eva, el gran musical argentino*, and a consideration of how the move between performing "as" Evita and "being" Evita operates onstage as well as within the larger context of a national politics that seems determined to conflate Eva with Argentina.

Chapter three, "Performing Evita's Afterlives," builds upon the previous chapter's analysis of the mythologizing process to examine the many performances of the Evita myth itself in what I argue to be a process of demythologization through surrogation. After first considering Evita's fetishized body-turned-corpse through various cultural phenomena, I turn to five theatrical productions—created within and outside Argentina—that overtly stage Perón's surrogated corpse in apparent response to a specific historical moment and its engagement with Evita-style Peronism: Copi's *Eva Perón*, whose 1970 Parisian premiere featuring a male actor in Evita drag caused controversy in France and Argentina, and whose two early twenty-first-century restagings in Buenos Aires provoked critical if not political discord; Mónica Viñao's 1998 *des/Enlace* [un/Link], in which the sole female character can be understood as both Evita and a *desaparecida*; and Buenos Aires performance troupe Pista 4's 1998 *Cadáveres* [Corpses], a staged piece of FM radio-theatre based on the disturbingly explicit poetry of exiled Argentine Néstor Perlongher. In tandem these two central chapters reflect upon Eva's multiple bodies, all mediated through staged representation, each reacting in its own way to the national (and international) polarizing Evita myth-making project. In both chapters I juxtapose a historical need to flesh out the myth to a critical desire to break down the flesh through mediation and effigy. The multiple staged Argentine "Evitas" presented in these two chapters reveal a telling slippage that casts doubt upon what is typically regarded as a distinctly national binarizing tendency and that instead suggests a national (and transnational) ambivalence toward Eva Perón as historical character, as mythologized figure, and as iconized effigy.

My final chapter, "Argentine Madonnas, Pop Stars, and Performances of Immediacy and Virtuality," begins with two examples of the convergence of the political and the devotional in Evita representation: Kogan's strategic substitution of Eva Perón for a Marian female figure in *La oscuridad de la razón*; and contemporary visual artist and scenographer Daniel Santoro's evocative political-devotional Peronist portraiture. However, instead of following the previous chapters' focus on a single female figure, here I draw upon Argentina's numerous popular devotional figures to examine how the "feminine" is performed, appropriated, and circulated throughout contemporary popular culture. The everyday texts analyzed encompass oral histories, folktales, prayer cards, Internet websites, and social networks; and my subjects range from Argentina's Catholic patron saint, the Virgin of Luján, to unofficial popular saint María Antonia Deolinda "Difunta" Correa (the legendary mid-nineteenth-century woman who died of thirst in the Argentine desert but whose "miraculously" full breast managed to keep her baby alive even after the mother's own death), and finally to the deceased pop singer Gilda, whose roadside altars, "Santa Gilda" websites, and Facebook pages, as well as YouTube pilgrimage uploads attest to her status as national popular devotional femicon. Gilda's career in the exploding Cumbia movement was cut short in 1996, when a truck hit her touring bus and killed the thirty-four-year-old singer. A sanctuary constructed near the fatal accident's site has become a pilgrimage destination for fans and worshippers. "Santa Gilda," known for her protection of the poor and infirm, has joined the pantheon of contemporary popular saints who, not unlike "Santa Evita," are venerated by hundreds of thousands of Argentines, sensationalized by the media, ridiculed by the upper classes, and exploited by big business. The chapter regards the role of the digital in contemporary iconography and iconic performance, as I contend that the virtual has become the realm of popular cultural interactivity, mediating most if not all celebrity performances and devotional practices and confounding traditional expectations regarding femiconic embodiment.

I conclude my project with a return to the intersections of (trans) national politics, iconicity, and performance in the person of Argentina's current president Cristina Fernández de Kirchner and her own complex relationship with Evita femiconography. Ultimately, although my project has a specifically national frame, I intend it to serve as a model for reconsiderations of the intersections of globalized celebrity and national myth-making, and thus is conceived as a timely investigation into the confluence of performance, nation, gender, and iconicity. Through an examination of the porous borders between mythology and history, the inseparability of embodied performance and popular iconography, and the role of virtuality in contemporary celebrity, the chapters that follow approach the many questions of iconographic representation through the making of multiple Argentine femicons.

ONE

Camila O'Gorman and the Making of an Argentine Femicon

Argentina's Past Present—the Curious Cases Of Soledad, Camila, and Manuelita

It's difficult to shake off the image of a shaven-headed, handcuffed, hunger-striking twenty-four-year-old María Soledad Rosas flipping the double bird to the journalist's camera while three Italian *carabinieri* work to restrain her slight body.[1] After Sole's death in 1998, the defiant likeness was reproduced seemingly everywhere: appearing in multiple versions in all the major Argentine and European presses, gracing the cover of her single biography,[2] and circulating on the Internet (where it can still be found at multiple websites). Her brief life ended on July 11 of that year, when she allegedly hanged herself while under house arrest in a communal home three and a half months after the presumed suicide of her thirty-five-year-old lover and longtime squatter, Edoardo Massari (nicknamed "Baleno"—Flash or Lightning in Italian) on March 28. Soledad was a middle-class girl who didn't finish college, preferring instead to earn her way as one of Buenos Aires's many dog walkers. Traveling through Europe with a friend, she stayed on to join Italy's anarchist movement and cofound with Massari and Silvano Pelissero a Turinese *okupa*-squat.[3] Within the year, she would be in prison, accused with co-okupas Massari and Pelissero of ecoterrorist acts on excessive, inflated charges. The proof obtained through the use of GPS, tails, hidden microphones, and spying satellites to video- and audiotape the three squatters in their environs pointed to an obviously larger government campaign to incriminate and destroy the entire *okupa* movement.[4] It might be easy to dismiss Soledad's actions as those of a girl in love caught up in a conflict exceeding her experience. However, her comportment in prison and refusal to take on the role of an impressionable young woman under the sway of two older men suggest a commitment to and consistency with her professed anarchist ideals. Her death ostensibly triggered a series of protests, pickets, burnings, letter-bombs, and even other deaths, lending Sole's act a symbolic weight far heavier and more urgent (to use her biographer's apt term) than her ten-week romance with Edoardo might suggest.[5] Soledad Rosas's story acquires even greater urgency when regarded within a distinctly Argentine history of castigated female rebellion in the face of a male-dominated authoritarianism extending back to the mid-nineteenth century and Camila O'Gorman.

INDEED, NOT ONLY does Soledad's "urgent" life stand as yet one more example of young romantic rebellion excessively punished at the hands of a state; her ancestry links her to this chapter's subject and Sole's rebellious predecessor—another young woman who paid with her life for choosing to circumvent the laws of society and the state and, before Eva Perón, perhaps the country's most femiconized figure. In 1848, the twenty-year-old Argentine bourgeoise Camila O'Gorman was executed by firing squad, together with her lover and confessor-priest, the twenty-four-year-old Uladislao Gutiérrez. It was the scandal of the era: the couple had fallen in love and run away to the rural littoral, where they assumed other identities, lived as a couple, and cofounded and taught at the town's grade school. Discovered by a visiting priest and acquaintance of Uladislao, they were arrested and transported to a military headquarters, where they were summarily executed. It is popularly believed that Camila was pregnant at the time of her execution, and the couple's elopement and subsequent punishment provoked strong reactions in all social and political spheres. Essays, poems, and novels were published nationally and abroad, portraits and engravings were created, plays were staged and censored, and throughout the following century Camila's story would figure in films, novels, plays, poems, and other artistic works. These myriad cultural products inspired by Camila O'Gorman's short life provide the raw material for this chapter's investigation into the making of arguably the first in a long line of Argentine femicons.

By a strange quirk of historical coincidence, Soledad Rosas was a direct descendant of the nineteenth-century Argentine dictator Juan Manuel de Rosas (1793–1877), the man who infamously gave the orders to execute Camila and Uladislao. During his 1830s "Conquest of the [Pampean] Desert," Rosas had had a child with an indigenous Mapuche woman; he recognized their daughter, named Fénix, as his own, and in turn Fénix, who lived for more than one hundred years, had several children to whom she gave her father's surname, thus assuring the survival of this branch of the Rosas lineage. One of Fénix's offspring, Pascual Rosas, was Soledad's great-great-grandfather.[6] In strikingly ironic contrast to the rebellious Camila and Sole, Rosas's only legitimate daughter (with Encarnación Ezcurra y Arguibel) would end up exemplifying the very image of stultifying filial piety. Manuelita (Manuela Robustiana Ortiz de Rosas y Ezcurra, 1817–1898)—bearing her great-grandmother's name but with patronymic echoes (like her older brother Juan, 1814–1877?)—was born long before her half-sister Fénix. Like most Argentine girls of her class and time, Manuelita received only rudimentary education in reading, writing, and arithmetic.[7] However, early on she was interpellated into her father's political world, confirmed in at least one artistic rendition of the very young Manuelita accompanying her parents to view a celebration by one of Buenos Aires's Afro-Argentine "nations."[8] This supporting role would increase in importance when, after her mother's death in 1838, twenty-year-old Manuelita became the leading lady of her father's Palermo mansion and of the Confederation—Rosas's federalist organization and the bitter enemies of the centralist *unitarios* (most of whom by then were living in exile in Uruguay or Chile) in the power struggle over a recently independent Argentina.[9]

Manuelita played an active role in Rosas's international diplomacy, entertaining at their home and engaging in correspondence with visiting foreign dignitaries while her father ruled the country with a brutality often enforced by his "irregular" police force, called the Mazorca.[10] So critical was Manuelita's position to her father that he continued to postpone her marriage to her long-betrothed fiancé, Máximo Terrero, one of Rosas's *comisarios* in his provincial army and resident at the Rosas's Palermo mansion. It was only after her father's 1852 defeat and renunciation and the family's subsequent flight to England that Manuelita, at age thirty-six, would finally get to marry her Máximo, and only then after agreeing to her melancholic father's conditions that he not have to attend the wedding and that she move out of his house. She returned to her native Argentina only once, in 1886, spending the rest of her life and raising her two sons in South Hampstead, where she died in 1898 at the age of eighty-one. Her importance to her father's professional and private lives is perhaps best exemplified in her 1851 official portrait.

The painting, which was commissioned by the family and overseen by a select committee, was produced by the young Prilidiano Pueyrredón (1823–1870)—not yet established as one of nineteenth-century Argentina's great artists—and featured a thirty-four-year-old Manuelita in full Federalist crimson, from her dress and flower to the surrounding curtains, carpet, and chair.[11] Art director and historian Fermín Fevre interprets Manuelita's hand resting on the sheet of white paper (ostensibly a letter to her father) as representing her role as Rosas's "intercessor."[12] Her standing posture and slight smile speak to her elevated position and kindness for which she was well known. Yet even the privileged Manuelita did not enjoy sufficient sway over her father to intercede successfully on behalf of her childhood friend Camila O'Gorman, as we will see.

SOLEDAD, CAMILA, MANUELITA: not unlike Evita's own tale (recalled in the next two chapters), all three women's stories have been mythologized in the press, in historical fiction and nonfiction, and in artistic renditions. And the resulting versions blur easy distinctions between historiography and mythologization. For example, two weeks after Soledad's death, a Buenos Aires daily newspaper's "youth" supplement devoted multiple articles to her case and interviewed members of the Argentine and international anarchist movements in an effort to answer the question: "why must [Soledad Rosas] be converted into a rebel icon for posters and t-shirts?" One hypothesis was that "her story is ideal for myth":

> A sort of turn-of-the-century "love story"; a beautiful occupied morgue-turned-house in Turin; a middle-class girl who studied hotel management in a private university and in under three months gave herself over to a cause, lived in a commune, and followed a rigorous [vegan] diet in keeping with her ecologist principles. And, of course, the tragic end: jail and suicide in solitary confinement, three months after her boyfriend, 38[sic]-year-old Edoardo, had done the same thing in a high-security prison. Perfect.[13]

Whereas Soledad's story, as illustrated in the above excerpt, has been mythologized into the tragic love-story model, Manuelita's is typically rendered as a cautionary or exemplary tale of submissive femininity: mother, daughter, wife, and social secretary all in a single, self-sacrificing woman. Thus María Sáenz Quesada, in her 1991 book on Rosas's women, finds in Manuelita "something more" than simply the daughter of Rosas:

. . . the country's collective memory has elevated her to the category of myth; she is the angel of goodness; the beneficent fairy who, during a difficult period, fulfilled the feminine role par excellence: mercy, compassion, limitless supporter of the family's male figure . . . the most celebrated Argentine woman of her age . . . Halfway between legend and history, the Restorer's pleasant daughter has awakened few polemics among historians, be they supporters or opponents of her dictator father. This is because she somehow synthesizes the essence of traditional feminine virtues, of the self-sacrificing daughter, exemplary wife and mother, incapable of generating her own ideas, and faithful pillar of those [ideas] sustained by her clansmen. She thus becomes the antithesis of today's feminist conception of women, that privileges one's personal life project over the submissive adoption of outside values and projects.[14]

Historians, journalists, and novelists have portrayed both Manuelita and Soledad as women who sacrificed themselves for love, one out of devotion to her father and the state, the other for romantic love and state-condemned ideals.[15] Their stories seem ready-made for a genealogical saga of the complex and controversial Rosas family: Manuelita, the legitimate offspring of the region's most notorious nineteenth-century dictator; Soledad, the distant descendant of one of his likely numerous "illegitimate" liaisons. Manuelita's submission easily juxtaposes itself to Soledad's rebellion, just as her polished official portrait seems to epitomize the polar opposite of the "in-yer-face" photo of a scrawny, shackled Soledad. Manuelita's exemplary life stands in undemanding contrast to Soledad's resistant death.[16] Yet Manuelita ultimately challenged her father's wishes by marrying her longtime betrothed, while Soledad would typically spend her Sundays with Massari visiting his parents. Soledad's commitment to her principles—including a strict veganism that disavowed any animal products and incorporated the matutinal practice of urinotherapy as well as yoga—might strike us as far more monastic, even more "pure," than Manuelita's nineteenth-century lifestyle in a mansion that housed her fiancé as well as her father's lover (who bore him at least five unacknowledged children) and that was rumored to welcome prominent leaders, including clergy, and their mistresses.

Such seemingly facile contrasts are rendered more complex in the case of Camila O'Gorman. It is Camila, and not her childhood friend Manuelita, who has sustained the imaginative attention of Argentines

since the time of her arrest and execution. O'Gorman's romantic elopement with her confessor-priest has frequently been reinterpreted as symbolic of youthful resistance in the face of authoritarian repression, and
their passionate story has inspired many artistic works, including poems,
novels, plays, an early twentieth-century film, a recent musical, and even
an Oscar-nominated movie. After an initial examination of early Camila-
inspired historiographic practices, illustrated in memoirs, historical accounts, and theatrical versions of O'Gorman's life, this chapter traces her
impact on the Argentine national consciousness and creation as a national femiconic figure by pairing different versions of her story created
within the last forty years, a particularly difficult and violent period in
Argentina's history. Enrique Molina's 1973 novel, *Una sombra donde sueña
Camila O'Gorman* [A Shadow where Camila O'Gorman is Dreaming],
and Griselda Gambaro's 1982 play, *La malasangre* [Bad Blood], frame the
country's latest and most repressive military dictatorship (1976–1983).
Molina's lushly poetic novel purports to respect the available historical
data, yet it makes a fetish of the female body and ultimately victimizes
Camila as sexual object; in contrast, Gambaro's harshly unromantic play,
often narrowly read as historical dramatization, stages the reclaiming of
the Argentine populace—through the onstage female body and a controversial original production—of its theretofore silenced resistant voice
in the final years of military dictatorship. Such important politics of recovery and resistance notwithstanding, each artistic project participates
in the ongoing national mythologizing of Camila O'Gorman. On the
other hand, both María Luisa Bemberg's 1984 Oscar-nominated film,
Camila, and Ricardo Monti's 1989 play, *Una pasión sudamericana* [A South
American Passion-Play], restaged in 2005 at Argentina's national Cervantes Theatre (and the source of his 2002 *Finlandia* [Finland]), attempt
an alternative telling of Camila's story. While Bemberg's film ostensibly
reworks the Latin American romantic tradition of melodrama to con-
demn the immobile patriarchal structure for its continued oppression of
women and female eroticism, Monti's plays subvert the romantic tradition entirely by telling the story from the executioner's point of view and
taking audiences inside what has been called the shared subconscious
of victim and victimizer. All these artistic versions of Camila O'Gorman's
"tragic romance" (or, as I will argue in the majority of cases, romantic
tragedy) challenge easy distinctions between mythologizing and historiography, between fact and fiction—precisely what this chapter's analysis
of the ongoing creation of one of Argentina's earliest femicons attempts
to demonstrate.

Camila O'Gorman: A Political, Moral, and Historiographic Rorschach's Test

"Camila's crime wasn't what she did; it was that everyone found out what she did."[17]

Camila enjoys this brief but poignant defense in Marcos Carnevale's *Mercedes*, one of twenty-five short films commissioned by Argentina's Secretary of Culture on the occasion of the country's 2010 bicentennial celebration. In this film, femiconic Uruguayan actress China Zorrilla portrays Mercedes, a 212-year-old witness to the country's history who, if not among the country's great male figures, has "had tea with many of them, been the girlfriend of some of them."[18] During her historical romp, Mercedes briefly mentions her dear friend "Camila" (no surname required) and pointedly repositions her friend's crime away from any individual moral transgression and toward society and its politico-moral judgment. In so doing, Mercedes brings her interlocutor back to one of the key questions surrounding Camila's story and its multiple interpretations: "Who (or what) executed Camila O'Gorman?" The answer to that question tells us more about the respondent than it ever will about Camila herself.

The daguerreotype purported to be the only image of Camila O'Gorman produced in her lifetime reflects the young Argentine woman's class, background, and moment.[19] Camila's December 24, 1847, "wanted" bulletin [*filiación*] (circulated throughout the country and likely based on her own father's description included in a letter dated December 21) describes her as twenty years old, very tall, slim, and "well proportioned," with white skin, black eyes with a pleasant gaze, "average" nose and mouth, and dark brown hair. Her only distinguishing trait was a front tooth with cavities. She was said to be wearing "decent" clothing, among it mourning black.[20]

Camila O'Gorman was born in Buenos Aires in 1828.[21] She was the youngest daughter and the fifth of six offspring of Mauritian-born Adolfo O'Gorman (1793–1850) and his wife, the Buenos Aires-born (and Spanish-descended) Joaquina Ximénez y Pinto (1797–bef. 1852). Adolfo was the second son of Thomas O'Gorman (born Ennis, Ireland, c. 1760—d. bef. 1847, Spain?; sometimes confused with his firstborn son, Tomás). Thomas's wife, Marie Anne Perichon de Vandeuil y D'Abeille (c. 1775–1847, sometimes identified as Camila's great-aunt and not her grandmother), was born on the French-controlled Île Bourbon (today's Réunion) in the Indian Ocean, where Thomas O'Gorman successfully

Figure 2: An anonymous daguerreotype purportedly of Camila O'Gorman.

traded. Thomas and Marie Anne migrated to the River Plate region in 1797 with her parents and siblings, as well as their two male children, one of them Camila's father.

Historians and chroniclers typically make haste to draw readers' attention to the O'Gorman familial mix of accomplishment and scandal. Camila's paternal grandfather is thought to be related to Dr. Michael O'Gorman (1749–1819) of Ennis, who served as surgeon general in the Spanish River Plate viceroyalty, restructured Buenos Aires's school of medicine, and performed a key role in attempts to free the region of cholera, yellow fever, and smallpox. Thomas himself became wealthy through the less prestigious means, according to María Teresa Julianello, of "slave trade, saltmeat and dye industries, [and] sugar and indigo plantations in Paraguay."[22] A rumored contrabandist and spy for the British leading up to their 1806 invasion of Buenos Aires, Thomas left the city in the early 1800s and never returned. During his absences, his wife was also rumored to have spied for the British, the Portuguese, and the French as well as engaged in love affairs with some of Buenos Aires's leading figures, among them the soon-to-be-named Viceroy Santiago de Liniers, a French-born noble who had joined the Spanish navy and would become the hero of the 1806 Spanish "reconquest" of Buenos Aires. Liniers, increasingly criticized for his relationship with a suspected British spy of colonial French origin, sent Anita (as Marie Anne was often called) to

Rio de Janeiro, where she welcomed Argentine expatriates and continued her intrigues.[23] She would return definitively to Buenos Aires after Liniers's death but only after promising the provisional government of the newly independent region she would remain at her country estate. She died in Buenos Aires in December 1847, the same month her granddaughter Camila eloped with Gutiérrez.[24]

Notwithstanding this scandalous familial shadow, Camila—in accordance with her portrait—grew up in a privileged environment, where she was thought to have been a devoted reader of fiction as well as an accomplished musician. Her father, a fervent supporter of Rosas, apparently ran a strict household, in keeping with any self-respecting *porteño* family of the period. Camila's older brother Enrique would go on to become the chief of police during Domingo F. Sarmiento's presidency, as well as *gobernador* of the National Penitentiary in addition to organizing Buenos Aires's police force. Her younger brother, Eduardo, was a Catholic priest who would serve various terms as a national congressman. If not occupying the highest tier of Buenos Aires elite, the O'Gormans were solid members of the city's upper class, and Camila counted among her friends General Rosas's own daughter, Manuelita.

The agreed-upon plot points of Camila and Uladislao's brief life together are fairly straightforward[25]: In 1847, Camila met the recently ordained priest Uladislao Gutiérrez (b. 1824), the nephew of the governor of the province of Tucumán. The young Gutiérrez, who had come to Buenos Aires with his uncle's letters of introduction to Rosas and the clergy, was taken under the wing of Felipe Elortondo y Palacios—secretary general of the curate, dean of the Cathedral, and director of the Public Library—who apparently encouraged his ward to embrace a career in the church. Uladislao assisted the parish priest at Buenos Aires's Socorro Church, the O'Gorman family's place of worship. He was an acquaintance of Camila's brother and fellow priest, Eduardo, and attended the family's *tertulias* (the social gatherings typical of privileged households). Sometime during the night of December 11-12, 1847, O'Gorman and Gutiérrez eloped on horseback. While questions remain about the couple's exact itinerary, it is known that they crossed the Paraná River into Corrientes, an area that was not technically under Rosas's control. Under the assumed identities of a married couple from the northern city of Jujuy, Máxime Brandier and Valentina Dessau,[26] they settled in Goya, where they founded the town's first grade schools and were apparently so successful that the schools moved on three occasions, each time to a larger facility.

It seems that the O'Gorman family waited before approaching either church or state authorities. According to a January 17, 1848, letter signed by Rosas, Camila's father first informed local authorities of his daughter's disappearance on December 16, 1847. An obsequious, self-defensive January 22, 1848, letter from Elortondo y Palacios to Rosas states that the parish's curate [*teniente cura*], Manuel Velarde, had been approached by the family, who had requested that he not say anything. On December 21 Camila's father finally wrote to the minister of foreign relations, accusing Uladislao of having seduced Camila "under the cloak of religion."[27] The next day Buenos Aires Bishopric Vicar Miguel García wrote to Rosas, asking for his help in locating "those two inconsiderate young people."[28] Rosas, in his January 17 account, claims that he acted almost immediately thereafter, calling in the police chief, who said he had not been informed by the ecclesiastical curia. Evident from the *filiaciones* and other flyers circulated around the area, Rosas demanded the arrests of Camila and Uladislao, the former to be taken to a *casa de ejercicios* [spiritual retreat or convent] and the latter to be taken by cart to a public jail, each kept separate from the other.[29]

In June 1848 Gutiérrez was recognized at a local Goya social gathering by Fr. Michael Gannon, who informed the local authorities of the couple's true identity. After consulting with the region's governor, Benjamín Virasoro, local officials decided to return the couple to Buenos Aires. Upon orders from Rosas, they were taken separately in covered carts (with Uladislao—and maybe Camila—in chains), but instead of going to Buenos Aires, they were redirected to Santos Lugares (in today's San Andrés), Rosas's military headquarters [*cuartel general*] on the outskirts of Buenos Aires. They were both executed by a firing squad on August 18, 1848, in the headquarters' yard. Accounts claim it took three rounds of fire before Camila died.[30] According to the man who carried out Rosas's orders, the couple was placed in a single, albeit divided, coffin. The location of their burial has never been identified; they had already been buried when Camila's brothers arrived to retrieve her body.

Almost from the beginning, historiographic viewpoints diverge, especially regarding the motivations driving the various participants in Camila's story. Historians and artists often lead off with Camila herself, attributing her rebelliousness to either a stiflingly repressive society or an inherited "loose woman" gene from her father's side. Camila's father is characterized as overcompensating for his own mother's reputation, obsessed with his family's image and position at the expense of his daughter's life. Once the couple's flight was made public, Rosas's opponents unsurprisingly leveled the blame at the dictator and his corrupting influence on the easily impressionable youth of his social circle. High-placed clergy like Elortondo y Palacios sought to protect themselves and the Catholic Church from accusations of licentiousness and lack of supervision. Federalists condemned Camila's liberal reading habits, while Irish-Argentine clerics worried about her French grandmother's scandalous model. Interestingly, even though Uladislao appears as the frequent target of the period's accusations—variously as seducer, petty thief, and under-trained cleric—he fades into the background in the couple's later treatments, which center almost obsessively on Camila and her fate. Historiographic practices have denied Uladislao the iconic status accorded Camila.

Rosas's own motives likewise shift in their portrayal, unsurprisingly according to the individual historian's position with respect to Argentina's long debates over "civilization and barbarism": Rosas's 1880 signed letter claims full responsibility for the couple's deaths;[31] however, shortly after becoming aware of the couple's disappearance, he is said to have convened a committee of experts to review the legalities surrounding the two cases. Partisan accounts state that all but one recommended death for both.[32] Was Rosas an "Argentine Nero" (as one nineteenth-century playwright called him),[33] or a Pontius Pilate washing his hands of two cases already juridically, socially, and religiously predetermined? Was his decision to have the couple taken to Santos Lugares an attempt to shield his harsh decision from the Buenos Aires spotlight? Finally, what role did Manuelita play in the fate of her childhood friend Camila? In his memoirs, Antonino Reyes (1813–1897), aide-de-camp to Rosas and the Santos Lugares military head who carried out Rosas's execution orders, claims he wrote an urgent letter to Manuelita (with whom he had spoken shortly after the couple's disappearance), telling her of the orders to execute Camila and Uladislao and begging her to intercede on her friend's behalf. He relates that the letter never reached its addressee; rather, it was delivered by the messenger to the on-duty scribe, who in turn handed it to Rosas (and not Manuelita). Rosas returned the letter to Reyes, demanding that the aide complete the executions immediately.[34]

It would seem that in the end nearly anyone wielding any power in Camila's sociopolitical sphere wanted her dead: Rosas, the bishop of Buenos Aires, prominent Irish-Argentine community leaders, politicians and journalists for and against the government, and even her own father, who wrote to Rosas and asked that he exact extreme punishment. Yet once she was executed, some of these same voices clamored for her return, resuscitating her as the principal martyr of an undeniably violent regime.[35] One nineteenth-century lithograph portrays a blindfolded and seated Camila and Uladislao being carried by four prisoners into the yard, where soldiers wait in formation and other prisoners watch from high windows. Tellingly, while both wear white blindfolds, Camila occupies the center-foreground, with the black-clad Uladislao positioned further back and to the left.[36] Camila appears dressed in white in nearly all artistic renditions, including most plays,[37] centrally placed and increasingly absent her Uladislao. For these late nineteenth-century artists, as well as for most of those who would follow, Camila is the sole protagonist of this story.[38]

Nevertheless, and despite the debate regarding the execution of a young privileged woman from a prominent family, by far the greatest cry has been raised about the circumstances surrounding Camila's death, specifically whether she was pregnant at the time of her execution. Again, accounts vary wildly, from a false pregnancy claimed by a young woman desperate to live, to a nearly complete gestation that would have Camila becoming pregnant around the time of the couple's elopement.[39] One widely reproduced artistic rendition of Camila is an undated charcoal by the Italian Baldasarre (Baltasar) Verazzi (1819–1866), who resided in Buenos Aires between 1853 and 1865. The charcoal's title—"Baptism of Camila O'Gorman's Unborn Child Before Going to Punishment [suplicio]"—captures prevailing beliefs: we are taken inside Camila's cell, where a priest (possibly Pascual Alejandro Rivas or Félix Castellanos) blesses the fetus while a visibly pregnant (and, as usual, white-clothed) Camila drinks holy water.[40] In a potentially contradictory report, Miguel Bilbao—the Chilean lawyer and journalist who edited Reyes's memoirs in 1883—quotes Rosas's aide-de-camp: "And opening or pulling away from her womb a large black scarf that had been covering her, she said: 'Don't you see how I am?' And she accompanied her words by sticking out her womb." Reyes also reported that Camila told him she was sick and needed a doctor; he noted that her skin was not clear [empañado], her countenance haggard, and her hair messy, which he suggested might have been the result of her recent "life of agitation and hard work."[41] Nevertheless, and even though Reyes employed Camila's pregnancy as an argument in his plea for Manuelita's intervention, according to Bilbao, Reyes himself doubted "the truth of Camila's situation; because her young woman's body did not show it nor were there signs of such a pregnancy. If there were [a pregnancy], it could only have been very recent; but since it served him in that moment to save her, he alleged it, reaching an agreement with the camp's doctor, Martínez."[42] It was—and still is—Rosas's ordered double execution of a mother and her unborn child that has caused the greatest outrage. Their deaths continue to find national echoes in "the unusually high number of pregnant women among the victims of political assassination in the 1970's"[43] and in the five hundred children born to imprisoned mothers and then "adopted" by those complicit with the 1976–83 dictatorship.

Shifting attributions have resulted in conjectures today taken as facts, but no "fact" has caused so much furor as Camila's supposed pregnancy at the time of her execution.[44] We likely will never know for sure if Camila was pregnant. What interests me here, however, is how one version of an event becomes the dominating "true story"; how a single version-qua-fact can discredit or drown out other versions; how histories are written and how artistic products and their producers participate in historiography; and ultimately how mythology and history become inseparable when considering icons, iconicity, and iconography. Camila-as-femicon—both product and producer—sheds light on the limits of iconographical representation and offers, as we will see, a useful comparison to Evitist femiconography, particularly in the popular construction of Evita as "Madonna of the poor" and the public debates surrounding her own maternity.

Hayden White's caveats regarding historiography (historical interpretation/writing) prove useful when facing overtly partisan and extremely creative "histories," such as the majority of the cultural works composed out of or inspired by Camila O'Gorman's short life.[45] We might recall, for instance, that historical research is not the same as historical writing, that "events happen, whereas facts are constituted,"[46] and that, between archival research and the written (or otherwise composed) product, "a number of transformative operations must be performed," all of which are "culture specific."[47] Finally, and especially important for Camila historico-iconography, rather than considering fact and fiction to be mutually excluding opposites, White suggests it may be more productive "to view them as the poles of a linguistic continuum between which speech must move in the articulation of any discourse whatsoever, serious or frivolous."[48] Thus, rather than engage in the impossible debates over, for example, whether Camila was eight months pregnant at the time of her execution, I devote this chapter to reflecting upon *how* Camila's story has been told—through such "fictional" media as plays, novels, and films. In order to do so, I adhere to White's model of a fact-fiction continuum and consciously reappropriate his tropological theory for the discursive analysis of the artistic artifact. Further proof of the efficacy of the historical-artistic continuum, a surprising number of "histories" of Camila O'Gorman have emplotted her story as romantic tragedy or melodrama gone fatally wrong in near equal proportion to the surprising number of plays, films, and novels claiming to tell her "true story."[49]

"Camila vive": Staging the Life and Death— Mostly the Death—of Camila O'Gorman

Rosas lost control of Argentina merely three and a half years after Camila's and Uladislao's executions. Leading up to and following his fall was a flurry of cultural production centered on abusive dictators and victimized innocents, among them Camila and other young women. Shortly after the couple's execution, Hilario Ascasubi (1807–1875), a soldier once imprisoned by Rosas, published in Montevideo one of his famous "gaucho poems": an August 28 letter from the gaucho Donato Jurao to his wife about Camila and "the unfortunate priest." In his letter, Donato becomes so moved by his own highly dramatic recounting—"My God! In this moment / it gives me such an impulsive feeling [*corazonada*] / of desperate fury ... / that ... I don't know what I feel."—that he must take a breath before continuing his report. Ascasubi's conceit provides us with perhaps the first of what would be numerous fictionalized "eye-witness" accounts of the couple's execution.[50]

Dramatic versions of Camila and Uladislao's story followed similar suit. In 1856, the Uruguayan writer Heraclio Fajardo (1833–1867) published his Spanish translation of *Camila O'Gorman*, a novel by Felisberto Péllisot, a Frenchman living in Buenos Aires. Fajardo also adapted the novel for the stage.[51] Both the novel and the play fall squarely within the period's literary parameters. As Martín Rodríguez notes, Argentine romantic drama "was strongly tied to the political situation whose central theme was the fight against the Rosist government."[52] Fictional works of the period were often based—whether allegorically (especially before 1852)[53] or straightforwardly—on contemporary events and personalities, especially Rosas. Rodríguez points out that the two genres utilized to dramatize these histories were romance and tragedy, both modes that allowed for enormous liberties to be taken with historical "fact" while reasserting the fictional as factual.

Fajardo's 1862 play supplies a prime example of the period's dramaturgical mix of fiction and fact. Though subtitled a "historical drama in six acts [*cuadros*] and verse," it is much closer to "romantic pseudohistoricism."[54] Rosas stands as the chief villain in a play where at least half the characters seem determined to get Camila. Both Rosas and Gannon (here named Ganón) find vengeful motivation when their lustful overtures are rejected by the virtuous Camila, who loves the equally virtuous (and, of course, anti-Rosist) Uladislao. The play's characters refer to Rosas as, variously, a panther, despot, wild animal [*fiera*], monster, tyrant, butcher, and barbarian. All are, following Rodríguez, interchangeable terms that "form part of Republicanism's vocabulary, a language common to the lettered elites of the independence period throughout Spanish America."[55] Camila is abducted, not unlike her earlier Pampean counterpart and eponym of Esteban Echeverría's famous 1837 "captive girl" [*la cautiva*][56]; only in Fajardo's play it is Rosas and his supporter-cum-rival Ganón who are the "savages." Their opponents—and Camila's supporters—include a childhood friend-turned-Unitarian Lázaro; Manuelita, who stops her own father from violating Camila's honor; and Rosas's jester, Eusebio (the name of one of several "crazies" Rosas was rumored to have retained),[57] who saves Camila on multiple occasions. The text abruptly jumps in time, between its fourth and fifth acts, to the Brandier home in Goya, where Camila's reflections on her memoirs bring the spectator up to speed on her pregnancy just before the couple is denounced by a revenge-seeking Ganón. The final act unsurprisingly transpires in Santos Lugares. There Camila is visited in turn by her friends Lázaro and Manuelita, the latter of whom delivers her the good news of a pardon, only to see the order overturned two scenes later. The play ends with a brave Camila supporting a frightened Uladislao as they exit to their offstage execution, thereby affording Lázaro a last eyewitness plea to Heaven for revenge upon the "Argentine Caligula": "overwhelm this assassin with tremendous unequaled punishment."[58] Fajardo dedicates his play "to the spirits [*manes*] of Camila O'Gorman": "A new progeny rises / That now stomps the threshold of the future / And it will root out those germs of the crime / With the ease of his angered sole!"[59]

Even though Fajardo's *Camila O'Gorman* has been claimed one of the most popular of the period's many anti-Rosist plays[60] and "produced with great success,"[61] it did not elude controversy: Argentine theatre historian Beatriz Seibel writes that "its [Buenos Aires] premiere was hindered by censorship"[62] but notes that it premiered in Córdoba in 1873.[63] Abril Trigo and Graciela Míguez list a much-delayed Uruguayan premiere of June 6, 1875, in Montevideo's Cibils Theatre, with revivals in that city in 1879 and 1880.[64]

Fajardo's was not the last dramatic version of Camila's story to meet with controversy and prohibition. L. Mendoza Ortiz's early twentieth-century *Camila O'Gorman* (a "historical drama" in verse) was staged in Argentina's "interior"—Córdoba, Tucumán, and Salta, according to its author—despite having been prohibited by the government of Buenos Aires for its "immoral or anti-patriotic" representation of said historic event.[65] Mendoza Ortiz defended his play in a "Warning" that accompanied the published text, claiming that Camila O'Gorman's name could no longer be considered the exclusive property of certain persons "when history had appropriated it some time ago."[66] The play includes characters and characterizations present in earlier works such as Fajardo's, yet, if anything, their respective roles have become exaggerated: Uladislao is cleared of any possible crimes against the church when he repeatedly states that he entered the clergy against his will and only in fulfillment of his mother's death-bed request. Manuelita functions as her father's chief advisor and conscience figure, appearing at multiple and very melodramatic times to stay his violent hand and even lecturing him at length and in detail on the Mazorca's horrendously violent acts. The play omits entirely the couple's flight and new life in Goya, moving directly to the final act's imprisonment and executions, once again despite Manuelita's last attempt at intercession. Camila remains squarely center-stage in her final extended speeches, ending with a direct address to the audience: "Beloved fatherland! / Sun, that lit up my happy childhood; / receive the final farewell / that I send you from the edge of my monstrous grave."[67] However, and as Brenda Werth points out, it was likely not Camila's portrayal that inspired the negative official response of Buenos Aires's leaders but rather the reappropriative treatment of the gaucho figure: the doomed couple's death is avenged by Camila's *unitario* friend, Lázaro, who appears disguised as a gaucho and, wielding his *facón*, stabs the traitorous Banón (Gannon) while crying out the lyrics of Argentina's national anthem: "¡Libertad, libertad, libertad!" Werth argues that despite Mendoza Ortiz's attempts to reclaim the gaucho, long associated historically and culturally with Rosas and the federalist movements, "the place of Camila O'Gorman in the national imaginary [and] on the national stage [could not be] shared with the figure of the gaucho."[68]

By the early twentieth century, Camila was an infrequent yet recurring subject for the stage and the new medium of film.[69] The now-lost silent film *Camila O'Gorman* (1909), directed by Mario Gallo and featuring famed stage actress Blanca Podestá in the title role, was long considered the first scripted Argentine film.[70] Podestá and her company would later produce *Camila O'Gorman: poema dramático en cinco actos, un epílogo y en verso* [dramatic poem in five acts, an epilogue, and in verse], one of a dozen works created by Eduardo R. Rossi (here in collaboration with Podestá's husband, Alberto Ballerini) and characterized by their author as "poetic theatre."[71] Four years earlier Podestá had played Manuelita in Rossi's dramatic version of the life of Rosas's daughter (a role she reprised in the 1925 film version directed by Ricardo Villarán). In the Rossi-Ballerini play, Blanca of course portrayed Camila. The production premiered on June 3, 1927, as part of the company's season of local and foreign repertory at the Smart Theatre.[72] The published script expands the cast to include servants, Camila's parents, and a couple of slang-speaking *mazorqueros*.[73] Once again, Rosas's motivation appears to stem from a frustrated attempt to claim the resisting Camila, but the structural focus shifts from early intrigues (such as in Fajardo's play) to Camila's imprisonment and fate, with the final three of five acts alternating between Santos Lugares and Rosas's Palermo (Buenos Aires) home. The extended back-and-forth displays what is perhaps the play's most noteworthy modification in recasting Rosas's decision: at first intending to execute the couple (by "reason of state" and at Camila's own father's insistence that she be "condemned"), Rosas changes his mind in a moment of tragic anagnorisis triggered by Manuelita's "love" and "the sacred memory of the wife I have lost,"[74] but his counterorder does not arrive in time to save Camila and Uladislao. The play lets everyone but Camila's father off the hook, a judgment not unlike that suggested in Griselda Gambaro's *La malasangre*, discussed later in this chapter.

These plays of the late nineteenth and early twentieth centuries take artistic liberties with Camila's story (and maybe because the known historical record never easily fit into what John King calls "the River Plate Romantic mode" of which José Mármol's 1851 novel *Amalia* is a prime example).[75] Most noteworthy for this chapter's purposes are the repetitions in the "'falsifications'": Rosas is typically portrayed as the most powerful of Camila's multiple *pretendientes*, Manuelita is positioned as her father's conscience and Camila's beloved intercessor, Gannon is pathologically villainous, and valiant Camila is pregnant. Through repetition, these plot points acquire the patina of truth and, indeed, become taken as fact, as they in turn determine the later creation and reception of Molina's novel, Bemberg's film, and Monti's and Gambaro's plays.

When analyzed as what White calls "historical writing,"[76] the early Camila plays reveal other arresting and important commonalities: the mode of emplotment typically invokes romance and tragedy, both genres conventionally over-determined and often combined, especially during the period represented in this brief review of plays inspired by Camila O'Gorman's life and death.[77] Jennifer Wallace provides a succinct yet embracing definition of tragedy (in the sentence that opens her book-length study of the subject): "Tragedy is the art form created to confront the most difficult experiences we face: death, loss, injustice, thwarted passion, despair."[78] It is not surprising that nineteenth- and twentieth-century artists would turn to tragedy to engage with Camila's story and its larger Argentine context. And while scholars have tended to take a classical view of Camila's tragedy, looking comparatively to the Greek model, Romanticist conventions and values present in almost all versions suggest a template closer to Byron, Dumas *fils*, or even Ibsen.[79] Contemporary European genre practices—very much the conventional models followed by nineteenth-century Argentine playwrights—support my contention. As White notes:

> No doubt, the late eighteenth century and early nineteenth century was a period of what Michael Prince calls "genre instability" par excellence. It may have been precisely this "instability" that got codified and transformed into a solution to the problem of which it first appeared as only a symptom. The mixed genre, the fragment, the paragenre, and the metageneric genre are all celebrated in Romanticist theories of genre.[80]

For Wallace, "Romantic Tragedy" encompasses the nineteenth as well as early twentieth centuries, from Wieland to Chekhov. She states categorically that "[l]ate nineteenth-century tragedy is haunted by the Romantic legacy" that "established the basic Romantic dichotomy between the self and the rest of society."[81] Romantic tragedy has long been a favored genre of the "historical" play.

If we follow the romantic tragic model included in Augusto Boal's well-known typology, we abandon the classical model of the *hamartia* (or protagonist's tragic flaw) in conflict with a perfect social ethos. Instead, we might consider the region's Camila plays to be generic hybrids not unlike the dramatic version starring that other nineteenth-century— French—"Camille." According to Boal, the romantic (or, as he also calls it, dramatic) tragedy presents a negative tragic flaw (i.e., a tragic virtue) in conflict with a negative social ethos. The heroine must adhere to that negative social ethos with one exception, the "flaw" that leads to her destruction. Camila indeed belongs to the dominant social class: the daughter of a loyal Federalist, she performs all the duties expected of a young woman of her rank, and she is even friends with the daughter of the most powerful man in the country. Her flaw—a commitment to a love forbidden by family, church, and state—is punished by her own corrupt society driven by all three powers. Unlike classical tragedy, the spectator is not expected to identify with the dramatic world's social ethos but rather with the protagonist's sole "vice" and thus side with the playwright in an overarching condemnation of society. In Boal's words, the "author wishes to show a social ethics accepted by the society portrayed on stage, but he himself, the author, does not share that ethics, and proposes another."[82]

The romantic tragic mode provides additional insight into audience identification and empathy as well as character incorporation. Romantic or dramatic tragedy does not necessarily impede audience identification; on the contrary, "the romantic author hopes that the spectator will be purified not of the tragic flaw of the hero, but rather of the whole [negative] ethos of society."[83] With the spectator expected to identify with the romantic tragic protagonist, Camila's onstage portrayal acquires even greater significance. Incorporation not only speaks to Camila's onstage "embodiment" but also brings to the foreground the iconicity of an actress—such as the enormously popular, talented, and culturally powerful Blanca Podestá—playing the historical, romantic-tragic character. How did Podestá's onstage presence affect spectatorial identification with the character Camila? Extratheatrical elements also influenced this context of performance: more than a few plays saw delayed or censored productions, yet many productions successfully toured throughout the country. In what ways do these circumstances contribute to the larger construction of Camila as Argentine femicon?

During the twentieth century, Camila's story was told and retold in plays and films that often departed from a single straightforward narrative about the two lovers. Camila appears allusively in the first of three barely connected tales in Luis César Amadori's 1955 film, *El amor nunca muere* [Love Never Dies]. For the film, Amadori recycled the sets he'd recently created for his own Camila film slated to star his wife, Zully Moreno. Amadori then abandoned the project under pressure from supposedly Perón himself, purportedly concerned about the film's critique of the Catholic Church. Miguel Alfredo Olivera's 1959 play, *Camila O'Gorman: una tragedia argentina* [an Argentine tragedy], begins in 1885 with a return to an abandoned Santos Lugares and a deranged ghost, who may or may not be Camila. In Juan Batlle Planas's 1971 film, *El destino* [Destiny/Fate], Camila's story is paired with another famous historical execution. By 1989, there is even a musical version of Camila's life, by Agustín Pérez Pardella.[84] These final examples bring us to the period spanned by the 1976–83 military dictatorship and the context of the four artistic works that are the best known and widest circulating among the many artistic versions of the young woman's story. They form the remainder of this chapter's investigation into the making of a femiconic Camila O'Gorman.

Mythologizing the Femiconic Body:
Enrique Molina and Griselda Gambaro

Camila's story inspired two major Argentine works that framed the country's latest and most repressive military dictatorship (1976–1983): Enrique Molina's 1973 novel, *Una sombra donde sueña Camila O'Gorman*, and Griselda Gambaro's 1982 play, *La malasangre*.[85] The only novel written by an Argentine surrealist poet and visual artist might seem a strange candidate for inclusion in a chapter on the performed construction of Camila O'Gorman as femicon. Yet Enrique Molina (1910–1996)'s 1973 text, *Una sombra donde sueña Camila O'Gorman* (hereafter shortened as *Una sombra*), is so clearly connected to later Camila performances that this brief narrative digression is warranted.[86] First of all, the novel's publication coincides with a complex moment in Argentine history. As Fernanda Vitor Bueno notes, the 1973 novel's tone of "indignant revolt"[87] is also present in some of Molina's poems from the late 1960s, which Vitor Bueno suggests were written in response to the period's international and national turmoil. Orlando Ocampo positions the novel's writing on the wave of Argentina's return to "peace and freedom" after a period of sustained violence (the so-called Argentine Revolution and 1966–73 dictatorship period) but notes that the novel prophesied an even darker period initiated by violent unrest and the March 24, 1976, military coup. In some ways Molina's novel can be read as a companion text to Griselda Gambaro's 1973 play, *Información para extranjeros* [Information for Foreigners], which has also been deemed prophetic. But perhaps most importantly for our purposes here, and as we will see later, Molina's novel provided the "historical" documentation for Gambaro's 1982 play, *La malasangre*, and Bemberg's 1984 film, *Camila*, both of which are regarded as artistic responses to the "shadow" that consumed Molina's Camila and the more than thirty thousand *desaparecidos* abducted and "disappeared" during Argentina's last dictatorship.

Una sombra, called a "surrealist historical novel,"[88] was claimed by its author to be an act of "poetic analysis."[89] Much secondary scholarship has been devoted to interpreting the novel's mix of historical documentation (at times cited verbatim; included in an appendix are previously unpublished documents located in Federico Vogelius's extensive collection of historical artifacts[90]), analysis, and even correction; lyricism; and ideological essay.[91] While adhering to an overall chronological order, the novel's three separate sections are stylistically disparate: the lengthy initial section (comprising nearly half the novel) details associatively the world into which Camila is born. It does so through lyrical "impressions" often set off by brief titles, not unlike the novel's nineteenth-century models that mixed essay and novel, history and fiction.[92] As Ocampo notes, the proportion of narrative discourse to documentation begins to shift in the second section, which recounts the couple's flight to, settlement at, and discovery in Goya. By the final, third, section—narrating the couple's incarceration and execution—the reader finds "an accumulation of extranovelistic pre-texts that include private letters, historical and sociological studies, police reports, government flyers, eye-witness testimonies, [and] memoirs of the story's protagonists."[93] One of the novel's great contributions to artistic versions of Camila's story—in addition to a beautifully rendered, imagistic language—is its apparently omniscient narrator's refusal to position the blame entirely on Rosas, instead indicting both Unitarians and Federalists in a concerted, hateful effort to eradicate love, beauty, and dreams of a different, and better, world.

Literary criticism has typically centered on these ostensibly Bretonian "antinomies" of life/death, love/hatred, and desire/repression. While most scholars agree that Molina's "surrealist poetics" produced truly innovative results, most interpretive disagreement—implicit or explicit—has come over Camila's fictional representation. Molina's narrator insists that Camila *is* Poetry.[94] Thorpe Running considers Molina's Camila to embody "a repository of the major Bretonian values" polarized by her world's negative values as embodied in Rosas.[95] Said values are "incarnated" in Camila's dreams or visions, sometimes experienced in the first person but more often recounted by the unnamed narrator. Running claims that Molina's Camila inhabits four planes: 1) a personal (or "historic") Camila of a "true romantic tragedy"; 2) a national allegorical Camila symbolizing the "good and pure natural instinct" that threatened Rosist *caudillismo*; 3) a legendary or mythical Camila representing a "pure human ideal, a Venus personified"; and 4) a "real" Camila "who . . . lived out the surrealist ideal."[96] Marta Gallo more concretely acknowledges the participation of the reader's "imaginary perception" in the novel's three distinct perspectives of Camila-as-character: 1) Camila as statue—externalized, spatialized, outside time, the contemporary allegorical image of Camila; 2) Camila as a fugitive shadow-image—romanticized, predestined toward a tragic end, and dreamed by the narrator; and 3) Camila as fragmented—her body split into distinctive features, as envisioned and dismembered by her repressors.[97]

All three of these Camila-as-character perspectives are potentially problematic, but perhaps the most discomfiting for our considerations of representation and embodiment is her textual fragmentation. Gwen Kirkpatrick has drawn critical attention to the "problematics of surrealist characterization" ignored in Molina's novel and overlooked in Running's interpretation, especially regarding the surrealists' notorious tendency to fetishize the female body in their artistic creations.[98] For Kirkpatrick, Molina's "daring" project falls "captive of its own methods"[99]: by coding resistance in the "same fetishistic patterns most emblematic of repression,"[100] the novel renders Camila both erotic dreamer-creator and eroticized object of her repressors' violent fantasies. In attempting to rescue Molina and his character—whom she outright calls a "martyr"—from such criticism, Vitor Bueno has suggested that:

> Ultimately, the representation of Camila in this novel opens the discussion of the representation of historical violence through poetic violence toward a woman's body. In fact, the distinctive discourses of the narrative allow different readings of the representation of Camila. On one hand, she is "an element of plot-space, a topos" (De Lauretis 119) which guides the historical account of government and social violence. On the other, Camila is transformed into a muse, she is Poetry; she embodies the mythical hero, the subject of fables who crosses the boundaries of life and death surviving as a positive symbol of Poetry.[101]

Feminist scholars remain unconvinced. As Kirkpatrick writes, "Molina skirts close to creating a victimization of whatever is labeled the 'feminine.'"[102]

The frequently commented-upon fragmentation of Camila's body into parts perpetuates the romantic tragic mode of emplotment present in virtually all other artistic versions of Camila's story. Romance's idealization of a remote past of innocence's loss and attempted recovery in a heroic quest is blown apart by tragedy's inexorable move toward final cataclysm. Romantic metaphors appear to be decimated by tragedy's preferred trope, metonymically reducing (rather than synecdochically reintegrating)[103] Camila's parts to the site and origin of ongoing power struggles. The romantic quest for a transcendent whole is undone as Camila's body seems to disintegrate before the reader's eyes in "[t]he novel's fragmented vision of the body, its metonymic dispersions and fetishism."[104] Much like the earlier playwrights with their romantic tragedies, the most Molina's narrator can do is decry the obvious injustice. Once again we are confronted by the limitations of romantic tragedy, even when subsumed within a surrealist historical novel.

Vitor Bueno and Gallo make special note of how the male narrator emphasizes Camila's eyes and hair, not so unsurprisingly given that both are features conventionally coded and utilized in traditional fiction. However, one might argue that for the surrealist (and going back to Apollinaire's Tiresias), the idiosyncratically female feature remains the breasts; and indeed Camila's breasts receive the narrator's most devoted attention, evident even in the final physical description of her execution: "They placed their pistols at her temple and at his temple and pulled the trigger. From the orifice produced by the shot, a slight thread of blood began to run down Camila's neck and slipped away into the gully between her breasts."[105] No mention is made of what happened to Ladislao's body. The reader is left to interpret Molina's representation of Camila as commemorative, exploitative, or possibly both.[106]

Such debates over Camila's fictionalized embodiment recall other critiques of Argentine intersections of gender, nation, and cultural production in Argentina, most notably Diana Taylor's contention that many of the country's national battles "have been staged on, over, and through the female body—literally and metaphorically."[107] Ultimately, Molina's project is limited by its narrator's understandable inability to apprehend completely his subject. Like other male avant-garde artistic renditions, as Francine Masiello has argued, Molina's Camila is the result of a utopian vision of woman as the "non-codifiable, the empty space that introduces a mystery into the literary text."[108] The surrealist's fetish of the female body transforms Camila into victimized sexual object, and her agency is sacrificed once more to the generic strictures of romantic tragedy.

What interests me here, though, are the ramifications of Molina's novel and their manifestations in later Camila performances. There is, first of all, a historiographic consequence: Molina's project is not nearly as neatly "corrective" as he would lead us to believe: on at least two occasions there are obvious errors of calculation regarding Camila's age and history.[109] Given that such miscalculations are still present in the later editions, one wonders if a surrealistic counterhistory is being created to confound diachrony. Perhaps most problematically (and to the detriment of his very welcomed review of the record), Molina's narrator-historian unquestioningly accepts as fact Camila's pregnancy, thus contributing historiographically to the perpetuation of certain assumptions taken as "truth." Indeed, such was the novel's reputation as historically factual that when it was re-edited following upon the enormous national and international success of Bemberg's 1984 film, the new paperback edition came with a running banner that proclaimed the novel to be "the true life of Camila: the [hi]story the film didn't tell."[110] The 1994 edition includes on its cover one of Molina's own collages. Though untitled, the image captures the artist's view of his novel's heroine. In the foreground, a nineteenth-century woman—demurely seated, properly attired (in a white dress, wearing gloves, and holding a fan), and seen from the waist up—gazes off to her left; just behind her line of sight, a smaller woman—naked except for a white cloth partially covered by a red blanket, one breast exposed, a red rose in her upswept hair—stands and stares longingly at the full moon. Both female cut-outs float upon—are about to be consumed by?—the dark waters of what appears to be a lake below an equally dark sky, both barely illuminated by the moon, itself drifting behind cloudy threads. Molina's collage conjures up the romantic tragedy in which Camila's story up to that point had seemed doomed to be cast.

Griselda Gambaro's 1982 play, *La malasangre*, premiering on the eve of the country's return to democracy, takes a distinctly different stance regarding female desire and agency even as it too indicts a regime that sought to repress both. Gambaro (b. 1928), one of Argentina's most esteemed contemporary playwrights, left the country in 1977 after receiving death threats and seeing one of her novels officially banned. Upon her return from exile in 1980, she immediately recommenced writing plays, something she said she could not do while in Spanish exile and far from her Argentine audience.[111] Gambaro first wrote *Real envido* [Royal Gambit], a play that would not be staged until the eve of the country's 1983 return to democracy.[112] *Real envido*, a parodic revision of the classic fairy tale, inverts chivalry's traditional values to reveal the underpinnings of patriarchal despotism. The original production at the Odeón Theatre was closed down for one day in February 1983, when, according to director Juan Cosín, the censor saw in the production's vignette involving four puppets an allusion to the military triumvirate and soon-to-be-elected presidential candidate Raúl Alfonsín.

The year before, another recent Gambaro play, *La malasangre*,[113] had been the target of a midperformance attack by armed ultra-nationalists objecting to perceived criticisms of a nineteenth-century Argentine dictator in a play Gambaro claimed made "a very direct reference to the [current] dictatorship."[114] Gambaro and the play's director, Laura Yusem, had struggled to find producers for the politically charged work. The Nationalist Movement for Restoration (Movimiento Nacionalista de Restauración, its name a direct reference to Rosas's title as "restorer of laws") demanded that the city close down the production because of a perceived defamation of Rosas. Shortly after the play's premiere on August 17, 1982, at the Olimpia Theatre, about fifty men belonging to the above-named organization purchased tickets to a performance. When the actor playing the role of the heroine's father entered, the men got up from their seats and displayed their weapons. Brenda Werth describes the scene: "A somewhat chaotic sequence of events ensued as the [house] lights went on and the men advanced toward the stage, yelling 'Viva Rosas' (Long live Rosas!)[,] calling Yusem 'comunista' and [one of the actors] 'montonero.'"[115] The group's leader approached the stage, where he placed his gun. The actors apparently froze in terror, but the other spectators responded with "fury and outrage."[116] One older woman "pummeled the leader of the group with her purse while yelling, '¡yo quiero ver el espectáculo!' [I want to see the show!]."[117] Yusem recalls saying to one of the advancing armed men that "the stage is not to be touched!," and "he obeyed."[118] The police were called, and around twenty people were taken away. While some spectators objected to the show and were returned their money, the rest remained to watch the performance, which had been delayed for about an hour. However, only one paper (*La Nación*) covered the event, reporting that the protesters threw coins at the actors but making no mention of the weapons. When director Yusem tried to press charges, she was met with police refusal to pursue the matter. The production nevertheless continued without further incident, enjoying a very successful eight-month run.

Premiering only a few months after the Argentine military junta's humiliating defeat in the Malvinas/Falklands War, *La malasangre* clearly responds to the country's recent repressive past and its "bad blood" of "national inheritance of dictatorship."[119] The deceptively simple plot is easily read as a Camila-like tale: Dolores, the upper-class daughter of an abusive father and abused mother, falls in love with her tutor, Rafael, who has replaced an earlier (and now-disappeared) tutor hired by her father, assuming that Rafael's hunch-backed form will prove no attraction to the young Dolores. Over the course of eight scenes, we see Dolores's "homelife" in a violent world turned upside down, where melon-carts are filled with the heads of those who defy the regime, where Dolores's seemingly all-powerful father is named Benigno [benign], and where she is to be married off to a young business associate, and obvious abuser himself, Juan Pedro de los Campos Dorados [John Peter of the Golden Fields].[120] Dolores attempts to transform her life and her name (Spanish for sorrows or pains) by winning Rafael over to the idea of fleeing "across the river" to a world "where they don't shout 'Melons!' and leave heads. Where my father doesn't exist. Where at least the name for hate is hate."[121] In the final scene, the waiting Dolores learns that Rafael will not be coming; her mother has told her father, who has had his sadistic servant Fermín kill the tutor. After demanding to see Rafael's dead body, Dolores answers her father's command for silence, by giving him her silence but letting him know that "I will never close my eyes! . . . For as long as you let me live, I will stay awake, I will always be watching you."[122]

As Ana Elena Puga notes, a first reading suggests an Ibsenian realistic exhumation of a would-be rebellious woman destroyed by an unforgiving society. Puga, however, sees in the play a textual complexity, which she describes as concentric allegorical circles: "the superficial domestic drama," within which there is "the family as a microcosm of life under the brutal Rosas regime," and within that "the most dangerous metaphor: the Rosas dictatorship as a figure for the contemporary dictatorship led by a series of generals."[123] In interviews made during and after the play's premiere, Gambaro took pains to note that her play was decidedly *not* about Rosas: "If I'd thought of Rosas, I would have made a play much more careful from the historical point of view."[124] That said, both the written text and the 1982 production drew heavily from the earlier period's symbology: the stage directions set the action in the 1840s, in an affluent home colored with a red palette (evocative of both the required Federalist ribbons and Manuelita's famous portrait)—the walls, the upholstery, the costumes, and even, one expects, the wine. Noted set designer Graciela Galán helped open up the Rosas-Federalism connection by having all the costumes in varying shades of red (and not limited to the "Restorer's" crimson) and making sure to have the mother's arms bandaged in blood-red rags. Her design also worked against easy assumptions of turn-of-the-century realism by dispensing with the text's drapes and reducing the amount of furniture. Finally, the scenography acquired an even greater and less realistic symbolism of what Galán calls the "imprisonment" typical of Gambaro's characters, through a scale that "dwarfed the bodies on stage and heightened the atmosphere of terror with a series of arches in descending size that skewed upstage at odd angles, creating a labyrinth."[125]

Thus both the text and the production worked to engage with early 1980s Argentina through a distancing device. Censorship was still at work in the period (nor did it leave the country with the later return to democracy), so, in Werth's words, "recourse to metaphor was a necessary strategy."[126] Gambaro was nevertheless chided, even threatened, by Rosist supporters and critics, the former for defaming the dictator and the latter for returning to the past instead of focusing on the present.[127] A close look at the text reveals an aporetic duality in the play's symbolism: red signifies both a father's violence and his daughter's passionate defiance; *melones* [melons] are not only the dismembered heads of those who would dare oppose the order but also the fruit offered by Fermín to Dolores and Rafael during their first class; and, most importantly, Dolores is taken away but refuses to be silenced—shouting, as she's dragged offstage by her own mother and her father's henchman, "¡Yo me callo, pero el silencio grita!" [I am quiet but the silence will scream!][128] Silence, like the play's other symbols, is resignified; its negativity rendered resistantly positive as "part of a politics of the individual to say no to arbitrary power."[129] For many scholars, Dolores's final cry exemplifies a turning point in Gambaro's dramaturgy.[130] In contrast to her earlier plays of the 1960s and '70s marked by silenced or even absented women characters, *La malasangre*'s heroine refused to remain quiet, openly defying her autocratic father and claiming her own destiny as silent watchdog.

Even though we don't learn Dolores's fate (has she "disappeared" as well?), we know that "her defiance has repercussions,"[131] at least for an audience that identified with her rebellion. Such identification was further stimulated by the fact that Dolores was played by film and television icon Soledad "Solita" Silveyra (b. 1952).[132] Indeed, it was Silveyra who had asked Gambaro to write the play. Her *Malasangre* costar, Lautaro Murúa, who played Benigno, was a highly regarded film and stage actor recently returned from Spanish exile.[133] In casting two actors well known for both their performances and politics, Yusem pushed audiences further to identify with rebellion, resistance, and critical reflection.

Both Werth and Puga (to name two scholars who have weighed in most recently on this much-studied play[134]) mention Camila O'Gorman in their discussions of Gambaro's work, but they tend to see Camila's story as background to the "larger" Rosas period. I propose we briefly consider the twenty-year-old Dolores as a potential Camila figure and not as symbolic stand-in for Rosas's own daughter, Manuelita. How does Gambaro's play compare with the conventional romantic tragic emplotment of Camila's story? As Puga notes, Dolores and Rafael only fantasize about escape, whereas Camila and Uladislao actually flee and establish themselves on the other side of the river. The land Gambaro's couple envisions is white, the color of peace and the prevailing color in representations of Camila. Camila's pregnancy is evidence of the sexual fulfillment that Dolores and Rafael desire but do not appear to have consummated. Seen in such contrasts, Camila might be said to have actualized Dolores's dreams. Yet Gambaro's play—unlike the majority of Camila plays, novels, and films—ends in suspense; we do not witness what happens to Dolores. We know that Camila was executed for realizing what Dolores can only imagine. Nevertheless, I wonder if by play's end Dolores—much like her name, sorrows or pains—has begun to exercise a different agentive role from Camila's as typically emplotted: instead of activist dreamer, Dolores assumes the part of accusing witness to the abuses visited upon actors like Camila. In this way, Dolores seems more like Antigone (a version of whose story Gambaro would stage merely four years later)—or even Soledad Rosas—than Camila. It may be Suki, the heroine of Gambaro's next play, *Del sol naciente* [From the Rising Sun] (premiered in 1984), who functions most as a Camila-like figure. In this play, whose action ostensibly takes place in a "medieval" warlord Japan but which clearly speaks to the treatment of Malvinas/Falklands War veterans, the prostitute Suki embraces her own death by comforting an already dead tubercular beggar. Like most Camila historiographic texts, *Del sol naciente* presents a victorious but corrupt "warrior" society (centered on Suki's antagonist Oban) but proposes an alternative ethos, embodied in the self-sacrificing Suki. When portrayed by Soledad Silveyra in a production directed by Laura Yusem, Suki seems destined for parallels with Dolores, but the play's emplotment nears Camila's romantic tragedy as Suki takes on a larger social responsibility than either Dolores or even Camila. No longer Molina's fragmented victim, Gambaro's heroines assume an increasing agency regarding their own destiny.

Nevertheless and despite the author's own protests, some audiences (and scholars) have insisted upon seeing *La malasangre* as a historical critique, as a historical anti-Rosas play, with the most extreme response that of the armed intruders that one evening in the theatre. In a 1982 interview, Gambaro hazarded a guess as to why her compatriots insisted upon seeing Rosas in her play:

Well . . . confusions like this can be produced in a country that's afraid to inquire into its own history. The pretext of a prohibited topic enables such confusion, it's like what the play wants to say gets lost, by taking an anecdotal fragment that doesn't even work as a historically valid anecdote. We're not interested in knowing how these personages were in reality . . . but rather in appropriating these personages en masse so they can serve our ends . . . [. . .] These are the dichotomies we Argentines make. We need to have heroes or myths . . .[135]

According to Gambaro, then, interpreting *La malasangre* as a critique of Rosas constitutes an easy way out from confronting the country's actual circumstances and from considering the conditions that have resulted in repeated cycles of repression and violence. Such an interpretive tendency also speaks to what the playwright sees as a national "need to have heroes or myths" constructed upon such simplistic binaries as civilization/barbarity, love/hate, and even male/female. This chapter's examples demonstrate that, like Eva Perón, Camila O'Gorman continues to be used culturally to fill one pole of this dichotomized need: in such politically divergent statements as Fajardo's anti-Rosist romantic tragedy, Molina's condemnatory historical surrealist novel, and even in some critical and spectatorial responses to Gambaro's 1982 play.

Revising Femiconic Historiography: María Luisa Bemberg and Ricardo Monti[136]

Both Griselda Gambaro and Argentine filmmaker María Luisa Bemberg created works purportedly influenced by the events codified and consecrated as historical in Molina's novel. Indeed, Molina's novel would gain renewed attention and a new edition after the success of Bemberg's film based on O'Gorman's life and death. The 1984 Oscar-nominated film, *Camila*, was the first big hit of redemocratized Argentina's film industry, which had suffered the effects of censorship and economic decline.[137] The film would go on to be one of the most viewed movies in Argentina (seen by over two million in that country alone and at that time considered the largest audience for any national film) and jumpstart an international wave of Argentine film screenings. Ricardo Monti's 1989 play, *Una pasión sudamericana*,[138] did not enjoy the box-office fortunes of Bemberg's film, despite receiving the María Guerrero award for best national drama and being shortlisted by several critics as one of Argentina's best plays of all time. *Camila*, as might have been expected of a film premiering just as the country was leaving behind a brutal dictatorship, reflected the desire of many Argentines to denounce recent events. Nevertheless, the film's nineteenth-century triumvirate of Church, State, and Family (what Irish-Argentine history scholar María Teresa Julianello has called the "Scarlet Trinity") eclipsed the historical dichotomy of centralized Unitarian state and Rosist federalism.[139] Indeed, Bemberg emphasized the systematic and excessive authoritarian elimination of any infraction of established laws, be they those of a centralized state or a federation. The film's nineteenth-century Argentine references point to an immediate national past of detainment, exile, and disappearance, an indictment made explicit in its final two images, when a shot of the Argentine flag flying overhead is rapidly followed by a view from above of the two dead lovers side by side. *Una pasión sudamericana* also offers us a critique and proposed transcendence of traditional Manichaeistic oppositions.

In both the film and the play, Camila assumes a tragic protagonism. Bemberg and Monti alike portray the individual as victim of a repressive *socius* even as they institute said victim as the historic subject of her own tragic destiny. Both works function as historical revision and suggest a collective national imaginary long invested in creating what Diana Quattrochi-Woisson has called revisionist "countermemories."[140] Such similarities notwithstanding, whereas Bemberg's film condemns the immobile patriarchal structure for its continued oppression of women and female eroticism, Monti's play subverts the romantic tradition entirely by telling the story from the executioner's point of view and taking us inside what Argentine playwright-actor Eduardo Pavlovsky has called the victim-victimizer's shared subconscious.[141] Bemberg and Monti employ techniques that expose received history as historiography and suggest "other" ways of regarding an iconized Camila.

Nineteen years after her death and with only six feature films to her credit (in addition to several shorts and three screenplays), María Luisa Bemberg (1922–1995) deservedly remains one of Argentina's most respected contemporary filmmakers. The subject of many interviews and articles, MA film theses, and even an English-language essay and interview collection, Bemberg notoriously rejected the traditional roles assigned to her as a member of one of Argentina's wealthiest families in order to dedicate herself to film.[142] An avowed feminist (and founder of the early 1970s Unión Feminista Argentina [Argentine Feminist Union or UFA]), Bemberg did not begin making films until her fifties and frequently battled censors over her scripts, which centered on transgressive women striving to reinvent themselves in a male-dominated world. Her films' commercial success was such that the profits from one would fund the next, a phenomenon at the time almost unknown in Latin America, as John King remarks in his detailed overview of Bemberg's life and work.[143]

Bemberg began writing *Camila* during the final years of Argentina's dictatorship.[144] Daring her to do a "love story," Bemberg's longtime coproducer, Lita Stantic, had suggested the life of Camila. Bemberg read Molina's book and involved a friend and fellow former UFA member, Leonor Calvo, to help with the research. The filmed script was the seventh draft written under dictatorship, yet as many involved with the project have attested, the film could only have been released under democracy. Indeed, Bemberg and Stantic were so concerned about the country's political situation and the postponement of an Argentine release that they coproduced the film with Spain, thereby ensuring at least a European premiere. Argentina's Catholic Church, one of Latin America's most conservative, stalled on granting Bemberg permission to film in Buenos Aires's churches (which included the still-standing parish of Socorro where the O'Gorman family worshipped) and punished the priest who allowed her to film in neighboring Pilar.[145] Such obstacles notwithstanding, the film premiered in Argentina in 1984 as the first and soon-to-be largest box office hit of redemocratization. It opened in thirty countries around the world, went on to be nominated for an Oscar for best foreign film, and as film scholar John King points out, became instrumental in "Argentina's post-democracy internationalist strategy in film-making."[146] The film was so successful that, Bemberg claimed, "every day in Buenos Aires five or six infant girls were named Camila."[147] Argentines responded collectively to what David William Foster terms the film's assumed "continuity between Rosas's bloody Restauración de las Leyes (Restoration of the Laws) and, almost one hundred and fifty years later, the military's *guerra sucia* (dirty war) and the Proceso de Reorganización Nacional."[148]

Bemberg's film follows the major plot points as received through Molina's novel and other contemporary versions of Camila's story.[149] What stand out are the particularities of its imagery and storytelling. Among the various recurring elements are animals: after the film's initial scene (played out during the opening credits) in which a young Camila is seen greeting—with her family—her grandmother, who will remain sequestered in a tower under house arrest until her death, we first encounter the adolescent Camila in another tower with newly born but unseen kittens. Their mewling will be heard again when a family slave hurls a sack holding them into the river and drowns the kittens under orders of Ca-

mila's father. Soon thereafter Camila visits her grandmother, who holds
an adult cat as she listens to her granddaughter read old love letters from
Liniers. As with so many of the film's elements, a double symbolism operates: the kittens suggest innocence rewarded with persecution and death,
and while the adult cat is associated with libertinage, it still retains the innocent aura of its youth, thus aligning Camila's rebellion with her grandmother's notoriety, yet conferring upon both a certain innocence. Cats
contrast with dogs, whose barking in the film announces state-enforced
violence. As scholars have consistently noted,[150] Bemberg's attention to
the senses is crucial to the film: Camila "meets" Ladislao through a sequence of sensorial events—hearing his voice during confession, seeing
him give mass, and finally touching him at her birthday party during
a game of *gallina ciega* [blindman's bluff, literally "blind hen"]. Once
again, animals are invoked: the innocence of the party game turned sen-
sual encounter is bracketed by another discovery when Ladislao is recognized by Father Gannon at a cock fight in Goya. At their execution,
they both will be gradually stripped of their senses. The couple's violent
end is foreshadowed when the scene of their elopement (taking place in
Bemberg's film during an afternoon siesta) and suggested consumma-
tion during the carriage ride is abruptly interrupted by another scene in
which Camila's father somewhat disgustedly observes the decapitation of
a slaughtered cow, a reference to the couple's future execution as well as
the earlier murder of Mariano, Camila's liberal bookseller.[151] Bemberg's
images function as symbolic constellations, referencing larger symbolic
worlds and eluding easy dichotomies.

Although filmed entirely on location and with an enormous attention to period detail,[152] Bemberg's movie at first glance appears to
structure Camila and Uladislao's story as a romantic drama typical of
the nineteenth-century French model and not unlike earlier Argentine
Camila plays.[153] Much like Dumas *fils* with his readers of *La Dame aux
camélias*, Bemberg renders her spectators accomplices who experience
catharsis when confronting a society willing to inflict a punishment far
more cruel than the lovers' crime. Reminiscent of its narrative and theatrical predecessors, the film centers on the female victim, but through
her opposition to an overwhelmingly authoritarian and violently sadistic father, not unlike Benigno in Gambaro's *La malasangre*. Rosas is "a
remote presence"[154] permeating society in the film's condemnation of
a misogynistic patriarchy for its oppression not only of women but also
of female eroticism and pleasure. In this way *Camila* abandons national
revisionist historiography for a denunciation of an immediate national

past and its destruction of those perceived as questioning its "sacred" values of Church, State, and Family. The film's unhappy ending serves as an additional warning of the possible repetition of this very same violent cycle as long as these imposed, ostensibly collective values are privileged over the rights of the individual.

Many of the film's structural elements are reminiscent of Latin American melodrama, a genre which Bemberg consciously evoked in the film, stating in interviews that she wanted to move away from her earlier "psychological" themes toward "something like opera."[155] In the process—and not unlike other 1980s Latin American artists—she reclaimed a popular genre that had been derided by intellectuals of the largely masculinist Left for its sentimentality, false consciousness, and "reactionary populism."[156] John King suggests that such analyses simplistically equate "melodrama with failed tragedy or failed realism as a second-rate mass cultural form" and completely overlook the vast circulation of melodrama among, especially, Latin American women.[157] On the contrary, melodrama, as King notes, allowed Bemberg to position Camila (and Ladislao) as "objects of pathos, . . . constructed as victims of forces that lie beyond their control and/or understanding."[158] Bemberg's statements regarding her protagonist support this positioning: her Camila is entirely pure; "there is in Camila not a moment of guilt."[159] More importantly for audience reception, melodrama locates spectators in a position of knowing more than its protagonists and thus able both to understand *and* to feel for them. Melodrama permitted, as King states, both "clarification and identification": in Argentina "over 2 million people wept at [with?] the story of Camila O'Gorman" but they also evaluated "signs that the protagonists [could] not have access to."[160]

Bemberg's use of melodrama was more complex than the salvaging of a "woman's" genre. Like many of her contemporaries, according to Currie K. Thompson, she availed herself of postmodern aesthetics to doubly code *Camila*.[161] Thus, even as *Camila* appeals to spectators' emotions, Bemberg said she "spiced it with clues for those who could read them as a send-up of the wors[t] sentimentality: fallen lace handkerchiefs, vivid thunderstorms, rain and tears."[162] These ostensibly postmodern "winks at the audience" provoked a reflective melodrama in which the status quo could be challenged, be it the film's implication of both Federalists and Unitarians in Camila's demise or its challenge to patriarchy.[163] Such postmodern aesthetics are equally employed to challenge what in film scholarship has come to be known as the male gaze. Barbara Morris writes that "Bemberg inverts this relation between desired woman and desiring protagonist/public, rendering Camila ([the actress] Susú Pecoraro) the subject that gazes and expresses the full force of her sexuality in her gaze that passionately lays siege to Ladislao ([the actor] Imanol Arias)."[164] Bemberg's Camila seduces the always ambivalent, torn Ladislao.[165]

Bemberg herself claimed that *Camila* was a tragedy. "Tragedies are about people who are victims of their destiny. . . . She was destined to meet him, fall in love and die for him."[166] Nineteenth-century romantic tragedy has been defined as an "offshoot" of the earlier *mélodrame* and its mix of expositional monologue, music, heightened sentimentality, stock characters, and action-packed acts culminating in a last-minute happy ending.[167] Yet *Camila*'s melodrama ends in romantic tragedy, as the film's darkening colors and violent denouement make overtly clear. Bemberg's film thus subverts (or at the least slips away from) its own melodramatic genre, by having the lovers die in a tragically extended execution scene that lasts several minutes. Melodrama's happy ending—of disaster averted at the last moment, of the would-be victim saved by the hero—is replaced by final, definitive victory of the sick controlling ethos, the mark of romantic tragedy.

Despite her understood desire to break with traditional dichotomies and repressive cycles, Bemberg structured *Camila* in a way that still defines the individual in opposition to the oppressive Other, and thus the film falls victim to the very historical dichotomization it seeks to transcend. One indicator of this failed transcendence is Bemberg's treatment of Uladislao (named Ladislao in the film), who appears as an ambivalent subject incapable of choosing transgression over conformity. Given that the film tells the story of "a pair of star-cross'd lovers," we must wonder why it is not titled "Ladislao and Camila." Indeed, and like the majority of earlier plays and novels, the film focuses on Camila's experience and not that of Ladislao. The irony of this version of Camila's tragic story lies in the fact that her lover belongs to the same patriarchal order from which she seeks to free herself. In Bemberg's film, Ladislao, no matter how much he loves Camila, ends up participating in the destruction of his beloved. When offered the opportunity to escape Goya and Rosas's captors, his decision to spend the night praying instead contributes directly to Camila's capture and punishment. In contrast, Camila, first through her grandmother (in whose life we see the granddaughter's predestination) and then through her own readings, learns to dream of love and to desire a different world; and later, after both her grandmother and the bookseller Mariano—her putative guides to rebellious independence—have died, Camila finds herself able to claim her own subjectivity and escape with Ladislao.[168] In contrast, Bemberg's Ladislao appears incapable of claiming any such subjectivity. At first, he rejects Camila's romantic overtures, experiencing several moments of crisis that leave him confused, even after he has fled with Camila. "No sé quién soy" (I don't know who I am), he confesses after they've spent the night making love. It is only moments before the authorities arrive to detain them that he acknowledges his own incapacity to create the new life Camila has offered him: "Siempre seré Gutiérrez" (I'll always be Gutiérrez), invoking the patronymic symbol of social and institutional power. As Camila's sole companion on her journey, Ladislao is ironically the one who betrays her by not being ready, willing, or able to leave behind his own subjective virtuality.

Bemberg renders Ladislao's role ultimately passive, even objectified; her camera displays an erotic gaze that might be called female, and the film's action has Camila consistently taking the initiative in her relations with Ladislao: seeking him out, kissing him, giving him the first letter, and so forth. Camila's initiative is also related to her open gaze, contradicted by Ladislao's inability to see or turning his back. Peter Schumann has described *Camila* as "an album of images carefully elaborated with exquisite taste . . . , but in this film Bemberg does not manage to take a step forward in her emancipatory endeavor."[169] Said misstep—though I'm not sure I would call it that—might be owed to a schism between a "female" (and perhaps feminist) gaze and "a discourse still in disturbing proximity to the patriarchal visual mechanisms at play in the classical cinema."[170] A traditional narrative overdetermination ultimately predominates and is only occasionally broken with what David William Foster calls "significant punctuative ruptures."[171] In the film's final twenty minutes, which tell the expected story of the couple's arrest and execution, this traditional discourse takes over and stymies any possible rupture, most tellingly when for the first time the film employs a voiceover (rather than a voice-off that carries the action into the next scene), creating a voice without a body.[172] Up until the moment of the couple's incarceration, all sound effects—with the exception of the original sound track—originate in the dialogue or environment. The final minutes thus create a jarring contrast to what spectators have heard until then, as the two characters' voices begin to separate themselves from their bodies. While in jail Camila silently reads Ladislao's final letter as we listen to his voice. And at the film's end, as the couple's dead bodies lie in their shared coffin, we hear for a second and last time Camila and Ladislao's final dialogue: "Ladislao, are you there? / At your side, Camila." For

Foster, these voice-overs "[derail] the film completely into the thicket of conventional narrativity."[173] Bruce Williams more generously situates *Camila*'s filmic discourse at the *edge* of a patriarchal male gaze, thereby emphasizing the protagonist's transgressive attempts at manipulating the established social norms to which she falls victim. Ladislao is likewise constructed in this borderland though his ambivalence contributes to the very repression his lover defies. Contrary to Ladislao's reassuring profession, Bemberg's Camila is very much alone in this melodrama turned romantic tragedy.

In ways different from but not necessarily unrelated to Bemberg's "feminist" critique, Argentine playwright Ricardo Monti (b. 1944) has tenaciously focused his theatrical writing on what he perceives to be the failure of Western modernity and its aesthetic counterpart, modernism. His theatre suggests a critical project of investigation into modernity's complex consequences to create a heterogeneous theatrical critique of the modern world in full crisis. This critique is well exemplified in the 1989 *Una pasión sudamericana*. Ostensibly another retelling of Camila's story and, like Bemberg's film, mixing local period documents with structures from the Western performance canon, *Una pasión sudamericana* overtly marries historical critique and artistic revisionism. The multiple historical and cultural references notwithstanding, the text distances itself from Camila through characters that refer to other historical moments and geographies, gendered games of representation that mediate our heroine's protagonism, and a title that insists on looking at Argentina as American "frontier." But what happens when that spatiotemporal frontier itself shifts away from Camila's nineteenth-century Argentina? *Finlandia*, a 2002 streamlined version of the 1989 *Pasión sudamericana*, retains the prior text's basic story line but moves the action from Southern early independence to the North's frozen plains on the temporal Medieval-Renaissance border. How do such modifications function as their own revision of Monti's already revisionist take on modernity? I end this chapter with an examination of three Buenos Aires productions: the 2002 staging of *Finlandia* bracketed by two productions of *Una pasión sudamericana*—the 1989 premiere at the San Martín Municipal Theatre and the Cervantes National Theatre's 2005 radical restaging. These productions, I argue, attempted to release local spectators from the romantic tragic-melodramatic modes in which Camila's story has been unceasingly emplotted.[174]

With *Una pasión sudamericana*, like Bemberg's screenplay begun while Argentina was still under dictatorship but not finished until the country's return to democracy, Monti took his first theatrical steps outside his native land. Although set in "the hall of what remains of a ranch, located on the plains outside Buenos Aires,"[175] the play exists in a sort of borderlands space where nineteenth-century Argentine independence encounters a historical and mythical "America," a contested frontier populated by European, indigenous, and mestizo peoples, immigrants and creoles, men and women.[176] As the playwright put it in a 1992 interview: "I believe that there is a common destiny for America . . . We are living in a period of incredible transformations, of the dissolution of nation-states. Let's not talk about an absurd, romantic, nineteenth-century nationalism at a moment when it's obvious that broader structures are breaking through."[177] *Una pasión sudamericana* thus marks the expansion of Monti's critique of his native Argentina into a consideration of this common destiny, in other words, Western modernity.

Monti's two texts ostensibly retell the story of Camila and Uladislao, yet unlike practically all other artistic versions, neither centers exclusively on the lovers' story. Rather they extend the traditional narrative frame to include the man who orders their execution.[178] *Una pasión sudamericana*'s action takes place on the eve of a decisive battle against an unseen enemy (referred to in the play as the Madman [Loco]). The unnamed Brigadier, assisted by his aging Aide-de-camp and two scribes, meditates on the lovers' future, which he knows is inextricably tied to his own historical fate. As the night goes on, five buffoons (or "crazies") reenact Camila and Ladislao's "passion" in an inverted, carnivalized *Divine Comedy*. Despite the obvious Argentine resonances, Monti consciously distanced his play from its own immediate referent: some of the characters reinforce the nineteenth-century historical setting—the Brigadier is *and* is not Rosas, and the Madman's letters include fragments of texts by several of Rosas's historical opponents. Other characters suggest altogether different historical moments: British minister George Canning pays the Brigadier an anachronistic visit; the Biblical criminal Barabbas, an enormous gaucho "reeking of death," is chained in the Brigadier's quarters; the lead "crazy" goes by the name of Farfarello, one of the Dantean *Malebranche* demons guarding the fifth *bolgia* in Inferno's eighth circle, but claims he's really Pedro de Angelis, the Italian intellectual known for his never-explained yet radical shift from Unitarian liberal to Rosas defender; another buffoon is called Saint Benedict, whose monastic order has been credited with pulling Western Europe out of the Dark Ages; and there's even a war-mongering Murat, an apparent reference to Napoleon Bonaparte's marshal and allegedly Pedro de Angelis's brother-in-law.[179]

Taken together these elements—not intertexts but competing texts, according to Argentine theatre scholar Osvaldo Pellettieri[180]—create a collective yet self-contradictory mytho-cultural past that confounds linear historicity while hovering around the period historian Paul Johnson has deemed the "birth of the modern."[181] This "history" culminates in the play's most controversial revisionist modification—the birth of Camila's son—as the Brigadier swaddles the newborn in his own poncho.

Hermetically set in the Brigadier's world, *Una pasión sudamericana* dissects authoritarian thought and its preferred theatrical genre, tragedy, just as it also confounds both fictional and nonfictional treatments of Camila's life. Another theatrical form erupts onstage to challenge tragic dramaturgy and historiography: the lovers' own "passion-play." Neither Camila nor Ladislao appears onstage; rather the buffoons perform their story for the Brigadier in a carnivalesque mystery of the flesh, passing from lustful Inferno to the World of passion (told through a reworked *Song of Solomon*), then on to Purgatory and the fusion of the Mystic Rose with the sexual act, and finally ending in the lovers' escape to what we know will be a transitory Paradise. At times spectator and other times director, the Brigadier comes to identify so fully with the lovers' heroic elopement that by play's end he has arrived peacefully at his own solution. According to the norms of the Brigadier's world—where individualism, honor, and law prevail—the only way to respect *and* punish the lovers is to shoot them like soldiers. Yet despite his decision to execute both lovers, the Brigadier clearly identifies with Camila: at one point the buffoon who performs Camila's role in the company's retelling wears a crown of transparent roses, whose innocence contrasts with the violently red roses in the crown that inexplicably appears on the Brigadier's head; and the death and martyrdom of both characters seem to be foretold in the blood running down their respective temples. This is once again Camila's story, perhaps most tellingly revealed in the play's original title: *Camila, un misterio argentino* [Camila, an Argentine Mystery(-Play)]. Through the Brigadier's difficult decision—misunderstood by his Aide as cold-blooded decree—the two antagonists fulfill their individual destinies: Camila, by eloping, must assume the martyrdom required by the passion-play; likewise, the Brigadier chooses his tragic end as the monster who kills her. Each is the appropriate ending in a world of polar opposites and only two options: civilization or barbarism, the prevailing dilemma of Argentina's early independence. Nevertheless, the play ends in temporary stasis: the arrival of Camila's son offers the potential utopian hope of the foundling who can undo the established order and reclaim his lost parents, but it also suggests the dystopic possibility of future generations coopted by this patriarchal world, not unlike the *desaparecidos'* five hundred children born in captivity and appropriated by dictatorship supporters only a decade earlier than the play's premiere. The ending is rendered even darker by the Brigadier's unleashing of the criminal Barabbas, who disappears into the pre-dawn of battle.

Una pasión sudamericana precludes any identification, empathy, or catharsis on the part of the audience and subverts both melodrama and romantic tragedy in its avoidance of any easy resolution. The playwright himself has noted that "there is . . . a tragic movement . . . [that is] crossed and cut up by the mystery play, which in turn produces a very strong structural and aesthetic tension, because tragedy by definition is dynamic while a mystery play by definition is static. There's a tremendous tension."[182] In *Una pasión sudamericana*, product of dictatorship and post-dictatorship, Monti refuses to reconcile this tension. In the process the text stages and comments upon the tragic outcome of the authoritarian episteme confronting the unyielding mystery of passion. Despite a flawed original production, a short run, and a misguided general denunciation of Monti for refusing to "take sides" in the still-ongoing civilization-barbarism debate,[183] *Una pasión sudamericana* has come to be regarded by many as his greatest play.

In 2002 Mónica Viñao premiered her production of another Monti text, *Finlandia*, in Buenos Aires's independent performance space La Trastienda. A first glance suggests a streamlined version of *Una pasión sudamericana*, rewritten ostensibly to erase any local references and thus avoid the kneejerk nationalistic responses to the earlier play; a closer look, however, reveals some intriguing differences that suggest an even broader critique of Western modernity and mythologizing historiography. While the basic story remains unchanged, specific references to Argentine history have been removed. Instead, the action takes place on "the frozen plains of Finland, covered by a thick blanket of snow, at the end of the Middle Ages or the beginning of the Renaissance."[184] In this way Monti not only implies that the world of nineteenth-century South American independence scrutinized in *Una pasión sudamericana* owes its own limitations to earlier historical periods; but by playing upon the name Finland as Nordic country (with its own independence battles) and world's end, or *finis-terra*, he also opens geographic space to encompass the West's southern and northern hemispheres and the so-called

New and Old Worlds. *Finlandia*'s subject exceeds mere reflection upon the independence period's federalist-liberal struggles that have continued to haunt Argentine politics.

In Finlandia, Una pasión sudamericana's cast is reduced to four: the military leader Beltrami and his Aide-de-camp, with the earlier buffoons replaced by the Mezzogiorno twins—brother and sister whose genital conjoining keeps them in a state of perpetual orgasm. Eluding the potential freak-show strangeness of their physiological condition, the Mezzogiornos provide Monti with an opportunity to explore gender and power construction: there is no one leader as with the earlier play's Farfarello; and so fluid are the twins' sexual identity and power relations that often they themselves cannot tell which one is performing their version of the play's inverted *Divine Comedy*. Thus in lieu of a transvestite, male-mediated Camila, we encounter in *Finlandia* a refusal to determine sexuality—and passion—as either masculine or feminine, further extending Monti's critique of modern polarizing authoritarianism to include gender construction and categorization. While one might argue that a masculine/feminine dialectic has consistently been present in all of Monti's plays, in *Finlandia* the dialectic is complicated to the point of it becoming impossible even to determine the two terms in question with any certainty. This is not mere inversion of two poles but rather a suggestion that determination itself must be questioned.

The 2002 production in other ways confounded easy assumptions of *Finlandia* as merely a reduced *Pasión*: Viñao, trained by Japanese theatre practitioner and theorist Tadashi Suzuki and Argentina's leading teacher of his methods, slowed the play's pace, isolated the four actors physically, and created a simple design of pools of light into and out of which the actors stepped. The only onstage set piece was an oversized chair/throne onto which Beltrami jumped, the actor Eduardo Cutuli's rather short dangling legs contrasting with the chair's imposing dimensions. The supposedly conjoined twins were kept physically apart throughout nearly the entire performance, with their inseparability suggested through choral body language, operatic duets, and a brief, climactic coupling at the end of their performance of Purgatory's mystery of the flesh. With only four actors on stage,[185] the two worlds—military tragedy and lovers' passion—seemed almost evenly matched, with the Aide's intermediary, pro-leniency stand running counter to Beltrami's harsh decision and the Mezzogiorno twins fluidly exchanging roles. *Finlandia* revised *Una pasión sudamericana*'s earlier revisionist critique of modernity by extending its spatial and temporal borders as well as incorporating considerations of gender and emphasizing the dramaturgical aporia of "a tragedy crossed and cut by a mystery."

Ana Alvarado's 2005 restaging of *Una pasión sudamericana* continued this project of meta-revisionism initiated by *Finlandia*. Alvarado, one of the founding members of famed Argentine object-theatre troupe Periférico de Objetos, directed the production for the Cervantes National Theatre, at that moment in poor repair and slated for renovation. In the Italianate theatre,[186] worn and haunted by its own earlier grandeur, Alvarado exchanged the original text's "hall of what remains of a ranch" for the backstage of an abandoned provincial theatre. Thus, when Farfarello sang one of his many songs, he often directed himself to the onstage audience of the Brigadier, a chained Barabbas, and fellow crazies, seated in the upstage auditorium facing the Cervantes's audience members. The buffoons made inventive use of abandoned properties and sets: Camila and Ladislao's initial encounter, for example, was conducted through a tear in a flat painted in highly ornate pastoral detail. Farfarello, played by leading experimental actor Guillermo Angelelli, declaimed his ode to war from atop a wooden hobby-horse on wheels. Anachronistic set pieces added to the theatricality of temporal dislocation when, for instance, the scribes wrote on typewriters and not with quills or pens.

ALVARADO'S PRODUCTION also intensified the original text's self-referentiality and its refusal to provide a single, definitive historical narrative. By setting the play in a theatre, Alvarado not only doubled the audience,[187] she exiled the Brigadier from his own world. Daniel Fanego, the actor playing the role, noted that "a military rancher standing in the middle of a theatre is strange: it's like a woman with spiked heels in the snow."[188] Indeed, the 2005 production's theatrical setting opened up a space for reconsidering gender construction as performed; it also brought to the fore coercive practices of normativizing gender roles. For instance, rather than simply beating the buffoon Estanislao into playing Camila by forcing him to "see" her face reflected in an imagined fountain, in Alvarado's production the other crazies tortured him into the role by shoving his head repeatedly into a bucket of water. Normative gendering in this way became inextricable from such dictatorship torture practices as the "submarine." The 2005 production appeared to combine *Una pasión sudamericana*'s revisionist reconsideration of nineteenth-century independence with *Finlandia*'s broader critique of modernity, all filtered through contemporary postmodern theatrics and references.

Despite such a novel resetting and some very fine performances, the production was not successful at the box-office; the night I saw it, there were barely thirty of us seated in a theatre that holds 800. Among the various reasons for the production's lack of success, I noted a problem that perpetuated a skewed local reception of Monti's critical project: in pre-opening interviews, leading actor Fanego—himself a well-regarded director as well as seasoned stage and television actor—insisted upon identifying his character *as* Rosas. In doing so, he resurrected the general impression of *Una pasión sudamericana* as a "historical" play, reinforced by the Cervantes Theatre's own synopsis insisting that the play dealt with "an episode from nineteenth-century Argentine history"[189] and a publicity campaign centered on the Brigadier as sole protagonist. Once again, Buenos Aires audiences were urged to disregard the larger consequences of Camila's story and the inventive theatrico-historiographic strategies utilized in Monti's revisionist critique of modernity.

Monti has claimed that he seeks a "broader realism" when writing for the stage.[190] His is indeed a theatre that fuses realism and experimentation, a theatre cohabited by histories, myths, and dreams, a theatre where the personal is never separate from the social, the political, the historical, and the metaphysical. If we consider the postmodern as engaged in critical dialogue with the modern, Monti's theatrical corpus surely qualifies in its aporetic stagings of supposedly antithetical histories, aesthetics, and cultural models. Monti's eleven plays to date do not provide happy endings, conclusive catastrophes, or easy syntheses, but rather only a tenuous and temporary equilibrium poised on the cusp of sure-to-come chaos. It is a theatre that questions its own theatrical condition as a means of questioning the entire legacy of Western modernity, whether we locate that modernity in the frozen plains of a pre-Enlightenment Finland or in a recently formed Argentina, itself the conflicted revolutionary product of the Age of Lights. Seen in this broader, critical light, Camila is transformed from tragic romantic heroine into provocative mystery—the inexplicable thorn in the crown of post-independence Argentina. Argentine audiences still appear unready or unwilling to engage with a revisionist Camila. The critical and box-office failures of its two local productions have led their author to believe that *Pasión* is "doomed."

Bemberg's *Camila*—for all its feminist, postmodern critique—embraces an already accepted aesthetics and historical discourse; it thus, as Bruce Williams writes, never fully crosses the border separating conformity and transgression. Monti's plays—especially when regarded as a single project—break with the "facts" and the accepted aesthetics of their representation. The film's historic-sentimental eye is transformed in Monti's plays into the mind's eye of a collective national imaginary. Additionally, by having his spectators witness—through both concrete and symbolic events—what they might believe are the "facts" that lead the Brigadier-Beltrami to his final decision, Monti breaks with accepted Camila iconography and historiography to suggest an alternative means of representing and interpreting recent and not so recent Argentine history.

"At your side, Camila"

To rewrite bicentenarian Mercedes's words, perhaps our scholarly and artistic crimes are found not in our telling what Camila did but rather in how we've told and retold what Camila did. We might ask, for example, why does it matter whether Camila was or was not pregnant? Why do so many scholars and artists insist upon her pregnancy even though the historical record is inconclusive? What's at stake for us in a pregnant Camila? I would argue that it's a basic narratological requirement of Camila's "romantic tragedy" that she be pregnant: it multiplies the horror of Rosas's (and society's) act in executing her; it serves as proof that her relationship with Uladislao was a passionate—and not chaste—romance and further grounds her rebellion; and it ultimately positions her within the two roles typically accorded Woman, with her power derived from sexuality and motherhood. Camila is not alone in such positioning; indeed, Evita iconography has conventionally oscillated between hagiography—madonna of the powerless—and demonization—whore of the masses. Through the insistent writing of pregnancy into Camila's story, her own agency is biologically and socially reduced to fertility and reproduction. A film like Bemberg's dangerously positions such female agency right on the edge of conventional reconversion.[191]

Gambaro and Monti fight against standard historiographic practices: both refuse to allow their male character to be identified exclusively with a single historical, mythologized figure (Rosas) only to have their plays categorized as such by audiences and actors. Gambaro's Dolores is defiantly not a mother and thereby demands a different emplotment from the accepted Camila mode; Monti mediates Camila's physical body and radically alters the popularly assumed ending by having the (male) child born and then brought onstage after his mother's execution. In both playwrights' efforts, we see a conscious critique of the mythologizing process as well as potential models for other ways of telling Camila's story and thus alternatives to traditional historiography. In contrast, other versions of Camila's romantic tragedy may blur, but they do not problematize the distinctions between mythologizing and historiography, as this chapter's analysis of an attempted creation of an Argentine femicon demonstrates.

I say "attempted" because I'm not at all convinced that Camila has acquired femiconic status. Why has Camila's story been overwhelmingly limited to a single albeit heterogenized genre? Why have speculations about her life and, especially, death been so quickly and so emphatically rendered "fact"? I wonder if such anxieties as those displayed over Monti's alternative retellings point to Camila's shaky status as icon. When compared, as we will see in the next two chapters, to the seemingly endless artistic versions of Eva Perón's life and death, the aesthetic and historiographic restraint shown toward Camila O'Gorman is striking. I sense a different iconographic project at work. Did Camila achieve celebrity, or has it posthumously been thrust upon her? Chris Rojek distinguishes between "achieved" and "attributed" celebrity—reserving the former qualification for those with perceived accomplishments and ascribing the latter to those whose celebrity "is largely the result of the concentrated representation of an individual as noteworthy or exceptional by cultural intermediaries."[192] Rojek applies the phrase "pre-figurative celebrity" to those who achieved posthumous celebrity before the rise of mass media: "[T]hey were items of public discourse, and honorific or notorious status was certainly attributed to them. But they did not carry the illusion of intimacy, the sense of being an exalted confrère, that is part of celebrity status in the age of mass-media."[193] Since the prefigurative celebrity is not accessible to us (as, Rojek argues, would be the contemporary celebrity), I wonder if the fuss over the details of Camila's life and death doesn't constitute a collective attempt to retroactively create "a site of perpetual public excavation" required of the celebrity's "veridical self." Or is the ruckus proof of Camila's status as "celetoid," the term Rojek coins "to refer to a media-generated, compressed, concentrated form of attributed celebrity"?[194] Or is it simply a matter of timing—with Evita's celebrity construction paralleling that of Hollywood's blonde divas—that renders anachronistic any attempted categorization of Camila as celebrity? Artistic and critical overdetermination of Camila as myth suggests that she does not fully or clearly fit into any category of established celebrityhood.

Camila's slippage—between achieved and attributed celebrity, prefigurative celebrity and celetoid—brings me back to Manuelita and Soledad Rosas. While neither has achieved or been attributed Camila's historic-cultural status, both have been subjected similarly to monohistoriographies, as I described in the opening of this chapter. Like Camila and unlike Evita, they have been obsessively represented in a single mythologizing light—rebel icon, submissive daughter—and typically with an obsessively narrativizing approach—women who sacrificed themselves for love.

Is Camila an icon-in-progress?

Camila's execution was *the* event of her time, yet her story is rarely recounted in the male-dominated general "histories" of Argentina and, if present, is trotted out as one more example of Rosas's barbarism.[195] Might this suggest that Camila is more "iconic" than actual "icon"? Could her status as "not-quite-icon" explain why artists and scholars insist on rendering her as passionate Madonna? Might this explain why audiences have become so incensed when artists stray from her popularly accepted life-script? Is this why her story is almost universally and insistently told only one way—in selection of plot event as well as mode of emplotment?

Camila is linked to Eva through more than a popular evocation of the maternal and the reproductive. The novel, two plays, and film examined in this chapter followed the 1971 discovery of Eva Perón's missing corpse, which itself, not unlike Molina's heroine, had been subjected to abuse, fragmentation, and objectification. Popular melodrama, Bemberg's preferred genre, was also a key component of the historical Juan's and Eva's performances, and we will see that Evita's life, too, has been frequently rendered as romantic tragedy. Such commonalities notwithstanding, it would appear that only unquestionably established "femicons" like Eva Perón can be transgressed or pluralized in wildly divergent representations and accounts. And even then, Evita's myriad representations have not been without their own controversies. They constitute the subject of the next two chapters as I turn to performances of Evita's life and afterlives.

TWO

The (Many, Many) Lives of Eva Perón

Notes for a Femiconic Genealogy

One evening in 1973, we're told, the British librettist Tim Rice caught the last part of a BBC program about Eva Perón on his car radio. Intrigued enough to make a point of listening to a later rebroadcast of the program, he became fascinated with this woman, whose single saving grace—Rice wrote later—was that "she had style, in spades."[1] In late 1976, after more than two years spent researching (including one or two trips to Buenos Aires), writing, composing, and recording,[2] Rice and composer Andrew Lloyd Webber released the studio concept album of *Evita*, their rock-opera follow-up to the hugely successful *Jesus Christ Superstar*.[3] They would not work together again until they reunited to create the song "You Must Love Me" for *Evita*'s 1996 film version starring Madonna. The original staging of *Evita*, under Harold Prince's direction, premiered on June 21, 1978, in London's Prince Edward Theatre. The U.S. premiere came barely eleven months later, on May 8, 1979, in Los Angeles's Dorothy Chandler Pavilion. In December 1980, the Spanish-language version (translated and adapted by Jaime Azpilicueta and Ignacio Artime) opened at Madrid's Monumental Theatre. Although director Azpilicueta did not stray far from the original English-language staging, except for a few "Argentinizing" musical modifications,[4] on June 26, 1981, Prince premiered his own staging of the Azpilicueta-Artime Spanish translation in Mexico City.

Evita has gone on to be performed in more than fifty countries, including much of Latin America. Both Paloma San Basilio, who originated the Spanish-language role of Evita in Madrid, and the Argentine musical star Valeria Lynch, one of Evita's interpreters in the long-running Mexican production, performed for Buenos Aires audiences, singing selected songs from the Spanish-language productions.[5] "No llores por mí, Argentina," the rather liberally translated Spanish version of *Evita*'s signature tune, "Don't Cry for Me Argentina," remains a standard of Latin American *chanteuses* and drag lipsynchers alike.[6] Yet, Rice-Lloyd Webber's Latin American successes notwithstanding, when Azpilicueta's production traveled to Chile, unspecified pressures kept the company from performing in Argentina or even neighboring Uruguay. And although Argentine actress Elena Roger created a national sensation when she was tapped for the title role in London's successful 2006 revival (reprised less successfully on Broadway in 2012),[7] *Evita* has yet to be professionally staged in Buenos Aires.[8]

Such an absence is striking in a city that frequently imports U.S. musical theatre (usually in Spanish-language restagings by U.S. and local directors). Indeed, rock-operas such as *Hair* and Rice-Lloyd Webber's own *Jesus Christ Superstar*—after initial violent protests that postponed its premiere until well after the nation's return to democracy—were staged in Argentina with great success, in both English and Spanish.[9] The fact that *Evita* has never been professionally produced in Buenos Aires should not lead us, however, to assume that Eva Perón's own controversial life remains unstaged in her nation's capital. On the contrary, María Eva Duarte de Perón has been the subject of myriad musical and dramatic (as well as satiric) plays, films, and television dramatic programs, all produced in Argentina, and she has appeared as a character in many more.[10] Despite potential resonances with the Camila mythologization processes detailed in the last chapter, Evita iconography eludes easy generic classification. The widely complex artistic representations of the life of the now-femiconic Evita, and their equally diverse interpretations, occupy the center of this chapter.

ARGUABLY THE MOST successful Argentine play about Eva's life, *Eva, el gran musical argentino* [Eva, the Great Argentine Musical], premiered in 1986. *Eva*, a self-described *ópera-rock*, first played in Buenos Aires's commercial Maipo Theatre before touring Argentina's major cities. The production—with a supporting cast of twenty-one performers—starred Argentine femicon Nacha Guevara, who also directed and coauthored the libretto with playwright-historian Pedro Orgambide. Guevara's longtime collaborator Alberto Favero composed the music and also acted as the production's musical director. Still regarded locally as the quintessential Argentine rock-opera,[11] such is *Eva*'s repute that the Province of Buenos Aires underwrote the equally successful 2008 revival, again starring (and directed by) Guevara, who at 68 was more than twice the age of her subject at the time of her death. Despite such national success—and Nacha's own femiconic status—*Eva* has not achieved the international cachet of its British counterpart. While *Evita* productions are ubiquitous and accessible through multiple media, *Eva* has been restaged only once, and available documentation of the 1986 original Buenos Aires production is limited to one out-of-print collector's vinyl recording; programs, published interviews, and reviews archived in Buenos Aires libraries; online photographs; and recollections of cast and spectators.[12]

A comparison of *Evita* and *Eva*—two rock-operas about Argentina's most spectacular and spectacularized femicon—offers us a way into this chapter's discussion of the complicated politics and aesthetics involved in staging Eva Perón's life. Both are sung-through musicals that, in two acts, rehearse the well-known (or at least the well-believed) mytho- and historiographic highlights of Eva Perón's brief but intense life: the humble small-town beginnings that informed her anger at the privileged classes as well as her identification with and devotion to the underprivileged *descamisados* [shirtless ones]; her big-city arrival and determination to succeed as an actress in the theatre, on the radio, and eventually in film; her love affair with then-Colonel Juan Perón; their romantic and political union and combined rise to nearly absolute power; and Eva Perón's final struggle with and death from cancer at the age of thirty-three. The obvious differences between the two musicals also bear noting: *Evita* begins and ends with the protagonist's death, first announced as the audience watches a film in which the real-life Eva Duarte performs without distinction. From the beginning, *Evita* resists any consideration of the human Eva Perón, preferring to examine her public persona as a cautionary albeit captivating tale.[13] Much of the opera's biting criticism leveled at Evita comes from the character Che, whom Rice based on the "legendary revolutionary" Ernesto "Che" Guevara as representative of "a conventional radical opposition to Per[o]nism."[14] Che, Evita's "musical alter ego,"[15] comes close to upstaging the titular character as he dictates how the spectator is to judge her.

Eva, too, begins with a public Eva Perón; however, she is not seen overacting in a mediocre film but delivering her final speech (on October 17, 1951), during which, already dying, she needed to be supported by her husband and her doctor. Similar to the British musical, *Eva*'s action takes an immediate leap backward, but it ignores the problematically documented events of Perón's early years in Junín, preferring to begin the story with her optimistic arrival to 1930s Buenos Aires.[16] Thus, from *Eva*'s earliest scenes, we witness a contextualized, humanized Eva Perón. The musical centers almost exclusively on Eva, and Juan Perón is all but absent, appearing physically only in the opening tableau (which is repeated toward the musical's end), represented on banners and posters in selected scenes, and nearly always referred to in the third person. And even though *Eva* likewise includes a "conscience" figure, he bears few structural or critical similarities to *Evita*'s Che. Mario, former union leader and Eva's fictitious personal secretary, functions as "a kind of collective unconscious."[17] Mario is not Che; his is not the role of ironic dissenting narrator, and he never questions Eva's goals or motives but rather serves as their ethical touchstone.[18] Thus, notwithstanding a similar heterosexual binary (Evita/Che; Eva/Mario), *Eva* does not share *Evita*'s split focus. *Eva* is her own show, and in both versions Nacha Guevara appeared in nearly every scene of the two-hour-plus performance. Whereas *Evita* follows the standard "foreign" negative party line regarding both the Peróns and Peronism to deliver a rather predictable story of a woman driven to extremes by her apparently insatiable need for power and acceptance,[19] *Eva*, by focusing on the flawed but exceptional "national" individual, furnishes a more complex and more contextualized portrait.[20]

A brief retracing of *Eva, el gran musical argentino*'s genealogy, through its intersections with both its creator-star Nacha Guevara and the Rice-Lloyd Webber rock-opera *Evita* (and its various stars such as Patti LuPone and Elena Roger), will serve as the point of entry into this chapter's focus on the construction, rehearsal, and critique of the Evita "myth" through biographical narrative, film, and theatre. Here I look at four biographies (with Perón's own attributed autobiography, *La razón de mi vida* [My Mission in Life], hovering nearby): the two most widely disseminated Spanish-language biographies (by Alejandra Dujovne Ortiz and Marysa Navarro, respectively), as well as two broadly circulating and fairly recent English-language biographies (by Navarro with Nicholas Fraser and Shawn Fields's translation of the Dujovne Ortiz book). I examine in each text the manner in which two key moments in Eva Perón's story are recounted in order to demonstrate how each published "life" contributes in its own way to an overarching historiographic construction and reification of a certain Evita "myth" (or multiple competing myths). My analysis then develops through a consideration of two films and three plays—all created after Argentina's 1983 return to democracy—that attempt to reconstruct Perón's life from different generic vantage points: as quasi-documentary (Eduardo Mignogna's 1984 *Evita; quien quiera oír, que oiga* [Evita: listen if you want to]); as local feature film purportedly created in response to Alan Parker's 1996 *Evita* (Juan Carlos Desanzo's *Eva Perón*); as overtly politicized, "Peronized" Latin American play (Osvaldo Guglielmino's 1980s *Eva de América*); as a very local, even personal 1994 staging of Leónidas Lamborghini's Eva-dedicated poems, themselves a re-writing of his subject's autobiography (*Eva Perón en la hoguera* [Eva Perón on the Bonfire]); and as a long-touring imagined encounter between Eva Perón and Victoria Ocampo (Mónica Ottino's successful early 1990s play, *Eva y Victoria*), Evita's oft-perceived polar opposite in class, politics, and aesthetics. The chapter concludes with a return to Nacha Guevara and reflections on how the oscillation between performing "as" Evita and "being" Evita operates onstage as well as within the larger context of a national politics seemingly determined to conflate Eva with Argentina.

It should come as no surprise that approaches to artistic productions centered on Eva Perón's life have rarely enlightened but much more frequently reiterated and reified standard mythologizing practices. A contrastive analysis, such as the one I employed in my opening sketch of the two musicals, highlights one of multiple traps awaiting any cultural representation of Eva Perón. Traditional interpretations of Eva Perón's life, especially foreign versions such as the Rice-Lloyd Webber musical, typically fall into overly reductive saint-whore dichotomies. And while it may be tempting to pit "good" Argentine *Eva* against "evil" foreigner *Evita*, such simple binarism (as many scholars since Julie M. Taylor have noted) brings nothing new to the critical discussion. Our Lady of Hope Santa Evita and the Black Myth of "that woman" her enemies refused to even name ultimately are nothing more than two sides of the same misogynist coin.[21]

Another interpretive trap is causality. Neither simple cause-and-effect nor the accompanying concept of competition elucidates the genesis and reception of each musical: while it's true that *Evita* rehearses the standard northern hemispheric anti-Peronist "myth," the commonly held belief that Rice based *Evita* on Mary Main's extremely negative and frequently cited 1952 biography of Eva Perón is refuted by the librettist himself, claiming he did not read Main's book until it was published in Britain in 1977, well after *Evita*'s inaugural studio recording.[22] Given that Rice's libretto and Lloyd Webber's music echo many of the British stereotypes surrounding Eva Perón and Argentine (and even Latin American) culture,[23] it may be tempting to regard *Eva* as Argentina's response and corrective to *Evita*. All the same, and as one Argentine journalist noted on the eve of the Parker film's 1997 Buenos Aires premiere, despite "strong similarities and ambiguities," the two musicals really "have nothing to do with one another."[24] It would appear that both musicals elude basic cause-and-effect categories.

A third, and meta-iconic, trap awaits the would-be Eva interpreter. Many accounts of artistic-cultural productions centering on Eva Perón have resulted in little more than hagiographies, star-tales that recycle the same mythologizing events of her life, rehearse the already mentioned polarizations, and ultimately shed no new light on cultural reconstructions of the historical person. Yet it is difficult to avoid questions of celebrity when the actors performing Evita are not infrequently themselves femicons. Such is the case with *Eva*, where we are confronted by a dual femiconicity—Nacha as Eva—in a play that might easily but inadequately be dismissed as a "star vehicle." How to avoid (re)producing a doubled hagiography, of not only Eva Perón herself but also the now-femiconic Nacha Guevara?

What other ways might we—taking these two musicals as this chapter's initial examples—document and analyze the many, many Evita-inspired plays, films, and songs as they cross linguistic, cultural, and national borders? One alternative to the above-described contrastive Manichaeanism, simplistic cause-and-effect search for origins and ends, and reifying hagiography is through a reconsideration of genealogy, as conceptualized by Michel Foucault. In his 1971 essay "Nietzsche, Genealogy, History," Foucault revisited Friedrich Nietzsche's "originary" lexicon, discarding *Ursprung* [originary basis, literally "original leap"] in favor of two other, related terms: *Herkunft* and *Entstehung*. Foucault describes *Herkunft* as stock, descent, affiliation, not limited to mere identification but rather seeking "the subtle, singular, and subindividual marks that might possibly intersect in them to form a network that is difficult to unravel."[25] For Foucault, *Entstehung* denotes emergence, the moment of arising, but he cautions us to "avoid thinking of emergence as the final term of an historical development."[26] A Foucauldian genealogy would thus trace, record, and expose a network of singular incidents, accidents, even absences, and their intersections, as it avoided getting caught up in evolutionary trajectories or the fruitless search for beginnings and endings. Latin American transculturative theories can further enhance a Foucauldian theory of genealogy in understanding encounters between local and international cultures such as we've already seen with *Evita*.[27]

We might therefore begin this chapter's alternative genealogical project by tracing what I consider to be *Eva*'s local, transculturative affiliations. Buenos Aires's musical theatre tradition extends back to the earliest years of the Spanish colony. Indeed, one of the region's first Spanish-language plays was the one-act *El amor de la estanciera* [The Love of the Rancher's Daughter].[28] Like its Iberian counterpart, the River Plate *sainete* incorporated musical numbers, and *El amor de la estanciera* ended in a wedding celebration, complete with singing and dancing.[29] By the late nineteenth century, the local *sainete criollo* had been codified into a prescribed set of elements: the setting of the melodramatic, and frequently very violent, action in the shared inner patio of the *conventillo* [multifamily tenement dwelling]; the local-immigrant encounter replete with picturesque character-types and a Babelian mix of languages and dialects; and the obligatory songs and celebrations. Thus, long before Broadway-style musicals and burlesque/comic revues filled the commercial theatres lining Corrientes Street, Buenos Aires audiences were enjoying popular spectacles in which spoken text alternated with performed song.

Since the mid-twentieth century, another musical presence on the Argentine performance scene has been the *café-concert*—the intimate theatre-bar where solo artists or groups perform cabaret-style shows. *Eva*'s originator and star, Nacha Guevara (b. 1940), has long specialized in such shows. First trained as a dancer, then as an actor, and only later as a singer, Guevara found her performing milieu in the late 1960s in Buenos Aires's notoriously avant-garde Di Tella Institute.[30] She quickly became famous for her one-woman shows (with musical accompaniment composed and orchestrated by Alberto Favero), in which her rather thin soprano voice and fragile appearance contrasted with her enormous presence, highly dramatic performance style, and visually commanding stagings. Guevara was soon identified with Latin America's *nueva canción* movement. While not the exact equivalents of U.S. "protest" folk singers, these "new singers" were very sociopolitically engaged, extremely theatrical, and often quite humorous. One of Guevara's earliest and best-known shows, *Nacha de noche* [Nacha by Night, 1968], combined social satire with the lightly ironic material typical of the *café-concert* cabaret format, to which Guevara contributed her own lyrics as well as vocalized poems by Spanish and Latin Americans authors. Her 1969 one-woman play *Anastasia querida* [Dear Anastasia] was named "show of the year" by the leading Buenos Aires cultural magazine *Primera plana*, the first of the production's many awards. By 1970 Guevara was well aware of the contra-

dictions inherent in her own work as an award-winning entertainer singing of liberation in a rapidly polarizing and increasingly violent country:
"Musical protests don't do anything; some people like them because afterwards they feel justified for the rest of their lives. Or at least for the
rest of the month. . . . Disagreement has to make itself known through
direct means; otherwise, these songs become just another consumer
item."[31] Her own lyrics grew increasingly caustic as Argentina headed toward another dictatorship. After a paramilitary organization (the notorious Argentine Anticommunist Alliance, known as the Triple A) publicly
threatened Guevara with death, the performer and her family went into
exile in September 1974. She returned from Mexico in 1975 to perform
in *Las mil y una Nachas* [1001 Nachas]. When a midperformance bomb
explosion killed two spectators and wounded many others, Guevara shut
the production down and once again left the country, performing in
Latin America, Spain, and the United States.[32] She would not return to
Argentina until 1984, after the country's return to democratic rule.

Barely two years after returning from exile, Guevara premiered *Eva*,
whose lyrics, music, and staging were tied to the artist's own performance
aesthetics—developed over nearly two decades of solo performance—as
well as her personal history with her native Argentina. In 1986 *Eva* was
staged simply yet very dramatically, and Guevara did not claim any "historical accuracy" in her performance of Eva Perón.[33] Indeed, in an interview given the week *Eva* opened in Buenos Aires, Guevara said that her
wigs and makeup were the only elements employed to "recreate" Eva
Perón. She also observed that the costumes suggestive of Perón's famous
wardrobe were made out of "much more theatrical" fabrics. The program notes made the production's position clear: "This play is a free version of the life of Eva Perón. Only the protagonist's speeches belong to
historical reality."[34] In many ways, *Eva* played against not only its protagonist's star-tale but also Guevara's own diva status. Guevara's Eva was not
Rice-Lloyd Webber's hyper-sexualized Evita but rather under-sexualized,
her brief life played out against the backdrop of a much larger Argentine
class struggle. In obvious identification with some of Peronism's loftier
goals, Guevara transformed *Evita*'s tragic flaw of proud ambition into a
virtue: ambition as a model, a way out of poverty, neglect, and derision.
Guevara's Eva was not punished for having overreached her position;
rather, she was regarded as a young woman upon whom gigantic and
conflicting demands had been made and whose commitment to social
change blinded her to some, but not all, of the moral ramifications of
her choices.

Such a perspective—of a woman whose class and gender awareness is experienced collectively as well as individually—is highlighted in *Eva*'s signature tune.[35] "Si yo fuera como ellas" [If I were like (those women) . . .] is first sung privately by Eva, between takes in broadcasting the radio-theatre plays for which she performed the roles of famous women in history.[36] Guevara's Eva experiences her strongest musical moments alone; they are instances of doubt and renewed commitment to herself, her class, and her sex. When Eva reprises the initial verses of "If I Were . . ." just before being forced to reject the nomination for the vice-presidency, she reflects on her current dilemma, attempting to do what Perón and the military expect of her ("They told me to learn the prudence of living, / of keeping up appearances and even the art of lying.") while still honoring her self-imposed responsibilities to Argentina's dispossessed.[37] At the musical's end, the same rising melody slips in under Eva's final words, this time sung from her deathbed: "One day when I return / I will be with everyone / and that day with my people / that day . . ." Guevara's Eva Perón dies, still seeking to define her own personal identity through that of her Argentine "people."

Given Nacha's openly sympathetic attitude toward both Eva Perón and the more positive elements of her Peronist causes, it may be hard to understand why she even recorded "Don't Cry for Me Argentina" in 1977 (in what soon became one of the two best-known Spanish-language renditions).[38] It might baffle the reader even more to learn that she began to include the Rice-Lloyd Webber song in performances of *Eva* (to the rumored horror of colibrettist Orgambide) as the 1986 production toured Argentina.[39] The circulation of the Rice-Lloyd Webber tune appears to elude any traditional analysis of "origins," and an explanation might benefit from the more transculturative, genealogical approach I propose in this chapter. The lyrics for "Don't Cry for Me Argentina" were the first Rice wrote for *Evita*, and both he and Lloyd Webber have described them as their attempt to capture Evita's "'selling' herself to the full."[40] Many recorded versions of the hugely successful song are still in circulation—from Julie Covington's original concept-album studio recording to the London (with Elaine Paige) and U.S. (with Patti LuPone) stage productions, and the film version (with Madonna).[41] The Spanish-language version has resulted in multiple variations, including Argentine rock-star Charly García's bitter parody recorded while the country's military dictatorship was caught up in the ill-fated Malvinas/Falklands War: "Don't cry for the wounds that never stop bleeding. Don't cry for me, Argentina, I love you more every day."[42] Even the "original"

Azpilicueta-Artime Spanish-language translation alters significantly the Rice lyrics (and even led one frustrated Argentine to post an Internet complaint: "if you're able to explain this translation, then you deserve a prize").[43] Indeed, the slippages between the two versions are telling, evident even in the following brief comparison of the two choruses:

> Don't cry for me Argentina / The truth is I never left you / All through my wild days / My mad existence / I kept my promise / Don't keep your distance.

> No llores por mí, Argentina [Don't cry for me, Argentina] / mi alma está contigo [My soul is with you] / mi vida entera [My entire life] / la dedico [I've dedicated to you] / mas no te alejes [But don't keep your distance], / te necesito [I need you].[44]

The Spanish version, when combined with Nacha Guevara's *café-concert* intimacy, sociopolitical engagement, and intense theatricality, translates Rice's defensive, proud, commanding, and defiant Evita into a self-sacrificing, doubting, and even despairing Eva, whose relationship with her native country is experienced far more privately and soulfully than the original English lyrics and the majority of their many interpretations convey.[45] Difference is not limited to the linguistic: Guevara's performances transformed and enriched both the British original and the Spanish translation. Indeed, the translated lyrics as performed by Guevara do not seem at all out of place in the Argentine production, whereas they actually make very little sense within the context of the Rice-Lloyd Webber rock-opera, sung first at the top of act two shortly after Perón's 1946 victory and well before Eva had had the opportunity to exert much influence.[46]

Paul Rabinow has pointed out that Foucault's great contribution to studying "the problem of the subject" was to trace ways in which the human subject is objectified.[47] Ultimately, if *Evita* objectifies Eva Perón through the differentiating, split Evita-Che focus and the condemnation of her ambitions (witnessed in the social institutions that disciplinarily ended her political career), *Eva* looks at Eva Perón's own process of Foucauldian "subjectification" with Guevara's performance history standing as an example of her own icon-formation's "long and complicated genealogy."[48] Examining Nacha Guevara-as-Eva allows us to trace a double "articulation of the body and history," the task Foucault assigned to genealogy.[49] Although the 1986 production of *Eva* made no public claim to historical veracity, the subject Eva Perón—along with her interpreter Nacha Guevara—was (re)constructed as an historically articulated body.[50] By documenting *Evita/Eva*'s extraordinary incidents, accidents, absences, and intersections, we can turn our critical attention away from the dead-end models of narrative causality, polarizing rhetoric, and hagiographic myth-making and direct it more productively toward Eva Perón's iconically reconstructed body-in-history. The remaining pages of this chapter continue my proposed critical project, first by looking at how some recent Eva Perón biographers have christened her and cut her life, later by examining how that life has been reconstructed on stage and screen, and, finally, by illustrating how Evita's femiconicity continues to be played out in the national and transnational cultural and political arenas.

What's in a Name?

Eva Perón. Eva Duarte. Yo, Eva María Ibarguren, la Irreconocida. María Eva Duarte de Perón. Marie Eve D'Huart. La Chola. La Negrita. Cholita. Mi Negrita. Eva, María Eva, Evita.

La Puta. La Yegua. La Ramera. La Lujosa. La Enjoyada. La Descamisada esa. La Resentida. La Trepadora. La Santa. La Jefa Espiritual de la Nación. Evita Capitana. El Hada de los Desamparados.

Hay que aceptar todos esos nombres y apellidos. Soy, podría ser, todas y ninguna. . . . Pero en la etiqueta de la tapa del cuaderno puse *Evita*.[51]

So writes "Eva" in Abel Posse's 1995 novelistic retelling of Perón's story, *La pasión según Eva* [The Passion according to Eva]. In a novel that "shares traits of various established genres, such as the historical novel, biography, history, *testimonio* or oral history and fictitious autobiography,"[52] Posse attempts what he calls a "choral biography. Everybody's novel. Group biography, with a central character (helmeted [*de capelina*], smiling) and background chorus and people."[53] The "unrecognized" and illegitimate Eva María Ibarguren becomes the legitimate Eva María Duarte,[54] who in turn rechristens herself the actress Eva Duarte, later the wife María Eva Duarte de Perón, then Eva Perón, and finally her own preferred "Evita."[55] A woman beatified as popular devotional figure: Saint Evita, Spiritual Leader of the Nation, Captain Evita, the Fairy Godmother of the Helpless. A woman so despised that her opponents either refused outright to identify her by name— "that woman"—or sought onomastically to dehumanize and demean her as "mare," "whore," or "streetwalker." Her many names conjuring contradictory and antagonistic perceptions: a "showy" upper-class wannabe, jewel-encrusted "social climber" versus populist role-model and member of the "resentful," "shirtless" classes. A woman whose purported final words were the "perfectly musical" yet disconcertingly impersonal "Eva se va" [Eva is leaving].[56]

María Inés Lagos-Pope, building upon Rosi Braidotti's theory,[57] calls Eva Perón a "nomadic subject":

> Eva's journey from provincial town to Buenos Aires certainly contributed to her capacity for transformation. Her continuous process of renovation makes her especially modern, and the fact that Eva didn't feel tied to one type of image manifests a type of power as a woman, capable of rebelling against restrictions that certain sectors sought to impose upon her, especially Perón's rivals and the women of Buenos Aires's upper class.[58]

Eva's near-constant performance of self-transformation has become a central component in the femiconic construction of a larger national identity script, first created during her life and to this day still debated, deconstructed, and reconstructed. The historical Eva's many names point not only to her capacity for (self) reinvention but also to the challenges composing her life poses for those scholars, biographers, and artists seeking what Braidotti calls the nomad's "fixed routes."[59] Yet where Lagos-Pope sees only Eva's rebellious nomadic consciousness coming into conflict with the dominant powers (including her own husband's), I also see a clear challenge, even resistance, to representation itself, beginning with her own name and continuing through the contemporary issues of agency, authority, and authenticity that underlie this chapter's exploration of "historical" representation through biography.

Cutting a Life: Historicizing Eva Perón

Let's enter into biography through what is perhaps the most personal Internet appeal to a "truthful" telling of Eva Perón's life: the "official" Eva Perón website, "developed & maintained by the family of Evita Perón."[60] Eva's life story is retold in the section "To be Evita." Anyone familiar with the Evita-tale might anticipate this extended opening:

> Buenos Aires, July 26, 1952. Argentina is wrapped in silence as the country listens to the official communiqué from the Subsecretariat of

Information: "It is our sad duty to inform the people of the Republic that Eva Perón, the Spiritual Leader of the Nation, died at 8:25 P.M."

From that initial silence sprang forth the sound of weeping and the sound of corks popping from champagne bottles. These sounds reflected the love and the hate that Evita inspired. The sounds of weeping reached the street and took the form of interminable lines visible to all the world until the day of Evita's funeral on August 11th. The champagne glasses were raised in private.

Each Argentine knew who Eva Perón was; some, however, based their knowledge on their feelings while others depended on the rational interpretation of facts. Tangible reality began to take the form of myth and those of us who did not share Evita's chronological space in time but wished to know her found that for many years our way was blocked by silence. "We Do Not Speak of That" is not only the title of an Argentine film [María Luisa Bemberg's *De eso no se habla*, usually translated as "I Don't Want to Talk About It"] but also a signpost of our history.

The works that were published, the movies that were filmed, the voices that even today are raised in praise or condemnation confirm that Eva Perón has transcended both time and myth.

If life is a continual choice and we continue to evolve until the hour of our death, then on July 26, 1952, Evita, the child born thirty-three years ago in a small Argentine town, had reached the end of her journey: she had become forever Evita.[61]

Like Rice-Lloyd Webber's *Evita* and so many other versions of Eva Perón's life, this ostensibly official story begins with its protagonist's death before quickly moving on to other obsessively recurring dualities that have become the features of most biographic retellings: love/hate, emotion/rationality, reality/myth. The website's narrative reconciles these polarizations in Eva's physical death and transcendence through becoming "forever Evita."

The official website not only illustrates how Evita's "lives" often commence but also suggests how these lives have been configured or cut. The site divides Eva Perón's life into the following chronologically organized chapters: 1) "Los Toldos" of María Eva's birth and early childhood; 2) the family's 1930 move to "Junín" and the young teen's growing independence; 3) "Eva Duarte, Actress," which provides much information about her professional career while saying little about her highly speculated personal life[62]; 4) "The Day Which Split History: October 17,

1945,"[63] which begins with 1943's military coup before proceeding to Eva and Juan's meeting, Juan's release from prison, their marriage, and Eva's first steps into the political arena; 5) the presidency years "1945–1952" and Evita's growing participation; and 6) "From beneficence . . . to social justice," focusing on the Eva Perón Foundation's work and ending with her final public appearance, at Perón's second inauguration. Decisive to the narrative ordering is how nearly every section concludes with a comment about personal transformation; each is considered a phase in Eva Perón's life: from "the little girl of Los Toldos and Junín," to big-city actress, to Juan Perón's companion and leading proponent of his causes, to committed social activist, and finally to transformer of traditional charity into Peronist social justice.[64]

I cannot overemphasize the relevance of such configurations to femiconic historiography. They speak directly to what Karen Bishop deems "the roles that documentation, dissemination and politics play in the construction and preservation of 'historical fact.'"[65] Following Walter Benjamin's still-pertinent essay "Theses on the Philosophy of History," Bishop writes:

> What is at stake . . . in a reluctance to locate history outside of the boundaries afforded it by historical record is the opportunity to understand how history is decided upon—or rather, to ask ourselves according to what ethical principles, traditions and political motivations we construct it—and how events that may be labeled 'historical' in import or nature occur also in fields of vision not traditionally constructed by historians.[66]

This chapter's proposed metahistoriographic approach, based on Foucauldian genealogy and Latin American transculturative theory, responds to Bishop's call for a self-critical appraisal in order to reevaluate Evitist femiconic historiography.

Thus, before turning to recent plays and films about Eva Perón and building upon the previous chapter's historiographic project, I direct the reader's attention to four published biographies, all of which have circulated in English and Spanish (and in one case in French) and all of which are typically quoted in English- and Spanish-language Perón studies. A brief consideration of their publicity strategies, inferred readerships, and distribution will assist in later discussions of theatrical and film reception and circulation. Circulation and citation are not the only factors in this selection; each of the selected biographers consciously accepts the challenge of presenting and examining the multiple (and at times conflicting) versions of Eva Perón's life, a challenge that a standard biography (at least for the English-reading world) such as Mary Main's *The Woman with the Whip* does not. These biographers stand out precisely for their awareness of some of the hagiographic traps awaiting them. As María Inés Lagos-Pope asserts, the relationship between biographer and subject is not unlike that of the "postmodern" ethnographer and object of study.[67] The authors seem acutely aware of their own, and fluctuating, relationship to their subject and the power the femiconic subject can wield over her would-be biographer. Yet each published "life" contributes in its own way to an overarching historiographic construction and reification of a certain Evita myth or multiple competing myths.

Marysa Navarro (Aranguren)'s *Evita* was first published in 1982 and reissued as a "definitive version" in 1994 by Planeta Press. Navarro, originally from Spain, is a historian well known for her scholarship on Peronism and anti-Peronism.[68] Before *Evita*, she had coauthored an earlier Evita biography, *Eva Perón*, written with the British journalist Nicholas Fraser.[69] The Fraser-Navarro biography was first published by W.W. Norton in 1980 and reissued in 1996 with an updated introduction and epilogue. In 1995, Argentine Alicia Dujovne Ortiz's biography was published by the French publishing house Grasset (under the title of *Eva Perón: la madone des sans-chemise*); the Spanish translation, completed by the author herself, appeared that same year with Aguilar Press.[70] In 1996, St. Martin's Griffin Press published the English-language version of Dujovne Ortiz's biography.[71] While we might be tempted to consider these four books as representative of only two biographical projects (Navarro's and Dujovne Ortiz's), significant differences—in translation as well as style—render a review of all four profitable for tracing a transnational Evita biographical network.

Readers familiar with U.S. popular culture will not be surprised by the shared publication year of the two English-language texts. 1996 also saw the premiere of Alan Parker's film version of the Tim Rice-Andrew Lloyd Webber musical *Evita*, with Madonna in the title role. Indeed, both U.S. paperback editions capitalized on the timing: the cover of the Fraser-Navarro book proclaims that it deals with "the life that inspired the major motion picture," and on the back cover of the Dujovne Ortiz-Fields book, the Boston *Herald* reviewer urges, "If you already know Evita's story but want to read something new before you see Madonna's portrayal . . . get [Dujovne] Ortiz's book." The epilogue appended to the 1996 Fraser-Navarro reissue devotes most of its five-and-a-half-page discussion to recapping the history of the rock opera (much of it taking place far from Argentina), and only after a four-page account of *Evita* does it provide a one-page summary of Tomás Eloy Martínez's influential 1995 novel, *Santa Evita*, before simply and rather simplistically concluding, "¡Evita vive!"[72] The Rice-Lloyd Webber rock-opera's overly determinant role in the creation and circulation of recent Eva Perón biographies becomes especially apparent when we compare the Fraser-Navarro epilogue to Navarro's prologue to the 1994 edition of her sole-authored biography.[73] There Navarro makes only passing reference to the rock-opera as just one more example of the stereotyping process at work in Western sexism. She opts instead to place Eva Perón within the context of "First Ladies" who were maligned for not knowing their place, including in her list the later examples of Jian Qing and Hillary Clinton.

It's worth lingering a moment to consider the cross-authorship and resulting transformations in these four biographies. Marysa Navarro, after coauthoring an English version of Eva Perón's life obviously destined for a wide readership, went on to write a more academic, carefully documented, and annotated biography in Spanish (which unfortunately has never, to my knowledge, been translated to English—despite the fact that Navarro was a highly respected and U.S.-based professor of Latin American history).[74] Dujovne Ortiz's text undergoes a converse transformation: when we compare the Fields English-language translation (from the French) to the Spanish-language version, we note that entire passages have been excised, parenthetical asides omitted, and the author's Spanish-language rhetorical questioning style severely pruned.[75] The Fields translation surprises for not only its omissions (and at times problematic translations) but its transformation of an Argentina-identified text into an Argentina-as-other book. In the Spanish version, the first person plural is used consistently to refer to both the author's personal experiences (in interviews and in life) and *nosotros los argentinos* in a textual attempt to relate an individual life to a national way of being (what Argentines typically refer to as their *ser nacional*). Fields's translation—as very occasionally does the French source—removes the personal identification and any suggestion of a national predisposition.[76] The French and Spanish texts also avail themselves of (and some might say indulge themselves in) recent psychoanalytic theory to explain what might be perceived as an individual/national genetic and cultural predisposition. These connections, all present in the Spanish- and French-language editions, are missing from the English-language text, resulting in a far less original biography.[77] In the English version, Dujovne Ortiz-as-biographer, so vitally and compellingly present in the Spanish and French editions, disappears into yet another generalized story of Eva Perón.

It becomes obvious that a projected image of readership has played a determining role in the four biographies, one that takes into account readers' national(istic) preconceptions as well as the cultural-commercial marketplace. Both factors explain why the two 1996 English-language books seek to ride the Madonna-as-Evita wave, and why the two Spanish biographies feed even more information and analysis to an Argentine audience seemingly ever-starving for additional details about Eva Perón. Despite such differences in anticipated readerships, all four texts employ a similar strategy to position themselves within the polarizing truth/lie controversy surrounding virtually any discussion of Eva Perón. The cover of Navarro's 1994 *Evita* labels the book the "definitive edition," while Fraser/Navarro's 1996 reissue bears the title and subtitle: *Evita. The Real Life of Eva Perón*. Dujovne Ortiz's Spanish-language *Eva Perón* is subtitled *The Biography*, while the English version claims to be only "a" biography. All four texts dance around the veracity problem even as they market themselves as purveyors of what's real, definitive, and true.

Floating behind such labels as "definitive," "real," and even the use of definite or indefinite articles is an ethics of authority and authenticity. It is to this self-positioning as authoritative or authentic that I return over and over again in this chapter's examination of Eva Perón's many lives. Who speaks? Who writes? Who performs? Who's telling the truth? Whose truth? What's at stake in the answers to these questions? For the moment, I remain with the four biographies and their struggles with fact, authenticity, and originality, as well as with their companions fiction, myth, and pastiche. A brief comparison of how the four biographies begin and end their "lives" will also allow us a view into the structural and tropological project of each book, considerations that come into play when looking at other artistic versions of Evita's life.

Beginnings and Endings; Births and Deaths

A story must begin somewhere. Where to commence Eva Perón's biography? A life begins with a birth, and that birth must take place sometime and somewhere. Two of our four biographies begin their narratives with the birth of their subject, most likely on May 7, 1919, and most likely in Los Toldos (later renamed General Viamonte), a small town located on the Argentine pampa in the Province of Buenos Aires. Whereas Navarro opts for a detailed description of María Eva's birthplace, naming both the town and the newborn, Fraser and Navarro together create a more "dramatic" beginning for their story. The place-name is withheld until after it has been described; this suspenseful strategy is adopted for the subject as well, naming her only after the exotic details of her birth are provided (and the story of an Indian midwife delivering the fifth illegitimate offspring of an already married man and his mistress might be expected to titillate a U.S. reader). Yet even this apparently simple, obvious "fact" of birth represents a problem for Evita biographers: Eva María Duarte's official birth certificate inverts her two Christian names and records her as having been born on the same day but in 1922, and in the larger nearby town of Junín, where the family would later relocate. It also registers her as the daughter of Juana Ibarguren and the deceased Juan Duarte. María Eva was likely born shortly after her father left her mother to return to Chivilcoy and his wife and other family; thus the surname given on her certificate (which at the time would have distinguished between legitimate and illegitimate births) was Ibarguren, her mother's, and not Duarte, her father's and her older siblings'. When the family moved to Junín after her father's death in 1926, Eva was registered in school as a Duarte, thus effectively altering her name and legitimacy.

Even from its most logical beginning, birth, Eva Perón's life story thrusts the potential biographer directly into the problem of veracity and into potential complicity in the myth-making project. Navarro meets the problem of authenticity head-on, elaborating a complex "what-if" scenario that demonstrates both the unlikelihood of María Eva having been born in Junín in 1922—it is highly doubtful that a twelve-year-old girl would move alone to Buenos Aires to begin her acting career—as well as the benefits arising from having falsified her birth certificate, on the eve of her marriage to Juan Perón, to represent herself as the legitimate child of Juan Duarte, born in an urban center.[78] Throughout her biography, Navarro employs a retro-uchronic technique of presenting versions of a selected moment of Eva Perón's life, then taking each hypothesis to its (il)logical conclusion, and finally privileging the "most likely." Her goal appears to be one of correction through methodical analysis and citation of the various historiographic representations of Eva Perón's life. And while the Fraser-Navarro biography evinces a similar corrective inclination, it skirts issues of veracity regarding María Eva's birthdate and place by mentioning—without examining—the absence of birth certificates and baptismal records, by providing the 1919 birth date without question (which the authors revisit during their account of

Juan and Eva's marriage), and then by moving on to what would be for the other biographers the greater issue of María Eva's status as "illegitimate." Dujovne Ortiz in turn takes *ilegítima* as the title of the first chapter of her Spanish biography; indeed, "illegitimate" is only the first in a long string of "outsider" terms Dujovne Ortiz applies to Eva Perón.[79]

As the *New York Times* reviewer of the Fields translation rather unkindly notes, Dujovne Ortis "is a biographer . . . who never met a contradiction or a non sequitur she didn't like, who fearlessly piles on the bromides, gossip, conspiracy theories and psychology."[80] What the reviewer fails to recognize is Dujovne Ortiz's own awareness of how very personal her biographical project is. Dujovne Ortiz opens with an image of *alpargatas*, worn-out espadrilles, a metonym of poverty (what the Spanish version calls "the open abyss") that contrasts with the wealth represented by leather shoes. Dujovne Ortiz describes an early twentieth-century Argentina still polarized between the nineteenth century's "civilization and barbarity," between wealth and poverty, a country of dichotomized extremes. She portrays an Evita caught in-between those extremes, as the illegitimate daughter of a landowner and his "homeless" mistress.[81] Dujovne Ortiz, like many Evitographers, sustains throughout the biography that Eva Perón belonged to and almost always identified with other disenfranchised, illegitimate Argentines. The description she provides of Eva's place of birth further buttresses that division: the "two-color handshake" [*apretón bicolor*, inadequately identified by translator Fields as simply "crest"] between Indian and European portrayed in the town's crest erected in its square; the inviting maternal *ombú* tree "with its rolls of flesh" rejected by Evita, whose mercurial disposition and preference for tantrums made her more like a *sauce eléctrico* [twisted willow, *Salix erythroflexuosa*]; and finally, the contrast between the solitary, bourgeois Duarte family and the Núñez's *criollo* "tribal" matriarchy. Evita's disenfranchised working-class roots, upon which most Evitographies rely, easily justify her later class-conscious activism. However, as Marta Savigliano—following up on an observation made by historian Tulio Halperín Donghi—notes, it is problematic to consider Evita's maternal family as "lower-class, given that both her sisters married Argentine professionals (a lawyer and a military officer)."[82] In Halperín Donghi's suggestion that Eva's social commitment was more ideological than psychological, the possibility is created "for a political rather than a psychological analysis."[83] Such a consideration further complicates the simple causality or originary genealogy Dujovne Ortiz presents.

Thus not only does Dujovne Ortiz repeat the old cultural bipartite and polarized model so often utilized to configure Evita's life (and Argentina's national history, for that matter), she employs the well-used dichotomy to set up her argument for Evita's as a preordained life. In Dujovne Ortiz's retelling, Eva Perón would always surround herself with (or find herself surrounded by) people named Juan or Juana, beginning with her parents (Juan Duarte and Juana Ibarguren), the Coliqueo Amerindian midwife who delivered her (Juana Guaquil), and her brother bearing the patronymic, and continuing with her choice of husband (Juan Perón). Evita becomes just one more in a long line of "esos Núñez de por allá" (which Fields more specifically locates as "those Núñezes from the outskirts"), whose women were, according to two earlier biographers, "de esas cantineras ambulantes, trashumantes, que satisfacían las pasiones de los soldados durante la Campaña del Desierto" [traveling, nomadic barmaids who satisfied the passions of the soldiers of the (nineteenth-century) Desert Campaign].[84] This leads Dujovne Ortiz to ask (and for once Fields respects the interrogatory nature of Dujovne Ortiz's narrative approach): "¿Era 'trashumante' también ella, o se limitaba a llevar la trashumancia en la sangre, un vagabundeo ancestral, una capacidad de sobrevivir 'satisfaciendo pasiones', que Evita heredaría?" [Was (Petrona, Eva's maternal grandmother) 'nomadic' too, or did she merely carry nomadism in her blood, an ancestral wandering, a capacity for survival by "satisfying passions" that Evita would inherit?][85] From its opening pages, Dujovne Ortiz's biography would have us believe that María Eva/Eva María Ibarguren was destined to end up as Evita.

Dujovne Ortiz's first chapter ends—as do the initial installments of all four of the texts examined here—with Eva's train ride to Buenos Aires. The biographer adds the imaginative fillip of replacing Los Toldos/General Viamonte's town square in fifteen-year-old Evita's consciousness with Buenos Aires's landmark Kavanagh Building. The port of Buenos Aires raises itself above the flat pampas, much as, the biographers would have us believe, Evita will transcend the flatness of her humble beginnings. In 1935, the Kavanagh was Buenos Aires's first skyscraper and the highest building in all of Latin America, standing thirty-three stories tall. Dujovne Ortiz (with Fields) has Evita secretly identify with the skyscraper. In the Fields translation, "She would do whatever was necessary to rise higher than all the others,"[86] and even though Dujovne Ortiz also locates the identification in the fact that the Kavanagh's head "sobrepasa todas las otras" [surpasses all the others] without making explicit Evita's actions,[87] the biographer cannot resist a final predispositional nudge to note that the Kavanagh's number of floors paralleled Evita's age at the time of her death.

Among the scores of moments ripe for comparative analysis, Eva Perón's early death offers multiple and telling narratives, most notably for their inevitable conflation of the personal and the political: Evita's renunciation of the vice-presidential nomination and her terminal illness. Self-consciously or not, all four writers link the two—political apogee and terminal cancer—chronologically and narratologically.

Navarro signals her attempt to deal separately with these two defining elements of Evita's final years in her chapter titles: "La candidatura a la vicepresidencia" [the candidature for the vicepresidency] followed by "La enfermedad y la muerte de Evita" [Evita's illness and death]. With Fraser, she follows roughly the same division but with more arresting titles: "The Bridge of Love" and "Death and its Public." Both biographies begin in 1950 and the first public hint of Evita's illness before moving quickly to their subject's overwhelmingly active work schedule during what was to be the "height of Evita's power."[88] Fraser and Navarro conclude the chapter with the moment all four biographers consider captures the breadth and limitation of Evita's political power: the "Cabildo Abierto" of August 22, 1951. In conscious reference to May 25, 1810's Cabildo Abierto [citizens' assembly], during which Buenos Aires's residents gathered together to demand their independence from Spain, Argentina's most powerful labor union—the Confederación General de Trabajo [General Confederation of Work] or CGT—called the meeting to proclaim their support for a Perón-Perón ticket.[89] Nearly a million supporters attended, and in what most biographers interpret as an unscripted development in the middle of a heavily scripted event, Perón was caught off-guard when the multitude insisted not only that Evita run for vice-president but that she publicly accept the nomination at that very moment. The event's video and audio recording, documenting the body language and voices of Perón and Evita, has led most biographers to the conclusion that Evita and Perón were not in agreement on how to proceed. The crowd's cries of "now" whittle Evita's pleas for time to reflect down, from four days to one day to two hours, and it's only when she finally returns to say that she will do "what the people say" that the assembly disperses. Nine days later, Evita announced over the radio that she would not seek the vice-presidency. She would die on July 26 the following year.

Much speculation has surrounded the reasons for Eva Perón's "renouncing" of the vice-presidency, a decision that was most likely forced on her.[90] Chief among the other compelling arguments is that General Perón's military advisors would not stand for a woman vice-president, much less the president's own wife.[91] Yet while Perón's strained relationship with the military was certainly a factor in the decision, the story of Evita's rise to and loss of political power is always linked to her terminal cancer.[92] Dujovne Ortiz—in both the Spanish and English versions of her biography—makes the connection explicit in the chapter "Renunciante"/"Renouncer." The chapter opens on July 26, 1949, at a meeting between Evita and the Women's Peronist Party in Buenos Aires's Cervantes National Theatre. Dujovne Ortiz's choice of opening event becomes obvious when we remember that exactly three years later Evita dies. The biographer overtly links the personal to the political in this chapter, particularly in two connected subsections entitled "Mensajes cruzados: la enfermedad" and "Mensajes cruzados: el poder" (which Fields translates as "Crossed wires: the illness" and "Crossed wires: power" in the condensed English version). In Spanish we read that both Perón and Evita "hid and denied the illness behind an identical curtain," while Evita insisted on maintaining, when she could, her famously brutal work schedule.[93] The English version posits a personal reason for Perón's denial: having seen supposedly the same cancer take his first wife, Aurelia, "[p]erhaps he just couldn't watch the woman he loved die."[94] Both versions immediately move to the second crossed-wires chapter and Evita's inability to "intercept" the political messages that would decide her candidacy and deliver her to "the glory of failure" of the Cabildo Abierto. It is perhaps in this chapter that we can best detect Dujovne Ortiz's metonymic tendencies. Evita's final public speech (on October 17, 1951) is summed up in her weeping collapse onto Perón's jacketless shirted chest. And her final public appearance—at Juan's inauguration—is captured in the rumored cast she wore on her arm and body so that she could stand and wave during the long drive in the president's open car. Perón is reduced to a shirt, Evita to a cast. Both are props for the biographical staging of Eva Perón's passion and agony.

Navarro and Fraser are not immune to the occasional tropological twist either. In her chapter on Eva's vice-presidential bid, Navarro interrupts her narrative of the already-sick but hard-working Evita to discuss a parallel change in her wardrobe, noting that this was when she streamlined her appearance, wearing near exclusively her simple, "almost severe" suits and her hair styled in the equally restrained and simple chignon, with her single piece of jewelry the enormous gem-encrusted Peronist *escudo*.[95] Navarro takes corrective pains to note that Evita's sartorial practices were not reflected in her glamorous, gala-clad, jewel-bedecked images that dominated the press then and, I would add, continue to reign over most representations of Evita. Again, interpretations of such glamour diverge and, as Navarro argues, distract readers from Evita's focus on her work. Navarro ends her discursive aside by simply stating: "Evita's clothing, like her jewels, over time acquired an unusual importance as they were converted into one more symbol of what made her beloved to many Argentines and at the same time separated them from others."[96] Navarro, with Fraser, takes Evita's perceived lack of self-interest even further, describing her overwork and personal self-neglect (barely sleeping or eating) in ways that bring to mind an almost mystical self-martyrdom. Indeed, at one point they write: "Of all the many distortions surrounding her life the least outrageous and the closest to the truth is the suggestion that she elected to die for Perón and Peronism."[97] Time and again, even Evita's most self-aware and cautious biographers find it difficult to resist casting her life as either a melodrama or a passion play, or sometimes as both.

All four biographies end, unsurprisingly, with Eva's death and transfiguration—as embalmed corpse, as mythical subject, as History embodied. Evita's afterlives are the subject of the next chapter, and so I will not address these final sections here but leave these four biographies, concluding that each—despite attempts at demythologizing Evita and setting the record straight—do not avoid reinforcing the various Evita myths and thus the larger mythologizing processes still operating.[98] Evita dichotomies remain firmly in place, largely because all four authors to differing degrees perpetuate the mythical Peronist/anti-Peronist binary. Someone with even a passing acquaintance with A.J. Greimas's semiotic square might easily ask: are these the only options for mythologization? Where are, say, the non-Peronist myths—neither for nor against Evita? For that matter (and to complete the Greimassian square), we might ask where are the non-anti-Peronist myths? If we consider the Rumanian theorist's "square of veridiction," developed with Joseph Courtés and built upon the opposition of seeming and being, we can posit that our "truth" options are not only what's true (being and seeming) or false (not-being and not-seeming) but also what's illusory (not being but seeming) or secret (being but not-seeming). We might ask ourselves, how much of Evita mythologizing has been illusory, and how much is secret?[99]

Lagos-Pope concludes her comparative analysis of multiple Evita biographies as follows: "This lack of final truth, and the possibility of only *aproximaciones*, is precisely what befits a life [Eva's] that defined itself as a public image that, by not being constructed and political, stopped being effective and with very real consequences."[100] The Spanish word *aproximaciones* refers to approximations *and* approaches, and though it connotes closeness, it does not result in decisive arrival but rather rapprochement, as with politics the temporary establishment of cordial relations. In biography's case, for a moment we may believe we have glimpsed something approaching historical "truth," but we must remember that what we are reading is only one approach. Ultimately, all interpretations of Eva Perón—historiographic, biographic, cultural, artistic—must remain *aproximaciones*.

Reconstructing Eva's Life in Two Films and Three Plays

With these considerations firmly in mind, I turn to several avowedly "artistic" recent versions of Eva Perón's life, in which I perceive conscious decisions regarding how Evita is to be represented. Indeed, embodiment is a defining factor in all five productions, all premiering in postdictatorship and all in some way in dialogue with both contemporary practices of Peronism and the prevailing myths of Eva Perón. Of the many films centered on Eva Perón, two stand out for their variations on standard genres of Evita representation: as nonexpository documentary (Eduardo Mignogna's *Evita; quien quiera oír que oiga* [released under the English title of "Evita: let those who want to hear, hear"]), and as feature-film biopic (Juan Carlos Desanzo's *Eva Perón*). And from the numerous "Evita plays," I have selected three in which Eva-as-performed is central to the interpretation of the texts: a self-consciously politicized Latin American drama (Osvaldo Guglielmino's *Eva de América*); a staged version of Leónidas Lamborghini's Eva-dedicated poems, themselves a rewriting of her autobiography (*Eva Perón en la hoguera* [Eva Perón in the Bonfire]); and an imagined encounter between Eva Perón and Victoria Ocampo (Mónica Ottino's hugely popular *Eva y Victoria*). Both Mignogna's film and Guglielmino's play were created as Argentina emerged from its most violent authoritarian regime and thus might be interpreted as calls to reimagining Evita's role (and Peronism's place) in national redemocratization. *Eva y Victoria* and *Eva Perón en la hoguera* premiered under a different Peronism, made neoliberal and globalized under Carlos Saúl Menem's presidency. Finally, Desanzo's 1996 feature film, frequently counterpoised to Parker's *Evita*, is a fascinating case in point regarding the tensions that remain over how Eva Perón is to be performed.

The 1984 film *Evita: quien quiera oír que oiga* stands out among the myriad documentaries on Eva Perón for its almost palimpsestic approach to storytelling and attentiveness to historiography. Eduardo Mignogna's opera prima as a film director,[101] the movie shares many of the standard features of Evita documentary: interviews with eye witnesses and experts (such as psychologists and political scientists); documentary footage and photographs; clips from Eva Duarte's theatre, radio, and film career; radio broadcasts and other audio recordings; and credits pointing to additional archival research. However, the film is stylistically noteworthy for its overlay of multiple Evas: 1) the dramatization, starring Flavia Palmiero, of a young adolescent Evita boarding the train in Junín, traveling to Buenos Aires, and disembarking at the city's Retiro train station; 2) the documentary clips and images of the historical Eva Perón; and 3) the voice of Silvina Garré, who interprets fragments of some of Evita's best-known speeches as well as sings the songs composed for the film by Lito Nebbia (b. 1948), the influential Argentine rocker who had recently returned from exile. One of these songs—with lyrics by director Mignogna—provides the film's title: "If history is written / by those who win / that means there is another history. / The true history / those who want to hear it, listen."[102] As the young Eva makes her dramatized journey to Buenos Aires, the film uses historical footage to flash forward through the life that awaits her. It also repeatedly inserts the adolescent Eva into her own history by having the young woman briefly and anachronistically appear in future settings (e.g., riding in a taxi on October 17, 1945, or sitting on an airplane during the 1947 European tour). The film ends with the young Eva, off the train and walking quickly toward her future. *Evita: quien quiera oír que oiga*, by avoiding the often told (and always linked) stories of her (a)sexuality and power-hunger, presents an Evita full of promise and life. Through the overt use of imagined dramatization, Mignogna takes a clearly partisan position regarding an idealized "people"'s Evita. As Paola Judith Margulis notes, Mignogna employs the tools of documentary "not to impart knowledge with epistemic rigor but rather to move [his spectator]," thus reinforcing what she calls "the myth of Eva Perón in a moment of institutional crisis within Peronism."[103] Documentary mixes with fictionalization in a multiplicity of voices and images, some privileged formally and ideologically over others.[104] Margulis writes, "Far from proposing certainties, Mignogna's film restages Peronism's contradictions in a completely changed setting."[105]

That changed setting was an Argentina in the midst of redemocratization. Though Mignogna began filming during dictatorship, the movie premiered in April 1984,[106] shortly after the country's return to democracy and three years after its director's return from Italian exile. The film's original songs, and particularly the title's lyrics, connect Eva's story to an Argentina in transition from military dictatorship and the uncertain role of Peronism within redemocratization. Mignogna and Nebbia exhort us to remember the military repression as well as earlier Evitist idealism: "When we don't remember / what's happened to us / the same thing can happen again. / Those are the same things / that marginalize us / they kill our memory / they kill our ideas / they take away our words."[107] Within the premiere's context, the theme song's call for a counterhistory applies to both periods of twentieth-century Argentina; to read *Evita: quien quiera oír que oiga* narrowly—as exclusively an "Evita" film—is to ignore its moment of creation and strong reception in the early years of redemocratization.[108]

Another Evita cultural product of early redemocratization was *Eva de América*, published in 1983 but not staged until some four years later.[109] Its author, Osvaldo Guglielmino (b. 1921), is a well-known educator, public figure, poet, novelist, political essayist, and playwright. Perhaps most identified, like his friend José María Castiñeira de Dios, with Peronism's ideological wing, Guglielmino left his native Pehuajó (located in what he calls the "deep west" of the Province of Buenos Aires) for Buenos Aires in 1955 but stayed only a couple of months before having to leave when Perón was overthrown. He returned for a cultural position in Perón's 1973 government, as undersecretary of culture in charge of directing the national press Ediciones Culturales Argentinas. After the 1976 military coup he renounced the position to return to Pehuajó.[110] A self-described Argentina-focused *adentrista*,[111] Guglielmino has often spoken of the influence of place and region as his "point of view": "the country—man— needs to write about what is inside himself and inside the landscape where he lives."[112] *Eva de América*, like much of Guglielmino's writing, is easily compartmentalized as pro-Peronist. Written just as Argentina was emerging from dictatorship, the play can be understood as a call for Peronism's return but in the form of audience participation, which Sarah M. Misemer describes as "standing in for Evita": "Guglielmino suggests through his play that we are now to take up the performance where Evita left off."[113] Misemer notes that Guglielmino "exalts her to mythic proportions" and posits that within the play Eva Perón functions not as a protagonist but as the other characters' "ideal spectator . . . , their savior who never really appears to them, but whose voice is heard only in the final moments of the play."[114] It is only in the "outer structure" that all performances—Evita's included—"are directed toward another public, presumably an ideal one that will be receptive to Peronist rhetoric."[115] According to Misemer's interpretation, actors and spectators alike are interpellated as standing in for and embodying Evita's "will."[116] What does such a hailing mean for a 1980s Argentina returning to democracy under a democratically elected non-Peronist president? What role does Evita's "will" play in a text that calls upon its (Argentine) audience to commit to an idealized Evitism?

No actor embodies Evita in *Eva de América*. Guglielmino took his cue from Eva's own stated belief that some historical personages exceed the limits of artistic realism and justified her physical absence from his play in the following manner: "I decided to use suggestion, the character's spiritual force, her historical and social motivations, and not the representation of her human *criatura* [incarnation or creature]."[117] Should a director decide to place Eva on stage, according to the playwright's instructions it should be through "one of her most universally representative images," and he suggests her corporealization only in the play's final seconds, and only then as "motionless and dressed in white."[118] Such mediatized representation is key to Eva's *fatalismo protagónico* [leading-role destiny] in a play that positions her as the last link in a chain that for its author constitutes the "real" Argentina's rebellion over more than one hundred and fifty years of *mestizo* struggle.[119] The play's linear chronology threads its way through this chain of history, and it is only at the end of the concluding *porteño* (or Buenos Aires-based) act that we finally hear Eva's "voice," reciting selections from *La razón de mi vida*, together with fragments of celebratory Evitist texts easily recognized by an Argentine audience, including the famous "I will return and I will be millions."[120]

How does Guglielmino stage what he believes to be Evita's inevitable role as leading lady of the popular Argentine struggle in a play in which she does not physically appear? The playwright structures his text into four acts, and, utilizing what he calls the "primitive Greek" theatre's elements of chorus, protagonist, deuteragonist, and tritagonist, he creates a series of staged power struggles from which exemplary, martyred, and masculine lives emerge: in the first act, Mapuche *cacique* Llancamil rejects the European colonizers' offer of exile, resigning himself to death during full indigenous resistance; in the second act, the gaucho Molina advances the cause of Argentine Independence at its darkest moment; in the third, creole Juan Palavecino dies as a martyr of agrarian resistance to the new postcolonial, urban liberal politics. In the play's final act, after a sequence of dialogues among the various Buenos Aires types—pimps, prostitutes, socialites, oligarchs, and tenement dwellers—Eva's voice rises out of a blackout and above the many voices repeating "one day everything will change," particularizing the chorus's generalized call for transformation: "one day *all of this* will change."[121] Mestizo Argentina's ultimate martyr has spoken. And as she continues to speak—at times through actual recordings of Eva, at times interpreted by others, with the changes in voice and text marked by changes in tone, level, sound, light colors, and tempo—her various texts are punctuated and echoed by the multitude, calling "Oh, Buenos Aires, Buenos Aires . . . !" and later chanting "¡Perón!" and "¡Evita!"[122] In keeping with the playwright's general design, this now historicized and echoing chorus of the "people"—Evita-"millions"—has replaced any earlier antipopular, antihistorical ethos, still resounding as the curtain falls if we adhere to the published script.

The play's title and the author's professed desire to show Eva's "leading-role destiny" as symbol of social liberation notwithstanding, can we really say that Eva Perón is the protagonist of *Eva de América?* Is she, as Misemer contends, a stand-in for the nation and even the hemisphere, as the play's title might suggest? The principal characters of the three previous acts are all male and the typical martyrs of traditional Argentine historiography: indigenous leaders, local creole leaders, rebel leaders. Another reading suggests that the Eva of Guglielmino's America is really a continuation of the previous scenes' secondary, female characters: the first act's anonymous *machi* [a Mapuche spiritual leader, typically a woman as she is in the play]; the gaucho Molina's companion, Juana Carranza; the penultimate act's unnamed woman who hands the torch to the poor farmer so he can set fire to the harvests as a protest; and the final act's wife whose attempts to console her unemployed husband anticipate Evita's line as she assures him, "Someday all this will change." Oscar Rovito, in a brief note accompanying the 1994 edition, offers up a collective Eva, "all the Evas who played an important role in the creation and affirmation of a national and popular conscience."[123] An Eva-synthesis, arising out of Guglielmino's Argentina-of-the-rich/Argentina-of-the-people dichotomy, has come to "rescue [all Evas] and give them a battle-flag." Yet instead of developing Eva's "fatalismo protagónico," *Eva de América* relegates her to a secondary role, ostensibly that of Perón's companion, or *choregos*, but certainly not protagonist.[124]

We might argue that Eva is "embodied" aurally through the various recordings reproduced in performance. Yet even Eva's speeches do not belong to her: all are texts written by men, including her ghostwritten autobiography, whose published version was rumored to have retained very few of Eva's own words by the time Perón and his advisors finished editing it.[125] One version of Argentina's geosocial landscape is painted in *Eva de América*, but it is a world that consigns woman to a secondary role, that of companion and spokesperson. Her aggrandized titular role notwithstanding, Guglielmino's Eva is a voice without a body, a medium for the words and ideas of her leading men. At a historical moment when Argentines engaged in redemocratization were being called to *poner el cuerpo*—to commit body (and soul) to a cause—male bodies seem to be the only ones given physical protagonism in this supposedly eulogical play. In contrast to Mignogna's film of the same period and its multiple Evitas—embodied in one actor's body and another's voice, in film and photo stills, and in divergent expert opinions—Guglielmino's play ends up disappearing Eva into a mythic *vox populi*.

Performing Evita in 1990s Menemist Argentina

In the ensuing years (and as we will see in the next chapter), Eva Perón did not disappear from the national stage. Indeed, during the Menemist 1990s, with the president's pardoning of the dictatorship's leaders, his continuation of neoliberal economic policies resulting in elevated and artificially sustained consumerism as nearly everything seemed to be privatized, and his outright currying of a glocalized cultural capital (perhaps most notoriously through the support of Madonna and Alan Parker's biopic), Evita seemed more present than ever.

Premiering in the early 1990s,[126] *Eva y Victoria* overtly sought to stage the "human" Evita and render her iconized and idealized image flesh. To do so, journalist and playwright Mónica Ottino adopted a fictionalized, uchronic premise.[127] We witness two invented encounters between mid-twentieth-century Argentina's greatest femicons: first lady Eva Perón and her "paradigmatic nemesis" Victoria Ocampo, the upper-class writer, founder of the influential literary journal *Sur*, and, like her close friend Jorge Luis Borges, fervent anti-Peronist.[128] While Perón and Ocampo supposedly never met, they lived during the same period in Argentina's history and exercised enormous power in politics and culture, respectively.[129]

Eva y Victoria's first scene in which the women meet exposes the conflicts between the two figures, Argentine society's polar opposites; they are also conflicts that (stereo)typically represent the two poles of Argentine feminism at that time. Eva has come to Victoria's home to ask her to sign a petition in support of women's suffrage. Ocampo refuses to do so but not without sympathizing with the cause. The second scene takes place several years later. A now-terminally ill Eva calls Victoria to her home under the same pretext of women's solidarity. Once again, Ocampo refuses Perón, but the scene suggests that the two have now arrived at some degree of mutual recognition and understanding. In the first encounter, the two women make fun of their similarities. Victoria is ironic about their shared condition as motherless women: "There is too much of the masculine in us."[130] In the second encounter, though they remain at crossed purposes, all irony appears to have evaporated when Victoria says, "I think we're alike in some ways. We have to be someone, and since we live in a man's world we've gotten our dose of power through men."[131] The play ends close to some sort of reconciliation, suggested in the stage directions: "*Victoria . . . goes over to Eva [whose eyes are closed] and extends her arm as if she were about to caress [the resting woman]. Victoria's hand falls before it touches Eva, and she slowly leaves the room.*"[132] While there is a marked change between the first and third acts, Ottino's humanizing project is further developed in one other structuring element: the second act's two "private" moments that separate the two "public" encounters, one with Evita in her dressing room, the other with Victoria in her bedroom. These two intimate views reveal another goal, an attempt to relativize and ultimately transcend the old polarizations between these two women and their respective social orders, in order to see the similarities and ultimately the humanity that unites such two very different Argentines.

Eva y Victoria enjoyed a level of success unheard of in the Argentine theatre.[133] The 1992 production, directed by Oscar Barney Finn, ran until 1998 and traveled to more than one hundred cities in the country, including towns frequently excluded from the national touring theatre circuits.[134] Spectators returned to see the play over and over again. What were the reasons for the play's success and sustained appeal? Mempo Giardinelli, one of Argentina's best-known writers and a repeat audience member himself, volunteered the following explanation: "it's profoundly national and brings together two national styles without falling back on [the usual] Manichaeisms . . . ; it's a play that revises history from the imagination instead of from the 'truth.'"[135] *Eva y Victoria*'s national revisionist history, effectuated through the imagination and not through a search for the "truth," directly supports the play's humanizing objective. By having the two "national styles"—elitist intellectual and populist anti-intellectual—enter into dialogue rather than merely shutting each other out in the usual polarizations to which Giardinelli alludes, the play finds a feminist common ground, if not reconciliation, for these two supposedly antithetical national figures. Unusual especially for a self-described "patriotic" play, *Eva y Victoria* attempts to avoid the easy dichotomies of *Eva de América* and instead makes these two, so often mutually isolated "national styles" engage with one another. Viviana Paula Plotnik, in a book-length study of Eva Perón as "literary" character, goes so far as to call Ottino's subtitle "ironic" and postmodern in that the play questions "the binary oppositions [the two characters] embody."[136] She argues that the play "destabilizes" traditional borders and even "disarms" the old civilization-barbarity polarization in its symmetry and mirroring of the two supposed class and political enemies.[137]

Plotnik's examination of the dramatic literary text does not consider the play in performance, and her argument of resolution-in-the-same begins to fall apart when we consider the portrayals of Eva Perón and Victoria Ocampo in the play's original (1992–98) staging. The various times I saw the production (yes, I was a repeat spectator, too), I was always moved by how actress Luisa Brando performed Eva.[138] Working in a naturalistic style not unlike that associated with "American realism," Brando made almost palpable the physical deterioration of Eva's all too human body.[139] Her onstage counterpart, China Zorrilla, another celebrated actress of the Argentine-Uruguayan stage, also affected me but in a completely different way. Zorrilla's Ocampo (despite a physical resemblance far surpassing Brando's to Eva) never abandoned the iconic "Victoria Ocampo," just as China, a cultural femicon of her own,[140] never ceased being "China" onstage.[141] The experience of watching the meeting of two key figures of Argentine history, portrayed by two great actresses with such different acting styles, left me wondering if Ottino's play had a dual purpose: rescuing the person Evita from mythic fetishization while (re) claiming Victoria Ocampo's deserved place in the male-dominated national pantheon. If so, it made perfect sense that Brando would utilize a more naturalistic acting style, while Zorrilla would embrace a more "iconizing" approach. What can a staging that seeks to reconcile the human being with the icon tell us? Can it move us to discern in two acting styles, two models of self-construction? Does it not incite us to choose— between two acting styles, between two approaches to self-construction? Doesn't reducing a broader national debate to two "national styles" perpetuate Argentina's historic binarisms? Thus, I wondered, did the split performances undercut the play's apparent search for a common humanity and what Plotnik calls its postmodern critique of traditional Argentine oppositional politics? Or were they successful in making the spectator aware of choices being made?

It's interesting to note how these dual performing styles were actually accentuated in the publicity campaign: Two different promotional approaches were adopted, one in which Zorrilla's name appeared before Brando's, "as Victoria," and the other which listed Brando first, saying "Luisina is Eva." Not only did the two advertisements alternate in giving each actress top billing; they perhaps unwittingly pushed the production's audience toward considering Zorrilla's and Brando's performance styles as different: China appears "as" [*como*] Victoria, while Luisina "is" [*es*] Eva. In doing so, the ads neatly captured the two prevailing approaches to performing Argentina's femicons.

In 1994, Iris Scaccheri directed noted Argentine actress Cristina Banegas in a staged version of Leónidas Lamborghini's poem collection: *Eva Perón en la hoguera*. Banegas, since the 1970s an important presence on the national theatre, television, and film scenes, has operated her own independent performance space—El Excéntrico de la 18°—for over twenty-five years.[142] Scaccheri, known as a dancer and choreographer both in Europe and Argentina, created a one-woman dance-poem, which ran from April through November 1994 in the theatre space of the now-disappeared Gandhi bookstore in downtown Buenos Aires. (The production also played at another Buenos Aires theatre as well as in the nearby provincial capital of La Plata.) The two artists worked with images taken from the oversized photo book Banegas consulted in performance and a table on, under, and beside which the actress performed.

This was not the first time Lamborghini's text had been staged. An Italian version had been created in 1978 in Rome, and the year before the Scaccheri-Banegas production Mirta Izquierdo interpreted the poems at Buenos Aires's Recoleta Cultural Center.[143] As recently as 2006, I saw a three-woman version directed by Argentine artist Marsha Gall at New York's Dixon Place,[144] and the following year it was restaged in Buenos Aires by the group Todosjuntos. Nevertheless, Banegas's performance remains definitive, and she was awarded the 1995 ACE (Association of Theatre Critics) award for best actress in an independent production.

Lamborghini (1927–2009) first published his eighteen-part extended poem in 1972's *Partitas* [suites or variations] as part of a section entitled "reescrituras"—rewritings of known texts.[145] "Eva Perón en la hoguera" is, in its author's words, a "rereading" of *La razón de mi vida*, the radical result of cuts, repetitions, and reorganizations. A poet who described his own work as moving between parody and tragedy, Lamborghini published some twenty-five books of poetry, three novels, essays, and one dramatic monologue, *Perón en Caracas*. He was also an active Peronist forced into exile with his family after the 1976 coup. As Plotnik notes in her textual analysis, each section of the poem "takes a theme or idea that is repeated and expanded in diverse variations throughout the section."[146] Lamborghini combines what he sees as the key ideas in the original text and excises others he considers less or unimportant. Thus "revolution" is never far from "marvelous," but religious fervor is unhinged from social commitment. In this way, as Plotnik writes, "Evita's discourse is freed from *La razón de mi vida*'s messianic, mystic, and religious tone."[147] Lamborghini releases his Evita from her ghostwriters and censors; she is no longer, Plotnik states, "the mother of the workers or the intermediary between them and the Messiah."[148] Contrary to one published English translation of the poem, this Eva Perón is not martyred at the stake but rather has thrown herself fully into the social and political bonfire of the workers' cause.[149]

In performance, Banegas's voice—a rich, dusky, authoritative alto with enormous expressive range—beautifully carried Lamborghini's experimental text.[150] And though not a blonde, she adapted Evita's trademark no-nonsense chignon of her later years, as well as a version of the simple, tailored suits Eva favored for her work at the Foundation. Evita, as embodied by Banegas, was not the Dior-clad, jewel-encrusted, blondly ambitious bombshell adored and mocked by the international media. Hers—like Lamborghini's—was a radicalized Evita driven by passion and the fire ignited by ideas and emotions.[151]

Both Barney Finn's and Scaccheri's productions seemed determined to free Evita from an allegedly Peronist president who appeared hell-bent on putting the immediate dictatorial past behind by pardoning the military leaders and promoting a neoliberal economy that courted international investment but left little room for the working classes or the very institutions the Peróns had created to safeguard their wellbeing. *Eva y Victoria* presented a feminist Evita whose humanity reminded audiences of Peronism's loftier goals, while *Eva en la hoguera* recalled a revolutionary Evita willing to sacrifice herself for a better Argentina. Menem's Evita, in contrast, was Madonna, globalization's quintessential femicon.[152] It was thus not much of a surprise when the recently reelected Argentine president exploited the 1996 Alan Parker film opportunity by insisting that the pop-celebrity have lunch and pose with him before he would grant the British director permission to film a key scene at the presidential palace.[153]

It seems quite appropriate that Banegas would play Eva's mother, Juana, in Juan Carlos Desanzo's 1996 film, *Eva Perón*.[154] With a limited budget ($3 million, compared to Parker's $60 million) and a screenplay by the director and journalist, philosopher, novelist, screenwriter, and television personality José Pablo Feinmann,[155] *Eva Perón*, which premiered very successfully in Argentina some four months before *Evita* debuted there, is often described as the "local" counterversion to Alan Parker's "global" *Evita*.[156] When the Parker film opened in eighty-five theatres throughout Argentina (the wide distribution an indication of the film's anticipated success), it was received largely with derision: critics and viewers were eager to point out how the North had once again gotten things wrong, not only by buying almost exclusively into Evita's "black legend" but also by confusing the inversion of seasons, substituting Budapest for Buenos Aires, dressing extras in summer clothing for Evita's August funeral, having Evita renounce her vice-presidency from the wrong balcony, and, perhaps most egregiously, not crediting all of the quite limited number of Argentine actors who worked on the film. Local critics and artists had a field day: "like a remake of a Fellini film by a National Geographic documentarian," "Parker has invented the boring musical," "*Evita* ultimately poses the amusing irony of Walt's cold corpse uniting to commune with Evita's hot corpse and engendering nothing more and nothing less than a semifrozen cold cut," and "as boring as sucking on a straight nail, because sucking on a twisted nail is at least interesting."[157]

Early promotional strategies suggest that Desanzo's film sought to correct *Evita*'s historical record, despite the director and lead actress's protests to the contrary.[158] When initially released in Argentina, *Eva Perón* bore the subtitle "the true story," promising yet another definitive version of Evita's life. The film, however, centers on her final years and her political and charitable projects. Ending with the protagonist's death, the film—like other Argentine plays and films discussed here—omits her spectacular vigil and state funeral as well as the often sensationalized versions of her corpse's odyssey. Nevertheless, the events covered repeated the "habitual moments of all her biographies" and ultimately provided little insight into the film's subject.[159] One foreign reviewer called it "a weepy melodrama evocative of a South American TV soap opera" though she praised actress Ester Goris's "spunky" performance in the title role.[160] Goris's performance was unsurprisingly the focus of much critical attention, either hailed as believably detailed or criticized as overly mannered and grandiloquent. The actress, having briefly played Eva Perón before,[161] researched her role, working through much of the vast Evita bibliography and conversing at length with historians and Eva's friends. In at least one interview, Goris acknowledged that Eva Perón weighed much more heavily on her than Madonna's recent portrayal, and rumors still prevail about the actress having "lost herself" in the role for some time after filming ended.[162]

Goris's extremely thin frame (the result of losing fourteen kilos for the role), while effective in portraying a dying Evita, undermined the vitality of the younger Evita in the obligatory flashbacks; conversely, the strident commitment in the actress's voice worked well for conveying Evita's fiery speeches and legendary swearing but kept Evita's alleged vulnerability at bay.[163] Goris seemed encumbered by the screenplay's verbosity. In one local critic's estimation, the film's "flat and less than imaginative realism" resulted in a "humdrum, longwinded, and timid" portrait.[164] Desanzo had maybe played it too safe. As soon as *Eva Perón* premiered, everyone in Buenos Aires seemed to be arguing about Goris's acting choices rather than the film's possible contributions to Eva Perón biographical filmography. Goris's performance as Eva Perón, following so closely upon Madonna's, brought into sharp relief the landmines waiting for any actress assaying a portrayal of Argentina's premiere femicon.

"Yo soy Eva"

In one installment of the long-running Off-Broadway parody revue *Forbidden Broadway*, "Boyd Gaines" (the actor who starred opposite Patti LuPone in the 2009 revival of *Gypsy*) says to "Patti" that he will never forget her "as Evita"; "Patti" corrects him: "Patti LuPone *is* Evita."[165] Some of Evita's impersonators—like LuPone—have achieved femiconic status themselves, and chief among Argentines is Nacha Guevara, still recognized instantly as simply "Nacha."[166] In Mónica Ottino's *Eva y Victoria*, Luisina Brando "is" Eva, while icon China Zorrilla appears "as" Victoria. Ester Goris is accused of losing herself in the title role of Desanzo's *Eva Perón*, while Madonna, despite the hair, makeup, costuming, and protestations, never quite persuades us that she can play any femicon but herself. The slippage between performing "as" [*como*] and "being" [*es*] returns us to those complicated and possibly conflicted bedfellows, celebrity and mimesis, as this chapter concludes its considerations of

Figure 3: Eva Perón's official portrait by Numa Ayrinhac (c. 1951).

Figure 4: Nacha Guevara's publicity photo in handbill for the revival of *Eva* (2008).

femiconography. What is at stake in the above statement "Patti LuPone is Evita"? What happens when the Argentine musical's publicity image is transformed from *en*—in *Eva*'s 1986 poster ("Nacha *in* Eva")—to *es* in the early twenty-first-century revival's publicity ("Nacha *is* Eva")?

Nacha's 2008 performance capitalized on her abilities as impersonator. The lavish production claimed to tell "a story faithful to the life of this extraordinary, passionate, contradictory, and valiant woman."[167] The revival's search for fidelity resulted in a production far more complex and expensive than the initial 1986 show, which its creator said had been done with "lots of love and very few resources."[168] Effective use was made of enormous projections that convincingly superimposed Nacha's image onto the original Eva's and mixed historical and reconstructed footage. According to one local daily, the production had six hundred original costumes from the 1940s and '50s, including a restored Christian Dior original and replica of the black dress Eva wore on the cover of her quasi-autobiography [*La razón de mi vida*] and seen in Ayrinhac's now-lost painting.[169] Critics and bloggers took particular pains to note that this *Eva* could, in one reviewer's words, "compete with nobility [*hidalguía*] against the many, many deified [*endiosados*, also conceited] musicals coming from the septentrional side of the planet."[170] The fans, critics, and I were even won over by Guevara herself, who at the age of sixty-eight portrayed Evita from adolescence until her death at thirty-three.

Guevara had already dealt with the "ghost" of Evita in numerous interviews as well as in her own performance. Often called a chameleon who reinvents her public persona as frequently as Madonna, Nacha has long been known also for her irascibility and outspokenness (not unlike Patti LuPone in her autobiographic recollections regarding performing *Evita*).[171] But beyond the actor's obvious mimetic skills and the vehicle's impressive production values (far exceeding in budget and execution anything I've ever seen on Buenos Aires's busy stages), what struck me most about the 2008 performance was the audience's response to Nacha-Eva. Before the curtain rose, fervent Nacha fans gasped at the glossy Eva-Nacha photos in the production handbill. When historic dates were announced in the performance, the audience responded in unison. And at intermission, when I found one of my friends—a lifelong Communist and cynic—in tears, he explained to me that the production neared such a degree of verisimilitude that he was emotionally overwhelmed.

Just as any actor faced with portraying Evita, practically every Argentine woman politician finds herself forced to engage with (or disengage from) Evita as reigning femiconic political archetype. Even the country's current president, Cristina Fernández de Kirchner, has not been exempt from such ghosting. When the president attended the opening night of *Eva* at its "out-of-town" premiere in the provincial capital of La Plata, it seemed to be a calculated move to forge a defiant Evita-Nacha-Cristina trinity. Theatre and politics conflated; as the production logo's sky-blue-and-white rhinestones made clear, Nacha was Eva, and Eva is Argentina.[172] Theatre and politics intersected once again the week after *Eva*'s run ended, when Provincial Governor (and major revival underwriter) Daniel Scioli announced Nacha's candidacy for national congress on the Peronist Front for Victory (FPV) ticket, in the third slot behind former president, party head, and "first guy" Néstor Kirchner and Scioli himself, and allegedly replacing Eva Perón's own grandniece.[173] Suddenly the hefty provincial sponsorship of the *Eva* musical became fodder for political speculation: Was this so-called "Operation Evita" nothing more than another case of a political party hoping to capitalize on the aura of celebrityhood, or were the Kirchners planning to benefit from a "subliminal reference" to Evita in Nacha's uncanny impersonation of their party's iconic leading lady? Was this the Kirchners' attempt—in tandem with their longtime supporter Scioli—to reposition themselves within the fractured Peronist party as the "true" heirs of Evita-style populism? The motives behind Guevara's selection were further complicated by the fact that, in Argentine congressional elections, there are often "testimonial candidates," well-known figures who lend their star-power to the campaign but have absolutely no intention of taking office if elected. Which kind of candidate would the diva be?

On June 28, 2009, the Kirchners suffered their first major routing since Néstor assumed the presidency in 2003, with the FPV losing a parliamentary majority in Congress while retaining a bare majority in the Senate and causing Néstor to resign as head of the Peronist Party even as he continued on in Congress.[174] Despite the so-called emblematic defeat, certain FPV candidates were elected to office, among them Clotilde Acosta, also known as Nacha Guevara. Coming out of postelection seclusion in late July 2009 for fellow Evita-performer Elena Roger's opening night of *Piaf,* Nacha said that she would indeed serve in Congress and focus her term on promoting education and ending juvenile delinquency and violence.[175] She never took office. Far more than an auratic and much-lifted pretty face, Clotilde Acosta—born more than seventy years ago in the provincial ocean resort city of Mar del Plata—consolidated her national and international status as the diva Nacha Guevara. Like so many other femicons, her performances exhibit the as/is duality that has become a feature not only of theatrical characterization but also of a national politics that seems determined to conflate Eva (and any evocation of Eva) with Argentina.

Rita de Grandis concludes her essay on Evita-inspired films with a question: can Evita as a female political subject be represented outside the whore/saint dualism instituted by nineteenth-century melodrama?[176] It would appear that film has not been altogether successful in breaking the generic hold of melodrama. Rather, and as we'll see in the next chapter, it is in the theatre where we find a multiplicity of approaches to the representation of Evita Perón as national and transnational femicon.

THREE

Performing Evita's Afterlives

Deconstructing Evita's Body, Reconstructing Her Effigy

In February 1994, famed "underground" troupe Gambas al Ajillo opened their farewell production by hauling onstage a coffin,[1] ornately decorated in the distinctly *porteño* artistic practice of *fileteado*.[2] For a production whose very title—*Gambas gauchas*—signalled a send-up of Argentina's national self-image,[3] this was a telling move. Claiming the coffin was Evita's, the performers left it onstage, sometimes turned upright to be used as a podium but usually just there, along with all the other "national" paraphernalia spilling out of a cart positioned in front of the Argentine crest and a slew of cowhides. Gambas and their guests played drums and other musical instruments, twirled lassos and *boleadoras*, performed folk dances, recited gaucho poems, and sang snippets of popular tunes. All the while the coffin remained onstage, not only anticipating the troupe's own imminent demise but also reminding their exuberant audiences that even in death Evita was still part of the national "folk" baggage. For Diana Taylor, the coffin represented a distinct weight for Argentine women who "have to negotiate with Evita's image because she dominates the social imaginary and occupies one of the few spaces available to women."[4] As femicon Nacha Guevara's recent Eva performances on the theatrical and national stages—discussed in the previous chapter—suggest, Evitist Peronism still plays a strong role in contemporary cultural and state politics. Evita's coffin continues to weigh heavily on all. This chapter takes its cue from that 1994 onstage casket to focus, not on the living Eva Perón of biography, but on the deceased, ostensibly absent Evita and performances of her famously disappeared (and reappeared) corpse. I look at multiple theatrical productions—created within and outside Argentina—that overtly staged Peron's surrogated corpse in apparent response to a specific historical moment and its engagement with Evita-style Peronism. In doing so, these performances engaged with questions of corporeality, displacement, and disappearance, all issues that still inform, nationally and transnationally, the seemingly continual cultural resurrections of Eva Perón.

THE HISTORICAL Eva Perón was no typical "first lady": actively and influentially involved in Perón's presidency and larger Peronist politics, she maintained a brutal eighteen-hour workday as she ran her own foundation and served as Perón's strongest link to Argentina's working classes and labor unions. Only three years after Eva Perón's death in 1952 at the age of thirty-three, Juan Perón was overthrown by his own military after bombings of the Plaza de Mayo and the presidential palace killed hundreds of people. Perón was allowed to flee the country (first going to neighboring Uruguay before settling in Spain at the invitation of the country's dictator, General Francisco Franco), but his Justicialist Party itself was outlawed, and even mention of Juan or Eva's name prohibited. The Peronist decade of Juan's first two presidencies (1945–55) was over, and Peronism would not officially return to Argentina until the early 1970s.

Eva Perón's corpse became a key element both in the military regime's effort to abolish Peronism and in Peronist resistance activities. At Perón's request, Spanish physician Pedro Ara preserved Eva's cadaver through a method involving the use of paraffin.[5] This was no personal project of mourning but rather a politically motivated plan. As Sarah M. Misemer suggests, the preserved Evita "became a kind of incorruptible saint who did not decay."[6] Indeed, before his overthrow, Perón had approved plans for a gigantic mausoleum/monument that would contain Eva's paraffined remains. After the coup, not only was the project abandoned but the new military regime faced the challenge of dealing with the already venerated corpse. In November 1955, Evita's body disappeared from the labor union seat where it had lain in state. It is believed to have been taken by the Army Information Services [Servicio de Informaciones del Ejército, or SIE], under the command of Colonel Eugenio de Moori Koenig, whose relationship with the cadaver became the necrophilic subject of much conjecture. For months, Eva's corpse traveled around various military-supervised clandestine sites within Buenos Aires (including SIE's offices, homes of military officials, the water-works building, and even the backstage of a movie theatre) until, in early 1957, it was taken out of the country by plane. Once again it journeyed, now to Spain, Italy, Belgium, Germany, and Switzerland, before receiving secret burial in Milan's Maggiore Cemetery, under a false name (of one María Maggi de Magistris, born in Bérgamo and dead in a car accident in 1951 in Rosario, Argentina) and accompanied by an Army officer posing as the deceased's widower.[7] To further confuse would-be body-seekers, multiple effigies were said to have been deposited in different graves in various countries. At the same time, younger Peronist resisters sought to reclaim the corpse for their cause, and in 1970 the Montoneros (part of Peronism's left wing) kidnapped and executed General Pedro Eugenio Aramburu, the head of the military junta at the time of the cadaver's disappearance and presumed responsible party for ordering its kidnapping. By 1971, under growing political pressure and unrest, then-military junta president Alejandro Agustín Lanusse returned the corpse to Perón in Spain. As before, the body was accompanied by an officer, now posing as the dead Maggi de Magistris's brother. Perón, his third wife, Isabelita (María Estela Martínez Cartas de Perón), and their advisor (and founder of Argentina's most notorious paramilitary unit), José López Rega, received the body in Madrid. There it stayed until 1974.

During this period, the 1960s dictatorship ended, Peronism was extranominally reinstated as a political party, and the Peronist candidate, Héctor Cámpora, won the 1973 presidential elections, from which Perón had been banned. After serving under two months, Cámpora resigned, allowing Perón himself to take over as president; Perón died in office nine months later. In 1974, the Montoneros, through another act of kidnapping (this time taking the corpse of Aramburu, the military leader they'd executed in 1970), pressured then-President Isabel Perón to return Evita to Argentina. For almost two years, Evita's and Juan's corpses reposed together in the Olivos presidential crypt. Then, on July 22, 1976, only a few months after yet another military coup d'état, the new regime ordered Eva's corpse buried in her father's family crypt in Buenos Aires's Recoleta Cemetery, under what is reported to be a six-foot deep steel plank.[8] Taylor writes, "Evita's body, from the time of her death until Perón's return to Argentina in 1973, was the pivotal object in the struggle to control her image and the fetishistic power that continued to emanate from it."[9] I would extend that end-date to at least the body's 1976 burial, but not without first reminding the reader that Eva Perón's corpse continues to function as a pivotal, mythologized, object. Even in its absence (or at least hidden away in a sealed mausoleum under six feet of steel), Evita's body retains its "fetishistic power," as the performances this chapter examines attest.

Thus while in the 1950s Eva's dead body was venerated, then physically removed from view and all discussion thereof silenced, in the 1970s, with her body first the object of political power struggles and then later ostensibly "at rest" in the Duarte family's mausoleum, the mythologizing process shifted to Evita's image and its appropriation by various factions of a rapidly splintering Peronism. During this tumultuous period, Evita became synonymous with a militant Peronism of the left: "Evita revolucionaria," revolutionary Evita. In the mid-1970s, Peronism, together with Evita's femiconic body, was once again driven underground: after an aging and ill Juan Perón died in office, he was replaced by his third wife and vice-president Isabel, whose brief, disastrous tenure ended with the March 24, 1976, military coup that inaugurated the most repressive of Argentina's multiple dictatorships. By the time the country returned to democracy in 1983, over thirty thousand people had been "disappeared" while many others had gone into exile, some returning in the early 1980s. Peronism would once again be officially recognized, but now it was a "Peronism without Perón"—and without Evita.

Into the Peronist breach stepped the wealthy son of Syrians who had immigrated to northeastern Argentina before the end of World War I. A lawyer first known for defending political prisoners in the post-Peronist 1950s,[10] Carlos Saúl Menem (b. 1930) was elected to the presidency in 1989 (and reelected in 1995, serving until 1999). With his exaggerated sideburns and love of fast cars, Menem styled himself as a late twentieth-century "playboy" variation on the nineteenth-century *caudillo* [local-boss] model frequently associated with Camila O'Gorman's executioner, the dictator Juan Manuel de Rosas. Even though he ran for president on a traditional Peronist platform, as Tamara Falicov notes in her study of the period's films, "Menem proceeded to turn his back on all his promises of welfare state intervention."[11] Menem's power was instead achieved through globalizing neoliberal economic practices, first introduced by the 1976–83 military regime and developed in the 1990s as a key component of the president's larger project to establish Argentina as a global player.

Menem's Peronism—or, perhaps more accurately, "Menemism"—bore scant resemblance to Juan- or Evita-style Peronism, so little, in fact, that Peronism appeared to survive in name only. The Peronist void was rendered palpable in Ricardo Bartís's radical 1991–92 version of *Hamlet*, which played in the blackbox space of Buenos Aires's General San Martín Municipal Theatre.[12] In a production lasting only forty-five minutes and bearing the ambiguous subtitle "La guerra de los teatros" [the war of the theatres],[13] Bartís surveyed a Peronism in a state of crisis: Claudius-Menem sought to destroy a questioning Hamlet and stand-in for the "Peronist Youth,"[14] while Hamlet's father, Perón, remained onstage throughout most of the performance to be used as a physical punching bag in Claudius and Hamlet's confrontation. Gertrude bore traces of Evita's iconic style (the tailored suit, the blonde hair), but her behavior suggested a consumerist Zulema Yoma, Menem's recently divorced spouse, crossed with political weakling (and notorious shopper) Isabelita.[15] Audiences were left with the sickening feeling that the effects of short-term neoliberal, consumerist Menemism would prevail at the expense of any long-term investment in the country's future generations. There seemed to be no possible afterlife for Hamlet.[16]

Or for Evita for that matter. Gambas al Ajillo appeared to have gotten it theatrically right: in the 1990s the country had Evita's coffin but nothing to go in it. "[T]he most politically charged fetish of the twentieth century," Evita's body seemed to have gone missing by the century's end, even as her ghost remained ostensibly "the most politically powerful player in Argentine politics today."[17] Menemist Argentina had inherited the container but not its contents, an image lacking any substance.

In the post-Menemist early twenty-first century, what social theorist David Harvey has called Argentina's "rollercoaster experience with neoliberalization"[18] crashed, when several years of economic recession culminated in President Fernando de la Rúa's abrupt resignation on December 20, 2001.[19] Argentines had four presidents in less than a month; savings accounts were frozen (by *corralitos*, whose diminutive did not soften the blow of government-corralled funds); Congress openly declared the country's default on IMF loans (as if "it were an act of emancipation and not the recognition of bankruptcy,"[20] according to Uruguay's ex-president); 52 percent of the national population (including 70 percent of minors) fell below the official poverty line;[21] and generalized distrust of what Argentines call the "political class" even led one national Representative to perform a Catholic exorcism of the entire congressional building.[22] Out of the socioeconomic chaos emerged another Peronist power couple, the first since Juan and Eva. Both former and now-deceased president Néstor Kirchner and his wife and current president, Cristina Fernández de Kirchner, have defined their own style of Peronism through carefully calibrated evocations of Eva Perón. In apparently evermore complex iterations, Evita continues to play multiple femiconic roles in contemporary national and transnational cultural and political contexts.[23]

In each instance of the various resurgences and reinventions of Peronism in the years following Eva Perón's death, Peronism's own relationship to Evita has been transformed. From the state-supported veneration of her paraffined corpse and its subsequent disappearance after the 1955 coup; to its return and revolutionary repoliticization in the early 1970s, followed by yet another period of postcoup disappearance and silencing; to the 1980s redemocratization and 1990s Peronism without Perón; and finally to today's uneasy tension between a commodified, commercialized, and globalized Evita and a politically reclaimed populist Evita: nowhere are these transformations better evinced than in the ever-changing representations of Evita's dead body and the absent presence of her many effigies, on national and transnational cultural stages.

Evita's effigies appear seemingly everywhere, inspiring a range of politically, emotionally, and even metaphysically charged engagements. Jack Child, for example, documents that a series of Argentine postage stamps bearing Eva Perón's likeness was issued after her death, with executive orders that they be the only stamps sold and used for a period of one year.[24] Three years later, postal workers who had previously been instructed not to allow cancellation marks to mar the First Lady's face apparently celebrated Perón's fall by covering Evita's image in black ink.[25] In his 1960 microfictional narrative "El simulacro" [The Simulacrum],[26] Jorge Luis Borges locates a Perón impersonator and his blonde doll in a town in northeastern Argentina, where while Evita's corpse lies in state in the capital, people deposit two pesos to pay their respects to the miniature double. As Margaret Schwartz points out, the doll-effigy stands in not for the living Eva Perón but for her preserved cadaver: "This material object, itself a cipher for the problem of the simulacrum, is what haunts this text and mediates between a purely historical reading and a metaphysical reading, postmodern or otherwise."[27]

Thirty-five years later, another narrator—with an identity slipping toward his author's, whose name he shares—would find himself textually confounded by the enigma-effigy of the dead Eva Perón. In his best-selling 1995 novel, *Santa Evita*,[28] Tomás Eloy Martínez, whose early career included encounters with the historical Eva Perón and at least one onstage impersonator, created a generically hybridic fiction closely but deceptively aligned with received historical events surrounding the afterlives of Evita's corpse and its multiple effigies. Martínez's hypnotic text drives home Lloyd Hughes Davies's assertion, "Reality cannot be fixed but only reinvented."[29] Reinvention would later result in Martínez discovering a quotation he had invented for the Eva character when she whispered in Juan's ear in his earlier *Novela de Perón*—"gracias por existir"—presented as the historical Eva's own in an exhibit in a Buenos Aires museum. Martínez claimed that his novel *Santa Evita* inverted the rules of Capote's or García Márquez's New Journalism: instead of using fiction to narrate real events, "fictitious events are told as if they were real."[30] Much like an actor deciding whether to perform "as" Evita or "be" Evita (as discussed in the previous chapter), Martínez wrote that in his 1995 novel he took on "the challenge of the truth as if it were a challenge of verisimilitude."[31] The novelist, like the doctor preserving a corpse, attempts to transfigure historical bodies into "something they are no longer," returning them to the "fragile reality" of fiction transformed into "another icon of culture."[32] Effigies engender more iconized effigies.

Today, Evita's face and body circulate globally through practically every medium imaginable. For further proof of her "commodity fetishism," we need only make a cursory search of the Internet, where we can find for sale a Brazilian line of nail polish inspired by "women warriors" who "made a difference in world history," among them Cleopatra, Helen of Troy, Joan of Arc, Elizabeth I, Marie Antoinette, Queen Victoria, Princess Diana, and Evita Perón—represented by an intense shade of blue that only nominally brings to mind her country's flag with its sky-blue lines.[33] Surrounded by such a range of fetish- or effigy-effects, I take this chapter to look at performances of Evita with a specific focus on such events as they are historically, geographically, and culturally determined to reflect upon how and why, even after death, Evita is performed differently in different moments and places.

The Deaths and Resurrections of Eva Perón and Evitist Peronism

While many artistic media have lent themselves to countless representations of Eva Perón, living and dead, experimental live performance has been especially productive in reimagining her femiconic afterlives. As discussed in the previous chapter, films created both within and outside Argentina have frequently been constrained by a reliance on the "real" body and a predilection for biography and authenticity at creativity's expense. Musical theatre has likewise generally found itself restricted to a biographical impulse that almost inevitably ends with its subject's death.[34]

Instead, it is in experimental and independent theatre and performance where Evita's fetishized effigy appears to have undergone more complex reconsiderations. I therefore focus here on five performance pieces that address issues of corporeality, displacement, and disappearance through her death: Copi's *Eva Perón*, whose 1970 Parisian premiere featuring a male actor in Evita drag caused controversy in France and Argentina, and whose two twenty-first-century restagings in Buenos Aires have provoked a different kind of discord; Mónica Viñao's 1998 *des/Enlace* [un/Link], a three-person performance in which the sole female character can be understood as both Evita *and* a *desaparecida*; and Buenos Aires performance troupe Pista 4's 1998 *Cadáveres* [Corpses], a staged piece of FM radio-theatre based on the disturbing post–post-avant-garde poems of exiled Argentine Néstor Perlongher. These various productions respond to specific moments in Argentina's ongoing relationship with Peronism and its variations. Copi's play, product as much of the Parisian '60s as of the *porteño* '50s, becomes the site of twenty-first-century conflicting reiconizations of a transgressive Evita in domestic and foreign productions. The 1970 and 2004 Copi productions bracket Mónica Viñao and Pista 4's search in the 1990s for alternative modes of not only staging Evita's body but also representing the thirty thousand *desaparecidos* whose fate had not yet been acknowledged by any democratically elected government and whose victimizers had been officially pardoned by President Menem in 1990.[35] All five productions, through exhilaratingly different technologies of representation, complicate our historical and critical understandings of the Evita fetish-effigy.

Drag, Exile, and a 1970s Peronism (and Anti-Peronism) of the Left: Copi's Eva Perón

Copi's Eva Perón is so overdetermined, so openly mediated, and so outrageously substituted that Evita's death becomes nothing more than the birth of an image. Copi, the *nom d'artiste* of Raúl Natalio Damonte Botana (1939–1987),[36] was Argentine-born to a famously anti-Peronist family, Uruguayan-bred in exile, and from 1962 until his death in 1987 a French resident celebrated for his *Nouvel Observateur* cartoon strips, novels, outrageous one-man cabaret drag performances, and high-camp 1980s French television ads for Perrier.[37] Copi was also a gifted playwright and collaborated with fellow Argentine expatriate and stage director Jorge Lavelli on at least five different projects.[38] Although most of Copi's plays have finally been staged in his native Argentina (albeit posthumously), *Eva Perón* did not premiere in Buenos Aires until quite recently, and a local dialectal translation of the original French text was not published until 2000.[39] The possible reasons for this delay may lend some insight into the onstage representations of Evita's afterlives, as well as a more nuanced understanding of local popular and critical reception of later Evita embodiments.

In Copi's version of the Argentine femicon, Evita does not die but rather abandons the country, leaving everyone else behind to construct the Santa Evita myth over the corpse of her murdered nurse. As ostensibly a further slap in the faces of Evita mythologizers on both sides of the Atlantic, Paris production director and fellow Argentine expatriate Alfredo Rodríguez Arias cast Argentine male actor Facundo Bo to play Eva in a performance of high camp in aesthetic accord with many Copi productions.[40] Violent response kept pace with the production's popular (if not critical) success. Arias would later recall, "They condemned us. They held masses in Buenos Aires. In Paris the critics demolished us. . . . We received threatening letters."[41] After a mid-performance attack on the theatre, the play completed its three-month run under police protection.[42] Copi himself would not be allowed back into Argentina until 1984 after the country's return to democracy.

Copi called his play a "tragic farce," but, like Mónica Ottino's *Eva y Victoria*, its premise is uchronic: What if Evita never died? What if the famous corpse belonged to someone else, such as a young nurse stabbed to death at Eva's command? On the eve of its 1970 premiere at Paris's Théâtre de L'Epée de Bois,[43] Copi told an Argentine reporter (Tomás Eloy Martínez, who years later wrote *Santa Evita*), "I wanted [the play] to be a tragedy about power."[44] Nevertheless, tragedy ultimately cedes ground to black-humor ceremony: Eva escapes death and Buenos Aires, leaving behind her jewels so they can be displayed in future exhibits. Before departing, she gives her mother the number to one of her safe deposit boxes in Switzerland and bequeaths Perón and Argentina yet another box, the coffin containing the substituted body of the nurse, ready for transmutation into the Evita-myth. As Marcos Rosenzvaig notes, this is not a play about the historical Eva Perón but rather "a critical representation of a mythologized image."[45] Through conspiratorial surrogation, Copi's Evita saves her body from the myth that will be constructed around it, wresting her physical self away from Perón, her family, and Evita-obsessed Peronists and anti-Peronists alike.

The 1970 production included another body switch by way of its cross-gender casting. Director Arias justified his choice to have a male actor play Evita in terms that challenge our usual appreciation of camp mimetic transvestism: "the wider-set eyes and the greater distance between the chin and the mouth give [a man's] face a certain command without which the character would be self-contradictory."[46] Such commanding physical exaggeration came across in even some non-cross-gendered performances. Martínez described Michelle Moretti, the actress playing Eva's mother, as "a valkyrie with wild, red hair who looked like she'd escaped from some poem by Baudelaire."[47] Larger-than-life excess was not limited to the casting: whenever Evita or Perón walked across the small stage, Argentine designer Roberto Platé's set-pieces—all iconic images of Buenos Aires, including the national congressional building, the Obelisk, and the Opera movie theatre—would shake and groan. The production confused, intrigued, and outraged its audiences as it became, according to that same reporter, "impossible to know if the story [was] a nightmare of Carmen Miranda in 1940s Hollywood or the adventures of a tribe of rich King Kongs."[48]

A dream (or nightmare) of Hollywood, a drag demigoddess, a death, and hugely comical and obscenely ferocious dialogues:[49] who or what was this Evita as staged by Copi, Arias, and Bo? Given the conflictive history between the upper-middle-class Damonte family and the Peróns, it has sometimes been assumed that Copi's sole motive was to demonize his family's socioeconomic class enemy, Eva. Such a narrowly political perspective leads Viviana Paula Plotnik to dismiss Copi's Eva as "mentally unbalanced . . . [. . .] mediated by the black legend and his family's anti-Peronism."[50] Yet Copi himself confessed that when he was twelve years old, he was given to imagining Eva as "a fairy covered in diamonds,"[51] and she became a lifelong obsession.[52] Actor Facundo Bo's physical characterization of Copi's Evita—gorgeously exaggerated, deformed, obscene, grotesque, excessive, imposing, and transsexualized—returns us to the mythologizing project. Indeed, César Aira posits the idea of a "myth-dream" [sueño del mito] in order to explain the workings of Copi's play: Eva's invented "drag" condition affords her the opportunity not to comply with what the myth has programmed for her. That is, if everything is representation, she does not have to die: "Evita transvestite, the dream of the myth, survives in order to spread herself throughout the world as image."[53] In his book-length study, Aira elaborates a theory regarding Copi's artistic system in which the theatre is transformed into a world of miniatures, velocities, and Copi's stage. Evita, a standard character on the Latin American drag-performance scene, saves herself from cancer (just like drag Marilyn is saved from pills and drag Selena saved from the

Figure 5: Facundo Bo as Evita flanked by the cast of Copi's *Eva Perón*, Paris, 1970. Photo courtesy of Roberto Platé.

bullet).[54] Aira's persuasive case notwithstanding, Copi's and Arias's Evita is more or other than a female impersonator employed to make such a commanding presence believable, or Rosenzvaig's vehicle for a critique of gender construction,[55] or Aira's promise of a happy, myth-dream ending. In his consciously political use of transvestism, Copi dreams of monsters as well as myths. His Eva Perón is a demi-goddess, but she is also a ragingly grotesque, murderous creature, and she is ultimately a human being who will die a bodily death by terminal cancer and whose inevitable demise will be exploited by the state to immortalize and institutionalize the myth. By exaggerating and deforming the image of Evita, playwright Copi, director Arias, and actor Bo make it impossible for us to ignore her "performed" condition in the personal, political, and collective imaginary.[56] In *Eva Perón* the process of mythologization is deconstructed as the creation and anticipated performance of simulacrum.

It is therefore hardly surprising that *Eva Perón* was not staged in Copi's native Argentina until long after the country's return to democracy and the testing of the playwright's local reception through productions of nearly all his other works.[57] Fellow Argentine expatriate, the poet-anthropologist Néstor Perlongher (1949–1992) experienced a similar response to his equally, if not even more, complex and controversial renderings of Eva Perón.[58] This was most notoriously the case with his short story "Evita vive (en cada hotel organizado)" [Evita lives (in every organized hotel)], written in 1974–75 while Perlongher was still residing in Buenos Aires but not published in Argentina until 1987, after his self-imposed exile to Brazil; and even the 1989 Argentine reissue set off yet another scandal.[59] A transvestite prostitute narrates the first part of "Evita vive" to tell the interlocutor of her early 1970s encounter with another prostitute in a Buenos Aires brothel; the hooker is Eva, unmistakable in her blonde chignon and "that glossy, shiny skin of hers and the blotches of the cancer underneath."[60] Both the narrators of the second and third parts (respectively, a young gay hippie and a working-class male prostitute) swear to this identity, which Eva herself openly acknowledges, as she does her sexual and drug activities. The editors of Perlongher's collected prose frame the story in terms reminiscent of critical opinions regarding Copi's work; like *Eva Perón*, "Evita vive" is still capable of irritating "the emotional and political membranes of Argentinean mythology."[61] "Evita vive" is one of four texts—both poetic and narrative—that Perlongher composed about Eva Perón,[62] and coursing through all is what Ben Bollig terms the writer's own "difficult relationship" with the Peronist movement and especially his conflicted response to Evita-style Peronism.[63] Perlongher was a member, from 1971 to 1976, of the Frente de Liberación Homosexual [Homosexual Liberation Front or FLH], an organization famously rejected by the Peronist Youth in the 1970s. Bollig wisely reminds us that Perlongher's was "a personal and desiring politics on the margins, in keeping with his focus on desire rather than party politics."[64] The Perlongher scholar convincingly argues that his subject treats Evita much like he does the figure of the *travesti*,[65] both are capable of subverting patriarchal order in "questioning binary divisions between sex and gender, and linking desire to politics."[66]

José Amícola, in his book-length study of Latin American "camp," puts Copi's and Perlongher's combined politics another way. It is

> precisely the contrast of the sequins' or lamé's shimmer next to scatological revulsion that gives these two champions of camp, Copi and Perlongher, all the force of their political combat. This struggle between noble and ignoble surfaces is presented as juices coming out of bodies, bodies that have long been called "homosexual" and that now resist any essentializing in the pure exaggeration of their attributes.[67]

Like Copi's protagonist, Perlongher's Evita takes agentive control of her life, unlinking her own desire from the political aspirations of those who would later control her image.

In their respective "Evita" texts, both Copi and Perlongher make consciously political use of transvestism. Thus applying a somewhat moralistic standard to categorize these works as anti-Evitist, or even as generally anti-Peronist, overlooks the two writers' complicated relationships with Peronism and especially Evita-style Peronism. Not unlike Copi's fairy-goddess in disgrace, Perlongher's Eva Duarte is a plebeian princess who returns from heaven to distribute marijuana instead of blankets: she is Santa María in (but not *of*, as the city's official name states) Buenos Aires. According to Perlongher's two editors, both close friends of the writer, "*His* Eva was an unforgettable goddess, the girl next door [*novia de barrio*], a Peronist Amazon, resisting with her teeth and nails—always painted in Revlon polish—, who screamed 'treason' to those who manhandled her, who came down from heaven to give the cop a blow job and shack up in every dive hotel."[68] In other words, Perlongher imagines an Eva loved and hated, an Eva similar to Copi's protagonist, who creates a public corpse to assure her own private survival. Ultimately, both Copi and Perlongher—writing just before and after the turbulent return of Peronism (and Perón)—imply a relationship with Evita that refuses to be contained within the usual saint-whore dichotomies so frequently constructed around the historical Eva Perón and her cultural representations. Indeed, it is precisely the two artists' career-long artistic commitment to self-conscious overdetermination and excess, rather than any perceived simplistic anti-Peronism, that accounts for the ongoing unease that the play and the short story are still capable of provoking. As I discuss later in this chapter, such continued discomfort might also explain the mixed critical reception of two recent productions of *Eva Perón* in Buenos Aires. But before considering twenty-first-century Argentina, we must attend to the 1990s, the next moment of Peronist reinvention, and two other performances of a "disappeared" Evita. Both productions, coming out of late 1990s Menemism, offered not only aesthetically different approaches to performing Evita's absent body but also new models for staging what, by the late 1990s, was a ubiquitous subject whose cultural representation had become tragically clichéd: the thirty thousand desaparecidos still largely unaccounted for and only recently accorded official recognition.

In August 1999, I attended a performance of *des/Enlace* by Argentine director Mónica Viñao.[69] In striking contrast to Copi's *Eva Perón*, the piece's unnamed Evita is an underdetermined ghostly figure called "Sombra" [shadow or shade], who haunts the consciences of her two military torturers. The forty-five-minute work inventively conjoined two well-known national histories: Eva Perón's death and the subsequent disappearance of her body, and the still-then-unaccounted-for disappearances of at least thirty thousand people during the last military dictatorship. The production also utilized multiple intertextual and intercultural theatrical codes, which, I believe, may have precluded some Argentine spectators from recognizing both histories. *des/Enlace* stands as a remarkable example of the complexities involved in negotiating cultural memory, femiconic mythologization, and historical representation on the contemporary Argentine stage.[70]

I should first place *des/Enlace* within the specific contexts of Buenos Aires theatre and Viñao's own method and production history. Late twentieth-century Argentine performance bore the marks of contemporary mass media's overwhelming cultural and economic influences. Local actors aimed their sights on national and international film and television markets with the result that contemporary Buenos Aires actor-training programs, much like their North American and European counterparts, tend to offer some variant of Stanislavski-Method approaches. Stage directors complain that actors perform for the "little screen" and no longer possess the vocal and physical training necessary to reach a theatre audience. Economic realities have also dictated that most productions take place in smaller independently run performance venues. When the above factors are combined with the Argentine stage's "grotesque" aesthetic tradition when representing "real Argentines," performances can seem increasingly frantic and harder to understand while retaining an attractive hyperrealism.

Mónica Viñao, initially trained in set design, drawing, and painting,[71] began staging plays in the late 1980s and, since 1990, has been engaged in an ongoing working relationship with Japanese theatre practitioner Suzuki Tadashi.[72] With actors trained in her workshops, Viñao built upon Suzuki's method.[73] Early works such as the 1992 *Medea* found Viñao still seeking her own aesthetic path. Two Medeas moved in ways reminiscent of those prescribed by Suzuki in his "grammar of the feet": wearing traditional Japanese *tabi*, they employed sliding steps and stamping and especially favored Suzuki's "slightly pigeon-toed walk."[74] Viñao's earlier choice to work with classic Western texts in a non-Western mode also echoed her mentor's productions. By 1999's *des/Enlace*, however, she had developed her own hybridic method and was writing and staging distinctively Argentine texts.

Viñao's relationship to Suzuki nevertheless continued to shape local critical reception of her work, seen even in a cursory glance at the title of one review of *des/Enlace* published in a leading newspaper: "Yesterday's Ghosts, in an Oriental Key."[75] In fact, such critical compartmentalization of Viñao's work as Orientalist appeared to have skewed the production's reception. Critics and audiences tepidly responded to *des/Enlace*'s aesthetics while lauding Viñao's inventive attempts at calling forth the ghosts of the country's 1976–83 dictatorship. In doing so many of them completely overlooked another local referent and the text's inspiration, Eva Perón.[76] As a spectator I interpreted her character as both a recent desaparecida confronting those who had "disappeared" her *and* a dead Evita confronting her living husband, Juan Perón, and Carlos Eugenio Moori-Koenig, the colonel assigned to keep watch over her cadaver after her husband's overthrow. When I shared my double reading, Viñao responded: ". . . when I wrote it, I had in mind that strange relationship of the '*milico*' who fell in love with Eva, . . . but when rehearsals began, Perón appeared, unexpectedly, just like one more man who could and couldn't stand her. . . . With respect to the desaparecidos the subject is emblematic and unavoidable a cadaver without a tomb . . . something too obvious to leave out. . . ."[77]

Both historically grounded interpretations point back to the play's title—un/Coupling, un/Linking, un/Knotting, dé/Nouement—and its multiple interpretations of a single situation: two men linking themselves physically, emotionally, and mytho-historiographically to a woman who wishes nothing more than to uncouple herself from them and be left in peace. Yet the production's one-sided reception inspires me to ask questions with implications for femiconic representation: How did *des/Enlace* stage the historical figure of Evita? And why did so few see her on Viñao's stage? As the script is unpublished and the performance relied heavily on extratextual elements, I describe the production in detail.

des/Enlace begins in dark silence. Whispering voices are heard: an occasional word or phrase, "¿Quién es ella?" [Who is she?], cut off by shushes and an occasional slap. After a minute, the lights come up on a black stage and three actors, seated on identical white wooden chairs and all longtime Viñao collaborators. A spotlight focuses on the actress playing Sombra, whose black hat with netting, pearl choker, red wedge pumps, black lace gloves, and very pale street makeup recall 1950s Argentine fashion. Silvia Dietrich's blonde hair is loose, and the slinky asymmetry of her black knit top with one long sleeve is echoed in a reddish-brown skirt whose somber floral print ruffle cuts diagonally across crossed legs. Both arms are bent with one hand raised and the other in front of her torso, creating the effect of a slightly startled doll.

The other two actors are shrouded in shadow, but we can see that, to Sombra's left, Jorge Rod, playing Viejo [the old one], is dressed in a brown suit, with a white shirt, conservative tie, and white gloves. His hair is grayed and slicked back; his makeup whitened and somewhat exaggeratedly aged. One hand is on his hip, and his chin rests on the other fist. Joven [the young one], to Sombra's right, is the most ambiguously attired. Mariela Viñao's unbelted, brown silk trench coat covers a black blouse, buttoned to the throat and closed with a woman's silver brooch. She wears thigh-high hose. Such "feminine" touches are countered by heavy shoes, white leather driving gloves, slicked-back dark hair, and white masklike makeup augmented by blackened eyebrows, eyes, cheeks, and centers of upper lip and chin. Joven sits calmly, arms bent and hands slightly raised and crossed. At different moments, all three performers will adopt these individual "holding" poses of attentive stillness.

The motionless actors speak in deep, hoarse voices. Sombra unexpectedly shifts her body, dropping slightly to the left, reversing her arm placement, bending her right leg back while her left leg sticks straight out. She appears to be broken. Her voice shifts as well, into a higher, breathier, more "feminine" register, which she will maintain throughout the performance.[78]

Throughout the performance too, a single gesture—like the sound of one voice—seems to trigger others. Not only do individuals counter their own movements, often maintaining their bodies on a diagonal plane, but they balance the others' as well.[79] The first such example is also the first moment of interaction, four minutes into the performance: Joven turns to Sombra, who then extends her right arm outward in a gesture of rejection while turning her body and extending her left arm toward Viejo. Viejo leans toward Sombra, and then all three face forward, crossing left legs over right in unison. With rare exceptions, the movements are slow, and the gestures punctuated and then held.

des/Enlace's unpublished dialogue text is structured as three "moments of flight" [*momentos de fuga*] and an epilogue. In performance, all four sections are delimited by transitional scenes involving lighting shifts, repeated words, sounds of violence, and static poses. The first moment, entitled "a kidnapping" and created out of fragmented dialogues and private comments, leads us to surmise that the abduction has already taken place and that Joven has been carrying the victim, a half-naked (and presumably dead) doll-woman, around in a suitcase for a very long time. Viejo, frustratedly writing his memoirs, tells Joven to place the doll-woman on the table so he can return her to the wooden box kept in his armoire. The doll-woman in question is Sombra, clearly identified by the repeated references to her red high-heeled shoes. Sombra protests her mistreatment, claiming they have left her naked and stained and wishing she had instead been left at peace inside the box.

When Viejo exclaims, "The dead are not at peace," all three adopt Joven's initial pose as overhead lights cast them in silhouette. The next two minutes provide a transition from the first moment to the second, "the dance." The actors, held in the same attitude, speak simultaneously, overlapping and repeating words and sounds. Viejo commands Sombra to "Smile!" and complains that "the volume keeps getting louder." Joven commands Sombra to "Turn!" and attempts to insinuate himself into her life ("Are you inviting me to dance?"). Sombra objects: "Such intensity displeases me. . . . Why are you making this up? . . . It's not true!" During the dance, Joven and Viejo vie for control of Sombra even as together they seek to keep her safe from the marching "hooded ones" outside who wish to "burn her . . . make her disappear . . . send her to the waters." At times the young soldier obeys Viejo's orders, adopting a stylized military salute; at others, Joven speaks jealously of his love for the deceased and how her "death changed the destiny of my life."

Such multilevel role-playing is further complicated by the impossibility, in Spanish, of differentiating when Viejo and Joven are speaking *of* Sombra from when they're speaking *to* her.[80] Even linguistically Sombra is simultaneously present *and* absent as Viejo and Joven attempt to manipulate her in this perverse dance of after-death. Sombra contradicts their attempts at disappearance by insisting on her presence: at one point she slowly removes her right glove and drops it, forcing the other two to compete. Joven once again attempts to reduce Sombra to a fetish, by grabbing and placing the glove over his own. Sombra repossesses her glove, asserting authority over her own spectral shadow but in the third person, "Wrong. She wishes to rest in peace." When Viejo insists that she is just a corpse, Sombra violently shifts to her feet and the first person: "You force yourself onto me! . . . I said that I AM NO LONGER HER!"

In an apparent tactical change, Joven and Viejo begin to reminisce about a woman walking along the beach:

VIEJO: Then the woman in white passes by running among the rocks. Her blonde hair floating in the wind.
JOVEN: Can you see her?
VIEJO: Perfectly: she's crying.

Sombra has transformed into Ella [She], the woman in white who speaks at the beginning of the written dialogue and, lifting her bent legs up, leans back to the side of her chair, both arms raised in front, palms self-protectively facing outward: "Women always do that when they're raped. Some go mad. Others . . . even kill themselves." Maintaining this "violated" pose, her hands now close to her ears, Sombra speaks of the white gauze dress, shredded and bloodstained because "They forced themselves on me! After my death. I have an open wound."

Hearing the "others" at the door, Joven and Viejo demand to return Sombra to her box despite her protest that "I don't want to be buried without words." This dialogue, delivered by all three seated once again in their opening positions, precedes the transition into the text's third and final moment, "the rape." The performers motionlessly emit the odd phrase and repeated sounds of machine-gunfire, screams, ambulance sirens, and barking dogs. The sounds abruptly cease, and Sombra stands, adopts a stylized movie-star pose, and calmly repeats a line she had screamed seconds earlier in the transition, "I don't want to be photographed." Joven and Viejo consult each other behind Sombra's back, and as she sits down they raise her up, forcibly escorting her into the now glowing footlights. Although Sombra's attempts to leave are thwarted, the two men never seem to manage complete control of her. The final moment ends in apparent impasse as the three performers return to their initial positions. Ending where they began, Ella/Sombra repeats the opening line, "The Colonel has gone days without sleeping . . ."

A French *chanson* plays as the lighting shifts overhead to mark the performance's final transition. A sequence of movements is slowly repeated seven times: Sombra re-creates her earlier "violated" pose, Viejo raises his bent arms in an echo of his initial "pensive" pose, and Joven alternates between a drinking gesture and lunging suddenly at Sombra. The transition ends with all three frozen in the sequence's opening image.

For the epilogue, the performers gradually return to their original attitudes. Their stasis is punctuated twice, first by the snap of Joven's fingers, signaling a door closing behind him, as Viejo laments, "The wind drags me away. I'm lost in the mirror I look at myself and see only a hole. I extinguish myself slowly in the fire. But when I close my eyes she appears. *(Pause.)* Her voice resounds breaking the silence. She frees me." Ella/Sombra responds, "Who's calling me?" When she snaps her fingers, all lights are extinguished except for one, slowly fading on her face as she says, "I cross the panes of glass, freezing." Silence. Blackout.

To anyone familiar with twentieth-century Argentine history, *des/Enlace* possesses clear references to the received mythology surrounding the lives of Eva and Juan Perón. Sombra's costuming alludes to a 1950s Evita at the height of her powers and on the cusp of death, and the multiple references to Sombra's wax-doll appearance echo the descriptions of Evita's paraffined corpse lying in state in a glass coffin (as well as the rumored multiple effigies created to outwit would-be kidnappers). Perón appears as a haunted old colonel trying to rewrite history,[81] and Joven's military figure conjures images of both a Perón follower and his enemy, the army colonel assigned to keep watch over Eva's corpse after Perón's overturn and exile. It is commonly thought that the heavy-drinking Moori-Koenig went mad after falling in love with his enemy's corpse.[82]

However, *des/Enlace*'s constant citations of disappearance, torture, and rape also invoke the 1976–83 military dictatorship and its desaparecidos. The script's two female characters—Sombra and Ella—are played by the same actor, and no change from one character to the other is noted in production. Thus Sombra is not only the dead Evita; she is also Ella, a desaparecida, Derrida's ghostly *hantise*, "an obsession, a constant fear, a fixed idea, or a nagging memory."[83] Dietrich's conflated characterization of Sombra/Ella constitutes a shadow-figure of a "disappeared" Eva Perón, as Viñao's late 1990s representation of a national femicon takes place in the dual sociopolitical context of 1950s and 1970s Argentina. This duality is in fact present in all characters, as the two "colonels" are Perón and Moori-Koenig as well as the desaparecida's obsessed torturer-rapists. Despite such dualities, local critics tended to fix the two men in the 1970s, as seen in one published synopsis: "an unburied desaparecida's ghost torments her torturer, an old general."[84] I wonder if such narrow interpretations were the result of a staging that, despite the many details provided, remained culturally underdetermined.

Viñao's written description of Sombra provides an iconic portrait of

Eva Perón and the starting point for analyzing interpretive underdetermination:

> She is dressed in the style of the 1950s, high-heeled red shoes and a black tailored outfit that visibly traces the outline of her body. Her tight skirt has a slit that opens up above her knees. She is a thirty year-old woman and has a mysterious and elegant air about her. She wears her hair tied back behind the nape of her neck, and the netting of her hat barely covers her eyes. A pearl choker peeks out from under her lapels.[85]

Ella, in contrast, is textually described as a disheveled woman wearing a torn, bloodstained white dress. In performance, the two roles collapsed into one, and there were no changes in costuming or attitude to suggest an alteration in character, except for Dietrich's above-described vocal shift (from low to high pitch) early in the performance. Onstage Ella's bloodstained white gauze dress was replaced by Sombra's skirt, the color of dried blood. Dietrich's loose blonde hair substituted Evita's characteristic double-chignon, and, instead of Evita's beautifully tailored 1950s black suit, she wore more contemporary stretch-knit. Sombra's costume, the "period" accessories notwithstanding, favored an overall interpretation of her as desaparecida. The characterization lacked the now-canonized details that make up the Eva-myth.

Dietrich's performance of the Evita-desaparecida double trace introduces a second issue regarding the production's partial reception: the *mise en scène* incorporated multiple intercultural theatrical codes that may have ultimately served to distance the Argentine spectator from "seeing" Evita in Sombra. One intercultural element came from the Japanese performance tradition. Suzuki notes that "the classical Japanese dramas were often set in spots where spirits were thought to dwell, the site of a burial, for example, or a raised grave mound."[86] Performers' stamping might be understood "as a means to help in the calling forth of the spiritual energy of the place, a summoning of the ancestral spirits to come and possess the body of the performer."[87] Although *des/Enlace*'s actors at no point stamp but are either attentively seated or moving very slowly through a very limited space, they call forth their own spirits. This haunting—of a spectral woman, a sleepless colonel, and a young man dragging around a suitcase and a corpse—may have informed one spectator's impression that the production spoke of "genocide and the unburied dead."[88] Ironically, the very "Orientalism" that distanced critics from Viñao's work helped reinforce the more contemporary reading.

Other elements might have served to distance a spectator accustomed to "Argentine" theatrical idioms. Many movements and poses—such as Joven's modified military salute, Viejo's initial evocation of Rodin's "thinker," and the not-quite-right dance—were recognizably pedestrian, yet their carefully stylized transformations rendered them less familiar. Additionally, the characters' many references to themselves and others in the first and third person created confusion at times regarding whether one character was speaking to or about another. This not only confounded spectators' understanding but also kept them from identifying too closely with and possibly recognizing the characters.

Nevertheless, such slippage (e.g., between first-person subject and third-person object) functioned very effectively to stage the struggle between a tortured and raped woman's ghost demanding to be acknowledged and her two torturer-lovers desperately trying to contain her within the memory of an idealized love affair. Viñao's eclectic style imbued the production with an enormous corporeal, vocal, and emotional vitality that portrayed the struggle to claim a space for a national heroine and the resisting traditions attempting to render her invisible through cultural representation. Viñao's Evita defied her condition as desaparecida, attempting to physically reclaim her place in the Argentine imaginary.

At the core of des/Enlace is another kind of struggle, over the possibilities of local aesthetico-cultural transformation. Such possibilities conform to Viñao's stated belief that "the audience does not attend a performance but rather participates in a transformation."[89] In 1999, there was apparently little critical participation in such a transformation, considering that des/Enlace was reduced to deliberately slow motions and distorted voices, an "acting code that devoured the story . . . scaffolding holding up the rest of the work."[90] Such resistance to transformation did not go unnoticed by Viñao, who stated two years later, "I'm a little tired that they always connect me to the Oriental [mode], because I'm from here."[91] In the same interview, Viñao announced a change in her work, a rejection of her previous experimentation and a move, ironically, toward hyperrealism and action "in order to get out of myself."

Critical rejection and artistic frustration notwithstanding, Viñao's hybrid mix of intertextual and intercultural theatrical codes traced the mythocultural shadow of Evita and the disappeared in unexpected, unanticipated ways that could only have occurred in a postdictatorship Argentina still attempting to come to terms with its official legacy of unacknowledged disappearance. des/Enlace's spectral traces eloquently captured the struggle between objectified disappearance and subjectified presence in a nation Tomás Eloy Martínez has deemed "a country of ghosts."[92] *des/Enlace*'s Evita possessed a physical presence, a vital force that countered her mythical disappearance and relegation to history's shadows. Viñao's Evita-desaparecida rebelled against her condition, and her overtly physical presence reclaimed a noncommodified, non-Madonnified place in the Argentine imaginary, "something too obvious to leave out."

Evita, Radiophonics, and Disappearance: Pista 4's Cadáveres

The year before Viñao staged *des/Enlace*, another Buenos Aires production had addressed the same twinned themes of Evita and the desaparecidos through a strikingly different approach to representation. On Sunday evenings during the 1998 Buenos Aires theatre season, in the bar-café of the now-gone experimental theatre space Babilonia, performance troupe Pista 4 presented *Cadáveres* [cadavers, corpses]. For forty-five minutes, the four performers—longtime Pista 4 members Luis Ziembroski, Gabriel Correa, and Luis Herrera, together with guest artist María Inés Aldaburu—spoke, chanted, and effectively deconstructed six poems written during Argentina's 1976–83 military dictatorship by renowned and controversial Argentine poet-anthropologist Néstor Perlongher (whose short story "Evita Lives" I compared to Copi's play earlier in this chapter). The performance I attended began with the three men winding through the bar and playing trombone, trumpet (in some performances a clarinet), and bass drum; the opening four-note dirge was quickly transformed, first into a Brazilian carnival tune before finally settling into a Peronist march. The musicians proceeded to accompany Aldaburu's recitations with discordant, at times barely articulated, sounds before they moved to individual microphones set on a table covered in a black cloth. There Correa, Herrera, and Ziembroski played off of one another as they experimented with their amplified voices and a prerecorded sound track, which they controlled by using a tape player set atop the onstage table. The performance ended with an apparent nod back to Italian futurist *sintesi*: confetti fell over four pairs of legs (two male pairs wearing fishnets), these being the only parts of the performers' bodies made visible below the table, as the performers together recited the evening's final poem.[93]

Five of the six texts performed came from Perlongher's initial published book of poetry, *Austria-Hungría*.[94] The poems in this 1980 collection are littered with the dead—Anne Frank, carnival ghosts, flayed boys, and human-animals in extinction—and include, most importantly for my purposes here, the corpse of Eva Perón. Indeed, the performance opened with "El cadáver" [The Cadaver/Corpse], a poem Perlongher begins by juxtaposing Evita's official time of death (8:25 p.m., during which, under Perón, all radio broadcasting would observe a daily minute of silence) and funeral cortege with the speaker's indecision about entering a hallway filled with danger and pleasure, an image the poet associated with Peronism itself. While Perlongher, like many of the 1960s and early '70s generation, was attracted to "revolutionary" Evita's embrace of the marginalized, he grew to regard Peronism as a dangerous shortcut to liberation.[95]

It was nevertheless Perlongher's best-known and ostensibly non-Evita-themed poem that lent the production its title and most immediate historical referent. "Cadáveres" appeared fourth on the bill; and its eighteen-minute recitation took up over one-third of the entire performance. Legendarily written on a 1981 bus-ride as Perlongher left behind dictatorship Buenos Aires (as well as multiple arrests and beatings) for a permanent move to Brazil's São Paulo, the poem howls about the thirty thousand disappeared by the repressive regime. The initial verses provide a sense of the poem's unrelentingly hypnotic rage:[96]

> Under the bushes
> In the rushes
> On the bridges
> In the canals
> There are Corpses
> Along the tracks of a train that never stops
> In the wake of a sinking ship
> In a small wave, vanishing
> On the wharves the steps the trampolines the piers
> There are Corpses.[97]

Working against the text's merciless litany and interacting with Edgardo Cardozo's ornate sound track, the Pista 4 performers constantly changed sonic directions: one actor spoke inaudibly or distorted his voice by placing a glass over his mouth, while a second countered the rhythms of the third actor's animated radio announcer covering a soccer match with the melancholic swoop of a tango-crooner, and all came together as if they were members of an out-of-tune neighborhood *murga* band.[98]

Before beginning the Babilonia run, the troupe had performed *Cadáveres* at an experimental music festival in Buenos Aires and at various poetry encounters; and until 2003 the piece was reprised for theatre festivals and art fairs. Such diverse artistic venues confounded easy synopsis of a performance that already eluded obvious categorization. Pista 4 member Ziembroski attempted one description in a pre-opening newspaper interview: "It's an intermediate zone between a poetry recital and a more theatrical schema. Voices come out through microphones, and there are traces of acting."[99] The Babilonia production's handbill even added a suggested mode of reception to its own brief summation: "A structure of tempi and chance mathematical combinations began to create a sort of score on top of which the poem was mounted. *Cadáveres* should be listened to as a radio-play, like the ones we'll never get to hear on FM."[100] A live performance of a radio-play that was never broadcast: Was this radio-theatre? Experimental music? A poetry slam? Performance art?

I can say with certainty that *Cadáveres* was the product of a group that had achieved local and international fame for extreme innovation during a time when experimental performance was itself the norm in Buenos Aires: the late 1980s and early 1990s "underground" theatre movement.[101] Notwithstanding, or perhaps because of, the group's notoriety for defying easy labels, its members' eclectic backgrounds in theatre, music, and circus clowning (the last evident in the name Pista 4 or [Circus] Ring 4),[102] and its dedication to fusing different arts and techniques, Pista 4 has never received much critical attention beyond its inclusion in nearly every list of important experimental groups to come out of the nation's mid-1980s return to democracy.[103]

In seeking alternatives to representing Evita and these absent-yet-present national bodies, the Pista 4 production revisited three cultural phenomena of 1980s and '90s Argentine redemocratization: post–post-avant-garde poetry, the theatrical staging of disappearance, and FM radio. The result not only materially resituated the performance of disappearance but also constructively responded to the tyranny of visual representation in contemporary cultural production, including the staging of Eva Perón.

Perlongher belonged to a third generation of Argentine avant-garde poets, and his "post–post-avant-garde poetry,"[104] while not as overtly politicized as the previous generation's, eclectically combined experimentation with protest. Perlongher's highly experimental poetry reflected his multiple praxes: ex-Trotskyite, ex-sociologist, an academic with graduate degrees in social anthropology, a pioneer in Argentina's gay liberation movements, an avid reader of Deleuze and Guattari, an expert on male prostitution in Brazil (and author of one of the most influential academic essays on the subject), and a practitioner of the ecstatic drug-enhanced Santo Daime religion at the time of his AIDS-related death in 1992. Perlongher referred to his poetry as *neobarroso*—an homage to favorite writers, the Spanish baroque poet Luis de Góngora and Cuban neobaroque author José Lezama Lima, as well as a play on the words *barroco/barroso*: "baroque: irregular pearl, nodule of mud [barro]."[105] Perlongher's other preferred poet was Antonin Artaud,[106] a rather unsurprising choice when we think of the Argentine writer's personal and creative search for "spaces for desire and communities based on desire."[107] Perlongher's post–post-avant-garde poetry was a rich and eclectic mix built upon "expanding the poetic lexicon, using everyday language, writing about sex or perversion, mixing avant-garde techniques with political denunciation."[108] His "corrosive gaze," Jorge Monteleone suggests, was largely the consequence of a repressive environment; he wrote with a "latrine tongue, ass eye. Porn[ographic] if not golden graffiti, the voice of the orifice."[109] His disturbing experimental poetics were nevertheless formally concrete: verse combined with prose, line lengths radically varied, entire poems written in italics while others mixed typefaces, certain nouns capitalized at certain times, and ellipses and spacing employed to exasperating effect. Most, if not all, of these elements are present in the printed text of "Cadáveres," which, like much of the author's dictatorship-era poetry, attempts to give form to all that has been repressed or erased or disappeared. The poem concludes:

> She's the one who . . .
> You could see the harp standing there . . .
> In the carpeted room . . .
> Villegas or
> There are Corpses
>
> . . . .
> . . . .
> . . . .
> . . . .
> Isn't anybody there? is what the woman from Paraguay asks.
> Answer: There are no corpses.[110]

Perlongher's own decidedly visual treatment of the missing bodies encountered its theatrical counterpart in the staging of disappearance in postdictatorship Buenos Aires theatre. Throughout the 1980s and early 1990s, embodiment seemed a prerequisite for any play on the subject.

From the first explicit representations of the disappeared (such as Carlos Somigliana's 1982 *Oficial primero* [Official Number One], where the stage ended up buried in bodies), throughout the 1980s and early 1990s embodiment was emphasized. Bodies abounded on local stages: there were mute corpses, victims yanked under tables, loudly furious Antigones, and lamenting Eurydices. Even when the individual was split into two, the body separated from the voice, the corporeal dominated staging and reception to such an extent that, for example, in production and publicity photos for Eduardo Pavlovsky's *Paso de dos* [Pas de deux], the photographer didn't even bother to include the third performer who, seated in the audience, provided the voice to her muted physical counterpart.[111] The disappeared were so emphatically embodied on the Buenos Aires stage that it became nearly impossible to think of their representation as taking any form other than corporeal ghosting.

However, what had made dramatic sense in early redemocratized Argentina—when it was urgently necessary to unearth and give human form to all that the military regime had covered up—dangerously neared fetishism and aesthetic exhaustion ten years later. The more realistic of Buenos Aires theatrical productions insisted on incorporating the desaparecidos into the historical pantheon through the most literal of embodied performances, while many experimental artists of the late 1990s avoided overt theatrical engagement with their country's recent history. Pista 4's *Cadáveres* constituted an important exception and challenge to Argentine theatrical representation of disappearance.[112]

To fully understand Pista 4's detour from the representational dead-end of privileging the visual in experimental poetry and traditional embodied performance, I turn to yet another phenomenon of early redemocratization. The return to democracy also witnessed the explosion of "unidentified," reduced-range FM radio stations as an outlet for expression in a country testing its still-precarious freedom. FM not only provided an alternative to commercial AM stations but, from 1988 on, became some of the most listened-to radio in the country. There were—depending on one's perspective—clandestine, illegal, free, neighborhood, and community radio stations transmitting all over a city, albeit at a reduced range (similar to U.S. college radio stations), and their impact was astounding. FM stations transmitted programs from inside mental hospitals, geriatric homes, and jails—the programs were created by their inhabitants; they communicated vital information to otherwise isolated dwellers in slums and to non-Spanish speakers; and they welcomed artistic experimentation.[113]

Even so, Argentine FM radio has never tested the limits of theatrical performance beyond the continued broadcasting of radio-plays (much like those in which the actress Eva Duarte performed in the 1940s) and the occasional "soundscape." Conversely, radio's performance potential has rarely been explored by Argentine artists, one noted exception being 1960s *happenista* Marta Minujín, who used radio as a medium for achieving experiential "simultaneity."[114] Performance's radiophonic potential—even on the almost-anything-goes FM dial—has not been exploited, as Pista 4's program notes imply: "*Cadáveres* should be listened to as a radio-play, like the ones *we'll never get to hear on FM.*"

The performance of the evening's final poem ("Por qué seremos tan hermosas"/Why must we [women] be so beautiful) recalled another, much earlier experiment with radio and live performance. At the beginning of the twentieth century, the Italian futurists created "radiophonic theatre"—live performances that were recorded and later pressed into disks. Pista 4's exposure of their legs under the table as the final poem's sole "visual" performance element echoes F.T. Marinetti's 1915 theatrical "synthesis," *Le Basi* [Feet], whose legs-and-feet photo still occasionally circulates on the Internet.[115] The group's selection of an image from theatrical (and not radio) *sintesi* might cause us to suspect a reversal in direction: whereas traces of the radio body were seen on the early twentieth-century futurist stage, the late twentieth-century *Cadáveres* suggests an attempt on the part of the overdetermined visual stage body, such as Eva's, to (re)gain radiophonic existence.

Joe Milutis builds his study of the relationship between radio art and avant-garde performance on Allen Weiss's concept of radiophonics.[116] In contrast to our common understanding of radio airwaves as extracorporeal signals, for Weiss, Milutis, and Gregory Whitehead, the body itself becomes the mediating term in radiophonic signification. As Milutis states, "[T]he body is source, substance, and medium of radio. [. . .] The radio artist is both producer and consumer, audience and performer, of his own electroacoustical surroundings."[117] Milutis contends that "[r]adio's most fundamental, ontological feature is precisely [its] ability to break down ontological borders," a process he claims is very similar to certain forms of psychosis.[118] Avant-garde radio thus performs a kind of "paranoid-schizophrenic stereophony": it is paranoic—"the radiophonic universe takes the voice away from the body, stealing words . . . and transmitting them everywhere"—and "schizophonic"—"radio loads more voices into the head than the body can withstand."[119] We might recall that Antonin Artaud wrote several pieces for radio, and the recording of his last written work, the 1947 radio-play *To Have Done with the Judgment of God* (recorded but then censored by French radio), concluded with Artaud's own voice calling for a "body without organs," one of his most enduring images.[120] Indeed, radio's "interiorizing technology" promises an Artaudian "spectacle that is more felt than seen," as David Graver has put it.[121] Nor is the physical radiophonic experience necessarily solitary (or unidirectional, as Brecht feared). Weiss makes this clear: "In radio, not only is the voice separated from the body, and not only does it return to the speaker as a disembodied presence—it is, furthermore, thrust into the public arena to mix its sonic destiny with that of other voices."[122]

If Italian futurist radiophonic theatre, according to Milutis, presented "a mad body . . . , a body beyond the modes of reason that reason has presented," vibrating "erotically through contact with out-of-body signals,"[123] then Pista 4's very Argentine *Cadáveres* sought to reclaim radiophonically the paranoid-schizophonic madness that mimesis had excluded from national theatrical representation. The production effectively disrupted body-voice identification as it created layers of voices impossible to track, its sounds mixed with those of its audience in a spectacle more felt than seen. Yet this was not a radio-play but ostensibly a *performance* of a radio-play; that is, the performance's materiality was visual as well as aural. By "staging" a radio-play, Pista 4 achieved a goal shared by body- and radio-artists, Milutis asserts, that of "dematerializ[ing] the art object into performing present."[124] This spatiotemporal shift held an important consequence for Argentine cultural production: by disrupting sign and referent in a staged (not broadcast) performance, *Cadáveres* freed Perlongher's words from literary visual representation, much as it freed the performing body from mimesis.

This shift might also explain why the group ultimately decided not to include Perlongher's own recorded voice in the performance after months of working with the cassette. I deduce that the recording (taped by Aldaburu herself during one of Perlongher's visits to Buenos Aires), though aural and not visual, was still not sufficiently disruptive of the vocal sign and its referent, Perlongher's own now-disappeared body. The recording was not incorporated into the final sound track, designer Cardozo noted, "in order to distance ourselves a bit."[125] The group's decision highlights the risks of the mimetic, even if it is disembodied through aurality. If, as Milutis writes, "the art of radio . . . paradoxically recuperate[s] the referent without mimetically reproducing 'life,'"[126] *Cadáveres* managed to recuperate multiple explicitly Argentine referents without mimetically reproducing their "deaths."

Cadáveres also provided Argentine performance with the possibility of a simultaneous future-present-past. Instead of condemning theatre to representing past horrors in present bodies, *Cadáveres* made "the future strange by the avant-garde use of an 'obsolete' technology."[127] All the poems performed, each written during the 1976–83 dictatorship, dealt with the effects of repression in its myriad forms (political, historical, cultural, sexual . . .), but by freeing these effects from the aesthetics of visual mimesis through an insistence on aural experimentation using "old" media (like the radio-play and the onstage tape-player), the production reinserted the political and the historical into Argentine experimental performance and forecast a future made strange—a radio-play we'll never hear on the radio.

Cadáveres mediated its own theatrical condition by (re)emphasizing the materiality of the aural in performance. It thus became an attempt not only to work against the privileging of Perlongher's poetry as visual artifact (or even as authentic "spoken word"); it also provided an alternative for the staging of historical corpses. By radiophonically disrupting the identification of disappearance with the (re)appeared body, *Cadáveres* provided an alternative to Argentine theatre's apparent choice of mimetic embodiment as the only means of re-presenting and re-membering disappeared bodies such as Eva Perón's.

VIÑAO'S AND PISTA 4's innovative approaches to the staging of disappearance introduced Evita into the multitudinous pantheon of Argentine desaparecidos. Pista 4 added Eva Perón to a list of tens of thousands through their selection and performance of Perlongher's poems, while Viñao created a character whose underdeterminacy caused Evita to slip practically unnoticed by audiences predisposed to certain national representational codes. While both productions provided much-needed alternatives to the embodied performance of disappearance, each remained an exception to the rules of Evita performances still firmly in place in the twenty-first century, as my concluding examples of two recent versions of Copi's *Eva Perón* attest.

Copi, revisited: Myths, Effigies, and a (Trans)national Femiconic Evita

In 2004, after more than a thirty-year wait, Buenos Aires audiences were able to see not one but two productions of Copi's *Eva Perón*, the infamous "tragic farce" that had supposedly never before been staged in Argentina after the uproar surrounding its 1970 Parisian premiere.

The general impression of Copi's play as unstageable in Argentina has prevailed until very recently, and the reason typically given is that loyal Peronists would not tolerate either the play's sacrilegious historical revisionism or its foul-mouthed drag Evita. Both justifications conveniently ignore local performance history just as they reinforce the traditional saint-whore dialectic in which so many Evita debates have found themselves deadlocked. These rationalizations also point to certain historiographic prejudices regarding critical acknowledgement of actual local practice. One example comes from the academy, often overlooked by local critics: the National University in Tandil, located in the Province of Buenos Aires 360 kilometers outside the national capital, included *Eva Perón* in its 2000 academic season.[128] Might this university production's omission from most accounts of the play's performance history be the result of critical myopia on the part of Buenos Aires-based reviewers, often blamed by other Argentine scholars of willfully ignoring theatre taking place outside the megalopolis? Another example comes from critically under-acknowledged performance practices: ever since the global success of the 1970s Rice-Lloyd Webber rock-opera, local drag Evitas have been lipsynching "No llores por mí, Argentina," proof of the presence, at least within certain performance circles, of cross-dressed Evitas. Such counterexamples notwithstanding and given the received impression of Copi's *Eva Perón* as unstageable in Argentina, having two independent versions of *Eva Perón* participate in the same 2004 Buenos Aires theatre festival, *Tintas Frescas* [Fresh Tints], was historically and critically noteworthy. One production came from France, while the other was locally produced; together they shed light on current national and transnational representations of Eva Perón.[129]

In 2001, Argentine-born and now French-resident theatre artist Marcial Di Fonzo Bo (b. 1968, Buenos Aires) and his Paris-based company, Théâtre des Lucioles, created the self-proclaimed "first" Spanish-language production of Copi's *Eva Perón*, starring noted Chilean actor-director Alfredo Castro in an all-male cast and staged on a bi-level set with moveable semitransparent scrims reminiscent of Copi's own cartoon boxes.[130] Di Fonzo Bo's French-language version arrived in Buenos Aires in 2004. In it, Di Fonzo Bo played a muscular, often unwigged Evita, taking on the very role his uncle, Facundo Bo, had so notoriously originated some thirty years earlier.[131] The other Buenos Aires production was distinctly homegrown. Staged in a more intimate theatre, it was directed by Argentine actor and Pista 4 member Gabriel Correa making his directorial debut,[132] and the role of Eva was filled by the actress

Alejandra Flechner, former member of Gambas al Ajillo, whose farewell production, *Gauchas gambas,* opened this chapter's commentary.[133]

Given the coincidence of performance, local reviewers perhaps unavoidably pitched the two *Eva Peróns* against one another, with many concluding that they were diametrically opposed. Di Fonzo Bo's production was commended for preserving Copi's "transgressive" spirit in a staging that bore traces of vaudeville, burlesque, and the grotesque. In contrast, Correa was admonished for straight-jacketing his talented lead in a perceived naturalistic staging. One reviewer even implied that self-censorship (femiconophobia?) had predetermined the director's choices: "[Correa] couldn't get past the fear of hurling himself into the pool [of Evita camp performance]; whether out of admiration for his character or out of simple caution, he tried to render formal something that resisted [formality] . . . Of course, he stays here, and the Frenchman has already gone back to France."[134] We might wonder whether this was a case of directorial self-censorship—as Rómulo Berruti, the critic cited here, suggests—or perhaps an act of critical censorship on the part of a reviewer uninterested in considering a more "feminized" and distinctly noncamp Eva. Such an alternate consideration led another reviewer, Hilda Cabrera, in apparently the critical minority, to contend that the production's move away from 1970's transvestism was precisely the motive informing Correa's choice to cast the nonblonde Flechner.[135] The two images here capture neatly the differences in Evita characterization.

The implication of censorship's role in determining local and international staging leads me to larger critical issues: Did the majority of local critics embrace Di Fonzo Bo's production because they regarded it as aesthetically (and even genealogically, in the case of the lead performer/director) closer to the original Paris production? What roles did the "myth" and legacy of censorship, with particular respect to the 1970 production, play in the 2004 Buenos Aires critical response?[136] Most local reviewers appeared to seek an experience that reproduced the scandalous 1970 premiere, thereby reifying the play's own mythic censored "'6os" status. In so doing, though, they critically discarded a version that wildly diverged from the original, now-canonized production to propose a renewed engagement with 1970s-era feminist Evitism and a twenty-first-century metacritical reappraisal of Evita femiconography.

THE PLAYS AND performances examined in this and the previous chapter artistically take up the body of Eva Perón: the historical body rendered mythically invisible yet omnipresent (*Eva de América*); the human-

Figures 6 and 7: Alejandra Flechner and Marcial Di Fonzo Bo as Eva in 2004 restagings of Copi's 1970 *Eva Perón*. Photos courtesy of Gabriel Correa and Marcial DiFonzo Bo.

izing re-corporeality of a previously dehumanized, mythologized image (*Eva y Victoria*); the disappeared presence of a shadow made flesh (*des/Enlace*); one corpse among tens of thousands of desaparecidos heard but not seen (*Cadáveres*); and the invented female body that seeks immortality through mythic substitution (*Eva Perón*). All Eva's bodies, all mediated through staged representation, each reacting in its own way to the national (and international) polarizing Evita femiconographic project.[137]

In both chapters I have juxtaposed a material "historical" need to make the myth flesh to a "critical" desire to demystify, to break down the flesh through mediation. Thus although both *Eva de América* and *Eva y Victoria* attempt an immediate portrayal of the "historical" Eva Perón, one project is undone by relegating its protagonist to supporting player status while the other complicates its own message of commonality through a production that juxtaposed two very different approaches to mimetic performance. Both of these supposedly transparent historical plays demonstrate an ambivalence toward their subject. Ambivalence is likewise overtly present in both *des/Enlace* and *Eva Perón* as they push their not-always-willing audiences to see Eva's as a demystified, mediated presence.

The multiple staged Argentine "Evitas" presented in these two chapters reveal a telling slippage that casts doubt upon what is typically regarded as a distinctly national binarizing tendency and instead suggests a national ambivalence toward Eva Perón as historical character, as mythologized figure, and as femiconized effigy. Not even the most theatrically conventional of these productions (e.g., Guglielmino's *Eva de América* or Ottino's *Eva y Victoria*) manages to present a wholly essentialized body of Eva Perón; rather, each reconstructs her body as a "network of effects" under constant re-elaboration. Consciously or not, they all end up questioning what Frantz Fanon called, albeit in a different context, "cultural mummification"—of turning Evita-as-body into a fetish by fixing it, stereotyping it, preserving it, commodifying it—and thus they undermine any attempt (even their own) at essentializing Eva Perón.

At the same time, however, Evita continues to be culturally mummified on the transnational stage, beginning perhaps with Rice-Lloyd Webber's rock-opera, itself an international *revenant* haunting the global cultural economy through ubiquitous revivals in myriad languages and reaching its Madonnified extreme in Parker's 1996 film. Latin American playwrights, too, continue to call forth Evita's spirit, as in the case of Venezuelan Gustavo Ott and Argentine Mariano Vales's 2009 Spanish-language musical *Momia en el clóset [Mummy in the Closet]: The Return of Eva*

Perón, whose very title points to a different configuration of Evita-corpse and its famous coffin. Rendered literally a mummy, Ott and Vales's Evita dances to salsa music while she slips in and out of her dressing chamber's closet-coffin.[138] Director Mariano Calegaris's notes emphasized that this Evita, product of "our cultural 'melting pot,'[. . .] is the object of the passions she has engendered in life . . . profoundly Latin American."[139] Evita-product, Evita-object: no longer the Gambas' empty coffin, to be filled by the national weight of cultural representation, this twenty-first-century Latin American Evita's "closet" overflows with Latino-America's cultural artifacts, and Eva herself becomes one more victim of national and hemispheric power struggles. The artistic tensions engendered by Eva Perón's dead body—politicized overdetermination and apoliticizing underdetermination, Evita-agent and Evita-patient, romantic tragedy and melodramatic farce, excess and repetition—will not be resolved any time soon. Nor should they be, I contend, as we shall see in the final chapter's examination of how the "femiconic" Santa Evita and other devotional figures are performed, appropriated, and circulated throughout Argentine popular culture.

FOUR

Argentine Madonnas, Pop Stars, and Performances of Immediacy and Virtuality

Santa Evita—Politics, Religion, and Artistic Reenvisioning

The Pietà tableau concluding Ricardo Monti's 1993 play, *La oscuridad de la razón* [The Obscurity of Reason], leaves no doubt as to the imminent resurrection of its protagonist, a nineteenth-century messianic Orestes returned from Europe to an Argentina torn apart by postindependence struggles: "Mariano, resting motionless on the Woman's lap, appears to wake up; he slowly gets up, smiling, and submerges himself, dancing in the ever-growing light."[1] Monti's text—with its mystery-play structure and Christian symbolism—posed an interesting staging challenge for director Jaime Kogan, who began his career in Buenos Aires's independent Yiddish Folk Theatre.[2] In Kogan's production,[3] the Woman leads Mariano over to the indicated place, but she does not sit with him. Mariano instead lies alone in the very spot where he appeared at the play's beginning. No Pietà in sight, Mariano rises unaided and dances, while the Woman watches from the sidelines.[4]

In Kogan's staging, this "Woman" was Eva Perón, performed by longtime Payró regular Felisa Yeni, and it was through Evita that Kogan channeled the play's Christian imagery.[5] In performance, the Woman sported Eva Perón's trademark fitted suit and chignon, yet Kogan avoided the easy deification of Perón's own now-iconic Marian representation as "Santa Evita," our lady of the dispossessed. The dark-haired Yeni smoked cigarettes and spoke in an earthily local *porteño* dialect. Far more involved in the performance than suggested by her bookended appearances at the beginning and end of Monti's dramatic text, the Woman frequented (but never sat on) the stage, and her entrances were underscored by a pealing bell, as she periodically intervened in the play's action by handing props to the others and moving across the stage—none of which is scripted in the published text.[6] Despite the iconic Eva Perón markers, Kogan's performed Woman remained every bit as enigmatic as Monti's written character, and only in her final appearance did she lift her veil, exposing herself as Evita while she uncovered her plan to redeem the lost Mariano and break the tragic cycle of violence and revenge created by Argentina's colonialist, patriarchal past. In translating the Virgin Mary to the stage as Eva Perón, Kogan clearly directed the character's redemptive and trans-formative powers toward a late twentieth-century secular Argentina and the more positive aspects of Peronism, especially as practiced by Evita herself: the privileging of the local over the imported, the protection of the working-class underdog, and the promise of immediate sociopoliti-cal change. Nevertheless, the 1993 production also underscored Monti's own thwarting of any easy utopian expectations: the Woman remained dressed in black, her white-cloaked angels still estrangingly deformed, as the "dark ray" of Mariano's Electra-like sister, Alma, lurked nearby, hav-ing elected to wait in resistant albeit "defeated obscurity."

The strategic convergence of Monti's Virgin Mary and Kogan's Eva Perón is not the only time an iconized Evita has functioned as Marian de-votional surrogate. Indeed, Eva Perón, even before her death at the age of thirty-three, was already inspiring among certain Argentines a venera-tion not unlike that of other popular devotional figures. Representations of a "benevolent" Santa Evita began to circulate in poems, songs, novels, plays, films, and the visual arts.[7] Today she is a ubiquitously exhibited and still-venerated figure in the pantheon of Argentine popular female devotional, particularly Marian, figures, the most prominent of whom are the subjects of this chapter and its study of contemporary devotional practices, whose performances of iconicity interpellate the practitioner as much as, if not more than, the devotional femicons themselves.

Perhaps the contemporary Argentine visual artist most closely identi-fied with Evitist and Peronist iconography is Daniel Santoro (b. 1954). He is also the artist whose work has most attracted and confounded me, in near equal parts. Astoundingly prolific, Santoro has produced a body of paintings and other objects determinedly (and, some would say, ob-sessively) focused on the icons of Peronism, especially Peronism's ulti-

Figure 8: Daniel Santoro, "Altarcito" (oil, gold leaf, and objects, 40 x 70 cm, 2002). Courtesy of the artist.

mate femicon, Evita, and in the process he has constructed his own very personal Peronist symbology that frustrates definitive interpretations.[8] The son of Calabrian immigrants, Santoro grew up in the Buenos Aires working-class neighborhood of Constitución, combining formal artistic training (at the National Fine Arts School) with political activism. Between 1980 and 1991, he worked in the Colón Theatre's scenic shop, and toward the end of that decade he was invited to Singapore to participate in an exhibit. Success led to other trips to Asia and the study of Chinese language. Soon Santoro was incorporating Sanskrit, Hebrew, the Kabbalah, and Chinese cosmography into his images of Evita, Juan, and Argentina's larger gallery of icons. Santoro has continued to work occasionally as a scenographer (and designed the set for Gabriel Correa's 2004 production of *Eva Perón* discussed in the previous chapter).[9] His very theatrical paintings frequently exhibit an almost proscenium framing as well as the suggestion of staged events. In the recent "Victoria Ocampo Observes the Indian Raid's Return" (2011), for example, historical periods and persons are mixed, with the resulting impression that the nineteenth-century event is being (re)created for the spectating Ocampo, Evita's contemporary and class nemesis. As the anonymous collective author of Santoro's Wikipedia site notes, "The theatricalization of politics is a permanent visual feature of Santoro's work."[10]

Before surveying Santoro's vast Evita-iconography, one might anticipate a saintly Evita. She indeed appears as Perón's enigmatic sphinx, as companion to solitary children, and even as devotional object in a quasi-religious altar (fig. 8) that recreates the famous image from the cover of her autobiography and incorporates not only the gold leaf typical of religious icons but also the *milagros* [amulets] offered to a devotional figure as physical representations of a prayer made or realized. Nevertheless, the serenity inferred from such an Evita-*retablo*,[11] signed by her devoted *grasitas* (the pejorative term for the "greasy" disenfranchised Evita would transform into a blessing), is easily troubled by other, possibly more complex images, like the painter's 2008 oil "Pietà: Eva Perón devours Che Guevara's entrails" (fig. 9).

Evita-Madonna (her halo is firmly in place) does not cradle a dead Che-Jesus on her lap but rather turns him over and devours his intestines, evocatively linked in a rosary. Flanked by two rows of cypresses—themselves traditional symbols of death and immortality—and seated below the headquarters of Argentina's largest labor union, the General Confederation of Labor (where Eva's preserved corpse lay until the 1955 military coup), Evita and Che, as stand-ins for Peronism and the

Figure 9: Daniel Santoro, "La Piedad. Eva Perón devora las entrañas del Che Guevara" (oil, 200 cm, 2008). Courtesy of the artist.

Argentine Left, are locked in "a ritual of communion, a recirculation of visceral energy taking us back to the old rituals of cannibalism, habitual in many original cultures of America," in Santoro's own words.[12] In this scene caught between "camp and kitsch," Santoro creates what critic Guillermo Saccomanno calls an "adopted mythology," which from an "orthodox" Peronist position provides a critique of Peronism's syndicalist and right-wing betrayal of the youthful Left even as it presents a "disciplinarian and miracle-worker Evita."[13] Though positioned in the painting as the mother of the Left, she feeds upon the Left's dead body, destroyed—we might assume—by her own movement and husband's later rejection of a militant younger generation. Is Evita's populism as represented by Santoro radical? Conservative? One critic cautiously asserts, "In 'La Piedad' a cumulus of significations—from anthropophagy to political metaphor—coexists and as happens in many of Santoro's pieces proposes such an excessive eulogy of Peronism and its symbols that it's not easy to tell if this is a celebration or a mockery."[14] The painting's combined figures recall Harold Prince's decision to render the Lloyd Webber-Rice Che as a "revolutionary" opponent of Perón-style populism. Santoro's Evita, however, is a far more complex and provocatively enigmatic figure.

One thread runs throughout Santoro's Evita-iconography and joins her multiple and historically opposed images: in objects that now include the two enormous metal mural-portraits of Eva recently installed on downtown Buenos Aires's broad Avenida 9 de Julio,[15] Evita appears as the militant protector and embodiment of Justicialism's "third position,"[16] an alternative to the two Cold War models of U.S. capitalism and Soviet communism. For Santoro, Peronism's third way is a void, a tension and oscillation between Right and Left, "a vagabond of the ideological field,"[17] Yin and Yang, and ultimately a still-to-be realized utopia. His representations of Evita compose the setting of that unfulfilled alternative.[18] According to the artist,

> If we were to ask ourselves if it's true that Eva Perón's simple profile says more about Argentine history than all the others in our pantheon of founders, the answers would range from absolute denial to unconditional support. But what lies beyond any dispute is that this profile constitutes the vertex of the construction of a political imaginary [in] which . . . some of the limits of our identity are drawn.[19]

In Santoro's own work, Evita's femiconic silhouette pops up as the opening left in an arched rock in the ocean, a Greek mask floating on a beach, a silhouette of a dark jungle, the blueprint for a "cultivated garden," the remains of a destroyed culture, and a monolithic stone supporting a dwelling.[20] In yet another recent painting, "Mantel de hule" [Plastic/Oilskin tablecloth], milk spilling out of a knocked-over blue-and-white striped glass (itself suggestive of the Argentine flag) pools into Evita's unmistakable profile before dribbling off the working-class table. Santoro recreates his void, a ghost, a white (blank) canvas onto which the viewer can project her own imagined Evita, Peronism, and an Argentina still under construction.

Santoro, Kogan, and Monti, all artists influenced by Peronism, exhibit many of the complexities attached to that influence. Santoro's art exemplifies particularly well some of the complicated relations inherent in contemporary devotional performance practices, sites of the confluences of art and religion, politics and socioeconomics, celebrity and tourism. Alberto Ciria suggests that in order to understand Evita's beyond-the-grave power, we must look to "widespread cults of the dead, local shamans, even great popular artists such as Pancho Sierra, Madre María, and Carlos Gardel."[21] In cultural representations of Evita, the majority of which oscillate between radical defender of the dispossessed and standard-bearer of a conservative populism, we see the contradictions underpinning today's religious practices and pitting a conservative, nationalistic Catholicism against popular devotional practices and their undeniable mix of religious and popular iconicities.

Santa Evita is only one among the many femicons featured in Argentina's pantheon of popular devotional figures. In this final chapter, I move away from my project's primary focus—the physical onstage and onscreen embodiment of a single historical female figure like Camila O'Gorman or Eva Perón—to a consideration of Argentina's popular devotional figures in performance and an examination of how the "femiconic" is performed, appropriated, and circulated throughout popular culture.[22] The subjects here include the country's patron saint—the Virgin of Luján—and such unofficial popular devotional figures as Argentina's preeminent folk saint, María Antonia Deolinda "Difunta" Correa, the legendary mid-nineteenth-century woman who died of thirst in the central-western Argentine desert while trying to reach her ailing husband—a military conscript in the mid-century civil wars—but whose "miraculously" full breast managed to keep her baby alive; and the deceased pop singer Gilda, whose roadside altars, "Santa Gilda" websites and Facebook pages, as well as YouTube pilgrimage uploads, attest to her status as national popular devotional icon-in-the-making.

As simultaneously a symbol of orthodox conservative Catholicism and the nationalistic Argentine state *and* a popular devotional figure and religious icon, Our Lady of Luján and her veneration have been subsumed into a larger, complex national history of class, race, politics, culture, and religion that continues in twenty-first-century Argentina,[23] where ongoing socioeconomic challenges coexist with rapid technological advances and cultural transformations. Devotional practices centered on Evita, Deolinda, Gilda, and the Virgin of Luján are all typically framed as reaffirming maternal adorations, but in each we encounter contradictions and conflicts not easily reconciled in the popular "Madonna" archetype despite frequent representation and (in some historical cases) self-representation as such. Over the last century the Virgin of Luján has accumulated local and national resonances that challenge her identification as simply the "Mother of God." We might rightly regard as "maternal" the political practices of the Madres of the Plaza de Mayo,[24] just as we might understand as Madonna-like the popular devotions surrounding such unofficial "saints" as María Antonia Deolinda "Difunta" Correa and Gilda. Nevertheless, performance of the maternal alone—as *mater dolorosa*, self-sacrificing martyr, or miraculous healer—does not account for the powerful longevity of the Madres and their sustained demand for an accounting of their disappeared children's fates, or for the many devotional and other performance practices and their contradictions. This chapter looks beyond the initial maternal explanation of these devotional femicons to examine the contexts and complexities involved in performances of their advocations.

This chapter has a further purpose regarding the changing roles in contemporary iconography and femiconic performance practices, as I—like many others—contend that the virtual has become the realm of popular cultural interactivity, mediating most if not all celebrity performances and devotional practices. If virtuality is indeed replacing embodied orature as the medium and site of popular performance, including devotional practices,[25] it also is extending the possibilities of performance (beyond the elite borders traced by much contemporary theatre) even as it thwarts traditional expectations regarding embodiment and devotional and celebrity practices and questions how far our discussion of digital embodiment might extend in determining the limits of theatrical performance through the female iconic body. In the past decade, increased scholarly attention has been paid to the intersections of virtuality and devotion, in examinations of the proliferation of Internet activities ranging from virtual altars and pilgrimages to videos of devotional performances by artists and followers alike. However, scholars have yet to consider how these various Internet devotional practices intersect with performance; class and economics; ethnic, racial and other cultural identities; and Argentina's recent and ongoing "Latin Americanization." This chapter considers such intersections—through the visual arts, film, and especially live and mediated performance—and the complex devotional, touristic, and celebrity practices surrounding Argentina's most-revered popular devotional female figures, all of whom could now arguably be deemed "traveling virgins."[26]

Over a one-month period in September-October 1997, Argentine folksinger María Celeste Lores completed a five-thousand-kilometer pilgrimage-performance tour. The journey symbolically reunited two colonial advocations of the Virgin Mary, whose images had been separated since the early seventeenth century. In a memoir bearing the same title as her sixty-minute performance piece, *De Luján a Sumampa por el Camino Real* [From Luján to Sumampa following the Camino Real],[27]Lores recounts the official impetus for her pilgrimage to ten of the more than fifty "stations" along the colonial-era "royal highway" connecting the Buenos Aires provincial city of Luján (sixty-seven kilometers west of the nation's capital) to Sumampa in the interior province of Santiago del Estero: the 110th anniversary of the "Pontifical Coronation" of Nuestra Señora de Luján. Lores had earlier encountered more personal inspiration in a tune she would incorporate into performances offered along the route, where she sang her "Grito lujanero," a Luján "cry" set to a traditional *chacarera doble* beat that described the miraculous obstinacy of Luján's "gaucha Virgin" and Argentina's future patroness—the Virgin of Luján.[28]

According to what historian Linda B. Hall dubs a "discovery story" that is also a foundational myth,[29] in 1630 and some fifty years after Buenos Aires's second and successful founding, the Virgin herself chose Luján. A Portuguese rancher [*estanciero*] based in interior Córdoba, Antonio Faría(s) de Sáa had requested an image of Saint Mary of the Immaculate Conception to be delivered from northern Brazil (whose colonial Pernambuco artisans were renowned for their terracotta creations) to his Sumampa estate's private chapel. The transporting boat's captain—also Portuguese, by the name of Andrea Juan—arrived to the port of Buenos Aires with not only one small terracotta statue but two, the other representing the Mother of God in her archetypal pose cradling the Baby Jesus.[30] The two wooden boxes were added to a caravan of carts heading toward Santiago del Estero. On the second night of their journey, the company camped near Rosendo de Oramas's *estancia* [ranch]. The next morning, the cart carrying the two statues could not be budged. When the boxes were removed, the vehicle easily moved forward, only to stop again when the two boxes were replaced. It was finally determined that only one of the containers was impeding the journey, the box carrying the effigy of the "Purísima Concepción." Amid cries of "¡Milagro! ¡Milagro!," the statue was taken to Don Rosendo's home. After a few days' rest, the caravan continued its journey, delivering the

Figure 10:
A statuette of the
Virgin of Luján.

other effigy—and not the image Faría had originally requested—to her final destination in Sumampa, where today she is venerated as "Our Lady of Consolation." The other Virgin stayed behind, taking up residence on a simple altar created in Rosendo's country home. Over the centuries the image would be moved within the immediate area, as increasingly larger chapels were built in her honor,[31] until arriving at the late nineteenth-century basilica sited on the place where purportedly the Virgin first chose to stop the cart.[32]

The fragile terracotta statue—a commercial reproduction of which appears in this section—is barely fifteen inches (thirty-eight centimeters) tall. She resembles the early seventeenth-century Zurbarán and Murillo paintings so influential in popular depictions of the abstraction that is the Immaculate Conception: a young woman, dressed simply in a red dress with a blue star-spiked robe, holds her hands together in a prayerful attitude. She stands upon clouds out of which appear four cherub heads and the half-moon typical of period representation. In keeping with seventeenth-century custom, the statue would have been covered in additional cloth, often described as a white tunic with a sky-blue robe. Her presentation today, however, is far more ornate: in 1887 the fragile figure was covered by a thin layer of silver, provided a bronze base as well as the background of Gothic rays and an aureole of twelve stars, and given the inscription "The Virgin of Luján is the first Founder of this Town." The "imperial crown" she now wears was created in Paris and blessed by Pope Leo XIII as part of the eventual ceremony conferring on the Virgin of Luján status as America's first Pontifical Coronation. The responsible cleric, Jorge María Salvaire (1847–1899), had earlier fulfilled his promise to the advocation (made when the French missionary recovered from supposedly fatal wounds sustained during an Indian attack) by writing the two-volume *Historia de Nuestra Señora de Luján* [History of Our Lady of Luján], published in 1885. He would go on to be named Luján's parish priest and devote himself to the construction of today's basilica. Today, the effigy resides within the enormous Gothic structure, where, shrouded in the ornate stand, halo, crown, embroidered robes, and crescent moon embossed with the national crest, the only visible elements of the original effigy are her face and praying hands.[33]

This chapter looks at several of Argentina's many devotional figures to examine how the "femiconic" is performed, appropriated, and circulated throughout the country's contemporary popular culture. The Virgin of Luján stands as my sole example of a canonized (and thus officially recognized by the Catholic Church) devotional figure; the other female figures examined here are "popular" saints that, as Argentina's leading folklorist, Félix Coluccio, reminds us, are "real and even imaginary persons to whom oral tradition has attributed the realization of true miracles."[34] Such useful distinctions notwithstanding, the official and the popular are not necessarily exclusive categories.[35] Indeed, María Gisela Hadad and María Pía Venturiello argue that Our Lady of Luján is an even more potent advocation for being both an official *and* a popular religious symbol.[36] As we will see, it is nearly impossible to consider her devotion otherwise.

In popular devotional practices surrounding the Virgin of Luján, two performative features stand out. Both are unsurprisingly related to her saga, and both have been transformed in recent decades. La Lujanera is not only the "first founder" of Luján, she is also known as the "pilgrim" [*peregrina*] or "wandering" [*andariega*] virgin, who legendarily chose where she would remain, who has been credited with traveling to perform her miracles, and whose now mass-reproduced effigy is frequently taken to other locations.[37] She thus connotes both the object and the agent of pilgrimage. Such ostensibly contradictory connotations are resolved in the performative practices of her devout, who travel the seventy kilometers separating Buenos Aires and Luján but who also walk in a circular fashion within the basilica. Hadad and Venturiello note that traveling to as well as walking inside the rarely empty basilica constitute orientation practices that allow the devout "to live the [site's] foundation and position themselves in the center of the world."[38] Indeed, pilgrimage rituals play a central and very particular role in devotional practices: the Luján pilgrimage traditionally begins at 2 p.m. in the northwestern Buenos Aires working-class neighborhood of Liniers and the sanctuary of another saint, Cayetano [Cajetan], Argentine Catholics' patron of work and prosperity.[39] There are "special-interest" pilgrimages with their own histories: on the last Sunday in September, the "gaucho" pilgrimage features some seven thousand horseback riders with their families, and the following Sunday more than a million young people travel on foot in a special "youth" pilgrimage that began in 1975. The Virgin's feast day is May 8, but featured throughout the year are other Virgin-centered activities, including a "nautical" pilgrimage on the December 8 Feast of the Immaculate Conception as well as a mid-summer marathon.[40] A festive mood typically prevails, whether the pilgrims travel alone, with family and/or friends, or in organized church groups. Songs are sung, pilgrims are cheered on, and even in the final exhausting blocks, according to Venturiello and Hadad, there is "great enthusiasm and emotion."[41] Many stay for mass in the plaza before heading home.

Let us regard the fascinatingly complex Lujanera devotional figure through some of her dramatic representations. Playwright Osvaldo Guglielmino notes, in the preface to his 1991 oratorio for the Virgin, that the "miracle of Luján . . . can be interpreted as historically, culturally, and socially associated with the genesis [*hecho genésico*] of a new people [*pueblo*]."[42] Guglielmino divides his verse retelling into two acts. In the first part, the Soloist and Chorus recount the "miracle" through dialogue and exposition, concluding with the separation of the two Marian figures. In this section, the Soloist plays the roles of the story's various "heroes": Farías Sáa, his Pernambuco contact, the boatman Andrea

Juan, the estanciero Rosendo, and even a nameless gaucho poet. The Chorus alternates here between individual interlocutor and undifferentiated mass. The second part of the play quickly moves forward through the standard historical account, touching briefly upon the subsequent constructions of temples to the Virgin and concluding with the basilica. Of greater interest than what might be regarded as a telescoped rehashing of the famous and likely retroactively constructed saga, however, is the second act's insistence on the Virgin's role in protecting the Spanish-descended creoles from both indigenous and foreign attack and in abolishing slavery. Indeed, the act begins with the Soloist lauding the Virgin of Luján as "the first American Mother of Restoration / of man to the inheritance of his person; / the first to break the chains / that the ignominy of the skin bound, / destroying the human condition."[43]

Guglielmino here alludes to another central character in the Luján tale. Popular and religious histories tell us that the Portuguese boatman Andrea Juan had an African slave, Manuel, who accompanied the effigies on their caravan but elected to remain behind to care for the Virgin. Manuel (together with his wife, according to Catholic historian Juan Antonio Presas, "a *criolla* named Beatriz, slave of the González Filiano family [Manuel's new owners]"[44]) would devote his entire life to caring for the statue, and various curative miracles were attributed to his work as her instrument. Accounts vary, however, regarding the details of his emancipation. Guglielmino, for example, writes that Andrea Juan freed Manuel before continuing his journey north to Sumampa. The more generally accepted version, similar to the one set forth in a Claretian-published children's play about the Virgin of Luján as "told and sung by her faithful slave, the black Manuel,"[45] has it that Manuel remained a slave, with title passing to the (Rosendo de) Oramas family (and political relatives of the González Filiano family) after his Portuguese owner's death. When the Virgin's effigy was sold to one Ana de Matos, Manuel refused to obey the family's orders that he abandon the statue. In 1674, the case went to court, and a community collection was taken up to buy Manuel's freedom.[46] He is believed to have died a free man in 1686 after serving as the Virgin's constant companion in her various peregrinations.

Regional politics of race and class in fact have played a key role in almost all depictions of the Virgin of Luján. Despite the advocation's Europeanized features, she is typically referred to as the *morena* Virgin for her somewhat darker skin, yet she is not considered to be a *mestiza* or indigenous advocation (like, say, her Mexican counterpart, the Virgin of Guadalupe, or the Bolivian Virgin of Copacabana). Instead, as Hall implies, hers is an imported effigy,[47] linked to a racialized colonial politics that included regional slavery practices as well as Spanish-descended creole domination of the region and struggles with resisting indigenous populations. Though Hall omits from her discussion of the Virgin of Luján any reference to Manuel, she nevertheless carefully notes that, unlike some of the other Marian effigies of the Americas, the Argentine patroness has a home disconnected from any earlier, pre-Hispanic religious cult: "Rather than being established on an indigenous spiritual site, it was the site of an Indian attack on Spanish troops in the year 1536—on the date of Corpus Christi."[48] Many of the miracles recounted, including that of the advocation's nineteenth-century defender, Father Salvaire, are thus set within the context of Indian attacks, with the Virgin's miracles defending the Spanish and later creole populations. As Eloísa Martín sums up, "The Virgin of Luján is constituted as a symbol of white culture that revalorizes and responds to a Hispanic tradition, denying any possibility of aboriginal roots."[49] The Luján foundation myth thus bears the contradictions of a Virgin who freed at least one African slave yet supported European colonialist domination and the ultimate erasure of entire indigenous populations.

Other contradictions continue to surround historical and artistic representations of Our Lady of Luján. As I have recounted, the Virgin of Luján received official pontifical coronation in 1887, but she would not be declared patroness of Argentina (and neighboring Paraguay and Uruguay) until October 1930. The naming ceremony, which symbolically marked the incorporation of the Virgin of Luján into Argentine "nation-building iconography,"[50] was carried out by a recently installed military regime that, while not particularly religious, sought to utilize Catholicism as part of its larger nationalistic project. In a country abounding with regionally distinct Marian devotions, the timing of this declaration was crucial: under the sway of the increasingly influential Spanish Primo de Rivera model, the military regime sought to Hispanize Argentina by returning it to Catholicism's "traditional values." The regime worked in tandem with an official Catholic Church that sought to "homogenize the diversity of Catholicisms" present in a country that in recent decades had undergone massive migrations,[51] from European countries as well as from the Argentine interior to its capital of Buenos Aires. Authoritarian church and authoritarian state joined forces in consolidating "a model of an integrally Catholic Argentina,"[52] united under the banner of, in the words of the period's monsignor (Miguel de Andrea), "God, Fatherland, Family, and Property."

As the twentieth century advanced, the Virgin of Luján was increasingly associated with a nationalistic, militarized, fascistic Argentina of the Right.[53] Indeed, each of the century's multiple military dictatorships incorporated her image and devotion into its campaign for national consolidation under authoritarianism, and, even after 1983's return to democracy, the military continued the association.[54] As Martín writes, democratically elected governments found themselves contending with Argentina's strong church-state alliance through "either cooperation or cooptation."[55] The Virgin of Luján thus became inseparable from a constructed national identity that frequently found itself leaning far to the right.

The Virgin of Luján's association with both conservative Catholicism and the nationalistic, typically militarized and authoritarian, state has not gone unchallenged. In, for example, the political performance practices of the Madres of the Plaza de Mayo, we find very different deployments of the Virgin of Luján's femiconographic power. While the singer María Celeste Lores, like Linda B. Hall, leaves the seventeenth-century African slave Manuel out of both her memoirs and performance of the Lujanera's story, she nevertheless appears to participate in a counterproject of popular yet "official" reclamation of the Virgin of Luján. Undertaking a physical pilgrimage retracing the old colonial roads, the artist Lores and the effigy symbolically reunite a contemporary Argentina that from colonial times has been divided, not only geographically but ethnoracially and socioeconomically. Martín wisely intuits that geography must have played a role in the political-religious selection of the Virgin of Luján as Argentina's national patron. As a provincial city, Luján enjoys a proximity to the nation's capital while lying outside the capital's boundaries. Located at the edge of the pampas, the city can be seen as symbolically linking interior and capital. "Sufficiently close . . . and sufficiently distant," Luján could "establish a dialogue with the Argentine political, economic, social, and cultural center [Buenos Aires] as the country's 'spiritual center.'"[56] Yet while Buenos Aires—and its national power brokers—might see Luján as gateway to the interior, the people of northern Sumampa do not. In his sermon at the mass celebrating the final station in the Virgin's (and Lores's) 1997 pilgrimage, Sumampa parish priest José Jaime was adamant:

> Attention! The beginning of Marian devotion in Argentina is rooted here . . . . Luján is nearing her origins. [. . .] It would appear that Argentina ends where the center of the country ends; for the north,

no, and I have to say it. María Celeste knows that we here are [also] Argentina, but with the poverty of Argentines, and we live at this extreme. I ask the Mother of Luján to return us our Argentineness . . . to make [everyone] recognize that . . . Argentines aren't only those who are in the south.[57]

At each station in her pilgrimage Lores and her band offered a carefully selected program of folkloric music that symbolically united the polarized regions, a southern *huella* followed by a northern *chacarera*. Even in a marginalized Sumampa, the Virgin could not be separated from the nation; when the priest placed her replica on the sanctuary's altar, symbolically reuniting the two separated virgins, spontaneous shouts rang out: "Long live the Virgin of Consolation! Long live the Virgin of Luján! Long live the pilgrims! Long live the people of Sumampa! ¡*Viva la Patria*!"[58]

Like Guglielmino's oratorio, Lores's performance accounts appear to respond to the popular insecurities generated in neoliberalized 1990s Argentina. Where Guglielmino makes general reference, in the preface to his play, to a contemporary "universal uprooting that purposefully assaults cultural identity,"[59] in her final pilgrimage-performance, Lores prays to the Virgin to help and protect: "This is our *patria* [fatherland], this is our *hermandad* [brotherhood]. We're Argentines, children of God and of our Mother."[60] Hadad and Venturiello remark that, in their interviews with Luján's pilgrims (conducted in 2002 and 2003), there was constant "reference to the socioeconomic and political situation Argentina was undergoing in that moment and even today is undergoing. The feeling of a generalized anxiety was expressed in the petitions made to the Virgin."[61] Requests for personal and family members' health and work were accompanied by desires for an improved Argentina. Analyzing the various collected testimonials, Hadad and Venturiello characterize contemporary Luján pilgrimage practices as creating a potential space for the "channeling of collective anguish and hope."[62]

Today it seems more symbolically charged than ever that San Cayetano—patron saint of work—and the Virgin of Luján—the national patroness—remain linked through physical pilgrimage. Despite the seeming continuity provided by such physical pilgrimages as Lores's or the annual Lujaneros', Argentine popular devotional practices have been transformed in the fragmented, chaotic new century. Working-class and disenfranchised Argentines found their already precarious situation disastrously exacerbated in the wake of 2001's economic crisis; and increased internal and international migration to Buenos Aires resulted in a broad ethnic plurality in the capital's working-class suburbs, euphemistically described as the "Latin Americanization" of Argentina and especially its capital city. With the "north" now living in the middle of the "south," Lores's performance pilgrimage seemed almost quaint barely five years later. Her preferred medium might also strike us as somewhat outdated: by the middle of the century's new decade, the majority of devotional performances seemed to be taking place virtually on the Internet, and not in the churches. In light of such rapid technological developments and increased accessibility, the huge numbers of pilgrims who annually journey to another site of popular devotion complicate easy replacement hypotheses.

La Difunta Correa: Traditional Popular Devotional Performance (and Touristic) Practices as Spectacle

An *estampita* I received on a Buenos Aires subway train some years back bears the now-iconic traits identified with Difunta [Deceased Woman] Correa: a young woman, having perished from thirst, lies on the desert ground surrounded by a few dried shrubs. Her only companion is her infant, who continues to nurse at his dead mother's breast.[63] The young woman is dressed in red, her long black hair hangs loose, and her left arm is extended while her other arm clings to her child. The sun's rays not only depict the region's heat but also celestially illuminate the dead woman's body.[64] Printed on the reverse of my card was a prayer:

> "DIFUNTA CORREA" Holy Spirit, enlighten me so that I may accomplish God's commands loving and helping my brothers and sisters with the same generosity and fidelity as did our remembered Difunta Correa, example of the true Christian woman. Give me, O Lord, the Grace that I ask of you today.

The young mother who handed me the card had used a piece of tape to attach a photocopy of a handwritten note: "Fellow passengers could you help me with what you can for milk and bread many thanks in advance and God Bless you." In keeping with local cultural practices, I gave the woman some coins, kept the card, and maybe had my own prayers answered as well.

Over one hundred and fifty years after María Antonia Deolinda Correa's legendary death in Argentina's Andean semidesert, her devotion remains livelier than ever, with nearly a million people visiting her

Figure 11: A prayer card received on a Buenos Aires subway train, mid-1990s.

shrine every year—the majority during Holy Week[65]—and making her "the most prominent of the many Argentine folk saints."[66] As visitors arrive by bus or car, on horseback or on foot, it becomes nearly impossible to separate the tourist from the pilgrim. Indeed, religious tourism surrounding Difunta has been increasingly promoted since 2002, when direction of her shrine was subsumed under the provincial government [the Difunta Correa Administration] and the site exploited as an opportunity for local economic development.[67] An entire town has grown up around the popular devotional industry, enhanced by 2010's completion of an aqueduct: "from a handful of people running temporary kiosks and grills, it became a stable town, with varied culinary offerings, a hotel, campground, public baths, church, convention center, museum and parallel altars donated by some of the millions of people who annually arrive on foot, bicycle, horse, cart, auto, truck, or bus."[68]

Devotional practices surrounding Difunta Correa serve not only as an example of traditional embodiment in performance; her story, like the Virgin of Luján's, is distinctly localized, yet it cannot be extricated from a larger socioeconomic and sociocultural national context. Official pilgrimages to the sanctuaries of the Virgin of Luján and Difunta Correa are today advertised on municipal and regional websites as these practices become integrated into the larger economic model. Poverty, crisis, and tourism go hand in hand with penitent pilgrimage and charitable exchange, such as my retention of the prayer card, made when I gave the young mother some coins requested to help her buy milk and bread.

Local and now national and international legend tells us that around 1830–1840 (though some stories place it as late as 1850), there lived a young woman by the name of Deolinda Correa. Deolinda was the daughter of Pedro Correa, who had fought for independence from Spain but, during postindependence power struggles, fell on the wrong side of local *caudillo* Facundo Quiroga (whom future Argentine president Domingo Sarmiento would later render as the image of nineteenth-century Argentine barbarism) and sought safety in moving his family from San Juan to neighboring La Rioja. Both Pedro Correa and Deolinda's husband were forcibly conscripted to fight in the ensuing civil wars. Some more melodramatic versions—rehearsing the now-familiar civilization-versus-barbarity dichotomy—have an "extraordinarily beautiful" and now abandoned Deolinda pursued by the very same "barbarous" official who had persecuted her father and husband. Other versions find her accused of collaborating with the enemy "Unitarians" and seduced by a colonel.[69] In all the many retellings of Deolinda's story, she desperately sets out in search of her husband (sometimes appearing named Clemente or Baudilio Bustos and varyingly recounted as having taken ill, been imprisoned, or already died), carrying their infant child and a small supply of water, some say on foot, others on burro. Never quite catching up with the soldiers (and perhaps lost), she finally collapses near the summit of a small peak. The first miracle occurs to the devotional figure's own body: "Feeling herself die," in Argentine folklorist Félix Coluccio's reconstruction of the legend, "she asked heaven to give life to her breasts so that her child would not die of hunger and thirst like she."[70] Her corpse was found by cattle drivers (in other variants, travelers), who buried her near where she died, marked the site with a wooden cross, and rescued her son.[71] Soon thereafter local dwellers began to visit her simple grave, bringing offerings of colorful paper flowers. Her first attributed miracle occurred in 1898,[72] when a cattle driver retrieved his lost five hundred head of cattle after promising to build a chapel to cover her tomb and wooden cross. Don Pedro Flavio Zeballos kept his promise and constructed Difunta's first chapel. From patroness of migrant herders and lost travelers, Difunta Correa moved with the changes in transportation to protectoress of trains and, by the mid-twentieth century, patron saint of truck drivers. Today multiple shrines—with their trademark filled water bottles—dot the roadsides throughout northern Argentina.

In a story narrated, filmed, sung, and dramatically staged,[73] Difunta Correa easily fits into the European archetype of the self-sacrificing mother,[74] and related devotional practices generally resemble those surrounding the Virgin Mary. That said, different from Luján, the site of Difunta Correa's sanctuary bears indigenous traces of the pre-Conquest Atacameña custom of leaving a sign of passage, and local versions evince a syncretic historiography suggesting incorporation and adaptation of local Huarte legends and the indigenous belief in Pachamama, or Mother Earth.[75] As Bibiana Apolonia del Brutto puts it, both the sanctuary and the legend's structure are "highly pagan."[76] Such is Difunta's ongoing power that conservative factions of the Argentine Catholic Church have been consistently unsuccessful in dissuading Catholics from praying to her.[77] Today, she has the largest following of any popular devotional figure in Argentina.

While the unusual details surrounding the advocation and its devotional site are very specific to the region's geography and preconquest, colonial, and postindependence cultural history, perhaps the most striking aspect of the Difunta's devotional practices are the practitioners—the *promesantes*, or promise-makers.[78] Her followers say that "la Difunta Correa cumple pero se lo cobra" [the Difunta Correa comes through but she charges for it];[79] one asks her not for a gift but for a loan, which must be paid back with interest. Thus, offerings made to her, in a variation of the standard devotional practice of *ex-votos* directed to a divinity in gratitude or devotion for a favor received,[80] actually constitute repayments, collected and organized in the theme-based *capillas* [chapels] that house car parts, uniforms (in a security forces chapel), bridal gowns and first-communion dresses (including shoes, gloves, veils, and bouquets), athletic trophies and boxing gloves, filled water bottles, and photos of same.[81] Some of the costlier offerings—such as automobiles—are sold at auction, and the funds are used to maintain the sanctuary. And still others, especially offerings made by the famous, will be displayed in a planned museum that will also exhibit some of the ex-votos now housed in the capillas.[82] Hanging from posts lining the steps leading up to Difunta's hilltop shrine (and the grotto where her remains are rumored to be buried) are thousands of license plates, along with tires and car parts, all reminders of her patronage.[83] Filled water bottles encircle the area, while inside the sanctuary there is a plaster life-sized effigy of the devotional figure. A "town of kept promises" covers the surrounding hill, and its miniature city of tiny houses, pizza shops, car garages, and even a discotheque makes the local church's normal-sized billboard seem gigantically out of place.

Pilgrims may borrow many of the ex-votos, which they then return in the same condition they were received. An employee explains the singular system: "Each promesante gives a ring, a guitar, whatever he or she can . . . She gives her bridal gown, which the Vallecito Cemetery Foundation loans to young women with limited resources. Afterwards they return it. It also loans money to people in need, without any signed documents, just their word. It's never happened that someone didn't return what was received."[84] An entire economy has developed out of Difunta's ex-voto loan system: not only is there an infrastructure built to accommodate visitors (operating not unlike other popular devotional sites), but there exists the above-described barter-based economy built upon trust, not promissory notes, and accommodating those without resources. Contemporary devotional practices surrounding the Difunta Correa are far more complex than truckers leaving license plates in thanks or travelers making sure she is never without water. The Difunta Correa is a popular saint for hard times.

More striking than the unique need-based bartering system is another ex-voto practice that involves the pilgrims' own bodies in a performed act of devotion: in what Coluccio calls "sacrificial ex-votos" [exvotos de sacrificio], the promesantes climb to the site's highest point and shrine. Coluccio describes the scene:

> While we still had some kilometers before arriving, we came across on the road hundreds of men, women, and children who in trucks, cars, buggies, on horseback, and on foot shared our destination—climbing up the Cuesta de la Vaca. It was a stiflingly hot day; the hot northerly wind sent out its quick, hot puffs. [. . .] As we drew closer, our progress became slower and more difficult; the pilgrims numbered hundreds and hundreds; collective transportation vehicles from all over the Cuyo and La Rioja regions were packed with promesantes, many of whom would spend the entire day in the place, asking for or fulfilling promises made to the Difunta Correa, visiting all the capillitas or building their own, chopping wood to prepare a fortifying asado [barbecue], or acquiring in the kiosks souvenirs to take home.[85]

The promesantes typically initiate their penitential journey at night, either from the city of San Juan (some thirty-eight miles away) or the slightly closer village of Caucete (twenty-one miles distant), so that they reach the shrine during the hottest hours of the day. The majority arrive during the latter part of Holy Week, with the greatest crowds on Good Friday; thus their own suffering can be interpreted as penitentially emulating not only Difunta's death but also Jesus's martyrdom. The penitent make their way up the stairs by foot, on their knees, and even crawling on their backs. In 2011, Argentine filmmaker Dolores Montaño directed a sixty-nine-minute documentary about this performative devotional phenomenon, filmed over three years and titled simply *Promesantes*.[86] Montaño decided to make the film after first visiting the sanctuary as a tourist in 2006 and being surprised by "the materialization of faith in plaques, bottles, candles, and gifts." In each promesante she saw "a story, and in each story, a way of life."[87]

Among those whose stories Montaño tells is Rosa, who credits Difunta Correa with dissuading the seventeen-year-old unwed mother from aborting her child. In return, Rosa has promised to make the pilgrimage every year until her child reaches the age of fifteen. The documentary shows the mother in obvious pain as she struggles to hold on to her now three-year-old child while working her way up the hard steps lying on her back. Afterwards she requires physical assistance to descend.[88] I cannot but interpret such penitential practices as Rosa's face-up climb as an embodied performance of Deolinda Correa's own self-sacrificing journey to protect her child. As such, it firmly locates Correa femiconography in the body of the promesante in ways quite different from popular Evitist or other Marian devotional practices.

It would appear that, Difunta Correa's own Facebook page notwithstanding, the devotional practices of her many devoted seem decidedly and performatively lived.[89] Yet, despite the ostensible continuity provided by such annual, physical pilgrimages as Rosa's, Argentine popular devotional practices are undergoing transformation. Indeed, the majority of devotional performances appear to be taking place virtually, on the Internet and not in shrines. Nevertheless, while most scholars recognize that the lower socioeconomic classes constitute the devout majority, they often overlook the Internet's devotional potential, dismissing it as the province of the more privileged sectors. Recent statistics contradict such easy dismissals: according to 2012 data, twenty-eight million Argentines, or 66.4 percent of the national population, use the Internet. In 2008, only 41 percent of those users had bank accounts; pay-by-the-minute Internet centers and cybercafés followed home computers as the most popular sites of usage; and at least three out of ten Argentine Internet users pertained to the "lower socioeconomic strata."[90] In the intervening four years, usage continued to grow across sectors; however, by 2012, rapidly transforming technologies and national and capital-city delivery projects resulted in internet cafés being superseded by mobile phones, workplaces, Wi-Fi hotspots, and schools, with an overwhelming usage (92 percent) occurring at home.[91] Such statistics suggest a far different Argentine Internet-user profile than has been typically painted. This profile is critical to any consideration of Argentina's most recent object of Marian devotion and femiconography: the popular singer Gilda.

Santa Gilda: Virtuality as Devotional and Celebrity Performance

If, as it has been argued, virtuality is replacing physically embodied orature as the medium and site of popular devotional performance,[92] we should ask what roles the Internet plays in the performances of Argentina's devotional practices surrounding such femicons as deceased Argentine pop singer Gilda. While most scholars note that the lower socioeconomic classes constitute the devoted's majority, they often overlook the Internet's potential, dismissing it as the province of the more privileged sectors known to disparage popular devotions and cultural practices as *cosa de negros*.[93] In doing so they ignore an Argentina undergoing rapid social, economic, and cultural transformation—the Argentina of the musical phenomenon Cumbia, whose initial marginalization and later exploitation echo the tango's national history half a century earlier[94]; a working-class and disenfranchised Argentina, whose precarious situation was exacerbated in the wake of 2001's economic crisis; and an Argentina of internal and international migration, which has resulted in a broad ethnic plurality in Buenos Aires's working-class suburbs.[95] "Santa Gilda"'s online veneration sits squarely at the confluence of a changing Argentina's popular devotional practices and fandom.

Gilda was born Miriam Alejandra Bianchi on October 11, 1961, in Villa Devoto, a middle-class neighborhood located on the northern edge of Buenos Aires and famous as the "city's garden." Nicknamed Gilda by her mother, Tita, in homage to Rita Hayworth's film character,[96] the young woman had hopes of becoming a flight attendant or pediatrician, but, during her father's protracted illness (he would die when she was seventeen), she began studies to be a kindergarten teacher while working in the afternoons as an administrative employee.[97] Gilda married at eighteen, within two years gave birth to two children (Mariel and Fabrizio), and continued working as a teacher in the Catholic-run kindergarten where she also organized school performances. A chance encounter with a childhood friend on a public bus led to her new career: Gilda invited her old friend, Carlos "Toti" Giménez, to join her at a school show in which she was to impersonate popular Cumbia singer "La Bomba Tucumana."[98] Toti, classically trained but at the time working as a musician for "dance king" [*rey del baile*] Ricky Maravilla,[99] was so taken by Gilda's performance that he convinced her to record a demo, which he took to an agent, who in turn took Gilda into the studio to make her first record, which was released in 1992. When the school director, a nun, told her she had to choose between her two professions, Gilda chose music. Shortly thereafter she left her husband for Toti, who was by then playing piano in her band and managing her career. Despite the hardworking rags-to-riches narrative in which her hagiography is typically cast, Gilda's was not an overnight success story: unable to get on television or attract high-profile producers, who preferred voluptuous blondes and cute boy bands, the petite brunette Gilda gradually built her fan base by performing throughout Argentina, often playing six or seven different clubs in a single evening.[100] Between 1994 and 1996, she recorded three more albums, toured to Peru and Bolivia, and finally gained recognition in Buenos Aires, with her fourth album going "gold."[101] On September 7, 1996, while traveling northeastern Argentina's Route 12 to a midnight gig in Chajarí, Entre Ríos, at kilometer 129 her tour bus was hit by a truck, killing the singer, her daughter, her mother, and four band mates, and injuring fourteen others, including Toti and her son. Gilda and her family members were all buried in Chacarita Cemetery in Buenos Aires. Seven months after her death, on April 7, 1997, Cumbia radio stations released Gilda's posthumous tune "No es mi despedida" [It's not my farewell], written only days before the singer's death. Toti included the song in a fifth album, which eventually sold more than six hundred thousand copies; he would go on to release two more posthumous collections whose combined sales surpassed 1.2 million copies. Homages to Gilda accumulated: a Tucumán street was named after her; a traveling museum of personal artifacts was created; and various altars were erected, the most important of which was constructed on the site of the fatal accident by family friend Carlos Maza. Both the Route 12 sanctuary and her Buenos Aires Chacarita burial site are now pilgrimage destinations, especially on the dates of Gilda's birth and death as well as during Holy Week.

Although Gilda's actual career as a Cumbia artist lasted only four years, it coincided with *tropical* music's meteoric popular and commercial rise in postdictatorship Argentina.[102] A musical form that succeeded the

Santa Gilda
Canta por nosotros

Figure 12: "Santa Gilda canta por nosotros/Saint Gilda sing for us." Prayer card image circulating on the Internet.

rumba and first achieved popularity in the 1960s, Argentine Cumbia—not to be confused with, say, Colombian or Chilean Cumbia—is a heterogeneous fusion of Andean cadences and folk genres like the Italo-Spanish *cuartetazo*, the delta *chamamé*, and Paraguayan polka, with each region marking its own distinctive version.[103] In Buenos Aires, these regional rhythms came together in *bailantas* [dance clubs], where working-class locals socialized with Paraguayan, Bolivian, Chilean, Peruvian, Uruguayan, and national migrants. Around 1989, the media and commerce caught up with the burgeoning suburban dance scene,[104] and musical groups were marketed on FM radio, on television, in specialized magazines, and in the clubs themselves. By 1992, the year Gilda recorded her first album, Ricky Maravilla was performing in Buenos Aires's most exclusive—and definitely not working-class suburban—neighborhoods.

In life, however, Gilda never achieved Ricky's popularity. As Eloísa Martín notes, "it was only in the years following her death that her presence grew in visibility in the public sphere."[105] Martín details Gilda's posthumous fame through newspaper and magazine articles, TV specials, a documentary, a feature-length biopic (which has yet to be made though casting was announced), special CD collections, posters, and books. Her recordings can still be heard on televised soap operas, and her lyrics have been covered by artists working in various musical genres and even transformed into professional soccer club anthems.[106] Martín documents as well the many fan clubs that have sprung up, some before but many more after Gilda's death, throughout Argentina.[107] Despite club members' obvious devotion to the Cumbia singer and perhaps contradicting their own charitable practices carried out in her name, Gilda's fans should not be assumed to be Gilda's religious devotees. In fact, as Martín's research demonstrates, there is a tension among various constituencies stemming precisely from questions of her divine status. Gilda's followers see in the artist a spectrum of roles, ranging from the divine to the human, from *santa* to *ángel* to *princesa* to *mejor amiga* [best friend] and even from *almita* [little soul] to "un muerto como cualquier otro" [a dead person like any other].[108] Martín concludes that simply calling Gilda a "saint" overly reduces the number of roles she plays for many of her devoted. In many ways, Gilda's celebrity—secular or divine—has yet to be consolidated.

Nevertheless, there are elements that position Gilda within the pantheon of Argentina's popular devotional figures: special commemorative dates are reserved for her veneration;[109] many of her followers wear her violet-blue devotional color, perform acts of devotion and sacrifice, and regard themselves as *promesantes*; pilgrimages are made to her sanctuary; special numbers are assigned to her;[110] and original prayers are delivered to her.[111] Accounts exist of at least two miracles attributed to the singer while she was still alive,[112] and nearly every biography makes mention of her own personal sacrifice and physical suffering.[113]

A televisual trip to Gilda's route 12 sanctuary, such as one made for commercial broadcast on the occasion of the thirteenth anniversary of her death,[114] takes us first to the destroyed touring bus, now transformed into a shrine covered with photos, flowers, homemade banners, and other offerings from those one Cumbia FM station calls, with no apparent irony, "the devout of the tropical mystic."[115] We then enter the sanctuary, where we see practically every sort of Gilda object imaginable, along with ex-voto offerings, candles, flowers, photos, images of Jesus

Christ and the Virgin of Luján, no-longer-needed canes and other artifacts attesting to prayers fulfilled, notebooks in which to write one's
name and plea, and even a photo of a politician considered sympathetic
to Gilda's rural followers.[116] The television reporter's attitude falls somewhere between sensationalizing and respectful, perhaps in bewildered
acknowledgment of Gilda's continuing fame. The broadcast makes little
reference to the profits from Gilda's beyond-the-grave fame, where attributed miracles have pervaded even marketing campaigns. Perhaps the
most notorious example surrounds the posthumously released album,
Entre el cielo y la tierra [Between heaven and earth], which included several songs Gilda recorded on her own shortly before her death. According to the record company, the tape was "miraculously" recovered from
the accident site one month later; in reality the tape had been stored in
Toti's home. As the *América Noticias'* reporter notes, without much self-
reflection, "everything is faith."[117]

The most theatrical act of faith—most are carefully excised from the
footage—comes toward the end of the six-minute note with the appearance of a woman dressed in full Santa Gilda costume. The woman attests to Gilda's many miracles, but it was when the saint, "together with
our Lord Jesus Christ," cured her of breast cancer that she became one
of Gilda's *promeseras* [pilgrims] who now must fulfill a promise made to
the *santita* in exchange for her own miraculous cure. The violet-blue
dress and crown of flowers repeat Gilda's cover photo for her last album
(*Corazón valiente* [Brave heart]). Viewing the woman's devotional performance together with the Marianesque altar set within glass and mounted
to the sanctuary's wall and Cumbia singer Celeste's own posted photo
on her Myspace site,[118] it becomes difficult to differentiate between impersonation and veneration, as Gilda's celebrity mixes with devotion in
practices not unlike those of Difunta's tourist-pilgrim.[119]

Scholars have repeatedly emphasized the role popular devotion plays
in the lives of the disenfranchised, and it is perhaps here that Gilda's fans
and devoted find the greatest common ground. In Gilda's last recorded
interview,[120] she spoke of the differences between Bolivia's and Argentina's Cumbia scenes, noting that in Bolivia the music isn't as socially
"sectarian" and relegated exclusively to the popular clubs. Her observation holds: Argentina's "intellectual class" has tended to infantilize,[121] at
best, or simply dismiss out of hand popular cultural practices as cultist in
a country where, as one journalist smugly wrote, "anyone can be transmuted into a messiah."[122] The growing numbers of Argentine Cumbia
bailantas were indeed accompanied by increasing poverty and alienation

exacerbated in the 2001 crisis and off-the-chart statistics surrounding unemployment, underemployment, and numbers living below the poverty line.[123] Cumbia culture swelled in the big cities and reflected a sea change in cultural identity: Buenos Aires was becoming less tango, the mythical Palermo neighborhood, and the high culture of Jorge Luis Borges, and more Cumbia, the gritty Constitución train station, and the "foolish realism" of Washington Cucurto, a working-class writer of color whose 2003 hit book, *Cosa de negros*, contains a novella titled after a Gilda song.[124] In death, Gilda became patron saint and symbol of this "new" Argentina.

In fact, popular devotional figures like Gilda, theologians note, humanize an institutionalized Catholicism that, in Argentina's case, has rarely responded to the needs of its less-privileged devoted. Furthermore, from the vantage point of liberation theology studies, popular practices can undo official culture.[125] In Gilda's particular case, religious cult and celebrityhood intersect, and nowhere is that meeting place more evident than on the Internet. While references to virtual performances have already peppered this chapter, they have largely been examples drawn from the media and music industries. In this final section I turn to Internet performances by Gilda's followers themselves to begin to trace the roles virtuality plays in contemporary popular devotional practices.

Potentially useful models for understanding Gilda's multiple Internet users and sites may be drawn from recent studies. George Edward Brandon, following Stefania Capone, identifies six types of Yorùbá Internet users: Recruiters, Lost Souls, the Suspicious Ones, and Cyber Elders respectively search for new followers, attempt to connect with fellow devotees, use the Internet to verify religious beliefs, or dispense (typically unsolicited) advice; Web Bricoleurs seek to cobble together a belief system across religious traditions without having a clear "home"; and Border-Crossers wish to "establish a relationship between their religious identity and [in Brandon's case] Yorùbá religion."[126] Joseph M. Murphy describes five kinds of òrìṣà [deity] sites: organizational, individual, devotional, academic, and commercial.[127] Organizational sites provide information sanctioned by some institutional authority; individual sites self-presentationally focus on the sole priest or priestess, whereas devotional sites center on the òrìṣà through virtual altars and holy sites; professional scholars run academic sites; and commercial sites are engaged in the business of selling items for òrìṣà ritual. Yet, as Murphy notes, rarely does any site fall into one exclusive category; rather, "[e]ach site displays, and at times merges, the concerns of institution and identity building, information dissemination, and commerce."[128]

My examples represent what I consider the three prevailing genres of Internet Gilda-based devotion and fandom: virtual altars; virtual pilgrimages; and virtual performances.[129] All demonstrate the fluidity of the above-mentioned categories as well as illustrate the permeability of the distinction between fans and devoted, among recruiters, lost souls, bricoleurs, and border-crossers, in sites where commercial and individual projects often become indistinguishable.

The "Homenaje a Gilda" [Homage to Gilda] website (http://www.homenajeagilda.com.ar/inicio2.htm) may be a good place to start. Filled with Gilda images and clips, celebrity and fan tributes, and magazine and newspaper clippings, the site is a virtual album for Brandon's "lost souls." Despite the two listed e-mail addresses (where you can send your own photo with Gilda), the site has no clearly identified author. While the site refers to Gilda as "angel," its thrust is archival fandom. Earlier Google searches for "Santa Gilda" connected me to now-disappeared sites that repeated her hagiography (http://argentinamisteriosa.totalh.com/gilda.htm) *and* had clearly commercial interests in selling her recordings and other merchandise (http://www.muevamueva.com/grupo/gilda/). I rarely found any sites that were overtly devotional (and the few that I located in the past several years have subsequently been removed). Far more popular are fan sites such as the still-active http://www.fotolog.com/admiradoresdegil/69231495, where I found the announcement for a 2009 commemorative birthday "caravan" from Buenos Aires's downtown landmark obelisk to Chacarita Cemetery and Gilda's tomb. Indeed, different from devotional sites such as those where you can light a virtual candle to a favorite saint (for instance, at the site http://www.arcangelgabriel.com/altares/indexdealtares.htm or at individual saints' Facebook pages), Santa Gilda sites more closely resemble the "virtual altars" dedicated to teen heartthrobs.[130] As earlier website or blog activity moves to social networks, it remains difficult to distinguish between the fans and the devoted creating Facebook pages for Gilda that list her present location as "heaven."[131]

YouTube offers a somewhat more complex sampling. In addition to the many expected video clips of Gilda herself performing, one finds professional and homemade music videos. Two in particular provide a generically challenging mix of virtual pilgrimage, music video, and home movie. The first upload (http://www.youtube.com/watch?v=tW5BW1p9 tR8&feature=related) comes from an episode of a very successful late 1990s Argentine soap opera, *Muñeca brava* [Wild Doll]. Filmed to one of the artist's posthumously released and signature tunes ("Se me ha perdido un corazón" [I've lost a heart]), the scene recreates a pilgrimage to Gilda's sanctuary.[132] The second upload (http://www.youtube.com/watch?v=cN28BldwtFY&feature=related) is clearly a home video. It too begins with the journey before carefully documenting the group's visit to the sanctuary. How different is the produced *telenovela* clip from this "home movie" or any number of pilgrimage virtual photo albums (such as http://www.youtube.com/watch?v=Gl2vLDCdoxA with accompanying Gilda song "Fuiste") regularly posted on YouTube? Religion scholar Mark W. MacWilliams notes that virtual pilgrimages range broadly in format and content, from informational sites about physical sacred places to participative simulations of actual or invented travels. He contends that such pilgrimages construct an immaterial reality that not only entertains but allows for the experience of divine presence and a sense of *communitas* through engagement with online traveling communities.[133] A key author on virtual spirituality, Philip Carr-Gomm, puts it another way: "Maybe one day you will visit [sacred places], maybe not, but the connection will be there nevertheless. Spiritually you will have 'plugged into' a network that covers the planet, and that is linked by lines of energy that create a matrix around the globe."[134] Despite *Muñeca brava*'s clearly commercial exploitation of the Gilda phenomenon, its careful documentation of the sanctuary and respectful treatment of its subject point to a level of networking that I would argue is not exclusively commercial.

What community then is created through such Gilda-related YouTube clips? It is clearly one that brings together, crosses, and exploits the various intersections discussed throughout this chapter: Gilda's complex status as devotional figure and popular artist; Cumbia's popular and commercial reach; and a demographically transforming Argentina. Race, popular fandom, Cumbia, and digital performance all come into focus in my final example, a self-declared "parody" of Gilda's "Paisaje" [Countryside] by "La Nadu y un Ponja que pasó por ahí" [Nadia and some Ponja who dropped by] (http://www.youtube.com/watch?v=ykgh_Oc8nKg). In an Argentina where "ponja" [the reversed syllables of *Japón* or Japan] is the popular but ultimately pejorative term for someone of Asian descent, this "performance" so typical of the hundreds of thousands available to us on YouTube features a duo barely imaginable ten years ago. Today's Gilda-inspired uploads feature faces that have rarely appeared in Argentine cultural performances and continue to be absent from television and film, but they also bear the traces of the conflictive views of nativism and immigration (Nadu's friend doesn't get a name but an ethnicized marker, Ponja), as well as commerce and art, celebrity and spirituality.

A 2009 trip to Buenos Aires coincided with Gilda's birthday. Through Internet sources, I learned of the above-mentioned "caravan" and so decided to take advantage of my stay to experience a physical Gilda celebration and document what I projected to be a mix of devotion and fandom. Before leaving for the obelisk (a city landmark and the caravan's meeting-point), I watched up-to-the-minute coverage on one of the local television stations, and the images led me to expect a gathering not unlike the many popular demonstrations I'd seen and participated in before in a city where large public assembly is not at all uncommon. When I arrived, one and a half hours after the appointed meeting time, I found thirty shivering souls holding five banners and apparently engaged in socializing or talking to reporters, who represented at least three different television stations. By the time I left, some forty-five minutes later, no one else had joined the proceedings, nor had the march begun.

My "non-experience" serves as a cautionary note regarding the uses and expectations surrounding the visual and the virtual. Televised close-ups led me to expect a far larger convocation, and upon reflection I was struck by how I'd been taken in by the televised images and so quick to cast the Gilderas as lost souls just because so few of them made the physical pilgrimage, temporarily forgetting the thousands of hits at the hundreds of YouTube clips dedicated to the goddess of Argentine Cumbia. Simply put, I was looking for the performance of popular devotional practice in the wrong place. If the virtual has indeed become the realm of popular cultural interactivity, it now plays a pivotal role in celebrity and devotional performance practices. There exists today a productive tension between the physically embodied pilgrimages of Difunta Correa's promesantes and the virtual expressions of devotion to Santa Gilda, just as those devotions themselves are complicated by twenty-first-century immigration, tourism, and celebrity practices. It would be unwise to underestimate the power and potential of the virtual in popular cultural performance practices.

Concluding a Tale of Two or More Femiconic Saints: Cumbio, Celebrity, and Another Argentina

At the 2009 Buenos Aires Book Fair, Argentine author Martín Kohan stated adamantly that fellow Argentine Washington Cucurto couldn't be a popular writer, because the popular masses "don't have a writer; they have a TV host . . . Those who venerate Cucurto are 'modern kids' that get off doing *cosas de negros*, the same way they do when they dance to Gilda."[135] The cultural elite, embodied here by Kohan, continues to dismiss popular culture as nonexistent or, at best, as coopted and fetishized by the bourgeoisie, even as Cumbia stubbornly remains identified with the Buenos Aires of suburbs, working classes, recent immigrants, and popular cultural responses to the recent economic crisis. It is also the music identified with one of Argentina's newest candidates for femiconic status: Agustina Vivero (b. 1991), the young flogger—Internet photo-logger—known to her fans as "Cumbio," a nickname she received in school for her love of Cumbia music. According to her 2008 autobiography, *Yo Cumbio*, Vivero began taking and posting photos of herself on the Internet when she was thirteen. By seventeen not only had she penned her memoir, she'd starred in a Nike ad campaign, raised awareness about HIV, become the subject of a documentary,[136] lunched with femicon Mirtha Legrand on her daily television show, made the rounds of news and talk shows, and still found time to hang with her fans and friends at their gatherings on the steps of a shopping mall located in a historically working-class Buenos Aires neighborhood and on the site of the old Abasto market. In 2009 alone, her fotolog site logged over thirty-six million visits.[137] Today she is one of the best-known "out" celebrities in a country that has led the world in legalizing civil rights for all its citizens.[138]

In many ways, too, Cumbio personifies the current trends, tensions, and blurred boundaries of popular devotional and celebrity practices. Cumbio herself claims that iconicity was attached to her; she's a "queni" [doesn't] celebrity: "que ni baila, que ni canta, que ni actúa"—she doesn't dance, sing, or act.[139] Her fame is instead constructed and sustained through a mix of constant online self-revelations and personal appearances—not only at the Abasto mall but in clubs [*boliches*] throughout the country—where she's paid to pose for photos with her fans. As Cumbio puts it, "I moved from being a phantom idol who only existed on the Internet to a close-up idol who travels all over the country."[140] Born in the northeastern Argentine city of Corrientes and coming from a solidly working-class home and neighborhood (her father is a plumber and her mother is a stay-at-home mom living in Buenos Aires's San Cristóbal), Cumbio stands as an example of the internal migration of Argentina's working classes. And while she and her television-producer older brother have profited from Argentina's strong media industry, she does not easily conform to prevailing mediatized standards for celebrity status. Cumbio is openly bisexual, writes frankly about her relationships, and often poses with girlfriends in her fotolog (creating a minor scandal when she appeared on the cover of the Argentine edition of *Newsweek* with her girlfriend); and she dresses in the androgynous style favored by her fellow floggers, sports piercings and brightly dyed hair, and does not diet or use makeup. In short, though benefitting from Argentina's mediatized culture, she refreshingly does not conform to the prevailing televisual image of Argentine women as suffering from eating disorders and obsessed with cosmetic surgery.[141]

Cumbio's memoir touches upon the femiconic subjects of this chapter and reminds us of just how porous the line between fandom and devotion is. Near the end of the book, Cumbio writes of her own devotional practices as a Catholic who goes every other week to Buenos Aires's San José Church to pray to San Expedito, a canonized saint popular among *correntinos* like Cumbio's parents and known for his "fulfillment of urgent needs."[142] She recounts "thousands" of family visits to the popular saint Gauchito Gil's sanctuary on their way to and from seeing her grandmother in Corrientes. The brief chapter ends with "Cumbio's Prayer," a version of the "Lord's Prayer" posted by another flogger: "Mother Cumbio who art in Abasto / Direct to FFs [Facebook Friends] be Your name."[143] While Cumbio writes that one should not joke about the "Lord's Prayer," her decision to include the re-gendered petition acknowledges her status as potential object of devotional practices.

Cumbio's passing identification with Eva Perón is more explicitly framed but still suggests an already culturally established relationship between an Argentine femicon and her followers:

> For a short while, I felt I was Evita. Eva Perón, yes! What? Is it so weird to think about an Evita-flogger? It was one Sunday in Abasto, I arrived and everybody was following me, I had a lot more people behind me than I was used to. And so like Evita going out onto the Casa Rosada balcony to talk to the people and throw them kisses like a diva, I also turned around and threw kisses at the floggers. And that was the closest I came to the image I have of politics. Period.[144]

Cumbio immediately follows up this anecdote with a description of her "Peronist" home and their support of the current president, concluding the section with a rejection of the Evita-Cumbio comparison as a load of rubbish: "¡Qué pavadas, ¿no?!"[145] Nevertheless, this scene from her memoir is one of the few described in a *New York Times* profile—one more example of the implication that every Argentine woman of any note must inevitably be held to the Evita femiconic standard.

Cumbio exemplifies an Argentina that appears to be coming into its own in the twenty-first century. Not only is she from the working-class interior and a younger generation, Cumbio is also cofounder and icon of a new community that is both virtual and physically embodied: the "flogger community" has been deemed an "urban tribe" born on the Internet but just as importantly maintained in its mass Abasto gatherings. Today Cumbio and her tribe constitute Argentina's leading example of what media scholar P. David Marshall has called a new "user-subjectivity" that "has begun to modify the sources of our celebrity."[146] As presented in the 2011 documentary by Andrea Yannino, *Soi Cumbio*, Vivero retains some ambivalence toward her self-created celebrity: the somewhat solitary girl nicknamed for being the only Cumbia-lover at her school finds her community online and meets it in person, which leads to the media fame she both enjoys and finds overwhelming. Cumbio also has a tenuous relationship with the idea of "tribe," famously saying that floggers are a style [*moda*] that does not require exclusive allegiance. Cumbio maintains her fotolog—http://us.fotolog.com/cumbio/mosaic/—and her complicated relationship with those she calls interchangeably her friends, fans, and followers. And she still loves Cumbia music. As Argentine working-class rocker Pappo reminds us, "When people despair, they listen to Cumbia."[147] Santa Evita, Santa Gilda, Difunta Correa, and perhaps even the young Cumbio reign at the virtual-embodied crossroads of a complexly forward- and backward-looking twenty-first-century Argentina.

Conclusion

Toward a Complicated Understanding of Eva Perón and Argentine Femiconicity in Performance

"I identify with Eva Perón of the chignon and the clenched fist,
not with my mother's miraculous Eva,
the Colón Opera House Eva, the good fairy
that came to hand out jobs [and] the right to vote."

—CRISTINA FERNÁNDEZ DE KIRCHNER[1]

When diva Nacha Guevara opened her much-anticipated revival of *Eva, el gran musical argentino*, seated in the audience that spring 2008 evening was Cristina Elisabet Fernández de Kirchner, Argentina's first woman president and leading member of the Peronist party. The current president's own humble and still rather mysterious beginnings in provincial Buenos Aires have recalled Evita's life and are often given as reasons for the president's "in-yer-face" brand of coalitionist Peronism. A career politician, Cristina—as she's popularly called—has consciously embraced Evita's more rebellious image, to which my opening epigraph attests. Her presence at fellow Peronist and onetime political candidate Nacha's opening-night performance of Eva completed a femiconic Peronist trinity: Nacha was Eva, Eva was Argentina, and Cristina Argentina's first elected woman president and steward.[2] It seems only fitting that I conclude this extended study of Argentina's femicons with a final consideration of the political performances of Argentina's current leader and internationally known femicon.

At the beginning of the twenty-first century, Cristina (b. 1953) and her husband, Néstor Kirchner (1950–2010), emerged as the new Peronist power couple, the first to achieve and sustain such a profile since Eva and Juan. The Kirchners, who met while law students at the National University of La Plata (the capital of Buenos Aires Province) and active members of the Peronist Youth, consolidated their political careers in provincial Patagonia. There they practiced law and engaged in Justicialist politics, with Néstor serving as mayor of his native Río Gallegos before being elected governor of Santa Cruz Province in 1991 and Cristina representing the region in Argentina's legislature. The couple's national emergence came just as Argentina's neoliberal '90s went crashing into the new millennium: on December 20, 2001, President Fernando de la Rúa abruptly resigned, and Argentina plummeted into social, political, and economic chaos. Néstor would be tapped to run for the national presidency after interim President Eduardo Duhalde moved elections up by six months amid demands that all politicians be thrown out of office—"que se vayan todos." In 2003, Kirchner was elected president by default, winning—with only 22.2 percent of the first-round vote and the lowest percentage of any successful Argentine presidential candidate ever—when former president (and chief architect of the previous decade's neoliberal economic policies) Carlos Saúl Menem withdrew from the race. Néstor's four-year term saw the country begin a gradual economic recovery, and his government has been credited for the long-overdue official acknowledgment of the 1976–83 military regime's abuses and overturning of amnesty laws for military officials and others involved in the torture and disappearance of tens of thousands of Argentines.[3]

While Néstor was a Peronist insider at the time of his presidential campaign, he had not yet matched his wife's national profile. Cristina embarked upon a career as an elected official in the mid-1990s, when she moved from the Santa Cruz provincial legislature to the national congress. Once there she would serve continuously—as senator, then *diputada* [congress-woman], and once again as senator—from 1995 to 2007.[4] In October of that year, she was elected president of the nation with 45.3 percent of the vote and a 22 percent advantage over her closest competitor. Néstor became the "first gentleman" to the country's first woman president, even as he remained politically active (as president of the Justicialist Party), fanning rumors of a tag-team Kirchner presidential "diarchy."[5] Any possible dream of an open-ended Kirchnerist presidency, however, ended on October 27, 2010, when Néstor's unexpected death brought hundreds of thousands to the presidential Casa Rosada to pay their final respects to his body lying in state. Cristina and their two adult children stayed by the coffin for nearly twelve hours, receiving from citizens, celebrities, and hemispheric leaders personal condolences, commemorative gifts, and at least one spontaneous performance, when an unidentified man sang a haunting *Ave Maria* that silenced everyone in the room.

The day after Néstor's death was the national census, which the government had decreed a federal holiday. Banks were closed, only emergency personnel were supposed to go to work, and restaurants and markets did not open until eight that night so that the census-takers would find the heads of household at home as they went door to door completing their questionnaires. As a foreigner in Buenos Aires, I could not participate in the census, but I stayed home anyway, watching on television the endless line of mourners at the Casa Rosada and finding myself fascinated by Cristina's own marathon vigil. Indeed, it was her attention to detail—the care she took personally to place items such as the Madres' signature head scarf on her husband's coffin, greet dignitaries, respond to the countless others, and even arrange the many bouquets of flowers—that impressed me as much as her remarkable stamina and commitment to conducting her private mourning in public.

Over ten years into the Kirchners' tandem presidencies (which Cristina has called the "won decade"), the Argentine economy continues to be cited in the international press, often as point of comparison for Europe's own economic calamities. Even as the Kirchners have been praised for advancing human and civil rights causes, critics are quick to point to rapidly increasing prices, the ongoing high peso-to-dollar exchange rate (and illegal "blue-dollar" market), suspected fiddling with inflation numbers, and continuing international battles over the country's defaulted debt. Cristina's presidency has been marked by polarizing controversy, in itself not an unusual occurrence for almost any president, and she is often paired in the international press with other "left-leaning" and "controversial" South American leaders like Bolivia's Evo Morales and Venezuela's now-deceased Hugo Chávez. At the time of Nacha's 2008 revival, Argentine ranks were clearly split over the president, particularly regarding her insistence upon taxing Argentina's profitable soybean industry, to which industrialists responded by cutting off highways and staging protests, including a near-daily ritual of noontime banging of pots and pans in the capital. Cristina's latest battles have also been international, as she threatens to stir the global pot by renationalizing the country's various industries (most notoriously its oil reserves by reclaiming national and local control over the YPF from the Spanish-owned company Repsol) and by questioning the United Kingdom's territorial rights to the Malvinas/Falkland Islands.[6] Reviled and praised, Cristina and Argentina maintain a charged international profile.

Despite such recent national and global-market frays, the leading international obsession continues to be with Cristina's style, which one foreign analyst lauded as "a refreshing girl-next-door kind of image"[7] even as local detractors have ridiculed her as "the Botox Queen."[8] Cristina herself has deflected criticism of her long, loose hair, strong makeup, and preference for breezy shirt dresses and high heels with self-deprecation and humor: "I was born wearing makeup" is her most-frequently quoted response to such comments.[9] For some three years after her husband's death, she dressed in mourning, only to be criticized yet again for supposedly owning over two hundred "little black dresses."[10]

It seems inevitable that, given her combination of glamor and guts, Cristina has unendingly been compared to Evita. Cristina Fernández de Kirchner today occupies a political position exceeding that to which Eva Perón aspired but was never allowed to occupy.[11] Two months before her October 2011 reelection to office (with an impressive 54 percent of the vote), Forbes ranked her seventeenth on its list of the one hundred most influential women in the world.[12] As one Argentine commentator put it, "Cristina is Perón and his wife wrapped in a single package."[13] Such a concentration of power, nevertheless, has not kept the twice-elected president from having to field questions whether she is "the new Evita," "the next Evita," "not just another Evita," "the auburn to Evita's blond," or even "sexier than Evita."[14] Rumors have abounded as to whether Cristina will run for a third term as president of the country where Evita still reigns in the national imaginary through near-constant cultural and political iconic circulation.

Cristina herself has made very effective political use of Evitist symbolism, perhaps most obviously through her commission of two enormous (15 tons, 31 by 24 meters) metal cut-out murals of iconic Evita profiles that now hang one hundred feet above downtown Buenos Aires's widest avenue. Sculptor Alejandro Marmo (b. 1971), known for his recycled metalwork, conceived the idea of hanging a silhouette of Eva Perón from the Health and Social Development Ministries Building, the former Public Works Ministry Building where some sixty years earlier, on August 22, 1951, Evita had appeared in response to the assembled crowd's demands that she seek the vice-presidency for Juan's second term. A few days later and under extreme pressure, she would decline. One of Evita's best-known photos—taken at the August rally and showing her in profile, shouting into a microphone while gesticulating—would serve as the model. Cristina so liked the idea that she backed it through presidential decree. At her behest, though, there would be two murals: the "angry" militant Evita directing her ire toward the city's northern upper-class neighborhoods (fig. 13) and, facing south toward the country's suburban and provincial poor, the bejeweled "kind" Evita—inspired by Ayrinhac's now-destroyed painting and likely Eva's most recognizably iconic image (fig. 14). Another visual artist, Daniel Santoro, was brought on board to design the two murals. A painter whose subject matter and very personal symbology have long centered on the Peróns and Peronism (and whom I discuss at some length in the previous chapter), Santoro is perhaps the artist best qualified to execute the designs. Cristina carefully oversaw the process, and Santoro recounted to me the remarkable experience of sitting in the Casa Rosada with the president correcting his lines. In one published interview, he told of her displaying his drawings to a group of ministers and secretaries:

> The drawings of Evita facing north were lined with traces of a black marker [with a special emphasis on her mouth]. [The president] spoke to me of the strong relationship between the mouth delivering the speech and the microphone in front of her, a large microphone typical of the era. I realized that she had already imagined how the silhouette would look once it was installed on the ministry's walls. She also told me to take care with the lines of the upper part of her head, so she wouldn't look bald, and with the chignon so that the final product wouldn't look like a helmet.[15]

Santoro considered the project a collaborative effort, and neither artist signed the final works. The timing for inaugurating the two murals was charged with Evitist symbolism: the south-facing mural was unveiled on July 26 at 8:25 p.m., the day and hour of Evita's death, while the north-facing unveiling coincided with the fifty-ninth anniversary of the inspirational speech. Both are iconic images, and both, according to the artist today most closely identified with Evita, are destined "to transform Buenos Aires's visual [landscape] as the Obelisk once did."[16]

Evita dominated the capital city during a June 2013 trip: not only were her two murals visible from just about any vantage point along the city's broad 9 de Julio Avenue, but she seemed to pop up everywhere I went. There were at least three Evita-inspired plays running (including Cristina Banegas's restaging of *Eva Perón en la hoguera*), and she ghosted several others.[17] In trendy Palermo Soho, a friend took me to Los Octubres, a resto-store devoted to 1950s and '70s Peronism. After lunch over a "Perón" Malbec ordered from a menu with Evita's image embossed on its cover, we walked past the Chagall-inspired stained glass window showing key historical and invented Peronist moments that included an impossibly pleased Che reading Evita's quasi-autobiography to look at the store's wares, among them reproductions of 1970s Peronist Youth jackets, "Peronist Kid" mugs, and even "Perushkas"—a Peronist pantheon of *matryoshka*-style nesting dolls: Perón, Evita, Cámpora, Néstor, and Cristina. Evita's image graces the new one-hundred-peso bill, coveted by collectors but rejected by businesses, because "it's difficult to tell if the new Evita bills are true or false."[18] A duplicated Evita even traveled to the 2013 Venice Biennale, where she occupied Argentina's National Pavilion in a performance installation by Argentine multimedia artist Nicola Costantino: four works that included *Eva los sueños*, a four-hour video installation in which the artist embodied six different "iconic" Evas, projected simultaneously onto a circular screen as well as onto the mirrors of Eva's reconstructed bedroom; *Eva la fuerza*, a chrome-plated "machine-dress" that recalled Eva's last public appearance, supported by a metal stand for Juan's second inauguration; and *Eva la lluvia*, a steel table piled with ice teardrops evoking the rainy two weeks following her funeral.[19] Despite Costantino's claims of artistic freedom from "dogmatic and ideological representation," her *Sinfonía inconclusa* [Unfinished Rhapsody] was renamed by the president as "Eva-Argentina: a contemporary metaphor" and her installation followed by a "video hagiography,"[20] with historic Eva footage and Cristina's voice bringing home the metaphoric trinity—Eva-Argentina-Cristina.

Another Argentine artist present at the Biennale, Daniel Santoro, shared with me the draft of an essay intended for the catalog of a 2013 exhibit of Evita iconography. In his review of five iconic images of the historical Eva Perón, Santoro notes that "Eva Perón presents us [with] complications of ambiguity and multiple vanishing points."[21] Costantino's installation and Santoro's essay bring to mind Martin Kemp's work on how images are transformed into icons. There Kemp discusses the role of the "matrix": "the template for a range of variants exploiting the key visual signs in the image."[22] A matrix seems required for an iconic image's "extraordinary robustness" as it is reproduced serially.[23] The two Evita murals' choice of material and design aesthetics draw parallels with

Figure 13: Daniel Santoro's "militant" north-facing Evita mural. Courtesy of the artist.

Figure 14: Daniel Santoro's "kindly" south-facing Evita mural. Courtesy of the artist.

Argentina's other icon, Che, and his metalworked silhouette that over-looks Havana's Plaza de la Revolución.[24] As Kemp points out, the Che-icon's matrix-template is Alberto Korda's famous 1960 photograph, the source image for the Cuban mural. Most iconic figures like Che have one matrix; however, as Santoro implies but with a different terminol-ogy, multiple matrices have informed Evitist iconology. Cristina's choice to have Marmo Santoro's two sculptures overhanging the city reflects her awareness of the power of Evita's plural iconicity, and the fact that two different sources were chosen for these images suggests an even more complex understanding of iconographic possibilities and multi-plications. While, like the Che matrix, the "angry" Evita matrix bases its configuration on a well-known and widely reproduced photograph, the "benevolent" Evita matrix references a now-missing portrait that has been artistically reinterpreted and associated with Eva's autobiography and particularly the scholastic editions distributed throughout the coun-try. Argentina's current president demonstrated once again her uncanny awareness of how femiconicity operates. Though Cristina may herself identify with only the "Eva Perón of the chignon and the clenched fist," she knew that her mother's "miraculous Eva, the Colón Opera House Eva, the good fairy that came to hand out jobs [and] the right to vote" needed to be iconographically present to jointly validate what Santoro calls a "collective imaginary that no one is going to question."[25]

Cristina skillfully invoked the dual matrix of a femiconic Evita as part of her campaign to reverse earlier neoliberal economic moves toward globalizing privatization, first by renationalizing Argentine airlines and pension funds, and then through the renationalization of the country's oil reserves. Accompanying her in the nationally televised and inter-nationally published announcement of the country's reclamation of a majority stake in YPF were multiple images of Evita that included an iconic photo of the "angry" historical Evita that neatly contrasted with a mock-up of the new mural's benevolent image. Cristina calculatedly made sure that both Evitas were present: the twice-removed artistically rendered "good fairy" Evita was utilized for close-up personal identifica-tion (fig. 15) while the historical photograph of "Evita of the clenched fist" loomed above and larger than life. Although their placement lacked the symmetry of the two murals hanging from the nearby building, the images seemed perfectly positioned for Cristina's press conference per-formance, reinscribing the double matrix, creating opportunities for side-by-side photos with the caring Evita (and the recent mural project)

Figure 15: Cristina holds up a flask of "renationalized" Argentine oil. Daniel García/AFP.

while still underscoring the president's claimed preference for the militant "real-life" Eva Perón and reminding us of her own political power, to which Evita aspired but was never allowed to attain.

Cristina's political performances complicate our understanding of iconographic performance as surrogation or effigy. Hers is not a secondary elaboration or a double performance, yet she evinces an awareness of an icon's dual function as cultural agent *and* cultural product. Cristina is not Evita, nor does she theatrically embody Evita, and, through her careful actions, biting wit, and sheer political longevity, she has resisted the international media's reductivist attempts at, once again, equating any Argentine woman of weight with the country's premiere femicon. However, like the many artists who have performed Evita, Cristina-the-politician has repeatedly demonstrated her remarkable knowledge of and ability to channel femiconicity's powerful and charged symbology for a particular moment and place. Like her rejection of certain neoliberal market practices, Cristina's cultural repoliticization of Evita's multiple iconic matrices serves a larger renationalization project. Argentine icons in Cristina's performance assume an "Argentinicity," much like other iconic manipulations that rely on a reified sense of nationhood. At the same time, and as we have seen throughout this project, icons travel. Evita-femicon is not exclusive to Argentina. While the 2012 revival of the Rice-Lloyd Webber musical relocated her as "the First Lady of Broadway," YouTube clips of multiple twenty-first-century productions of Copi's dark French-language comedy abound, and Evita still functions as shorthand for and analog of any ballsy woman politician, especially if she's deemed conventionally attractive. Even in the most "national" of femiconic performances, such as Cristina's, and in the ongoing transnational circulations of Evita-femicon, we can detect a productive ambivalence toward Eva Perón as historical character, mythologized figure, and femiconized effigy. Possessor of multiple matrices, Evita-femicon remains to this day the most complex of any Argentine icon.

She nevertheless does not stand alone. In fact, one of my aims has been to trouble the standard cult of singular iconic personality by placing Evita within the much larger national and transnational historical, political, and cultural context and within a pantheon of other Argentine femicons and femicons-in-the-making. In this project, she's been accompanied by Camila and Gilda, with their mythologizing, iconographic performances spanning over one hundred and fifty years and technological transformations that have taken femiconic representation from the embodied to the mediated and enabled a degree of popular performance agency unimagined at a time when Camila's and the Difunta Correa's tragic lives were first being reconstructed on the region's melodramatic stages. Today, as Cumbio has shown us, any Argentine teenager with a government-supplied laptop and a camera can imagine herself a femicon, and physically performed popular devotional practices can be documented and uploaded to YouTube. The femicons' many performers have included stage and film actors, *café concert* divas, and cabaret transvestites; and among would-be femiconographers we've noted photologgers and penitents; musicians and painters; novelists and historians; playwrights and filmmakers. In concert, the many performances studied here have served as material for reconsidering the intersections of globalized celebrity, national myth-making, popular iconography, and cultural and artistic performances.

And yet, we return, inevitably, to Eva Perón. If this book has accomplished anything, it has directed its reader away from the forever unanswerable question of who or what was the historic Eva Perón and toward the more productive interrogations of where, when, and most importantly how she has been staged and restaged femiconically. In the many Evita performances examined here, we have witnessed the national and transnational robustness of her plural images. I find in her iconic multiplication, excess, and even surplus an opportunity: Evita-icon's matrices can expand our understanding of iconicity as they constructively disrupt and defy our attempts at equating the icon with the person. If Evita-femicon's matrices are multiple, then so must be our intellectual engagements with them.

Notes

INTRODUCTION

1. Recent award-winning examples include Tristán Bauer's documentary *Che, un hombre nuevo* (2010) and Walter Salles's *The Motorcycle Diaries* (2004, screenplay by Puerto Rican playwright José Rivera), but let's not forget the 1961 *Che!*, directed by Richard Fleischer with Jack Palance playing Fidel to Omar Sharif's eponym. Memorable non-Argentine theatrical productions featuring Che include Culture Clash's (the self-proclaimed "original exploiters of Che") *A Bowl of Beings* (1991); José Rivera's 2007 *School of the Americas* (about Che's final days); and Zhang Guangtian's *Che Guevara* (premiering in Beijing in 2007, http://app1.chinadaily.com.cn/star/2001/0308/wh26-1.html [accessed 11 January 2012]).

2. Nina Gerassi-Navarro, "Las tres Evas: de la historia al mito en cinemascope," in *Evita: Mitos y representaciones*, ed. Marysa Navarro (Buenos Aires: Fondo de Cultura Económica, 2002), 65–100, 66. Unless otherwise noted, all translations are mine.

3. Javier Auyero, *Poor People's Politics: Peronist Survival Networks & the Legacy of Evita* (Durham, NC: Duke University Press, 2001), 145, especially chapter four, "'We will fight forever, we are Peronists': Eva Perón as a Public Performance." It could be argued that Argentina's current president, Cristina Fernández de Kirchner, has created her own political persona, but as we'll see in this book's concluding chapter, it is a persona engaging with selected Evita-identified aspects. Peronism generally refers to the political movement founded by Juan Perón and to the Justicialist Party (after its central tenet of "social justice"). Peronism's complexities and some of its many variants will be discussed in detail in subsequent chapters.

4. See, for example, John Heilemann's essay on Hillary Clinton's presidential campaign ("The Evita Factor," *New York*, 11 February 2008, 20–23). Heilemann quotes one of Clinton's advisers: "It's happening again, right now, in Argentina, for example. I guess you could say that Hillary is benefiting from the Evita effect" (20). In the middle of the 2008 U.S. presidential campaign, Gregory Bergman (with Paula Muner) published *101 Things You (and John McCain) Didn't Know about Sarah Palin* (Avon, MA: Adams Media, 2008), in which Eva Perón appears eighth on a list of "Top Ten Past Lives for Palin" (sandwiched between Jimmy Swaggart and Mata Hari!), 186. And on 17 January 2011, a *Washington Post* op-ed piece excavated the Palin–Perón comparison:

"The way Palin portrayed herself as not only a popular champion but also a martyr reminded me—not for the first time—of Eva Per[ó]n. If she chooses this unpromising route to higher political office, I suggest she find a suitable balcony from which to deliver her next address to the nation." Eugene Robinson, "Sarah Palin's Egocentric Umbrage" http://www.washingtonpost.com/wp-dyn/content/article/2011/01/17/AR2011011702851.html (accessed 18 January 2011). Here, and typical of U.S. analyses, Evita is trotted out as cautionary negative role model. Another recent example of Evita sensationalizing is Juré Fiorillo's pop-historical collection *Great Bastards of History: True and Riveting Accounts of the Most Famous Illegitimate Children who Went on to Achieve Greatness* (Beverly, MA: Fair Winds Press, 2010), where out of fifteen "bastards," Eva is one of three Latin Americans (with Bernardo O'Higgins and Fidel Castro) and one of three women (with Elizabeth I and Billie Holiday). The summary captures the fourteen-page bio: "She began life poor, plain, and illegitimate. An iron will, relentless ambition, and her own sexuality transformed herself [sic] into the wealthy, glamorous, and controversial first lady of Argentina" (228).

5. Respectively, Adolfo Díez Gómez, *Una mujer argentina: doña María Eva Duarte de Perón* (Buenos Aires: Biblioteca Infantil "General Perón," 1948); and Kathleen Krull, "Hair like a Halo: Eva Perón," in *Lives of Extraordinary Women: Rulers, Rebels (and What the Neighbors Thought)* (New York: Scholastic Inc., 2000), 78–81. The English-language book, written for readers nine to twelve years old, illustrates Evita as a lavishly dressed and peso-dropping fairy godmother who carries her own halo and cavorts with two of Perón's poodles. The Spanish-language book, in contrast, bears a cover drawing of a simply dressed and head-scarved Evita surrounded by twinkling stars suggesting a celestially divine status.

6. The itinerary and quotation come from one of the many Evita–Buenos Aires tours: http://www.embraceargentina.com/evita.html (accessed 10 January 2012).

7. "The President Wore Pearls" (broadcast 16 November 2003), a parody of the Rice-Lloyd Webber musical through daughter Lisa's Evita make-over, was the third episode premiered during *The Simpsons'* fifteenth season. Lady Gaga's 2010 video "Alejandro" has been said to resurrect Evita, or at least Evita as imagined by Madonna.

8. Julie Taylor, *Paper Tangos* (Durham, NC: Duke University Press, 1998). At one point, during anthropologist-tango dancer Taylor's extended reflections on her relationship with Argentina and the tango, she wonders if her supposed physical resemblance to both Evita and images of the Virgin Mary contributed to her positive reception by Argentines (50–52).

9. "The theatre, by performing history, is thus re-doing something which has already been done in the past, creating a secondary elaboration of this historical event." Freddie Rokem, *Performing History: Theatrical Representations of the Past in Contemporary Theatre* (Iowa City: University of Iowa Press, 2000), 6.

10. Martin Kemp, *Christ to Coke: How Image Becomes Icon* (Oxford: Oxford University Press, 2012), 3.

11. Like me, Kemp is not "concerned to arbitrate in the often bilious disputes about Che's virtues and vices." Instead, he examines "key episodes in how the familiar visual image acquired its extraordinary status." Kemp, 170.

12. W.J.T. Mitchell, *Iconology: Image, Text, Ideology* (Chicago: University of Chicago Press, 1986), 9.

13. An icon's duality is very much present yet left unacknowledged in Jens Andermann and William Rowe's parenthetical observation regarding the "equivocal trajectory" of both Eva Perón's image and her body. Andermann and Rowe, "Introduction: The Power of Images," in *Images of Power: Iconography, Culture and the State in Latin America*, ed. Andermann and Rowe (New York: Berghahn Books, 2005), 3.

14. Sarah M. Misemer, *Secular Saints: Performing Frida Kahlo, Carlos Gardel, Eva Perón, and Selena* (Woodbridge, UK, and Rochester, NY: Tamesis, 2008), 1.

15. Ibid., 9.

16. Marvin Carlson, *The Haunted Stage: The Theatre as Memory Machine* (Ann Arbor: University of Michigan Press, 2001); Jacques Derrida, *Specters of Marx: The State of the Debt, the Work of Mourning, and the New International*, trans. Peggy Kamuf (London: Routledge, 1994); and Joseph Roach, *Cities of the Dead: Circum-Atlantic Performance* (New York: Columbia University Press, 1996).

17. Roach, *Cities of the Dead*, 36. Roach re-cites the passage in *It* (Ann Arbor: University of Michigan Press, 2007), 235, n.26.

18. The photo, taken on 17 April 2008, can be found at http://www.flickr.com/photos/maisagua/3702379207/. The caption contains the multilingual comment: "Qué dupla, hein?" [What a pair, eh?].

19. Michael Shaw's June 2013 post attempts to differentiate between Internet memes and icons through a photograph taken during a protest in Turkey: "an icon is a picture of someone or something that is widely seen to capture and define the essence of a situation," whereas a visual meme "is a[n] image or scene which not only hits a nerve, but serves as a catalyst, through humor or exaggeration, to drive home the essence (and, typically, the pathos or irony) of a situation." Shaw concludes that the image under analysis—of red-dress-clad Turkish academic Ceyda Sungur with her hair standing on end as she turns away from a policeman's pepper spray—is more meme than icon for the ironic ambiguities created through comparison with other images: the UC Davis cop's "virulence," Marilyn Monroe's elevated skirt from *The Seven-Year Itch*, and the Turkish flag. The memetic result for Shaw is "three-fifths state terror, one-fifth Dadaism, and one-fifth Marx Brothers." See "Icons, Memes, and the Hair-Raising Turkish 'Lady in Red,'" *Bag News*, 7 June 2013 http://bagnews notes/2013/06/icons-memes-and-the-hair-raising-turkish-lady-in-red/ (accessed 24 June 2013). I find meme's current connotative relations to social media and near-requisite ironic or parodic commentary, as well as implication that memes operate independently as "viruses," too constraining a category for my present discussion of performance practices.

20. Dennis Hall and Susan Grove Hall, "LebowskIcons: The Rug, the Iron Lung, the Tiki Bar, and Busby Berkeley," in *The Year's Work in Lebowski Studies*, ed. Edward P. Comentale and Aaron Jaffe (Bloomington: Indiana University Press, 2009), 321–40, 321. The examples I provide are theirs.

21. Ibid., 322.

22. Michael L. Quinn, "Celebrity and the Semiotics of Acting," *New Theatre Quarterly* 6, no. 22 (1990): 154–61.

23. Chris Rojek, *Celebrity* (London: Reaktion Books, 2001).

24. Richard Dyer, *Stars* (London: British Film Institute, 1998). I direct the reader to Paul McDonald's supplementary chapter, which summarizes some of the develop-

ments in film and "star" scholarship since the initial publication of Dyer's book in 1979.

25. Roland Barthes, "Myth Today" (1956), in *Mythologies*, trans. Annette Lavers (New York: Hill and Wang, 1972), 109–59; and "Mythology Today" (1971), in *The Rustle of Language*, trans. Richard Howard (New York: Hill and Wang, 1986), 65–68. It is important to recall that, in the later essay, Barthes rejected his own earlier demythification project while retaining language's repoliticizing potential.

26. Susan Hayward, *The Key Concepts in Cinema Studies* (London: Routledge, 1996), 304. Michael Casey, in his study of Che's "afterlife," provides the fascinating example of how Korda's photographic portrait "has taken on a kind of postmortem life of its own." *Che's Afterlife: The Legacy of an Image* (New York: Vintage, 2009), 7. Casey's book traces this image-as-icon as it has moved around the world.

27. Marysa Navarro, "La Mujer Maravilla ha sido siempre argentina y su nombre verdadero es Evita," in *Evita: Mitos y representaciones*, ed. Navarro (Buenos Aires: Fondo de Cultura Económica, 2002), 11–42, 19.

28. Casey, 17. Toward the end of his book, Casey reminds us of our own participation in the globalized capitalist economy of the Che image: "Adopting the brand is a very personal act" (344).

29. Rojek, 10.

30. Ibid., 11.

31. Roach, *It*, 8 (emphasis his) and 36.

32. P. David Marshall, "New Media–New Self: The changing power of celebrity," in *The Celebrity Culture Reader*, ed. Marshall (New York: Routledge, 2006), 634–44, 644. The term "user-subjectivity" comes from Marshall.

33. Regina Janes, "Femicons," *Salmagundi*, nos. 135–36 (Summer/Fall 2002): 107.

34. Roach, *It*, 36.

35. See, for example, Diana Taylor, *Disappearing Acts: Spectacles of Gender and Nationalism in Argentina's "Dirty War"* (Durham, NC: Duke University Press, 1997).

36. Seibel's original list: 1) Theatre: *Eva Duarte en el espíritu de Eva Perón* (Cargasachi/Jamandreu, 1981); *Evita la mujer del siglo* (Pérez Pardella/Lo Cane, 1984/1985); *Eva* (Orgambide, 1986, with Nacha Guevara); *Eva de América* (Guglielmino, 1987); *Eva y Victoria* (Ottino, 1992); *Eva Perón en la hoguera* (Lamborghini, 1993); *Compañera* (Loisi/Rubertino, 1994); . . . *cariñosamente Evita* (Cabrera, 1996). 2) Television: *Eva Perón inmortal* (1990); *Eva Perón ha desaparecido* (1994). 3) Film: *Evita (quien quiera oír que oiga)* (Mignogna, 1984); *El misterio Eva Perón* (Demicheli, 1987); *Eva Perón* (Desanzo, 1996). I provide production and bibliographic details when discussing the individual plays and films.

37. Beatriz Mosquera, *Gotas de rocío sobre flores de papel*, 1994.

38. *Juan y Eva*, directed by Paula de Luque, distributed by Primer Plano (2011) http://www.imdb.com/title/tt1920980 (accessed 11 January 2012).

39. *Eva de la Argentina*, directed by María Seoane, produced by Azpeitia Cine and Illusion Studios (2011). Well-known stage actor Carlos Portaluppi provided the voice of narrator Walsh. http://www.imdb.com/title/tt2086840 (accessed 11 January 2012).

40. Rodolfo Walsh, "Esa mujer." Walsh's widely circulating short story—a barely fictionalized account (and excellent example of documentary fiction) of the journalist's interview with the colonel assigned to watch over Evita's cadaver kidnapped

shortly after Juan's 1955 overthrow—first appeared in *Crónicas del pasado*, ed. Julia Constenla (Buenos Aires: Jorge Alvarez, 1965). The intensely hypnotic text, in the words of a later editor, "articulates the chronicle of denunciation, in oblique form through dialogue of strong, dramatic content—likely helped by Walsh's experience in the theatre during those years—with an impeccable narrative structure highly configured by crime story elements: allusion (clues), a mystery to be solved, interrogation and confession, scenography, etc." Jorge Lafforgue, "Noticia," in Rodolfo Walsh, *La máquina del bien y del mal*, ed. Lafforgue (Buenos Aires: Clarín/Aguilar, 1992), 118. The author can be heard reading his own story at journalist Juan Alonso's blog: http://leyendadeltiempo.wordpress.com/esa-mujer-por-rodolfo-walsh (accessed 10 January 2012).

41. See, for example, Silvia [Sirena] Pellarolo, "The Melodramatic Seductions of Eva Perón," in *Corpus Delecti: Performance Art of the Americas*, ed. Coco Fusco (London: Routledge, 2000), 23–40. Pellarolo analyzes the construction of Evita's own "performing body" and her political activist performances that incorporated a melodramatic style she had learned and rehearsed while working as an actress in theatre, film, and, most importantly, radio.

42. See the various analyses of Copi's controversial 1970 play, *Eva Perón*, discussed in chapter three.

43. Matthew B. Karush and Oscar Chamosa, eds., *The New Cultural History of Peronism* (Durham, NC: Duke University Press, 2010). Theatre is absent from an otherwise performatively rich collection of essays constituting a "theoretically informed cultural history" of Perón's first government (2).

44. "Santa Gilda" in *Radar* supplement to *Página/12*, 24 May 1998 http://www.pagina12.com.ar/1998/suple/radar/mayo/98–05–24/vale.htm (last accessed 5 October 2009).

CHAPTER 1

1. One source for Soledad Rosas's widely distributed photo (which also appears on the cover of her sole biography, see below) is Punksunidos/Nodomutante. "Soledad Rosas, Amor y Anarquía" (posted August 2010) http://www.punksunidos.com.ar/2010/08/soledad-rosas.html (accessed 17 February 2013).

2. Martín Caparrós, *Amor y anarquía: La vida urgente de Soledad Rosas 1974–1998* (Buenos Aires: Planeta, 2003). Caparrós, an Argentine journalist and fiction/nonfiction writer forced into exile during the 1976–83 dictatorship, not only interviewed members of Soledad's family but traveled to Italy, retracing Sole's life in Turin (and spending several weeks living in one of the occupied buildings) as well as interviewing her colleagues, friends, and lawyers, as well as police officers and other officials involved in the case. In his biography he quotes extensively from Soledad's own letters and diaries. Caparrós has called this his least ironic book: "I wanted to respect her." Qtd. in Mariana Enríquez, "La vida breve," *Página/12*, 6 July 2003, *Radar* supplement http://www.pagina12.com.ar/diario/suplementos/radar/9–820–2003–07–09.html (accessed 10 September 2010).

3. Intentionally misspelled from the Romance-language *ocupa*, *okupa* can be applied to both the squatter and her squat. Robert Neuwirth estimates there are some

one billion squatters around the world. *Shadow Cities: A Billion Squatters, A New Urban World* (New York: Routledge, 2004).

4. The charges leveled against the three far outweighed their actions, as Caparrós details in his biography and multiple interviews. The Italian state sought to criminalize an entire movement through punishing the three "ecoterrorists." According to Caparrós, one police tape has Massari proposing the burning of an ATM, while others have them discussing paint "bombs." Okupas typically do not participate in "terrorist" acts but rather engage in activities like shoplifting (because money is not recognized) to back up their subversion of the "system." Enríquez, "La vida breve."

5. As Caparrós notes, other deaths followed upon Sole's: the owner of the house where she lived while under arrest committed suicide, as did her Argentine ex-boyfriend. Pasquale Cavaliere, the proecology politician and one of few officials the couple would speak with, was found hanged in Argentina while seeking information on Italian *desaparecidos*. "No one knows what happened." Qtd. in Enríquez, "La vida breve."

6. See Caparrós, 23–24.

7. See María Sáenz Quesada, *Mujeres de Rosas* (Buenos Aires: Planeta, 1991), for a chapter-length discussion of Manuelita's life, environment, and relationship to her father. Manuelita's brother, Juan, is rarely mentioned in most accounts of the Rosas family. Far greater critical and popular attention has been paid to the patriarch and the women surrounding him.

8. I refer to Martín Boneo's 1820 "El Tambo Congo," today part of the Museo Histórico Nacional's collection (Buenos Aires). One image source: http://lacu erdaweb.com/site.html (accessed 13 June 2012).

9. The Buenos Aires-based *unitarios* were centralists, associated with the oligarchs and plutocracy, and seen as Europeanist (and U.S.-identified) "modernizers." The federalists (or *federales*) were identified with the rural provinces and regionalist autonomy, and often associated with the more conservative, Hispanic, and Catholic doctrines of earlier *criollo* settlers. For information on both the period and the two factions, see David Rock, *Argentina: 1516–1987: From Spanish Colonization to Alfonsín* (Berkeley: University of California Press, 1985); and Nicolás Shumway, *The Invention of Argentina* (Berkeley: University of California Press, 1991).

10. Rock describes the *mazorca* as "a ruthless vigilante police force." *Argentina*, 106. As the "archsymbol of the Terror," the name suggested both 1) *más-horca* [strangle more], "an etymology referring to the gallows, although their procedure was in fact to slit the victim's throat with a dull knife"; and 2) corncob, a reference "to the use of this agricultural byproduct in a final indignity practiced on the corpses of the vigilantes' victims." David W. Foster, *Contemporary Argentine Cinema* (Columbia: University of Missouri Press, 1992), 19.

11. Prilidiano Pueyrredón's famous 1851 portrait of a thirty-four-year-old Manuelita Rosas today hangs in Buenos Aires's Museo de Bellas Artes [Fine Arts Museum]. Image available at the museum's "Visita virtual" http://www.mnba.org.ar/detalle_obras_sala.php?piso=0&sala=24&obra=700&opcion=VISITA_VIRTUAL (accessed 17 February 2013). Alberto Passolini's 2008 parody, "Manuelita and the Terror," attests to the painting's ongoing presence in the national imaginary. The knocked-over vase of flowers suggests Passolini's opinion regarding Manuelita's complicity in her fa-

ther's violent regime. Image available at artist's website http://www.albertopassolini.com/ (accessed 17 February 2013).

12. Fermín Fevre, "Retrato de Manuelita Rosas/Cómo ver la obra," *La Nación*, 24 August 2003, http://www.lanacion.com.ar/nota.asp?nota_id=520737 (accessed 22 September 2010). Though Fevre's name no longer appears on the site, the author's biography is clearly his text. See also María Lía Munilla Lacasa, "Siglo XIX: 1810–1870," in *Nueva historia argentina: Arte, sociedad y política,* ed. José Emilio Burucúa (Buenos Aires: Editorial Sudamericana, 1999), 105–60, 144–45.

13. Mariana Enríquez and Máximo Eseverri, "¿Nace una estrella?," *Página/12,* 23 July 1998, 4, *No* supplement.

14. Sáenz Quesada, 111, 111–12, 112.

15. Caparrós goes as far as pronouncing both possible explanations for the young woman's actions—rebellion or love—as "anachronistic." In an interview the biographer explains his reason for writing the book: "What attracted me was that it wasn't clear if Soledad had killed herself for love or for a cause, but both reasons were so anachronistic that they caught my attention. I found out about her death, and later her life interested me." Qtd. in Enríquez, "La vida breve." On YouTube there can be found various accounts (and interviews with friends, fellow anarchists, and Caparrós) as well as dedicatory photo albums with music clips (more often than not borrowing from Argentine rockers Los Fabulosos Cadillacs' "Matador") posted—and still being uploaded. See, for example, "Soledad Rosas 1974–1998: L'ultimo Gesto di Liberazione," *Soledad Rosas–Anarquista,* marcelotrotamundo video, posted May 2009, http://www.youtube.com/watch?v=FEhVxF1SYCk; and *Sole e Baleno-There Will Be Trouble In Town-Andrea Sigona,* Cubaparma video, posted 2 April 2010, http://www.youtube.com/watch?v=juCoGKt8FDI.

16. In fact, Caparrós begins his biography of Soledad by stating categorically that "the first thing that caught my attention was her death." *Amor y anarquía,* 9.

17. My approximate translation of dialogue from "Mercedes," a short film commissioned for Argentina's 2010 bicentennial celebration. *Mercedes,* directed by Marcos Carnevale (Argentina: MC Millecento, 2010), 8 min.

18. According to director Carnevale, in the "making-of" film found at the government's project website: http://www.25miradas.gob.ar/cortos/mercedes/ (accessed 26 November 2010).

19. The daguerreotype, considered the only living image of Camila and taken by an unknown photographer, has been reproduced in Juan Gómez, *La fotografía en la Argentina* (Temperley, Argentina: Abadía Editora, 1986), 47; and Vicente Gesualdo, *Historia de la fotografía en América* (Buenos Aires: Ed. Sui Generis, 1990), 16. It can be found reproduced at multiple electronic sites, such as "Iurisdictio-Lex Malacitana" http://iurisdictio-lexmalacitana.blogspot.com/2009_11_01_archive.html (accessed 23 November 2010). In a post dated 19 November 2009, the blogger conjectures that, given the daguerreotype's reduced size (one-ninth of a plate or approximately 2 inches by 2 ½ inches, instead of the more commonly commissioned quarter or sixth), Camila may have had it made for her beloved Uladislao. The same blogger wonders if the image was removed from Camila's "bloodstained clothes." On another site, a blogger interprets the sitter's silk dress as winter wear and her accessories as typical of the period and the woman's age, and suggests that the image was made in 1847,

one year before Camila's death (though both these sources for the reproduced image list the date as 1848, the year of her death, while others list it as 1846). If the model is indeed Camila, she could have posed for the unknown photographer in Buenos Aires, Montevideo, or even Corrientes, all cities where the new technology was already being used. The second blogger also suggests that Camila's mouth remained closed because she was hiding the cavities that her "wanted" bulletin stated were prominent in one of her front teeth. See "Reflejos del Plata" http://reflejosdelplata. blogspot.com/2009/11/camila-ogorman-fue-victima-de-los.html (accessed 24 November 2010). Until 1998, the daguerreotype was said to have been in the collection of Uruguayan historian Augusto Schulkin, who identified the image as Camila's.

Another, highly idealized, lithographic portrait of Camila created after her death (possibly in 1860) has been attributed to Juan León Pallière (1823–1887), a French-Brazilian painter who resided intermittently in Buenos Aires. It has been conjectured that Pallière, though present in Buenos Aires at the time of Camila's execution, prudently waited until after Rosas's fall to create the portrait. In it, Camila wears a *peinetón*, a rather restrained version of the combs popular among Argentine women at the time and whose occasionally exaggerated sizes (up to three feet in height and width!), as Regina A. Root states, "became a symbol for the early nineteenth-century woman." We might cite Root, with some irony regarding Camila's own representation: "Authors and artists alike used the metonymical *peinetón*, which equated a woman's comb with public participation, to reflect on the breakdown of rigid gender roles and the transformation of public spaces." "Fashioning Independence: Gender, Dress and Social Space in Postcolonial Argentina," in *The Latin American Fashion Reader*, ed. Root (Oxford: Berg, 2005), 31–43, 33 and 43. The extensively reproduced lithograph appears on the cover of *Camila O'Gorman* (Buenos Aires: Planeta, 2001), edited by Argentine historian Félix Luna for his collection "Great Protagonists of Argentine History."

20. According to Eduardo Enrique Galiana, both Gutiérrez and O'Gorman's *filiaciones* are housed in the General Archive of the Province of Corrientes in the "Official and Judicial Correspondence 1848" section. They have been reproduced in many texts and recently by Galiana in *Camila O'Gorman y Uladislao Gutiérrez* (Corrientes, Argentina: Moglia Ediciones, 2009). Galiana, a lawyer and professor of law at the National University of the Northeast, reviewed the documents archived in Corrientes, the region where Camila and Uladislao made their brief home.

21. Galiana's book includes a detailed O'Gorman family tree. Another genealogy may be found at http://www.irishgenealogy.com.ar/genealogia/G/OGorman/Thomas.php (accessed 20 November 2010).

22. María Teresa Julianello, "The Scarlet Trinity: The Doomed Struggle of Camila O'Gorman against Family, Church & State in XIX Century Buenos Aires" http://www.irlandeses.org/julianello.htm (accessed 12 January 2009).

23. Among others, Leonor Calvera, who was historical consultant on Bemberg's film and published her own version of Camila's story, asserts that Perichon de O'Gorman was Camila's great-aunt Anita, who died before Camila's birth. See interview in Tamara Gould, "Transgressive Passions: María Luisa Bemberg's *Camila*," MA thesis, University of California, Santa Cruz, 1996, 102–7, 106.

24. Most biographers insist on using Perichon de O'Gorman's sobriquet, La Peri-

chona, and point out its negative word-play on the nickname of one of the great Latin American stage performers of the colonial period: the Peruvian actress Micaela Villegas, whose affair with the much-older Spanish Viceroy Manuel Amat y Juniet overshadowed her own theatrical achievements. Villegas's nickname, La Perricholi, is variously attributed to Amat's native Catalán *peti-xol* [jewel] or his mispronunciation of the racist insult *perra chola* [mixed-breed bitch] as "perri choli" in one of their lovers' quarrels. In Perichon de O'Gorman's case, the sobriquet was clearly intended to resonate with the more negative interpretation of Villegas's nickname.

25. I base these elements on my readings of memoirs such as Antonino Reyes's *Memorias del edecán de Rosas*, ed. D. Manuel Bilbao (1883; repr., Buenos Aires: Editorial Americana, 1943), and the various letters and other primary documents produced by officials and family members, verified and reproduced in texts such as Natalio Kisnerman's *Camila O'Gorman: El hecho histórico y su proyección literaria* (Buenos Aires: Universidad de Buenos Aires, Facultad de Filosofía y Letras, 1973; "Documentos para la historia del teatro nacional") and Galiana, as well as commonalities found in the following, otherwise very disparate and often ideologically incompatible, texts: Leonor Calvera, *Camila O'Gorman o el amor y el poder* (Buenos Aires: Editorial Leviatán, 1986); Julianello; John Lynch, *Argentine Dictator: Juan Manuel de Rosas 1829–1852* (Oxford: Clarendon Press, 1981); E.F. Sánchez Zinny, *Manuelita de Rosas y Ezcurra: Verdad y leyenda de su vida* (Buenos Aires: Ediciones de la Imprenta López, 1941); and Manuel Vizoso Gorostiaga, *Camila O'Gorman y su época* (Santa Fe, Argentina: Castellví, 1943).

26. Camila's assumed surname has been variously spelled as Desan, De San, Desand, or even Sand. Galiana bases his preferred spelling of Desau on primary documents (various official letters) archived in Corrientes.

27. Adolfo O'Gorman, letter dated 21 December 1847, reproduced in Kisnerman, 5–6, 5.

28. Miguel García, letter dated 22 December 1847, reproduced in Ibid., 6–7, 7.

29. Juan Manuel Rosas, letter dated 17 January 1848, reproduced in Ibid., 8–11.

30. Galiana writes that the eight marksmen did not even hit Camila in the first round (one marksman fainted while the others averted their eyes and missed); they wounded her in the arm on the second volley; and only during the third round did they take pity on their victim, shooting her "to death" [a balazos]. Galiana, 243–44.

31. Reprinted in many sources, most notably at the end of Reyes's chapter-long account of Camila and Uladislao. Rosas writes to his in-law Federico Terrero: "No person suggested to me the execution of the Priest Gutiérrez, Camila O'Gorman; nor did any person speak or write to me on their behalf.

On the contrary, all the primary persons of the Clergy spoke or wrote to me about this daring crime, and the urgent necessity of an exemplary punishment, in order to prevent other like or similar scandals.

I believed the same. [. . .] I governed according to my conscience. I am thus the only one responsible for all my acts." (Qtd. in Reyes, 370–71).

32. The dissenting opinion supposedly came from Eduardo Lahit[t]e. See Reyes, 362, and Galiana, 235–41. Nonetheless, Galiana writes, "Everyone collaborated in the assassinations of Camila and Uladislao" (242).

33. See Heraclio C. Fajardo, *Camila O'Gorman* (Buenos Aires: Imprenta Americana, 1856 [2nd ed., Buenos Aires: Imprenta Nacional, 1862, includes author preface;

repr. Montevideo, Uruguay: Imprenta Nacional, 1938]), 3.3, at 40. I discuss this play later in the chapter.

34. Reyes, 367–68. There is a letter signed by Manuelita and dated 9 August 1848, saying that she had personally appealed to her father and sending Camila "a thousand and one kisses from [her] very affectionate and loving friend." Qtd. in Calvera, 124; and Kisnerman, 18–19. The original letter is archived in Buenos Aires's Museo de Arte Hispanoamericano Isaac Fernández Blanco. It supposedly did not reach its intended recipient either. It is also said that Manuelita selected and purchased the few pieces of furniture Camila found in her room when she arrived at Santos Lugares.

35. Two examples reflect the many others published: Juan Manuel Beruti, in *Memorias curiosas* (orig. publ. *Revista de la Biblioteca Nacional* [Buenos Aires, 1956] 6–14, 37 n. 22, reprinted in *Biblioteca de Mayo* [Buenos Aires: Senado de la Nación, 1960], 4. 4076–77), complains "but this Señor, without paying attention to the innocent creature in her womb, without waiting for the mother to give birth, had her shot, an event unheard of in Buenos Aires, such that by killing two, three died." Rosas nemesis Domingo Faustino Sarmiento would later call it a "horrible tragedy, the assassination of that woman." (*Mi vida* [Buenos Aires: Estrada, 1949] 2: 78). Both are cited in Kisnerman, 20.

36. The lithograph entitled "Sacrifice of Camila O'Gorman and the Priest Gutierres" was created by Rodolfo Kratzenstein, a German who arrived to Buenos Aires in 1853, after the couple's execution. The image is housed at the Museo Histórico Nacional (in Buenos Aires) and is viewable at http://www.buenosaires.gov.ar/areas/cultura/arteargentino/00sigloxix/03gr_p2_10a.php (accessed 13 June 2012). A later watercolor, attributed to "N. Thomas" and housed in the Rosas Museum (in General San Martín), inaccurately portrays the soldiers in blue, rather than the obligatory Rosas crimson.

37. Two examples include the 1858 oil by Francisco Augero (an Italian who created the painting in Turin before traveling to Buenos Aires), whose "Execution of Camila" shows the couple in the same yard but standing and unbound; and the illustration included in the 1883 edition of Reyes's memoirs, which echoes the earlier lithographs but completely excises Uladislao. Camila had already become the artistic protagonist. Both images can be viewed at http://www.goyaopina.com.ar/?p=9040 with commentary by Héctor Daniel de Arriba, "Repercusiones de un fusilamiento," *La Opinión al Día,* 23 November 2010 (accessed 24 November 2010).

38. A recent exception to Camila's exclusive protagonism is the musical *Camila: nuestra historia de amor,* which opened at Buenos Aires's commercial Lola Membrives Theatre in April 2013. With current teen heartthrob Peter (Juan Pedro) Lanzani in the role of Uladislao, Fabián Núñez's musical grants nearly equal time and space to the two lovers, and both are sketched as idealistic, passionate rebels with an anti-Federalist cause. Twenty-four of the thirty-two scenes take place in the two playing areas of the church and the O'Gorman home, positioned side by side on revolving platforms. Postelopement bliss is limited to a single duet, performed by the lovers wrapped in sheets under a mantle of stars. When they are abruptly separated and jailed in facing cells, execution soon follows. Throughout, Camila is supported by other women, themselves victims of the masculine order: her mother and grandmother; her Afro-Argentine nanny; and her confidant, Manuelita. Despite the author-

director's assertions that this is "our love (hi)story" due to its alleged roots in "our popular culture" and the values of "freedom, loyalty, love, passion, and unconditional devotion," the musical disappoints as a schematic, barely historicized fairy-tale romance gone wrong, padded with superficial nods toward current politics and gender equality.

39. Camila's condition likely spurred her appearance a few years ago on the "Executed Today" blog: http://www.executedtoday.com/2008/08/18/1848-camila-ogorman-father-ladislao-gutierrez-traditional-family-values/ (accessed 28 November 2010). The entry calls Camila "virtually a lens for the contradictory currents of gender, class and power in her time," before proceeding to present her relationship with Uladislao as "torrid" and their elopement as "a grand gesture of romanticism."

40. The charcoal drawing is supposedly housed in Buenos Aires's Archivo General de la Nación. In response to requests made to the museum, I have been told that the work is in the collection but not available for viewing. It has been reproduced on multiple websites and in publications such as Doris Sommer's *Foundational Fictions: The National Romances of Latin America* (Berkeley: University of California Press, 1991).

41. Reyes, 364–65.

42. Ibid., 368.

43. Fernando Reati, "Argentine Political Violence and Artistic Representation in Films of the 1980s," *Latin American Literary Review* 17, no. 34 (July-December 1989): 24–39, 28.

44. In a telling example of the "fact"'s historiographic importance, María Luisa Bemberg recounts that when she showed the screenplay for her 1984 film, *Camila*, to her confessor-priest, the only point to which he objected was the unborn infant's baptism, saying that "it must be gossip, that no priest would ever do that. I told him it was in the historical record, part of the story that seemed so important that nobody had 'corrected' it." Qtd. in "Love as a Revolutionary Act," interview with Karen Jaehne, *Cineaste* 14, no. 3 (1986): 22–24, 24.

45. For a concise overview and defense of White's theories and contributions, see Keith Jenkins, "On Hayden White," in *Why History? Ethics and Postmodernity* (London: Routledge, 1999), 85–98. See also the extensive introduction to White's *Metahistory: The Historical Imagination in Nineteenth-Century Europe* (Baltimore: Johns Hopkins University Press, 1973).

46. Hayden White, "Literary Theory and Historical Writing," in *Figural Realism: Studies in the Mimesis Effect* (Baltimore: Johns Hopkins University Press, 1999), 18.

47. Ibid., 8 and 9. These operations include selection, organization, emplotment, troping, and argument.

48. Ibid., 17.

49. Indeed, and as a fine example of the fact-fiction discursive continuum, Julianello structures her Camila "history" into dramatic acts, each introduced by an epigraph from Shakespeare's *Love's Labour[']s Lost*. Julianello.

50. Ascasubi, *Aniceto el Gallo: gacetero prosista y gauchi-poeta argentino* (Paris: Paul Dupont, 1872), 391. As Brenda Werth notes, "In the literary versions of Camila O'Gorman's story, it's noteworthy the frequency with which narrators return to the place of the historic event, that is, to Santos Lugares." "Cuerpos y lugares de memoria: la genealogía de Camila O'Gorman en el teatro argentino," *Telóndefondo* 2

(December 2005) http://www.telondefondo.org/numeros-anteriores/numero2/articulo/20/cuerpos-y-lugares-de-memoria-la-genealogia-de-camila-o'gorman-en-el-teatro-argentino.html3 (accessed 27 March 2013). José Mármol's 1850s novel, *Amalia* (Paris: Casa Editorial Garnier Hermanos, 1854?), first published in serial form in Montevideo (during Mármol's exile), references the Camila-Uladislao story but through an inverted geography, by telling of the brief love affair between a young woman from Tucumán and the nephew of a prominent Buenos Aires leader.

51. Fajardo, *Camila*. In a brief but important comparison of the novel and the play, Christina Civantos notes how the Orientalist imagery employed in Pélissot's novelistic rendering of Rosas "drops out almost completely" from Fajardo's dramatic version. She suggests that Fajardo's transposition of the Orientalist French-Romantic imagery to a distinctly Argentine setting may account for the "filtering." See Civantos, *Between Argentines and Arabs: Argentine Orientalism, Arab Immigrants, and the Writing of Identity* (Albany, NY: SUNY Press, 2006), 83–84.

52. Martín Rodríguez, "El drama romántico," in *Historia del teatro argentino en Buenos Aires*, ed. Osvaldo Pellettieri (Buenos Aires: Galerna, 2005), 1: 305–28, 305.

53. See Sommer for an extended discussion of the role of allegory and the dialectics of erotics and politics in the novels of the period. Sommer's theories of narrative also apply to the period's theatrical production.

54. Abril Trigo and Graciela Míguez, "critical-analytical review" of *Camila O'Gorman*, from their "Critical Index of Uruguayan Theater" project (Ohio State University, 1976–1980) https://kb.osu.edu/dspace/html/1811/36396/Fajardo_Heraclio.html (accessed 2 December 2010).

55. Rodríguez, 324.

56. (José) Esteban Echeverría, "La cautiva," in *Rimas de Esteban Echeverría* (Buenos Aires: Imprenta Americana, 1837).

57. The fool's full name, Eusebio de la Santa Federación, is an overt reference to Rosas's "holy federation."

58. Fajardo, *Camila*, 85.

59. Fajardo, "A los manes de Camila O'Gorman" (dated 30 October 1856). English translation is credited to Jesse Hingson at http://chnm.gmu.edu/cyh/primary-sources/70 (accessed 2 December 2010).

60. José Juan Arrom, "Esquema generacional de las letras hispanoamericanas (ensayo de un método)," *Thesaurus* 17, no. 1 (1962): 123 http://cvc.cervantes.es/lengua/thesaurus/pdf/17/TH_17_001_110_0.pdf (accessed 3 December 2010).

61. Alfred Coester, *The Literary History of Spanish America* (New York: Macmillan, 1916), 175.

62. Beatriz Seibel, *Historia del teatro argentino. Desde los rituales hasta 1930* (Buenos Aires: Corregidor, 2002), 137. Osvaldo Pellettieri does not provide any Buenos Aires production information for the play in his chronology.

63. Seibel, 178.

64. Trigo and Míguez.

65. L. Mendoza Ortiz, "Advertencia," *Camila O'Gorman: drama histórico* (Buenos Aires: Impresora El Censor, 1900?), 5–6, 6. The play was staged in Argentina's interior by the Spanish-born actor Mariano Galé's company (Ibid.; Kisnerman, 27). Kisner-

man claims that the play was prohibited in Buenos Aires in deference to the feelings of both Rosas and O'Gorman descendents.

66. Mendoza Ortiz, 6.

67. Ibid., 106–7.

68. Werth, "Cuerpos," 5.

69. According to Ana M. López, "there is evidence that the first Argentine film—views of Buenos Aires—may have been produced as early as 1896." "Early Cinema and Modernity in Latin America," *Cinema Journal* 40, no.1 (Fall 2000): 51.

70. *La Revolución de Mayo*, Gallo's first film, is now considered the earliest scripted Argentine film. Most of my information regarding these early films comes from the following sources: Raúl Manrupe and María Alejandra Portela, *Un diccionario de films argentinos* (Buenos Aires: Corregidor, 1995); and López. López describes the early Argentine films like Gallo's as "proto-narratives" that were "linked to the project of modern nation building" and counted on the spectator's "extensive knowledge of the historical event being represented" (65, 63). It is likely that his *Camila* would have required a similar spectatorial competency.

71. Seibel, 619.

72. Seibel, 686. In 1967, the Smart would be renamed for Blanca Podestá and is the site of today's Multiteatro in downtown Buenos Aires.

73. Eduardo R. Rossi and Alberto Ballerini, *Camila O'Gorman: poema dramático en cinco actos, un epílogo y en verso*, in *Bambalinas* (weekly theatre magazine) 12, no. 573 (6 April 1929): 1–24.

74. Ibid., 22–23.

75. John King, "Assailing the heights of macho pictures: Women film-makers in contemporary Argentina," in *Knives and Angels: Women Writers in Latin America*, ed. Susan Bassnett (London: Zed Books, 1990), 158–70, 162. King elaborates: "Amalia has to bear the weight of [Rosas's] approval and thus remains as an ethereal cliché of perfect womanhood. In her life Camila O'Gorman subverted such neat Manicheism" (162).

76. I adhere to White's statement that "historical discourse should be considered . . . as a special kind of language use which, like metaphoric speech, symbolic language, and allegorical representation, always means more than it literally says, says something other than what it seems to mean, and reveals something about the world only at the cost of concealing something else." "Literary Theory," 7.

77. "Romantic tragedy" is sometimes used to classify "modern" tragedy that does not conform to classical Greek tragedy's norms. Such a conventional understanding appears in the following handbook entry: "It differs from the latter in its greater freedom of technique, its wider scope of theme and treatment, its greater emphasis on character (as compared with emphasis on plot), its looser structure, its freer employment of imagination, its greater variety of style, and its readiness to admit humorous and even grotesque elements." C. Hugh Holman, *A Handbook to Literature* (Indianapolis: ITT Bobbs-Merrill Educational Publishing Company, 1985), 392.

78. Jennifer Wallace, *The Cambridge Introduction to Tragedy* (Cambridge: Cambridge University Press, 2007), 1. As Sara Freeman rightfully evaluates, Wallace's book focuses more on the dramatic text than tragedy in performance. Review, *Theatre Survey* 51 (2010): 330–32, 330.

79. See, for example, Brenda Werth's otherwise perfectly viable suggestion that "[w]hen the source of the tragic representation is national and is based on a traumatic event, the spectator's emotional investment impedes the realization of catharsis and reestablishment of the social order indicated by classical tragedy." Werth, "Cuerpos," 6.

80. Hayden White, "Anomalies of Genre: The Utility of Theory and History for the Study of Literary Genres," *New Literary History* 34, no. 3 Theorizing Genres II (Summer 2003): 597–615, 600.

81. Wallace, 63.

82. Augusto Boal, *Theatre of the Oppressed*, trans. Charles A. and Maria-Odilia Leal McBride (New York: Theatre Communications Group, 1985), 44.

83. Ibid.

84. Werth cites critic Osvaldo Quiroga's review of the 1989 production. "Cuerpos," 6.

85. Enrique Molina, *Una sombra donde sueña Camila O'Gorman* (Montevideo, Uruguay: Seix Barral Biblioteca Breve, 1994); Griselda Gambaro, *La malasangre*, 57–110, in *Teatro 1* (Buenos Aires: Ediciones de la Flor, 1984).

86. Some of these influences are traced in Fernanda Vitor Bueno's dissertation, "The Myth of Camila O'Gorman in the Works of Juana Manuela Gorriti, María Luisa Bemberg, and Enrique Molina," University of Texas, 2007.

87. Ibid., 146.

88. Orlando Ocampo, "Interpretando el pasado histórico: El acto referencial en *Una sombra donde sueña Camila O'Gorman,"* Revista chilena de la literatura 40 (November 1992): 83–90, 86.

89. In one interview, Molina claims to have encountered Camila's story during a visit to an antique store and finding a "thick folder" related to Camila's arrest. He said what moved him was "that image of a woman illuminated by tragedy and poetry." Fifteen or twenty years later he would "feel the impulse" to write the novel. Interview with Raúl Vera Ocampo, "Un lenguaje nacido de la intuición y del asombro," *Zona franca* 3, nos. 13–14 (May-August 1979): 22–23, 23.

90. Vogelius (1920–1986) was no stranger to repression. The wealthy founder of the important cultural magazine *Crisis*, he was imprisoned by the dictatorship from 1977 to 1980 and saw much of his extensive collection of art, books, and historical documents stolen. His inheritors auctioned off what remained of his library in 1997.

91. See, among others, Ocampo; Marta Gallo, "La imagen de Camila," *Mujer y sociedad en América: IV Simposio Internacional*, vol. 1. (Inst. Literario y Cultural Hispánico de Baja California. Westminster, CA—Mexicali, 1988), 209–22; Susana López de Espinosa, "Discurso narrativo y representación histórica en *Una sombra donde sueña Camila O'Gorman* de Enrique Molina," *Alba de América* 12, nos. 22–23 (July 1994): 203–11; Thorpe Running, "Surrealist Poetics in Enrique Molina's *Una sombra donde sueña Camila O'Gorman,"* Chasqui 9, nos. 2–3 (February-May 1980): 23–29; and Miguel Espejo's chapter-length study, "El conocimiento poético," in *Senderos en el viento* (Puebla, Mexico: Editorial Universidad Autónoma de Puebla, 1985), 45–79.

92. I'm thinking specifically of Esteban Echeverría's late 1830s "El matadero" and Domingo Faustino Sarmiento's 1845 *Facundo*, both of which defy easy generic classification and are clearly referenced in Molina's novel. Sarmiento, *Facundo: Civiliza-*

tion and Barbarism, trans. Kathleen Ross (Berkeley, CA: University of California Press, 2003); and Echeverría, *The Slaughteryard*, trans. Norman Thomas di Giovanni and Susan Ashe (London: Friday Project, 2010).

93. Ocampo, 84.

94. Molina stated in one published interview that Camila "was passion in all its force and its complete challenge to the very special circumstances in which she lived." Jacobo Sefamí, "Itinerario de memorias: entrevista con Enrique Molina," *Chasqui* 23, no. 2 (November 1994): 143–49, 147.

95. Running, 25.

96. Ibid., 28.

97. Gallo, esp. 210–11.

98. Gwen Kirkpatrick, "The Poetics of History in *Una sombra donde sueña Camila O'Gorman*," in *The Historical Novel in Latin America*, ed. Daniel Balderston (Gaithersburg, MD: Ediciones Hispamérica, 1986), 139–50, 140.

99. Ibid., 141.

100. Ibid., 148.

101. Vitor Bueno, 151–52.

102. Kirkpatrick, 148.

103. While the two figures metonymy and synecdoche are sometimes used interchangeably as tropes synthesizing the whole and its parts, I follow Hayden White's model, in which metonymical troping is identified with the pessimistic tragic mode and a mechanistic, even reductive, search for causal laws, whereas synecdoche is linked to the optimistic comic mode and the reintegration of the parts into an organic "natural" whole. See White, *Metahistory*.

104. Kirkpatrick, 140.

105. Molina, *Una sombra*, 312.

106. This is by no means the only metonym Molina employs. For example, very suggestive use is made of *cabeza* [head], which links Rosas as dictatorial head to his decapitated enemies.

107. Diana Taylor, *Disappearing Acts: Spectacles of Gender and Nation in Argentina's Dirty War* (Durham, NC: Duke University Press, 1997), 32.

108. Francine Masiello, "Cuerpo/presencia: mujer y estado social en la narrativa argentina durante el proceso militar," *Nuevo texto crítico* 2, no. 4 (1989): 155–71, 157. As Ben Bollig points out, one exception is post post-avantgardist Néstor Perlongher, whose "hypersexual poetics" transgresses the limitations of Molina's heteronormative poetics, which Bollig also finds homophobic. See Bollig, "Néstor Perlongher and the Avant-Garde: Privileged Interlocutors and Inherited Techniques," *Hispanic Review* 73, no. 2 (Spring 2005): 157–84. I return to Perlongher's texts in future chapters, but for now I refer the reader to his poem "Para Camila O'Gorman," originally published in 1987 (*Poemas completos [1980–1992]* [Buenos Aires: Seix Barral, 1997], 77; first published in *Alambres* [Buenos Aires: Ultimo Reino, 1987]). An English translation by Liz Henry can be found at her blog: http://bookmaniac.org/poetry/nestor-perlongher/para-camila-ogorman/ (accessed 5 January 2011).

109. Susana López de Espinosa notes one error: Molina writes that Camila was seventeen (and not seven) years old in 1835 (205). A similar counting mistake occurs when the narrator claims that Camila and Ladislao lived in Goya only slightly over

four months, when, according to the sentence immediately following, they spent over five months, from 6 January to 16 June 1848. While these may seem to be minor errors, it merits noting that they were not corrected in subsequent editions.

110. In a mid-1990s interview with Gould, Molina emphatically and tellingly states that Bemberg's film has "very little in common with my book," describing the film as "completely realistic and naturalistic, fixed entirely in reality. Her Camila doesn't have the same aura. My Camila is the incarnation of liberty, of dreams and, above all, of love." Gould, 124.

111. Gambaro noted, "The playwright does not make his own confession alone." Griselda Gambaro, "Los rostros del exilio," *Alba de América* 7, nos. 12–13 (July 1989): 31–35, 35.

112. Griselda Gambaro, *Real envido* in *Teatro 1* (Buenos Aires: Ediciones de la Flor, 1984), 6–55.

113. Griselda Gambaro, *La malasangre* in *Teatro 1* (Buenos Aires: Ediciones de la Flor, 1984), 57–110.

114. See Ana Elena Puga, *Memory, Allegory, and Testimony in South American Theater: Upstaging Dictatorship* (New York: Routledge, 2008), 168, for the account. Brenda Werth also provides an overview of the events in *Theatre, Performance, and Memory Politics in Argentina* (New York: Palgrave Macmillan, 2010), 100–7. Their versions of the production's history coincide with those of published interviews with Gambaro, as well as my own personal conversations with Gambaro and director Laura Yusem in 1992.

115. Werth, *Theatre*, 101.

116. Ibid. In one conversation, Gambaro told me that Yusem also intervened, walking over and planting her high heel on the gun, stating that there was no place in the theatre for firearms. Personal conversation, 1992.

117. Werth, *Theatre*, 101.

118. Qtd. in Puga, 168.

119. Puga, 171. It also calls to mind the "topos of return" that Werth argues is present in the period's cultural production. Werth, *Theatre*, 103.

120. Marguerite Feitlowitz translates Juan Pedro's last name as "Paradise."

121. Griselda Gambaro, *Bad Blood*, trans. Marguerite Feitlowitz (Woodstock, IL: Dramatic Publishing, 1994), 51.

122. Ibid., 68.

123. Puga, 169.

124. Mona Moncalvillo, "Griselda Gambaro: la autora de *La malasangre*," *Humor* 90 (September 1982): 46–51, 50.

125. Puga, 171. For some of these details Puga draws upon her personal interview with Galán.

126. Werth, *Theatre*, 106.

127. I think particularly of Argentine historian Tulio Halperín Donghi's widely cited essay, "El presente transforma el pasado: el impacto del reciente terror en la imagen de la historia argentina," in *Ficción y política: la narrativa argentina durante el proceso militar*, ed. Daniel Balderston (Buenos Aires: Alianza, 1987), 71–95.

128. Gambaro, *Bad Blood*, 69.

129. David William Foster, "Two Feminist Dramatic Versions of Patriarchal Re-

pression," in *Violence in Argentine Literature: Cultural Responses to Tyranny* (Columbia: University of Missouri Press, 1995), 138. Foster devotes much of the chapter to *La malasangre*.

130. See, for example, Diana Taylor's afterword to Marguerite Feitlowitz's translations of three Gambaro plays: "Violent Displays: Griselda Gambaro and Argentina's Drama of Disappearance," in *Information for Foreigners: Three Plays by Griselda Gambaro* (Evanston, IL: Northwestern University Press, 1992).

131. Puga, 177.

132. Soledad Silveyra (b. 1952) has enjoyed a near-constant presence in Argentine film, television, and theatre since her 1964 TV soap opera debut at the age of twelve. By the early 1970s, she was a popular telenovela star but worked very little in television and film during the early years of the dictatorship. She is still one of Argentina's most recognizable actresses, with a career that runs from low to high brow, including hosting the country's version of the reality television hit *Big Brother* and performing in the two controversial Gambaro plays of the early 1980s.

133. Lautaro Murúa (Tacna, Chile 1926–Madrid, Spain 1995) began his acting career in the University of Chile's Experimental Theatre before moving in 1954 to Buenos Aires, where he continued acting in theatre and especially in Argentina's flourishing 1960s film industry. (He would go on to make over eighty films.) After receiving death threats, Murúa went into exile in Spain in 1976, returning to Buenos Aires in 1982 and working in film and theatre before returning to Spain in 1992.

134. See, in addition to the critical studies cited in this chapter, Sandra Messinger Cypess, "La dinámica del monstruo en las obras dramáticas de Griselda Gambaro," in *Ensayos críticos sobre Griselda Gambaro y José Triana*, ed., intro., and interviews Diana Taylor (Ottawa: Girol Books, 1989), 52–64; Kirsten F. Nigro, "Discurso femenino y el teatro de Griselda Gambaro" in *Ensayos críticos*, 65–73; Gail A. Bulman, "El grito infinito: ecos coloniales en *La malasangre* de Griselda Gambaro," *Symposium* 48, no. 4 (Winter 1995): 271–76; and Eric J. Nuetzel, "Of Melons, Heads, and Blood: Psychosexual Fascism in Griselda Gambaro's *Bad Blood*," *Modern Drama* 39, no. 3 (1996): 457–64.

135. Moncalvillo, 50.

136. A primordial version of this comparative analysis was published as "*Camila* y *Una pasión sudamericana*: Bemberg, Monti y un paraíso perdido argentino," in *Segundas Jornadas Internacionales de Literatura Argentina-Comparatística. Actas* (Buenos Aires: University of Buenos Aires, 1998), 102–10.

137. Steven Kovacs notes that Argentine film production dropped "from forty features per year in the early seventies to thirty-three in 1975 and twenty-one in 1976." Kovacs, "Screening the Movies in Argentina," *New Boston Review* 3, no. 3 (December 1977): 19–20. We should remember that, as John King stresses, film audiences during the 1970s and 1980s were shrinking "in every other part of the world." King, "Assailing the heights," 159. Clara Levín states that some seven hundred films were banned during the dictatorship. "Representations of Patriarchy and Censorship in Argentine Post-dictatorship Cinema" BA thesis (University of Cambridge, 1998) http://www.otrocampo.com/1/dictator.html (accessed 22 December 2004, no longer active).

138. Ricardo Monti, *Una pasión sudamericana*, first published in *Teatro/Celcit* 2, no. 3 (Fall 1992): 67–95; revised and republished in *Una pasión sudamericana. Una historia*

tendenciosa, ed. Osvaldo Pellettieri (Ottawa: Girol Books, 1993), 31–89; republished in *Antología del teatro argentino*, ed. Gerardo Fernández (Madrid: Centro de Documentación Teatral, Ministerio de Cultura, 1993). Unless otherwise noted, all subsequent quotations are from the published English translation, based, at Monti's request, on yet another revised but unpublished version. *A South American Passion-Play*, in *Reason Obscured: Nine Plays by Ricardo Monti*, trans. and ed. Jean Graham-Jones (Lewisburg, PA: Bucknell University Press, 2004), 207–45.

139. Indeed, Bemberg made this denunciation explicit in an interview: "What we have in *Camila* is a young woman who dares to oppose all three pillars." Qtd. in Jaehne, 22.

140. See Diana Quattrocchi-Woisson, *Los males de la memoria: Historia y política en la Argentina* (Buenos Aires: Emecé Editores, 1995).

141. The assertion comes from a personal conversation (1992) with Argentine playwright Eduardo Pavlovsky and can be observed in the majority of his plays created during the 1970s and 1980s.

142. As John King notes, the Bembergs arrived from Germany in 1850 and quickly married into local *criollo* "aristocracy." "By the time the fourth generation of the family had lived in Argentina (María Luisa's generation), the Bembergs were firmly established through marriage and through a diversified fortune" and most closely identified with the Quilmes beer company, which the first Bemberg established in 1869. John King, "María Luisa Bemberg and Argentine Culture," in *An Argentine Passion: María Luisa Bemberg and her Films*, ed. John King, Sheila Whitaker, and Rosa Bosch (London: Verso, 2000), 1–32, 4. Bemberg first worked in the theatre (cofounding the Teatro del Globo, which ran for five years) before turning to writing, which in turn led her to film, first as a screenwriter and then as a director.

143. King notes that Bemberg also worked with foreign coproducers, another rarity at that time in Latin American film.

144. Gould states that Bemberg "circumvented the censors by publicly announcing the project without having obtained official permission" (3). Gould's thesis includes an annotated retranslation of the screenplay as well as multiple interviews.

145. Among the many interviews with Bemberg which provide the information for this account, see, for example, Jaehne, and Caleb Bach, "María Luisa Bemberg Tells the Untold," *Américas* 46, no.2 (1994): 21–23. In another interview, Bemberg rather enigmatically suggests that having Camila seduce Ladislao "helped [her] with the Church." "María Luisa Bemberg," *Daily Telegraph*, 9 June 1995, 27.

146. King, "María Luisa Bemberg and Argentine Culture," 24.

147. Bach, 23. John King recounts the received statistic slightly differently, saying that "one girl in every six born in that period was named Camila." "María Luisa Bemberg and Argentine Culture," 23.

148. Foster, *Contemporary Argentine Cinema*, 16.

149. Some historical characters are named while others—such as Reyes—are identified by their function or station.

150. See, particularly, two essays by Bruce Williams: "In the Realm of the Feminine: María Luisa Bemberg's *Camila* at the Edge of the Gaze," *Chasqui* 25, no. 1 (May 1996): 62–71; and "The Reflection of a Blinded Gaze: María Luisa Bemberg, Filmmaker,"

in *A Woman's Gaze: Latin American Women Artists*, ed. Marjorie Agosín (Fredonia, NY: White Pine Press, 1998), 171–90.

151. William Childers provides a detailed analysis of these scenes in "La pierna quebrada: The Female Body and the Pre-Cinematic Gaze in *Tristana* and *Camila*," special issue on Cinematic and Literary Representations of Spanish and Latin American Themes, *Chasqui* 34, no. 2 (2005): 184–99.

152. Producer Lita Stantic recalls that "the team had to travel to five different locations we chose within a radius of 120 kilometers from the capital." Lita Stantic, interview, "Working with María Luisa Bemberg," in *An Argentine Passion*, 33.

153. Foster considers the plot to be a variation on the folkloric motif of Beauty (Camila) and the Beast (her father, and by extension the entire society). *Contemporary Argentine Cinema*, 23–25.

154. Ibid., 23. I would argue that Rosas is only as remote as Christ, given that both appear consistently throughout the film in iconographic imagery. There are multiple close-ups and pans of Rosas's portraits, much like the multiple crucifixes displayed. Indeed, the iconographic parallel is made overt when Rosas's portrait is prominently displayed inside the church where Ladislao delivers his "near-subversive" homily.

155. Bach, 23. For a detailed analysis of the film as politicized and feminized melodrama, see Stephen M. Hart, "Bemberg's Winks and Camila's Sighs: Melodramatic Encryption in *Camila*," *Revista Canadiense de Estudios Hispánicos* 27, no. 1 (Fall 2002): 75–85.

156. An oft-cited example of critical dismissal comes from Enrique Colina and Daniel Díaz Torres's essay, "Ideology of Melodrama in Old Latin American Cinema," in *Latin American Film Makers and the Third Cinema*, ed. Zuzana M. Pick (Ottawa: Carleton University Film Studies Program, 1978), 50 and 53, quoted by John King in *Magical Reels: A History of Cinema in Latin America* (London: Verso, 2000 [1990]), 38:

> Commercial Argentine cinema, impregnated with the prevailing pessimism, translated the collective state of hopelessness into a sentimental explosion, thus becoming a hindrance to the development of the people's political consciousness. Taking refuge in a frustrated skeptical individualism, promoting a fatalistic vision of existence and offering eternal sadness as an element of the Argentine character, this cinema is the refuse, the excrescence of a reactionary populism . . . God, Fatherland and Home make up the inseparable trinity of social equilibrium in these films.

157. King, "Assailing the Heights," 163.

158. Ibid., 164. Tim Dirks defines melodrama films as "a sub-type of drama films, characterized by a plot to appeal to the heightened emotions of the audience. Melodrama, a combination of drama and melos (music), literally means 'play with music.' The themes of dramas, the oldest literary and stage art form, were exaggerated within melodramas, and the liberal use of music often enhanced their emotional plots. Often, film studies criticism used the term 'melodrama' pejoratively to connote an unrealistic, pathos-filled, campy tale of romance or domestic situations with stereotypical characters (often including a central female character) that would directly appeal

to feminine audiences." http://www.filmsite.org/melodramafilms.html (accessed 5 January 2011). It merits adding that Bemberg's film makes very careful use of music, in both the score and the period songs performed by the actors. See Gould's interview with the film's composer Luis María Serra for a detailed description. 111–15.

159. Bemberg, qtd. in Jaehne, 23. Like the kittens drowned by her father in the film's opening minutes and the cows butchered while the lovers escape, Camila is a slaughtered innocent.

160. King, "Assailing the Heights," 164.

161. See Currie K. Thompson, "The Films of María Luisa Bemberg and the Postmodern Aesthetic," in *La Chispa 95: Selected Proceedings*, ed. Gilbert Paolini (New Orleans: Tulane University/Louisiana Conference on Hispanic Languages and Literatures, 1995), 367–76.

162. Nissa Torrents, "One woman's cinema: Interview with María Luisa Bemberg," in *Knives and Angels*, 171–75, 174.

163. "Melodrama is a very tricky genre [. . .] So I had all those little tricks, such as the handkerchief, the gold coin, the priest who is sick with love, and the thunder when God gets angry. They're all like winks at the audience." Bemberg, qtd. in John King and Nissa Torrents, *The Garden of Forking Paths: Argentine Cinema* (London: British Film Institute, 1988), 117; and S[heila] Whitaker, "Pride and Prejudice: María Luisa Bemberg," *Monthly Film Bulletin* 54 (4 October 1987): 293; repr. in King and Torrents, 115–21.

164. Barbara Morris, "La mujer vista por la mujer: el discurso fílmico de María Luisa Bemberg," in *Discurso femenino actual*, ed. Adelaida López de Martínez (San Juan: Editorial de la Universidad de Puerto Rico, 1995), 253–67, 256. In an interview made on the occasion of the film's New York premiere, Bemberg celebrated *Camila* as a "woman's film": "I'm elated when people say they can tell it was directed by a woman because I believe we see things in a different way from men. If a man had directed *Camila*, I'm sure it would have been the story of a gentle innocent seduced by a libertine priest. My story is about a passionate woman's intellectual sexual seduction of a man she found morally desirable." Qtd. in Carrie Rickey, "*Camila*: Argentina's Forbidden Story," *New York Times,* 7 April 1985.

165. Williams, "In the Realm of the Feminine," provides a persuasive case for the role the various physical senses play in Bemberg's filmic creation and destruction of the lovers' relationship.

166. Qtd. in Jaehne, 24.

167. For a brief overview of Western European melodrama and romantic tragedy, see Paul Kuritz, *The Making of Theatre History* (Englewood Cliffs, NJ: Prentice Hall, 1988), especially the chapter on the "Romantic Theatre," 276–78.

168. The film has other characters who, like Camila, question what is going on around them, but, unlike her, they fail to rebel: her mother and brother Eduardo, the Corrientes commander who gives the couple the chance to leave, and the soldiers who initially refuse to shoot the condemned.

169. Peter Schumann, *Historia del cine latinoamericano* (Buenos Aires: Legasa, 1987), 44.

170. Bruce Williams, "In the Realm of the Feminine," 69.

171. Foster, *Contemporary Argentine Cinema*, 16.

172. Mary Ann Doane notes: "'Voice-off' refers to instances in which we hear the voice of a character who is not visible within the frame. Yet the film establishes, by means of previous shots or other contextual determinants, the character's 'presence' in the space of the scene, in the diegesis." Voice-overs, in contrast, include a narrator's commentary, an internal monologue, or the voice of a character narrating in flashback. "The Voice in the Cinema: The Articulation of Body and Space," *Yale French Studies* 60, Cinema/Sound (1980): 33–50, 37, reprinted in *Narrative, Apparatus, Ideology* (New York: Columbia University Press, 1986), 335–48.

173. Foster, *Contemporary Argentine Cinema*, 25.

174. I have translated all but one of Monti's eleven original plays into English and quote from those translations whenever possible. *Reason Obscured: Nine Plays by Ricardo Monti*, trans. and ed. Jean Graham-Jones (Lewisburg, PA: Bucknell University Press, 2004); *Apocalypse Tomorrow, The Mercurian: A Theatrical Translation Review* 2, no. 1 (2009): 9–19. The published English translation of *Una pasión suadmericana* was based on a later (1999) version, at Monti's request. In this later version, Monti eliminated the fool Biguá as well as the characters of the British minister Canning, the chained criminal Barrabás, and one of the scribes.

175. Monti, *A South American Passion-Play*, in *Reason Obscured*, 208. By setting his play on a ranch and refusing to stage Camila's execution, Monti further confounds audience expectations of the Santos Lugares yard as site of "truth," historical authenticity, and the termination point of Camila's story, as nearly all other Camila-inspired artistic works do.

176. Brenda Werth describes its imaginary as "an impressive borderless memoryscape." Even though Werth examines in detail the embodiment and disembodiment of history, her project focuses primarily on the Brigadier as a Rosas-like figure rather than Camila. *Theatre*, 122.

177. Qtd. in Graham-Jones, "Introduction," in *Reason Obscured*, 7–35, 30.

178. In an interview preceding the 2005 revival, Monti takes pains to note that the play is not "historical theatre" but rather it is based on a "major mythical event." Qtd. in "'Una pasión sudamericana' Tragedia masculina," *La Nación*, 24 September 2005 http://www.lanacion.com.ar/nota.asp?nota_id=741336 (accessed 10 July 2010).

179. Rosas was known for having his own "crazies," the best known of which— Eusebio de la Santa Federación—appears in several of the earlier Camila plays.

180. Osvaldo Pellettieri, "Ricardo Monti: de la rectificación de la historia a la historia propia," in *Teatro argentino contemporáneo 1980–1990: crisis, transición y cambio* (Buenos Aires: Galerna, 1994), 87–108, 93.

181. See Paul Johnson, *The Birth of the Modern: World Society 1815–1830* (New York: HarperCollins, 1991).

182. Qtd. in Graham-Jones, "Introduction," 30.

183. Osvaldo Pellettieri says the production ran for six weeks, with scant audience attendance, "Ricardo Monti,"102. It's also worth noting, as Pellettieri does, that *Una pasión sudamericana* was Monti's first play to be staged in an "official" theatre, which almost certainly affected audience profile and response. The Argentine critic further notes that the play was "incorrectly" interpreted by spectators and critics from a "re-

alistic" aesthetic. Finally, Pellettieri writes about the difficult timing of the premiere, as audiences identified the Rosas-like caudillo with just-elected president Menem and thus tried to interpret the play in light of Menem's populist anticultural attitude. For another overview of the critical reception of the 1989 production, see Werth, *Theatre*, 119.

184. Monti, *Finland*, in *Reason Obscured*, 395.

185. The other actors were Andrea Bonelli and Ignacio (Nacho) Gadano as the twins, and Jorge Rod as the aide-de-camp.

186. See the Cervantes National Theatre website for a description of the eight hundred-seat theatre http://www.teatrocervantes.gov.ar/sitio/site/teatro/historia.php#h5 (accessed 10 July 2010).

187. Milton Loayza terms this audience doubling a "mirror vision" through which the Brigadier can never see himself clearly. Milton Loayza, "The Plays of Ricardo Monti and the Production of Space," PhD dissertation, CUNY Graduate Center, 2008, 245.

188. Qtd. in Camilo Sánchez, "La voz de Rosas fue lo primero que encontré," *Clarín*, 15 October 2005 http://www.teatroenmiami.net/modules.php?name=News&file=print&sid=3172 (accessed 10 July 2010).

189. http://www.teatrocervantes.gov.ar/sitio/site/programacion/obra3.php?obra=obra3 (accessed 10 July 2010). Further illustrative of this general impression was the summary provided at the popular website Alternativa Teatral: "Ricardo Monti's play is a metaphor about our own country, of the breaches and fratricidal battles, of our identity's construction on top of the terrible paradox: civilization or barbarity." http://www.alternativateatral.com/obra5212-una-pasion-sudamericana (accessed 10 July 2010).

190. Qtd. in Graham-Jones, "Introduction," 33.

191. The risks involved in such an "edgy" positioning can be seen in an essay like Richard Curry's "La estructuración del discurso fílmico en *Camila* de María Luisa Bemberg: 'filtros,'" in which the author declares, for example, "Throughout the film, the only way in which woman is realized as a person is through her sensitivity to the maternal instinct," which "elevates woman above (if not physically, then, morally) the masculine world." While laudable in its attempts to read the film through its various "filters," the article's language objectifies Camila, once again. *Letras femeninas* 18, nos. 1–2 (1992): 11–23, 15.

192. Chris Rojek, *Celebrity* (London: Reaktion Books, 2001), 18.

193. Ibid., 19.

194. Ibid., 20, 18.

195. For example, two highly regarded English-language scholars of the period, David Rock and Nicolás Shumway, make no mention of Camila in their accounts of this period. Camila's story is recounted in slightly over two pages by John Lynch in his biography of Rosas. Lynch's frequently cited text is unfortunately marred by an uncritical reliance on partisan accounts and the use of fictionalized inventions— including John Masefield's extensive poem, which Lynch acknowledges as "fact, imagination, and inaccuracy" but nevertheless incorporates into his narrative—as historical documents.

CHAPTER 2

1. Tim Rice, "Introduction," in *Evita: The Legend of Eva Perón (1919–1952),* Andrew Lloyd Webber and Rice (New York: Avon, 1978), n.p.

2. Rice mentions only the one 1974 visit, claiming he did not conduct any "major" research but wrote the initial synopsis of *Evita* while in Buenos Aires. Others state that he was in Argentina twice, first in 1973 and returning later with Lloyd Webber. See "Historia de un esfuerzo," appended to the Spanish-language edition of *Opera Evita (Versión en castellano. Texto íntegro de la Opera y documentos biográficos)* (Buenos Aires: CS Ediciones, 1997), 99–117, 103. The text also notes that Rice's visit(s) coincided with Perón's triumphant return to Argentina and intimates that Rice saw in Perón's third wife, María Estela (Isabelita), an "Evita II." Ibid.

3. My favorite description of the Rice-Lloyd Webber rock-opera "formula" comes from Argentine theatre critic Claudio España: "an ambiguous genre that allows for wide vocal registers and a scenic response to West End and Broadway audience requirements: individual melodrama; lyricism taken to the refined point of moaning romanticism; the drama of an identity reclaimed—the lack of a father and Evita's bitterness toward the bourgeoisie—in opera; and its recuperation within a collective epic, as in pre-Christian theatre." "Sueño de futuro convertido en mito," *La Nación,* 20 February 1997.

4. Musical director Juan José García Caffi "Argentinized" *Evita* by changing the instrumentation to include the *bandoneón* (a cousin of the concertina) and acoustic guitar; adding motifs drawn from such regional musical forms as *milongas*; and transforming Magaldi's first-act rumba into a tango. See "Historia de un esfuerzo," 114.

5. Both Paloma San Basilio and Valeria Lynch sang "Don't Cry for Me Argentina" in Buenos Aires. Lynch later performed this song (and "Buenos Aires") in a revue produced by noted comics Jorge Porcel and Alberto Olmedo in Buenos Aires's commercial Metropolitan Theatre.

6. A 1985 Buenos Aires "underground" show featured drag performers lip-synching tunes from the Rice-Lloyd Webber rock-opera, using recordings from British, U.S., Spanish, and Brazilian productions. According to two very negative press reviews, the show also included impersonations of popular Argentine stars, Edith Piaf, and even Disney's Cruella de Vil. See Luis Mazas, "Versión de 'Evita' con un pobre nivel," *Clarín,* 4 September 1985; and Néstor Romano, "Los transformistas de bajo nivel que pretenden ensuciar a Perón y Evita," *Flash,* 10 September 1985.

7. *Evita* opened at London's Adelphi Theatre on 21 June 2006. The first major revival since the 1978 Prince production, it was directed by Michael Grandage with choreography by Rob Ashford and design by Christopher Oram. The production included the song "You Must Love Me," written for the Parker film. Elena Roger (b. 1974), well known to Buenos Aires audiences for her performances in local productions of *Nine, Beauty and the Beast, Les Misérables, La fiaca,* and *Saturday Night Fever,* achieved even greater recognition for her award-winning performance in the 2003 musical *Mina, che cosa sei* (based on the life of Italian pop singer Mina Anna Mazzini and cocreated with director Valeria Ambrosio). Roger has continued on the London stages: as the Italian flight attendant in Matthew Warchus's 2007 retooling of Marc

Camoletti's French comedy *Boeing-Boeing* and in the title role in the 2008 Donmar Warehouse production of Pam Gems's *Piaf*. She has also recorded an album—*Vientos del sur*—of tango-inspired songs. For an overview of Roger's pre-London career, see her interview with Moira Soto, "Nacida para cantar y bailar," *Página/12* supplement *Las 12*, 5 December 2003 http://www.pagina12.com.ar/diario/suplementos/las12/13-894-2003-12-07.html (accessed 15 January 2008). The New York revival was Roger's Broadway début.

8. There have been local amateur and semiprofessional English-language productions of *Evita*, including one directed by Peter McFarlane at St. Andrew's Scots School in the early 1990s. I thank Elisa Legon for bringing this production to my attention.

9. *Hair* premiered in Buenos Aires in 1971 and ran for two years in the Teatro Argentino. Its producer, Alejandro Romay, bought the rights to *Jesus Christ Superstar (JCSS)* and began rehearsals with a cast of eighty-six (chosen from over three thousand aspirants). Andrés Avellaneda has documented the protests surrounding the first Argentine production of *JCSS*. Although Romay attempted to avoid religious controversy by emphasizing the text's sociopolitical elements, the theatre's burning forced him to cancel the production just before its scheduled May 1973 opening. In 1974, there were attempts to bomb the two movie theatres where the film version was slated to premiere. See Avellaneda, *Censura, autoritarismo y cultura: Argentina 1960–1983*, 2 vols. (Buenos Aires: Centro Editor de América Latina, 1986), 1:110–11; 114. *JCSS* would not see its Argentine premiere until the 1989 La Plata production, which received lukewarm response. The 1993 Buenos Aires production, sung entirely in English, was a great commercial hit.

10. In addition to those studied here, plays purportedly about Eva Perón include: *Eva Duarte en el espíritu de Eva Perón* [Eva Duarte in the Spirit of Eva Perón] (Cargasachi/Jamandreu, 1981); *Evita la mujer del siglo* [Evita the Woman of the Century] (Pérez Pardella/Lo Cane, 1984/1985); *Evita* (opera, Risso, 1990); *Compañera* [Comrade] (Loisi/Rubertino, 1994); *. . . cariñosamente Evita* [. . . Affectionately, Evita] (Cabrera, 1996); *La Duarte* [The Duarte Woman] (mise-en-scène, Vladimivsky, 2004); *Las 20 y 25 . . . Los mucamos de Evita* [8:25 p.m. . . . , Evita's Servants] (Suárez, 2005); *La eterna* [The Eternal (Woman)] (Giacometto and Suárez, 2005); *Eva Duarte, el musical* (Remón, 2008); *El evangelio de Evita* [The Gospel of Evita] (Balmaceda, 2009); and *Inevitable* (Mitre, 2011). Among films we find Amadori's 1952 documentary, *Eva Perón inmortal* [Immortal Eva Perón] (1990); *Una mujer, un pueblo* [One Woman, One People] (Serrano/Schroeder, 1970; banned in 1971 and repremiered in 1982); *El misterio Eva Perón* [The Eva Perón Mystery] ("semi-documentary," Demicheli, 1987); and *Evita: la tumba sin paz* [The Unquiet Tomb] (documentary, Bauer, 1997). As recently as 2011, two new films were released: *Juan y Eva* [Juan and Eva], directed by Paula de Luque and starring stage actor Osmar Núñez in an award-winning performance as Perón with Julieta Díaz as Eva; and *Eva de la Argentina* [Argentina's Eva], Argentina's first "political animated film," directed by journalist María Seoane (who cowrote the screenplay with Carlos Castro and Graciela Maglie) and animated by Francisco Solano López. These lists are by no means exhaustive. Eva Perón, as secondary character, appears in far too many plays, films, and television programs to be listed here; and it should be remembered that Eva Duarte herself performed in multiple radio-

dramas, plays, and films. I remain indebted to Beatriz Seibel for sharing her initial compilation with me.

11. Guevara's *Eva* would be eclipsed five years later—in popular success if not in critical opinion—by the super-production *Drácula*. In 1991, Pepe Cibrián's locally created and produced musical played in arenas to nearly four hundred thousand spectators during its 396 performances (both in Buenos Aires and on tour throughout the country), a box-office record for Argentine theatre.

12. I have read about, but have not been able to locate, a video recording of the 1986 *Eva* that was broadcast on Spanish television.

13. Marta E. Savigliano, in her thoughtful and provocative analysis of the Parker film, calls *Evita* "a melodramatic remythologization" and "a soap-operatic moral tale," with Evita-as-femme-fatale meeting her requisite destruction. While Savigliano's comments might be applied to the theatrical production (and contain fascinating insights into how globalization can erase the local and the national), they center on the 1996 film and its star, Madonna. Marta E. Savigliano, "*Evita*: The Globalization of a National Myth," *Latin American Perspectives* 24, no. 6 (November 1997): 156–72, 156, 164.

14. As España points out, it was Harold Prince who turned Rice's Che-as-people's-collective into a "metonymy" of the sixties (and possibly Peronist) left. Prince's interpretation would be echoed in most of the international productions of *Evita*. See "Sueño de futuro." In the 1996 film, Guevara is dehistoricized, as Argentine critic Fernando López notes, generalized into "some ubiquitous and reflective man of the people who will not be fooled." See "Lo inevitable de Evita," *La Nación*, 20 February 1997. Savigliano calls the film's Che "a transclass cultural translator whose ideology and interests can only be pinned down in his gender-specificity and heterosexual appetites" (157). Critics have derided Che's anachronistic 1960s revolutionary appearance in a rock opera whose action barely spans the first half of the twentieth century. I am more disturbed by *Evita*'s oversimplified dismissal of Peronism as simply "common or garden fascism" (Rice's phrase), with no interest in the complexities of Perón's Justicialist Party, a social and political movement that has included factions from the right, the center, the left, and just about anywhere else one might look. Other errors of fact and expression are contained in Rice's account (and found their way into the rock opera, to the ongoing consternation of Argentines and Argentinists alike). In the 2012 Broadway revival, Ricky Martin played the role, in a more period-specific and far less incendiary characterization.

15. The quotation comes from Andrew Lloyd Webber's essay, "The Music of Evita," in *Evita: The Legend*.

16. This is the "infamous decade" of 1930s Buenos Aires, whose poverty, corruption, and political fraud are captured in the beggars' mixed tribute: "Buenos Aires, we beggars love you, / and, if you kill us with hunger, we'll be screwed." I consulted the complete libretto at Nacha Guevara's website http://www.geocities.com/lanacha-guevara/ (accessed 15 May 2003, no longer available).

17. *La Nación*, 7 May 1986.

18. Nor is Mario *Evita*'s fictitious union leader Dolan Getta, who, at the end of act one, leads the Peronist "mob" in calling for "a new Argentina." Rice acknowledges that Getta is a stand-in for a real-life union organizer such as Cipriano Reyes, the head of the meat workers who ran afoul of the Peróns in 1945 and spent the next several

years in prison. Rice notes, "We cannot really recall why we did not use the name of a real union man such as Cipriano Reyes." See *Evita: The Legend*. For a brief historical account of Reyes's relationship with the Peróns, see David Rock, *Argentina 1516–1987. From Spanish Colonization to Alfonsín* (Berkeley: University of California Press, 1987), 282 passim. At *Eva*'s premiere, one Buenos Aires theatre reviewer noted, "Mario never separates himself from Eva Perón; more than her secretary, he attempts to be the voice of reason in the middle of a maze of power struggles. He believes in her and in her husband, but never blindly, which at one point even requires his own distancing [from Eva]. Perhaps he represents what purity or—if you prefer—sincerity can be found in a political movement." *La Nación*, 7 May 1986. Indeed, Mario is dismissed—midway through the second act—after asking Eva to release a jailed union leader critical of Perón administration. He and Eva reconcile when he comes to visit her on her deathbed.

19. As Rice puts it, "[T]he only political messages we hope emerge from the work are that extremists are dangerous and attractive ones even more so." See *Evita: The Legend*.

20. *Eva*'s script is not without structural problems. The second act seems to fall into a narrative trap of attempting to shoehorn a biographical checklist of Eva's overwork, illness, and death into little over an hour; the first act, in contrast, takes its time, tracing Eva's optimistic arrival to 1930s Buenos Aires and ending with the night of 17 October 1945, when she first claimed the political spotlight, helping to organize the mass rally leading to Juan's release from prison and his assumption of power.

21. Julie M. Taylor contends that these two, ostensibly contrasting, myths actually share underlying structures and values that relate to "the symbolism of female power." She goes on to posit a third myth: "Revolutionary Eva." *Eva Perón: The Myths of a Woman* (Chicago: University of Chicago Press, 1979), 9.

22. In fact, Rice suggests that *Evita*'s success triggered the British edition of Main's biography, which he deems "superb" and "definitive." See *Evita: The Legend*. That said, Rice's bibliography overlaps significantly with Main's. See Marysa Navarro, "La Mujer Maravilla ha sido siempre argentina y su verdadero nombre es Evita," in *Evita: mitos y representaciones*, ed. Navarro (Buenos Aires: Fondo de Cultura Económica, 2002), 38–39. Main published the biography pseudonymously after Eva's death. See María Flores [Mary Main], *The Woman with the Whip* (Garden City, NY: Doubleday, 1952). In her biography of Eva Perón, author Alejandra Dujovne Ortiz refers to Main as "the most ferocious and unforgiving of her biographers." *Eva Perón: A Biography*, trans. Shawn Fields (New York: St. Martin's Griffin, 1996), 26. Navarro justifiably pronounces *The Woman with the Whip* seriously defective, "ill-intentioned, gossipy, and without documented proof" (30). Yet despite the obvious shortcomings of the biography and its author, *The Woman with the Whip* continues to be cited in English-language texts as a reliable source, thus perpetuating the anti-Peronist position of most English-language cultural products, *Evita* included.

23. Lloyd Webber claims that he did not "self-consciously ape Latin American styles" except for the inclusion of the harp, because (even though the harp is found in Argentina only on the Paraguayan border) "it seems such an evocative sound of Latin America." See "The Music of Evita," in *Evita: The Legend*. We should also bear in mind that Britain and Argentina share a long history of mutual cultural admiration

and politico-economic frustration (of which perhaps the most extreme example is 1982's Falklands/Malvinas War).

24. "De Valeria Lynch a Miss Piggy," *La Nación*, 20 February 1997.

25. Foucault, "Nietzsche, Genealogy, History," in *Language, Counter-Memory, Practice*, ed. Donald F. Bouchard (Ithaca, NY: Cornell University Press, 1977), 139–64, 145.

26. Ibid., 148.

27. Regarding transculturative theories (which I consciously render plural), see Fernando Ortiz, *Contrapunteo cubano del tabaco y el azúcar* (Caracas, Venezuela: Biblioteca Ayacucho, 1978); Angel Rama, *Writing Across Cultures: Narrative Transculturation in Latin America*, trans. David L. Frye (Durham, NC: Duke University Press, 2012); and Néstor García Canclini, *Hybrid Cultures: Strategies for Entering and Leaving Modernity*, trans. Christopher L. Chiappari and Silvia L. López (Minneapolis: University of Minnesota Press, 1995). For an early reevaluation of transculturation, see Román de la Campa, *Latin Americanism* (Minneapolis: University of Minnesota Press, 1999). For its preliminary application to Latin American theatre, see Diana Taylor, "Transculturating Transculturation," *Performing Arts Journal* 38 (1991): 90–104. Ramian critical transculturation has been justifiably criticized for operating culturally "from above" and thus ending up as "a historical self-subjecting to Eurocentric modernity." John Beverley, *Testimonio: On the Politics of Truth* (Minneapolis: University of Minnesota Press, 2004), 69; Alberto Moreiras, *The Exhaustion of Difference: The Politics of Latin American Cultural Studies* (Durham, NC: Duke University Press, 2001), 188. Moreira's revised understanding of a "de-oriented" transculturation, always already happening everywhere, helps us to trace some of the complexities at work but often critically overlooked in femiconic performances (188).

28. The River Plate Viceroyalty was formed in 1776, and the earliest documented play (*Siripo*) dates from 1783. Scholars still debate the anonymous *Amor de la estanciera*'s date and place of performance. While early scholarship dated the play's composition to sometime between 1778 and 1792 and located its premiere at the Ranchería Theatre (destroyed by fire in 1792), today it is believed that it was written later in the colonial period and possibly performed privately.

29. Much like other River Plate *sainetes*, *El amor de la estanciera* pokes equal fun at the cultural clashes between the local *criollos* and newly arrived immigrants. Chepa's two rivals, Juancho Perucho and Marcos Figueira, respectively represent the rustic local rancher and the Portuguese merchant.

30. For more information on the Di Tella Institute, see John King, *El Di Tella y el desarrollo cultural argentino en la década del sesenta* (Buenos Aires: Ediciones de Arte Gaglianone, 1985). For more on the Institute's theatrical productions and relationship with the U.S. and European performance scenes, see Jean Graham-Jones, "Transculturating Politics, Realism, and Experimentation in 1960s Buenos Aires Theatre," *Theatre Survey* 43, no. 1 (May 2002): 7–21, and "Aesthetics, Politics, and *vanguardia* in Twentieth-Century Argentinean Theatre," in *Not the Other Avant-Garde: The Transnational Foundations of Avant-Garde Performance*, ed. James Harding and John Rouse (Ann Arbor: University of Michigan Press, 2006), 168–91. For an assessment of the Di Tella within the larger Buenos Aires avant-garde scene, see David William Foster, "The Argentine 1960s," *Works and Days 39/40* 20, nos. 1/2, Vectors of the Radical: Global Consciousness, Textual Exchange, and the 1960s (Spring/Fall 2002): 121–41.

31. Guevara, qtd. in King, *El Di Tella*, 149.

32. It was during this period that Harold Prince brought Guevara to the United States for apparently the first time. She performed *Nacha de noche* (New York and Chicago, 1978–79), *Nacha* (Washington, D.C., 1982), and *Nacha at the Top of the Gate* (New York, 1983).

33. Production handbill for performance given in Santa Fe, Argentina, on 9 April 1987 [archived in ARGENTORES (Buenos Aires) library, *Programas*, January-December 1987, n. 58]. Despite Guevara's claims that no historical veracity was sought, early publicity images were clearly modeled on Eva Perón's official portrait, painted by Franco-Argentine artist Numa Ayrinhac in the final year of his life and when Evita herself was terminally ill. While the original painting—reproduced on the cover and first page of her quasi-autobiography—has been lost, the image is among the most reproduced and circulated. See Andrea Giunta, *Escribir las imágenes* (Buenos Aires: Siglo Veintiuno Editores, 2011), 117–30, for a chapter-length discussion of the creation and circulation of Evita imagery in the early 1950s, the years in which, as Giunta notes, Peronist rituals became "crystallized" and clustered around the figures of both Juan and Eva.

34. Program handbill.

35. Two musical themes run throughout *Eva*: one is the "Bienvenida" [Welcome] tune that is sung almost always by a choral collective (beggars, workers, young women, older people, etc.); the other is Eva's individual tune discussed here.

36. "They told me so many things / So many things I believed . . . / [that] I'm only a woman." Evita fantasizes how her life might be "if History had reserved a place for me"—"Here inside is another Eva / and she is better than I am"—and ends her reflections defiantly asserting her own future: "Someday I'll be Eva / and that day I'll be me." See Noemí Castiñeiras, *El ajedrez de la gloria: Evita Duarte actriz* (Buenos Aires: Catálogos, 2002), for a book-length study of Eva Perón's performance career.

37. "But I can't, I don't want to be safe / and I don't want to silence what I know . . . / But I can't, I don't want to be the cause / for another intrigue, another coup against your [Juan's] loyalty./ So I can't though I want to / but I can't tell them the truth."

38. Guevara recorded "No llores por mí, Argentina" for her 1977 album, *Amor de ciudad grande* (Hispavox, Spain). The other recording is by Paloma San Basilio, who played Evita in the original Madrid production (1980). There is also a 1981 Mexican recording with Rocío Banquells.

39. "No llores por mí, Argentina" was not included in the 2008 revival.

40. Lloyd Webber, "The Music of Evita." Lloyd Webber goes on to point out the lyrics' "slightly cynical use of sentimentality." Rice says that these were the first lyrics he wrote for the rock opera, in hopes that the words would "hint at" Eva Perón's "highly emotional speeches" made as Argentina's first lady. Peter Chumo interprets the Alan Parker-Madonna filmed version of "Don't Cry for Me" as follows: "The song itself is a kind of apology for making it to the top, for deserting one's roots. . . . At the same time, the huge audience of epic proportions allows Eva to revel in her newfound fame and privilege. The number thus expresses the essential duality of American success—craving fame and fortune and yet feeling compelled to make excuses for one's success when it's achieved." "'The greatest social climber since Cinderella': Evita and the American success story," *Literature/Film Quarterly* 29, no. 1 (2001): 32–36.

41. It would appear that "Don't Cry for Me" has been recorded in just about every contemporary Western popular musical idiom imaginable: ABBA, Joan Baez, Olivia Newton-John, the Carpenters, the Shadows, Will Oldham, Richard Clayderman, punk-rock supergroup Me First and the Gimme Gimmes, and even the cast of the television show *Glee* have provided versions. Tom Ewing, who has dedicated himself to tracking down and reviewing such recordings, deems Sinead O'Connor's the best: "confused, proud, grand, personal, involving and occasionally desperate." Ewing includes Guevara's version in his overview, calling it "elegant, pure and diva-distant" even though, as he admits, he "can't understand the words." "Every Word is True" (posted 2002) http://freakytrigger.co.uk/ft/2002/10/argentina1/ (accessed 29 January 2011). One of the funniest *Evita* spin-offs, *The Simpsons'* episode "The President Wore Pearls" (broadcast 16 November 2003), included parodies of five songs, most memorably young Lisa's rendition of "Don't Cry for Me, Kids of Springfield." I thank James Mitchell for reminding me of this episode.

42. García countercensorially turned Argentina into the name of a woman and the source of the male singer's anguish. In an interview published at the time of the song's release, García said that his version "speaks of the people who've left this country, of people who've returned because they miss it . . . . It's as if there were two Argentinas." *La Prensa*, 24 December 1982, qtd. in Avellaneda, 2: 226. García, as a member of the Argentine rock group Serú Girán, recorded "No llores por mí, Argentina" live in a 1982 concert in Buenos Aires's Obras Sanitarias; the recording was released in an album under the same title (PolyGram Discos, 1982).

43. Pablo Potenze, responding to an Argentine school teacher's request for the Spanish-language translation at http://boards1.melodysoft.com/app?ID=evita&msg=180 (accessed 25 September 2003, no longer available).

44. The complete lyrics for the original English version and the Spanish translation can be found in *Evita: The Legend* and *Opera Evita*, respectively.

45. The possible English-language exception might be Sinead O'Connor, who, to my knowledge, has never performed in *Evita*.

46. It is more appropriately reprised during Eva Perón's final broadcast, shortly before her death and the end of the play.

47. Rabinow, "Introduction," in *The Foucault Reader*, ed. Rabinow (New York: Pantheon, 1984), 3–27, 8. Foucault categorized the three modes as follows: 1) social "scientific classifications" that discipline and structure the individual; 2) "dividing practices" that differentiate the individual from the masses; and 3) the individual's own complicity in his or her "subjectification"—that is, "the way a human being turns him- or herself into a subject." Foucault, "The Subject and Power," in *Power*, ed. James D. Faubion (New York: The New Press, 2000), 326–48, 327.

48. Rabinow, 11.

49. Foucault, "Nietzsche, Genealogy, History," 148.

50. Silvia [Sirena] Pellarolo calls Eva Perón "a body that matters" and notes how Perón's body has been historically imprinted to become, "in the collective unconscious[,] a synecdoche of the plight of a people, a screen onto which a community's desires, hopes, and needs for visibility and representation are projected." See "The Melodramatic Seductions of Eva Perón," in *Corpus delecti. Performance Art of the Americas*, ed. Coco Fusco (New York: Routledge, 2000), 23–40, 24. Pellarolo analyzes the

construction of Evita's political activist "performing body," which she developed from the melodramatic performance style learned and rehearsed as an actor in theatre, film, and especially radio.

51. "Eva Perón. Eva Duarte. I, Eva María Ibarguren, the unrecognized one. María Eva Duarte de Perón. Marie Eve D'Huart. The half-breed. The little black one. Little half-breed. My little black one. Eva, María Eva, Evita. The hooker. The mare. The whore. The showy one. The bejeweled one. That shirtless one. The resentful one. The climber. The saint. The spiritual leader of the nation. Captain Evita. The fairy [godmother] of the helpless. All those names and surnames must be accepted. I am, I could be, all of them and none of them. . . . But on the cover of my notebook I put Evita." Abel Posse, *La pasión según Eva* (Buenos Aires: Emecé Editores, 1994), 30.

52. María Inés Lagos-Pope, "Género y representación literaria en la construcción de Eva Perón: narraciones de Abel Posse, Alicia Dujovne Ortiz y Tomás Eloy Martínez," *Revista Chilena de Literatura* 68 (April 2006): 73–103, 81.

53. Posse, "Nota," 11.

54. As Luis A. Intersimone stresses, "She was Eva María, not María Eva. The damned name of the one who made the human race fall precedes, in its origins, the sainted name of the one who redeemed humanity." "Las dos Evas, los dos Borges, los dos Perón," *Chasqui* 36, no. 1 (May 2007): 18–32, 23.

55. Intersimone, in a suggestive riff on Jorge Luis Borges's doubles, adds another name to the long onomastic list: Evita Durante, "a diminutive and an adverb" that Evita took on briefly as her stage name (23). This is also mentioned in Castiñeiras, 54. Alejandra Dujovne Ortiz, in the English-language version of her biography (discussed in detail in this chapter), links Evita to her chosen name in the following way: "Then who was she? Evita, as the people called her, which no other social class had the right to use. Evita in the form diminished by the diminutive but exalted by its tenderness. Evita, short and simple, without her father's, her mother's, or her husband's name." Alejandra Dujovne Ortiz, *Eva Perón. A Biography*, trans. Shawn Fields (New York: St. Martin's Press, 1996), 217.

56. In Fields's translation, Dujovne Ortiz writes that these last words, "Eva se va," are "perfectly musical, an ultimate understanding of her name, a syllable that comes back like an echo." Ibid., 277.

57. See Rosi Braidotti, *Nomadic Subjects: Embodiment and Sexual Difference in Contemporary Feminist Theory* (New York: Columbia University Press, 1994).

58. Lagos-Pope, 98.

59. Braidotti, 22.

60. The English-language version can be found at http://www.evitaperon.org/index.htm (accessed 11 June 2013). While the site asserts that "[o]ur purpose is to make known the life and legacy of Evita Perón," it quickly becomes obvious that the English-language version is designed for visiting tourists. For example, the "Evita Tour" has an itinerary created so that "[you] can organize your own Evita Tour when you visit Buenos Aires ["visiting" Buenos Aires is not in the Spanish-language version] by locating each place on a map, then deciding what you want to visit, either on foot, by bus, by subway or by taxi." (The tour is not advertised in the French-language version.) This is, of course, not the only tourist site featuring the "Eva

Perón" tours that have now become standard features of most travel and short-term rental agencies.

61. Ibid., trans. Dolane Larson.

62. Indeed, young Eva's move to the big city is one of the greater points of speculation and a key moment in subsequent femiconography.

63. As Alberto Ciria points out, in an extended review essay of the major Eva Perón biographies in circulation in 1982, Evita's participation in the October 1945 crisis was likely "much less decisive" than it has often been portrayed by "Peronism's official history," which substituted hers for "the actual participation of labor leaders Cipriano Reyes and Luis F. Gay." "Flesh and Fantasy: The Many Faces of Evita (and Juan Perón)," review essay in *Latin American Research Review* 18, no. 2 (1983): 150–65, 156, 162. For Ciria, the Fraser/Navarro biography offers "some welcome relief from the hollow Evitamania of the late seventies in the Northern Hemisphere" (155), with which I concur but to which I will simply add that said hollowness continues to the present day when English-language writers still insist on citing such problematic biographies as Main's *The Woman with the Whip* and John Barnes's *Eva Perón*, whose shortcomings Ciria neatly summarizes.

64. Noemí Castiñeiras, "Ser Evita," translated by Dolane Larson. As this is the site maintained by the "family," it is unsurprising that Castiñeiras comes down on the side of familial historiography; thus while other biographies are cited, recollections by such family members as Eva's sister Erminda are granted "definitive" status. As Castiñeiras is the author of a study of Evita's years in theatre, radio, and film, this might explain why the website's corresponding chapter is far more complete than most biographical overviews of Eva Perón.

65. Karen Bishop, "Myth Turned Monument: Documenting the Historical Imaginary in Buenos Aires and Beyond," *Journal of Modern Literature* 30, no. 2 (Winter 2007): 151–62, 154.

66. Ibid.

67. Lagos-Pope, 75.

68. Until her retirement, Navarro was the Charles Collis Professor of History and the chair of Latin American, Latino and Caribbean Studies at Dartmouth University.

69. Fraser has worked in New York and London as a journalist, perhaps most notably for *The Times* (London), and as a producer for the BBC. He is also the author of *Continental Drifts: Travels in the New Europe* (London: Secker Warburg, 1997) and *The Voice of Modern Hatred: Tracing the Rise of Neo-Fascism in Europe* (London: Picador, 2000).

70. Originally published in French, *Eva Perón* (Paris: Bernard Grasset, 1995); Spanish translation by the author, *Eva Perón. La biografía* (Buenos Aires: Aguilar, 1995). I refer to these various editions by their language and/or translator. Dujovne Ortiz emigrated in 1978 from her native Argentina to France, where she continues to publish poetry, narrative, and biography (most notably, of Argentine cultural figures such as María Elena Walsh and soccer star Diego Maradona), as well as contributes to various newspapers in Europe and Argentina. Dujovne Ortiz refers to herself as more of a novelist than a biographer. And, indeed, Grasset commissioned her to write the biography. See interview with Jason Weiss, "Alicia Dujovne Ortiz," *Hispamérica* 28, no. 82 (1999): 45–58.

71. Fields, raised in both Argentina and the United States, translated from the original French.

72. Nicholas Fraser and Marysa Navarro, *Evita: The Real Life of Eva Perón* (New York: W.W. Norton, 1980), reissued 1996.

73. Marysa Navarro, *Evita* (Buenos Aires: Planeta, 1994).

74. It is not clear whether the Argentine historian participated in the English biography's reedition; the 1996 introduction is signed by Fraser.

75. As Lagos-Pope notes in her extended comparative analysis, Dujovne Ortiz creates a personal voice within the biographical text: "[A]s we advance in our reading we realize that Dujovne has become a biographer with strong opinions [that are] often antagonistic and sarcastic, who loses her serenity and becomes exasperated with her character, whom she criticizes with unencumbered and ironic language." Lagos-Pope qualifies her characterization by suggesting that Dujovne Ortiz abandons this style in the book's final three chapters to provide an "extraordinarily perspicacious and candid reading of Evita's personality and actions, and her relationship with Perón" (79). Thus, for Lagos-Pope, "Dujovne is a biographer who participates in her reconstruction of the character and intervenes in history, constructing her own person throughout the text" (79–80). Although I agree with Lagos-Pope's assessment of Navarro and Dujovne Ortiz's books as "two different types of biographies," I hope here to demonstrate that there is more at work in Navarro's biography than "a historiographical study backed up by documented research." Lagos-Pope, 78 n. 10.

76. One example is the English translation's omission of both the French and Spanish editions' description of small-town "interior" Argentina cited from Manuel Puig's novel, *Boquitas pintadas* (Buenos Aires: Editorial Sudamericana, 1969), a description which notably both Navarro and Fraser incorporate into their texts.

77. A case in point is the quotation from Ezequiel Martínez Estrada's *Radiografía de la pampa* (Buenos Aires: Babel, 1933) on the first page of the initial chapter. No mention is made of Martínez Estrada's virulent anti-Peronism. Fraser and Navarro include Argentine texts but frequently without any context.

78. Dujovne Ortiz, citing Argentine historian Fermín Chávez, builds upon this speculation to suggest that, by changing her birth year to 1922, the year in which Juan Duarte's legal wife Estela Grisolía is believed to have died, Eva Perón was able to avoid a stigma even worse than illegitimacy. If María Eva were born before the death of her father's legal wife, then she would be considered a child of adulterers; furthermore, Perón, as a military officer, would not have been allowed to marry her. "In this way, the false document legitimized her" (Dujovne Ortiz/Fields, 11). Interestingly, both Perón and his brother were born before their parents married, but Perón never made public this information.

79. *Eva Perón para principiantes* [Eva Perón for Beginners] (Buenos Aires: Era Naciente, 2002) opens with a similar outsider juxtaposition, calling her poor, dark, rural, orphaned, savage, regionalist [*federal*], female, and finally plebeian in a country that has historically valued these qualifiers' polar opposites. Nerio Tello's text is illustrated by Daniel Santoro, whose portraits of Evita are discussed in chapter four.

80. Kate Jennings, "Two Faces of Evita," review of Dujovne Ortiz, *Eva Perón*, and Eva Perón [attributed], *In My Own Words*, *New York Times*, Sunday Book Review Desk, 24 November 1996.

81. Compare, for example, "¿Y esta doble pertenencia no era característica de un país mestizo, un país-espejo, desgarrado por su ansia de ser otra cosa, de hallarse en otro lado?" (31) and "Et cette double appartenance n'était-elle pas typique d'un pays métis, d'un pays-miroir, déchiré par son désir d'être autre chose, de se trouver ailleurs?" (30) with "This dual membership was typical of a mulatto country, a mirror country, torn by its desire to be something else, to find itself elsewhere" (21). The quotations exemplify the rhetorical slippage among the three versions, as the English translation removes the interrogative—however rhetorically formed—present in the Spanish and French. More problematic is Fields's translation of *mestizo* (*métis*) as *mulatto*, which does not adequately represent the assumed context of a Euro-indigenous ancestry.

82. Savigliano, 170 n. 1.

83. Ibid.

84. Dujovne Ortiz, 20, citing Otelo Borroni and Roberto Vacca's biography, *Eva Perón* (Buenos Aires: Centro Editor de América Latina, 1970). Fields translates this quotation as "ambulatory, semi-human saleswomen who satisfied the passions of the soldiers of the Desert" (9), incorrectly rendering the French *transhumantes* as "semi-human." The adjective is related to transhumance, the movement of livestock and their herders to different pastures with the changing of the seasons. A more appropriate translation might be "migrant" or "nomadic."

85. Dujovne Ortiz, 20. Fields translates the question as follows: "Was this a quirk of Petrona's, or did she carry this defect in her blood—an ancestral defect, an aptitude to survive by 'satisfying passions'—that Evita would later inherit?" (9).

86. Dujovne Ortiz/Fields, 27.

87. Dujovne Ortiz, 37.

88. Fraser/Navarro, 135.

89. In 1949, the government ratified a revisionist "Peronist" constitution that, among other changes (such as granting rights to senior citizens and abolishing the electoral college), allowed the president to run for re-election.

90. Fraser/Navarro, 147.

91. See Rock for an account of the military "veto" and subsequent unraveling of Perón's attempted alliance "between the Army and the people," 305.

92. While I discuss Eva's death and her cadaver's journeys in the next chapter, I should mention here that accounts vary as to the type of cancer she had. At times it remains unspecified as simply "cancer," other times it is identified as cervical cancer or uterine cancer, and sometimes the two cancers are treated interchangeably. Navarro and Dujovne Ortiz (going into much more detail in the two Spanish editions) identify Eva Perón's cancer as uterine. I will leave final diagnosis to the medical specialists, but it is frustrating not to see more detailed analysis of the information provided by the various involved doctors through reports and interviews, as recently as 1991. (See Navarro, 290, and Dujovne Ortiz, 276–77.) Both the earlier and later tumors were found in the *cuello del útero*, whose English equivalent is the uterine cervix. Detailed, thoughtful analysis might help correct the "medical" websites where Eva Perón is mentioned as an example of a woman who died from a cervical cancer most likely sexually transmitted (through HPV). The implications are that either Juan Perón "infected" both his wives or Evita was the victim of her own sexual activities. Either way, Evita's illness is exploited for mythologizing effect.

93. Dujovne Ortiz, 264.

94. Dujovne Ortiz/Fields, 260.

95. Navarro, 277.

96. Ibid., 278.

97. Fraser/Navarro, 135.

98. Karen Bishop provides a fascinating example of historiography's fragile relationship with Evita biography: in a 1998 interview given on the occasion of the publication of his novel *Santa Evita*, Tomás Eloy Martínez recounts that he invented the novel's dialogue from Evita and Perón's first meeting when unable to read Evita's lips in archival footage of the 22 January 1944 Luna Park benefit for earthquake victims. Martínez used Evita's attributed first words to Colonel Perón—"gracias por existir" [thank you for existing]—in his earlier *La novela de Perón*, a fictionalized narrative of the author's interview with Perón shortly after his 1973 return to Argentina ("a memoir of Perón writing his memoirs," in Bishop's description [160]). Both Dujovne Ortiz and Fermín Chávez, as Martínez points out in the interview, repeat the phrase in their biographies, and Dujovne Ortiz erroneously "attributes the phrase to Perón and not to his 'biographer'" (161). For Bishop, both biographers are "guilty of wanting *La novela de Perón* to be something that it is not" (160)—above factual suspicion: "Any biographer, Martínez warns us, is guilty of rewriting history." Bishop demonstrates how easily fiction can be transformed into biography, "the what-should-have-been-said-instead of history" (161).

99. For more information on Greimas/Courtés's theory, see Joseph Courtés, *Analyse sémiotique du discours. De l'énoncé à l'énonciation* (Paris: Hachette, 1991).

100. Lagos-Pope, 100.

101. Novelist Eduardo Mignogna (1940–2006) also enjoyed a very successful commercial film career as a director and screenwriter. Among his better-known films are *Sol de otoño* [Autumn Sun] (1996), *El faro* [The Lighthouse] (1998), and *La fuga* [The Escape] (2001), starring such major film and stage actors as Norma Aleandro, Ricardo Darín, and Federico Luppi.

102. "Quien quiera oír que oiga," music by Lito Nebbia, lyrics by Eduardo Mignogna. *Evita: Quien quiera oír que oiga*, original soundtrack. Nueva Dirección en la Cultura/Melopea Discos, 1984.

103. Paola Judith Margulis, "El montaje de la transición argentina: Un análisis de los films *La República perdida, La República perdida II y Evita, quien quiera oír que oiga*," *Culturales* 8, no. 16 (July-December 2012): 85–122, 110.

104. As an example, Margulis cites Ana Laura Lusnich and Clara Kriger on Mignogna's selection and sequencing of the interviews: "El cine y la historia," *Cine argentino en democracia, 1983–93*, ed. Claudio España (Buenos Aires: Fondo de las Artes, 1994), 83–103.

105. Margulis, 115.

106. And not in 1997, as Rita de Grandis misstates. Rita de Grandis, "*Evita/Eva Perón*: entre la Evita global y la local," *Revista Canadiense de Estudios Hispánicos* 23, no. 3 (Spring 1999): 521–28. Margulis quotes Mignogna saying that the film was intended to have premiered before the 1983 presidential elections but was delayed for budgetary and technical reasons brought on by "civil winds" (96). *La República*

perdida premiered on 1 September 1983 in clear support of Radical party candidate Raúl Alfonsín, who would be elected president on October 30. Its sequel premiered in 1987.

107. "Quien quiera oír que oiga."

108. For examples of the uniformly positive critical reviews, see the excerpts included in the film's entry in Raúl Manrupe and María Alejandra Portela, *Un diccionario de films argentinos* (Buenos Aires: Corregidor, 1995), 215. The film won awards at the Lisbon and Biarritz festivals.

109. Osvaldo Guglielmino, *Eva de América* (Buenos Aires: Temática, 1983), repr. in *Teatro* (Buenos Aires: Corregidor, 1995), 12–62. According to a note found in Argentores's library, *Eva de América* premiered on 25 July 1987 in a theatre located in the Centro de Empleados de Comercio [Business Employees Center], a space run by the SEC or Business Employees Union. I have been unable to find more information on the actual production.

110. Much of this information comes from an undated interview with Guglielmino, "Por algo Dios nos puso a vivir acá," *Noticias* (Pehuajo) http://www.noticiaspehuajo.com/index.php?option=com_content&task=view&id=835 (accessed 31 January 2011).

111. *Adentrista* roughly translates as insiderist or interiorist, as opposed to someone looking abroad for influences and validation.

112. Interview, "En busca de . . . Osvaldo Guglielmino, escritor," *La Opinión*, 29 July 2010 http://www.laopinion-rafaela.com.ar/opinion/2010/07/29/u072903.php (accessed 3 January 2012). Among Guglielmino's projects as undersecretary of culture was a playwriting contest in which the country was divided into seven regions, with competing dramatists writing about their native region. The finalists were invited to the Cervantes National Theatre, where a jury gave prizes to the best play and the best performers.

113. Sarah M. Misemer, *Secular Saints: Performing Frida Kahlo, Carlos Gardel, Eva Perón, and Selena* (Woodbridge, UK: Tamesis, 2008), 123.

114. Ibid., 120, 122.

115. Ibid., 123.

116. Ibid.

117. Guglielmino, 7. Guglielmino opens his preface with an anecdote about Evita, who, hearing about a film project on the life of José de San Martín, stated categorically that the great independence hero should not appear as a character. He notes that he learned of the anecdote after he had written his play.

118. Ibid., 7 and 56.

119. Guglielmino uses *mestizo* to denote "indio, gaucho, criollo" [Indian, Gaucho, Creole] in opposition to the Europeanized oligarchy (8).

120. These texts include Raúl Scalabrini Ortiz on "el 17 de septiembre," Jorge Melazza Muttoni's "El ángel humilde," and José María Castiñeira de Dios's famous "Volveré y seré millones." Shortly after Eva Perón's death, a grade-school text would be published with the title *Eva de América. Madona de los humildes*. Dujovne Ortiz, 286.

121. Guglielmino, 49.

122. Toward the end of the play, Eva's voice cedes for a moment to a "male voice" who speaks Raúl Scalabrini Ortiz's eye-witness account of the 17 October 1945 mass

gathering. Eva's voice returns to conclude the play, reciting the final fragment of "Volveré y seré millones," so frequently and erroneously attributed to Evita.

123. Oscar Rovito, "Eva de América," in Guglielmino, *Teatro*, 13.

124. Apparently Perón's greatness is such that he does not require even aural representation.

125. According to his own testimony, Catalonian journalist Manuel Penella da (or de) Silva met Eva in Argentina shortly before she left on her 1947 European tour. He encouraged her to write her memoirs and was engaged as her ghostwriter. However, he claims that Evita was not sure exactly how she wished to be represented, and that when Perón read the manuscript in 1950, he ordered it to be "corrected" by one or two (depending on who is telling the story) of his ministers: Raúl Mendé—Minister of Technical Affairs—and Armando Méndez San Martín—Minister of Education. Despite what Dujovne Ortiz calls its "censorship," the final product pleased Eva, who (according to Penella da Silva) called it "the child I never had" (Dujovne Ortiz/Fields, 253).

126. *Eva y Victoria* premiered on 8 April 1992 in Buenos Aires's Teatro de la Comedia. The play-text was published before the premiere. Mónica Ottino, *Evita y Victoria: comedia patriótica en tres actos* (Buenos Aires: Grupo Editor Latinoamericano, 1990).

127. Ottino has written other plays, published in two editions by Tiago Biavez: *Teatro 1* and *Teatro 2* (2000). *Madame Mao*—another "historical" drama—was staged by Barney Finn in 2001.

128. David W. Foster, *Sexual Textualities: Essays on Queer/ing Latin American Writing* (Austin: University of Texas Press, 1997), 150 n. 6. The counterpoising of these two figures is not accidental: "Probably the second most talked about woman in Argentina— the first is Eva Perón—Ocampo seems also the second most mystified." Janet Greenberg, "A Question of Blood: The Conflict of Sex and Class in the *Autobiografía* of Victoria Ocampo," in *Women, Culture and Politics in Latin America. Seminar on Feminism and Culture in Latin America*, ed. Emilie Bergmann and others (Berkeley: University of California Press, 1990), 130–50, 131. For further background on Ocampo and *Sur*, see John King, *Sur: A Study of the Argentine Literary Journal and its Role in the Development of a Culture, 1931–1970* (Cambridge: Cambridge University Press, 1986), and "Victoria Ocampo (1890–1979): Precursor," in *Knives and Angels: Women Writers in Latin America*, ed. Susan Bassnett (London: Zed Books, 1990), 9–25.

129. Daniel Santoro—whose Evita iconography is discussed in chapter four— captures one version of this opposition in his 2002 painting "Evita protege al niño peronista," in which a saintly Evita is seen protecting a sleeping, naked, and presumably defenselessly innocent "Peronist" child from the vigilant but excluded Victoria. Note how both are iconically attired. A reproduced image may be found at Santoro's website http://www.danielsantoro.com.ar/obra.php?anio=10&obsel=2680 (accessed 22 April 2013).

130. Ottino, 59.

131. Ibid., 98.

132. Ibid., 116. Foster suggests that in the play's second act "a homosocial female bonding takes place that, within the Adrienne Rich tradition, could be called lesbian." *Sexual Textualities*, 150 n. 6.

133. The play's "what if" premise apparently inspired other encounters. Several

years ago, Channel ATC organized a series of "Encuentros," invented encounters followed by discussion. Among the meetings they staged were between the author Leopoldo Lugones and the anarchist Severino DiGiovanni; Mariquita Sánchez de Thompson and Victoria Ocampo; and even the mothers of Borges and Sarmiento (*La Nación,* 23 December 1999). In the theatre, there were two productions centering on encounters: *Borges & Perón (Entrevista secreta)* [Borges & Perón (secret interview)], by Enrique Estrázulas, premiering in 1998 in the Cervantes National Theatre, and that same year, *Che, cuestiones con Ernesto "Che" Guevara* [Che: questions with Ernesto "Che" Guevara] (script by José Pablo Feinmann). Beatriz Mosquera's 1991 play, *Gotas de rocío sobre flores de papel* [Dewdrops on paper flowers], which predates Ottino's text, portrays the meeting of two mental hospital inmates who believe themselves to be, respectively, the "liberator" José de San Martín and Evita. Another text that predates the *Eva y Victoria* phenomenon is Gabriela Fiore's 1988 *Cuesta abajo* [Downhill], built around an encounter between Carlos Gardel and Rita Hayworth.

134. For example, during one week in 1998, the company of ten (traveling by private bus) performed in the cities of Goya, Concordia, and Chajarí. China Zorrilla restaged the play in 2007; that production—premiering at Buenos Aires's Comedia Theatre—toured as well but met with much less critical and popular success. The play has also been translated into various languages (an English translation is by Raúl Moncada) and staged in Europe and the Americas.

135. Mempo Giardinelli, e-mail message to author, 21 March 2000.

136. Viviana Paula Plotnik, *Cuerpo femenino, duelo y nación: Un estudio sobre Eva Perón como personaje literario* (Buenos Aires: Corregidor, 2003), 147.

137. Ibid., 151.

138. Luisina Brando (Luisa Noemí Gnazzo, b. 1945) is a much-celebrated stage and screen (TV and film) actress and was a favorite of Argentine filmmaker María Luisa Bemberg. Because of other commitments, she was replaced in 1996 by Soledad Silveyra, the well-known actress who originated the role of Dolores in Griselda Gambaro's *La malasangre*. Both Bemberg and Gambaro are discussed in chapter one.

139. Perhaps the emblematic moment of Brando "losing herself" in Evita occurs at the end of the second act, when Evita, dressed to attend the Colón Theatre, suffers a terribly painful attack.

140. China Zorrilla (Concepción Matilde Zorrilla de San Martín Muñoz, b. 1922, Montevideo) is truly one of Latin American theatre and film's *grandes dames*. She is adored in both her native Uruguay and Argentina, where until her ninetieth birthday she worked as an actress in film, television, and theatre as well as directed and produced for the stage. Her image appears on the website of "Uruguayan Icons," surrounded by eight others, including the musicians Leo Maslíah, Jaime Roos, and even Carlos Gardel, whom Uruguayans claim as a compatriot. http://www.uruguaytotal. com/99_extras/iconosuruguayos/iconosuruguayos.htm (accessed 7 February 2011).

141. Indeed, this is one of the very few criticisms one hears about the much-beloved Zorrilla. There are some notable counterexamples, one being her nuanced performance in Athol Fugard's *The Road to Mecca*, which premiered in Buenos Aires in 2003 and enjoyed a very successful multiyear run both in the capital and on various national tours.

142. See Banegas's website, http://www.cristinabanegas.com.ar/, for more infor-

mation on her extensive acting and directing career in theatre, film, and television (accessed 19 June 2013). Banegas (b. 1946) was recently named an "outstanding cultural personality" by the city of Buenos Aires and in 2012 won an International Emmy for Best Actress for her performance on the social-issues television series, "Televisión x la inclusión." For other images and commentaries from her extensive stage career, see María Moreno, "Escenas de la vida en escena" *Página/12*, 7 October 2007, *Radar* supplement http://www.pagina12.com.ar/diario/suplementos/radar/9–4163–2007–10–09.html (accessed 8 February 2011).

143. See http://www.fundacionkonex.com.ar/b3909-leonidas_lamborghini (accessed 8 February 2011).

144. The New York production made extensive use of a fairly complex video and sound design, which included original music, archival images and footage, and period and contemporary recordings.

145. Leónidas Lamborghini, "Eva Perón en la hoguera," *Partitas* (Buenos Aires: Corregidor, 1972), later published as "Eva," in "La palabra en la hoguera," *Las reescrituras* (Buenos Aires: Ediciones del Dock, 1996), 61–78. Lamborghini's rewriting of *La razón de mi vida* was part of a larger project of "reescrituras" that included Van Gogh's letters to his brother, tango lyrics, Spanish Golden Age poems, passages from the Gospels, and even the Argentine national anthem.

146. Plotnik, 113.

147. Ibid., 119.

148. Ibid.

149. "Eva Perón at the Stake (excerpt)," in *The Oxford Book of Latin American Poetry*, ed. Cecilia Vicuña and Ernesto Livon Grosman, trans. G.J. Racz (New York: Oxford University Press, 2009), 359–62.

150. I thank Cristina Banegas for sharing a copy of the 1994 production video and her own recollections of developing and performing Lamborghini's text.

151. Banegas restaged the text in June 2013 in an even more streamlined production. The black-clad actress stood behind a black podium covered by the Argentine flag, upon which was placed a large black lamp and a microphone. Banegas read Lamborghini's text, making full use of her expressive voice and hands to convey the text's many shifts and fragments. I thank Banegas's producers, Paloma Lipovetzky and Francisca Ure, for providing me with access to the recording of the 2013 revival.

152. At the time Rita de Grandis noted how the "Hollywood remythologization of Evita fit far too well with the current trend of political spectacularization of Menem's Peronism" (527).

153. See Savigliano on the relationship between the 1996 Alan Parker film and Menem's own involvement in Evita's "madonnification."

154. *Eva Perón*, dir. Juan Carlos Desanzo, Aleph Producciones, 1996.

155. Juan Carlos Desanzo (b. 1939) has directed some ten films, for four of which he wrote or cowrote the screenplays. José Pablo Feinmann (b. 1943) has enjoyed a multifaceted career and has written on, among other topics, the history of Peronism.

156. See, for example, de Grandis and Savigliano.

157. The respective sources are: "La Evita de Parker no está a la altura de Eva," *Clarín* http://edant.clarin.com/diario/1997/02/20/c-00801d.htm; Marcelo Figueras, "Parker inventó el musical aburrido," *Clarín* http://edant.clarin.com/

diario/1997/02/20/c-00904d.htm; Antonio Gasalla, "Aburrida como chupar un clavo," *Clarín* http://edant.clarin.com/diario/1997/02/20/c-01002d.htm (all published on 20 February 1997 and accessed 24 June 2013); and Rodrigo Fresán, "Un film casi embalsamado," *Página/12* http://www.pagina12.com.ar/evita.htm (accessed 11 September 2011, no longer available).

158. See, for example, Adolfo C. Martínez's article published during filming, "Una Evita que Madonna jamás imaginó," *La Nación*, 20 July 1996 http://www.lanacion.com.ar/172635-una-evita-que-madonna-jamas-imagino (accessed 6 December 2011).

159. Claudio España, "Evita, entre infinitas palabras," *La Nación*, 24 October 1996 http://www.lanacion.com.ar/173560-evita-entre-infinitas-palabras (accessed 9 January 2012).

160. Kristine McKenna, "A Weepy, Argentine Look at the Life of Eva Peron," *Los Angeles Times*, 18 December 1996 http://articles.latimes.com/1996–12–18/entertainment/ca-10064_1_eva-peron (accessed 4 January 2012).

161. Goris appeared briefly as Eva Perón in Spanish director Jaime Chávarri's 1995 film, *Las cosas del querer II*.

162. http://www.youtube.com/watch?v=WcTNBG87eFs (accessed 22 April 2013).

163. Susana Rosano claims that the film and its lead performance reinforced another image—of a "resentful" Evita. Rosano, *Rostros y máscaras de Eva Perón: Imaginario populista y representación* (Buenos Aires: Beatriz Viterbo, 2006), 66–67.

164. España, "Evita, entre infinitas palabras."

165. *Forbidden Broadway*, performance 27 February 2009, 47th Street Theatre, New York.

166. Glimpses into Guevara's cult status are available at her website www.geocities.com/lanachaguevara/ (accessed 15 May 2003, no longer up but accessible through http://www.archive.org/web/web.php [as of 11 January 2011]), as well as the website-blog and Facebook maintained by her fans: http://nachaguevaraweb.com/ and http://www.facebook.com/NachaGuevaraWeb (accessed 26 June 2013).

167. Program handbill.

168. "Nacha Guevara, de nuevo con 'Evita,'" *El diario montañés* (Spain), 17 September 2008 http://www.eldiariomontanes.es/20080917/sociedad/cronica-rosa/nacha-guevara-nuevo-evita-20080917.html (accessed 3 August 2009).

169. "Nacha Guevara vuelve a ser Evita," *Perfil*, 10 September 2008 http://www.perfil.com/contenidos/2008/09/10/noticia_0032.html (accessed 3 August 2009).

170. Pablo Gorlero, "Nacha, impactante como Evita," *La Nación*, 19 September 2008 http://www.lanacion.com.ar/nota.asp?nota_id=1051344 (accessed 3 August 2009).

171. See *Patti LuPone: A Memoir*, LuPone with Digby Diehl (New York: Crown Archetype, 2010).

172. I examine this conflation in detail in "Eva/Nacha/Cristina and the Argentine Trinity of Local, National, and Global Urban Politics," in *Performance and the Global City*, ed. D.J. Hopkins and Kim Solga (Basingstoke, UK, and New York: Palgrave Macmillan, 2013), 61–77.

173. In his announcement, Scioli justified the Party's choice: "Last night we were both at a dinner, and [Nacha] decided to commit herself at that moment after feeling she'd managed to realize her dream by restaging *Eva* . . . She really wants to serve

our country in another way . . ." "Scioli confirmó a Nacha Guevara como candidata a diputada," *La Nación*, 26 April 2009 http://www.lanacion.com.ar/nota.asp?nota_id=1122255 (accessed 5 January 2012).

174. Néstor Kirchner died unexpectedly on 27 October 2010.

175. In keeping with her outspoken and socially committed nature, Nacha publicly stated that Néstor Kirchner needed to "listen more" and that once in Congress she would back an educational plan designed to arrest violence and juvenile delinquency. "Nacha Guevara quiere que Kirchner 'escuche más,'" *Perfil*, 4 September 2009 http://www.perfil.com/contenidos/2009/08/04/noticia_0014.html; and "Nacha Guevara impulsará en el Congreso un proyecto para frenar la violencia y la delincuencia juvenil," *Perfil*, 28 July 2009 http://opencms1.editorialperfil.com.ar/contenidos/2009/07/28/noticia_0019.html (both accessed 14 September 2010).

176. de Grandis, 527.

CHAPTER 3

1. *Gambas gauchas* was the Gambas al Ajillo's final production, premiering in Buenos Aires's La Trastienda in 1994, before moving to the Maipo Theatre. The production was directed by Helena Tritek, and, in addition to some of the usual Gambas (Alejandra Flechner and María José Gabin; the other two Gambas, Laura Markert and Verónica Llinás, did not perform), Andrea Politti and Gabriel "Puma" Goity appeared as guest artists. Formed in 1986, the Gambas became a key performance troupe of the many that emerged toward the end of the 1976–83 military dictatorship, despite their having created only four shows in the eight years the group was together. Their name, literally the Spanish dish "Shrimp in Garlic Sauce," plays also upon local slang for legs, *gambas,* and captured the group's manic and wonderfully comic style. See María José Gabin's "unauthorized biography," *Las indepilables del Parakultural* (Buenos Aires: Libros del Rojas, 2001), for an irreverent but compellingly written account by one of the company's members.

2. *Fileteado* (or filleted) is a style of painting and drawing that can be traced back to the nineteenth century and the heavily decorated carts that transported food products through the streets of Buenos Aires. With its recurrent themes and use of local colloquial expressions, it is a distinctly *porteño* artistic tradition. For an illustrated historical overview, see Alfredo Genovese, *Filete porteño* (Buenos Aires: Comisión para la Preservación del Patrimonio Histórico Cultural de la Ciudad Autónoma de Buenos Aires, 2007).

3. The gaucho has long been the romanticized Argentine symbol of nostalgia for a lost time of independence, self-reliance, and individualism.

4. Diana Taylor, *Disappearing Acts: Spectacles of Gender and Nationalism in Argentina's Dirty War* (Durham, NC: Duke University Press, 1997), 51.

5. Evita's body was not "embalmed," as is frequently claimed. Pedro Ara (1891–1973) developed his own method of preservation that involved paraffin, not embalming fluids. Ara was rumored to have helped preserve Lenin's body. According to the Spanish doctor's memoirs, however, in 1929 he was approached to examine Lenin's embalmed body and report on a possible "remummification." He declined the offer, because of bad weather. Pedro Ara, *Eva Perón: La verdadera historia contada por el médico*

que preservó su cuerpo (Buenos Aires: Editorial Sudamericana, 1996), first published posthumously in 1974, 25–26.

6. Sarah M. Misemer, *Secular Saints: Performing Frida Kahlo, Carlos Gardel, Eva Perón, and Selena* (Woodbridge, UK: Tamesis, 2008), 101.

7. Army intelligence officer Major Hamilton Alberto Díaz supposedly posed as the widower Giorgio Magistris. The odyssey of Evita's corpse has been the source of much journalistic and fictional speculation. The two best-known examples of fact-fiction mixing are Rodolfo Walsh's 1961 story, "Esa mujer" [That Woman], which grew out of Walsh's frustrating interview with Moori Koenig, the colonel who took initial charge of the corpse but by the time of the interview did not know the cadaver's whereabouts, and Tomás Eloy Martínez's 1995 novel, *Santa Evita*, which builds upon that author's interviews and research (and which I discuss in further detail later in this chapter). Both are masterpieces of what we might call documentary fiction. Martínez, *Santa Evita*, trans. Helen Lane (New York: Alfred A. Knopf, 1996). The widely distributed Walsh short story may be found online: http://www.literatura.org/Walsh/rwmuje.html (accessed 9 January 2013).

8. Ironically, Evita is buried in one of Buenos Aires's toniest neighborhoods and the resting place of the country's major leaders, while Juan's remains reside in a family estate in suburban Buenos Aires after initial interment in the "popular" cemetery of Chacarita, located on the other side of the city. (Chacarita is also the burial site of such popular figures as singers Carlos Gardel and Gilda, folk healer Madre María, and numerous actors, musicians, and other artists.) In 1987, the Chacarita crypt was invaded and Perón's hands cut off. Among the illustrious buried in Recoleta are the former presidents Sarmiento, Mitre, Yrigoyen, Avellaneda, Celman, Illia, and the recently deceased Raúl Alfonsín, the nineteenth-century dictator Juan Manuel de Rosas, and famously anti-Peronist writers Victoria Ocampo and Adolfo Bioy-Casares. My necessarily brief account is based on varied sources, among them, María Seoane, "El último misterio de Eva Perón," *Clarín*, 23 January 2005 http://edant.clarin.com/suplementos/zona/2005/01/23/z-03015.htm (accessed 13 April 2011), the result of Seoane's research in the Argentine Army's archives. The story is far more complex and the evidence far more circumstantial than I can convey here.

9. Taylor, *Disappearing Acts*, 49.

10. Menem converted from Islam to Catholicism, it is believed, to comply with the then-constitutional requirement that the nation's President be Catholic. The 1994 Constitutional reform did away with this requirement. Menem has been linked to the more conservative branches of the Catholic church and has been outspoken in his opposition to abortion rights. In June 2013 he was sentenced to seven years in prison for violating arms embargoes and smuggling 6,500 tons of weapons and ammunition to Ecuador (then at war with mutual neighbor Peru) and Croatia during his presidency.

11. Tamara L. Falicov, *The Cinematic Tango: Contemporary Argentine Film* (London: Wallflower Press, 2007), 75. In this chapter Falicov links Menemist neoliberal politics to the 1990s rise of the Argentine blockbuster film.

12. Carlos Villavicencio composed the music, with costumes by Pablo Cremona and lighting by Bartís and Lito Pastrán.

13. There has been some speculation as to what Bartís intended with the subtitle,

which he claims is an allusion to the Elizabethan period as well as to the need for theatre to "fight for certain places of theatricality itself . . . , because the theatrical circulates more in other places . . . than the theatre itself." Ricardo Bartís, "No somos ingleses," in *Cancha con niebla: Teatro perdido: fragmentos*, ed. Jorge Dubatti (Buenos Aires: Atuel, 2003), 90. Potentially implicit also is a reference to the differences between the state-sponsored theatre, such as the one where the production premiered, and the "underground" theatre/performance scene that coincided with Argentine redemocratization. Finally, the title might also call to mind competing political theatres and the image-driven politics associated with Peronism and Menemism.

14. The *Juventud Peronista*, or Peronist Youth (JP), was founded by Gustavo Rearte in 1957 as part of the resistance movement against the military dictatorship that, after Perón's 1955 overthrow, prohibited the Justicialist Party. Some JP members would go on to form other, more radical parties within Peronism. The JP became identified with the early 1970s leftist and largely youthful militancy. (Ironically, Menem was instrumental in founding his home province's JP; he was also detained and imprisoned during the 1950s and 1970s dictatorships.) Thus, in Bartís's production, Hamlet not only stands in for young Peronists, he also likely represents a Peronism of the left, and most certainly is the antithesis of Menemist Peronism, condemned for compromising the movement's earlier held ideals.

15. The production also marked the "official theatre" debut of Alejandro Urdapilleta (1954–2013), who played both Polonius and the Actor. Urdapilleta, at that time best known for his work with Batato Barea and Humberto Tortonese and their outrageous original shows at Parakultural (one of the city's alternative performance spaces that sprang up during the country's return to democracy), became an acclaimed stage and screen actor with more than a bit of outrageousness still attached to his performances. Another actor who came to prominence during redemocratization, Pompeyo Audivert (b. 1959), played the role of Hamlet and is today a well-known stage, film, and television actor as well as director. Bartís (b. 1949) is regarded as one of Argentina's most influential directors. *Hamlet* was the only production he has ever directed for a state-supported theatre, preferring to produce his own shows—often original texts or radical versions from the national canon—in his studio-theatre in the Buenos Aires neighborhood of Palermo. For more information, see Jorge Dubatti's edited collection of plays by and interviews with Bartís, *Cancha con niebla*.

16. See Jean Graham-Jones's *Exorcising History: Argentine Theater under Dictatorship* (Lewisburg, PA: Bucknell University Press, 2000) and Diana Taylor's *Disappearing Acts* for extended discussions of Argentine cultural production under dictatorship. See particularly my fourth chapter, which discusses another production by Ricardo Bartís: the 1985 restaging of fellow Argentine Eduardo Pavlovsky's *Telarañas* [Spiderwebs/Cobwebs], whose 1977 premiere had been cut short when the play was prohibited by official municipal decree. See also Graham-Jones, "Transculturating Politics, Realism, and Experimentation in 1960s Buenos Aires Theatre," *Theatre Survey* 43 no.1 (May 2002): 5–19; and "De la euforia al desencanto y al vacío: la crisis nacional en el teatro argentino de los 80 y los 90," in *Memoria colectiva y políticas de olvido. Argentina y Uruguay [1970–1990]*, ed. Adriana J. Bergero and Fernando Reati (Buenos Aires: Beatriz Viterbo, 1997), 253–77, for overviews of Buenos Aires theatre both preceding and following the 1976–83 dictatorship years. Brenda G.

Werth's *Theatre, Performance, and Memory Politics in Argentina* (New York: Palgrave Macmillan, 2010) provides a detailed analysis of Argentine post-dictatorship theatre through the specific frame of embodiment. Finally, Paola Hernández directly examines the relationship between theatre and globalization in her book-length study, *El teatro de Argentina y Chile. Globalización, resistencia y desencanto* (Buenos Aires: Corregidor, 2009).

17. Diana Taylor, *The Archive and the Repertoire: Performing Cultural Memory in the Americas* (Durham, NC: Duke University Press, 2003), 144 and 152.

18. David Harvey, *A Brief History of Neoliberalism* (Oxford: Oxford University Press, 2005), 106. Harvey cites Argentina as an example of "how little neoliberal theory has to do with practice."

19. For an excellent historical overview of the crisis during its initial years, see David Rock's article, "Racking Argentina," *New Left Review* 17 (Sept.-Oct. 2002): 54–86.

20. Julio María Sanguinetti, "La Argentina todavía," *El País*, 27 September 2002.

21. Of those nineteen million poor (out of a population of thirty-five million), 7.5 million could not afford sufficient food.

22. The representative was Elisa Carrió, one of the front-running but unsuccessful candidates in the last presidential elections and still active in politics.

23. The historical Eva Perón has been analyzed from just about every angle imaginable. There are the inevitable psychoanalytic studies, such as Mario Deutsch, Alejandro Garbarino, Alejandro Raggio, and Hebert Tenenbaum, *Eva Perón. Una aproximación psicoanalítica* (Montevideo, Uruguay: Imago, 1983), which concludes that Evita possessed both feminine and masculine aspects, as well as "a markedly narcissistic libidinal orientation"(70). A book-length study analyzes her handwriting for clues to her personality: Liliana Conde Chamaza, *Eva Perón. Un análisis psicografológico* (Buenos Aires: De los Cuatro Vientos, 2005). And, possibly the most bizarre case for her exceptional personality is made in Lucia Fischer-Pap's self-published book-length argument for Evita as the reincarnation of the sixth-century Byzantine Empress Theodora: *Eva: Theodora. Evita Peron: Empress Theodora Reincarnated* (Rockford, IL: LFP Publications with Northwoods Press, 1982).

24. Jack Child, *Miniature Messages: The Semiotics and Politics of Latin American Postage Stamps* (Durham, NC: Duke University Press, 2008), 113.

25. Ibid., 114. Child provides examples of two stamps, from 1952 and 1955 respectively (figs. 6.9 and 6.10).

26. Jorge Luis Borges, "El simulacro," in *El hacedor* (Madrid: Alianza Editorial, 1995). English translation by Andrew Hurley, "The Mountebank," in Borges, *Collected Fictions* (London: Allen Lane/Penguin, 1998), available online http://www.google.com/url?sa=t&rct=j&q=&esrc=s&frm=1&source=web&cd=10&ved=0CF4QFjAJ&url=http%3A%2F%2Fdanestaniha.hmg.ir%2Findex.php%2Fsegment%2FSN%2Fitem%2Fdownload%2F5_ef17a032e3fd703297087c34e0d34297&ei=SEzDUYjsCMzH0AGrooCQCQ&usg=AFQjCNF3O6XDdIrxXu-Kxm6-PacYUPJR1g&sig2=wmE6y67uMZjIcQa F3Z8p5Q (accessed 20 June 2013).

27. Margaret Schwartz, "Dissimulations: Negation, the Proper Name, and the Corpse in Borges's 'El simulacro,'" *Variaciones Borges* 24 (2007): 93–111, 97.

28. Tomás Eloy Martínez, *Santa Evita* (Buenos Aires: Planeta, 1995).

29. Lloyd Hughes Davies, "Portrait of a Lady: Postmodern Readings of Tomás Eloy Martínez's 'Santa Evita,'" *The Modern Language Review* 95, no. 2 (April 2000): 415–23, 417.

30. Tomás Eloy Martínez, "La construcción de un mito" (1996), in *Réquiem por un país perdido* (Buenos Aires: Aguilar, 2003), 345–65, 350.

31. Ibid., 354.

32. Ibid., 364.

33. See L'Apogée's winter/spring 2010 collection of nail polish for "women warriors like you." http://www.flickr.com/photos/maniadeesmalte/4857875282/ and http://www.fotolog.com.br/maniademakeup/93830735 (accessed 20 June 2013).

34. One exception is Gustavo Ott and Mariano Vales's 2009 *Momia en el clóset*, discussed in this chapter's conclusion.

35. During the presidencies of Néstor Kirchner and Cristina Fernández de Kirchner, many of those pardoned—and others—have been or are being retried.

36. The similarity of Copi's name to his father's (Raúl Natalio Damonte Taborda, 1909–1982, journalist and politician) has led to some biographical confusion. Scholars have attributed Damonte senior's scathing indictment of Perón, *Ayer fue San Perón: 12 años de humillación argentina* (Buenos Aires: Gure, 1955), to his son (who was still a teenager when the book was published). While both father and son suffered under and went into exile during Peronist rule, their political positions were not identical. Much conjecture has also been made about the influence of Copi's maternal grandmother, who gave him the nickname *Copito de nieve* (little snowflake), a shortened version of which he would later take as his *nom d'artiste*. Salvadora Medina Onrubia de Botana (1894–1972) was married to Natalio Botana, the wealthy founder of the Buenos Aires daily *Crítica* (which Salvadora ran after her husband's death). She was also the daughter of a circus écuyère, an anarchist from the age of fifteen, and a feminist playwright, known in later years for shouting revolutionary slogans from the back seat of her Rolls Royce. See Marcos Rosenzvaig, *Copi: sexo y teatralidad* (Buenos Aires: Editorial Biblos, 2003), 144 n. 6.

37. Copi, nevertheless, claimed to have retained his Argentine citizenship. Clips of Copi's stage, film, and television performances are available online. See, for example, a montage of excerpts from his 1983 Theatre Fontaine production of *Le frigo* http://www.dailymotion.com/video/x20rnj_le-frigo-de-copi_creation (accessed 10 February 2012).

38. After staging his first play in Buenos Aires, Copi moved to Paris in 1962. Known for his irreverent *Le Nouvel Observateur* cartoon strips, "Montmartre's transvestite" wrote and performed in France, Italy, and Spain. Copi's dozen plays (including his solos *Loretta Strong* and *The Refrigerator*) take place in the hyperreal space of what critic Rosenzvaig calls a "theatre-comics" aesthetic: "A sketched [*dibujado*] theatre that happens at the speed of the skits. There's no pause, everything is one continuum separated by cartoon boxes, drawings. Copi sketches with actors, and this way of conceiving theatre makes him the creator of a [new] language." Rosenzvaig, 17. (Rosenzvaig claims that very few directors, with the exception of fellow Argentine expatriates Alfredo Arias and Marilú Marini, have explored this type of relationship with their actors.) Copi's exuberant inversions were theatrically amplified by Jorge Lavelli, who directed five works, including *L'Homosexuel ou la difficulté de s'exprimer* [The Homosex-

ual, or the Difficulty of (S)expressing Oneself] (1971), *Les quatre jumelles* [The Four Twins] (1973), and *Une visite inopportune* [An Inopportune Visit] (1987). In the 1960s, Lavelli (b. 1932) moved from his native Buenos Aires to Paris, where from 1987 to 1996 he headed the Théâtre de la Colline. A stage and opera director who has worked throughout Europe, he frequently returns to direct in Buenos Aires. For further information on Lavelli's theatrical career, see José Tcherkaski, *El teatro de Jorge Lavelli: el discurso del gesto* (Buenos Aires: Editorial de Belgrano, 1983); and Alain Satgé, *Jorge Lavelli, des années 60 aux années Colline: un parcours en liberté* (Paris: PUF, 1996).

39. Copi, *Eva Perón*, trans. Jorge Monteleone (Buenos Aires: Adriana Hidalgo, 2000).

40. Both Arias (b. 1944) and Bo belonged to the theatrical group, TSE, which, after forming in Buenos Aires in 1968, traveled to Caracas and New York before settling in Paris. The group's first Parisian production was *Eva Perón*. Fellow Argentine company member and scenographer Roberto Platé created the set design. http://www.alfredo-arias.com/groupe-tse/biographie (accessed 8 April 2011). Arias went on to stage other Copi shows, including *La femme assise* (with Marilú Marini), *Loretta Strong* and *Le frigo* (with Copi performing), *Les escaliers du Sacre Cœur*, and *Cachafaz*. He continues to work in theatre and opera, in Europe and Argentina. Platé's design career is profiled in a beautifully illustrated book: Marie Binet, *Roberto Platé, tableaux de scène* (Paris: Editions ArtLys, 2013).

41. Alfredo Arias, "1970, Evita," *Página/12 (Primer Plano)*, 28 June 1992, 5. See also Tomás Eloy Martínez, "Teatro: Los muertos que vos matáis," *Panorama*, 17 March 1970, 44–46, 45.

42. There are many versions of this event; see, for example, Tomás Eloy Martínez, "El revés de la trama," *Panorama*, 24 February 1970, 43–44; and Alfredo Arias, "1970, Evita," 5.

43. *Eva Perón* premiered 2 March 1970 in the Théâtre de l'Épée de Bois with the Group TSE. In 1993 the Théâtre National de Chaillot revived it as a "classic" (under Laurent Pelly's direction in the Salle Gémier). See Jason Weiss, *The Lights of Home: A Century of Latin American Writers in Paris* (New York/London: Routledge, 2003), 111. See also Thomas Quinn Curtiss's negative review of the revival, which he calls "a straight melodrama of crude cut." He contrasts the 1993 production to Arias's original staging, which "created on a small platform a spectacle of enormous intensity, swift movement, exotic costuming and theatricality, a Daliesque version of the text." "Copi's 'Eva Perón,' Minus the Absurd," *New York Times*, 30 June 1993 http://www.nytimes.com/1993/06/30/style/30iht-copi.html (accessed 8 April 2011).

44. Martínez, "El revés," 43.

45. Rosenzvaig, 140.

46. Martínez, "El revés," 43. In his review of the production, Martínez called Bo's casting "understandable": "with his well-rounded voice, violent gestures and the fever he manages to pull out of his eyes, Bo confers upon the character the authority and charisma that didn't come across in Copi's text. It's a performance of the first order . . ." "Teatro: Los muertos," 44.

47. Martínez, "El revés," 43.

48. Ibid.

49. Evita's first spoken word (and the first line of the play) is "Merde," which, as

David William Foster notes, "becomes a veritable motif" of the text. Foster, *Sexual Textualities: Essays on Queer/ing Latin American Writing* (Austin: University of Texas Press, 1997), 28. The play exaggerates the historical Eva Perón's attributed predilection for the invective and local slang stereotypically associated with the popular classes. At one moment Evita screams at Ibiza (a fictitious character and amalgam of Evita's inner circle, including her brother, Juan): "Sale cochon de merde de putain de couillon de bordel de lâche" (Copi, *Eva Perón* [Paris: Christian Bourgois, 1969], 58). In his recent Spanish translation, Jorge Monteleone somewhat abbreviates the line but renders it ably into very local *porteño*: "Cobarde de mierda de la puta madre que te parió" (63). In her English translation, Anni Lee Taylor truncates the expletive and cuts short its florid absurdity (especially the original French's exhilarating repetition of the preposition *de*): "Dirty, pig-shit coward! Filthy whore!" Copi, *Plays, Volume 1*, trans. Taylor (London: John Calder, 1976), 26. A more complete if less felicitous English translation of Copi's original French might be: "Get out of here you shit-pig of the naked whore from the coward's brothel."

50. Viviana Paula Plotnik, *Cuerpo femenino, duelo y nación: un estudio sobre Eva Perón como personaje literario* (Buenos Aires: Corregidor, 2003), 106, 108. Plotnik rejects any transgressive interpretation of *Eva Perón*, stating rather emphatically that the play functions as "a kind of caution about the phallic woman that, when she is not subdued by the patriarchal regime (as would be the case with a weak husband), results in a lack of control of irrationality, abuse, arbitrariness, and madness with serious consequences for society." Plotnik's analysis is further limited by her consideration of only the dramatic text and not the text in production.

51. Martínez, "El revés," 43. Copi was thirteen years old when Eva Perón died, so this memory could have predated her death.

52. The tension in Copi's obsession is present in an anecdote Martínez recounts in his performance review. At the post-opening celebration, Copi responded to a French architect's question about the real Eva Perón: "She was a fairy who tried to turn herself into a goddess. But what does that matter? From tonight on, she'll be a goddess in disgrace, a useless bejeweled cadaver." "Teatro: Los muertos," 45.

53. César Aira, *Copi* (Buenos Aires: Beatriz Viterbo, 1991), 107.

54. This search for a happy ending can be extended to Copi's larger gay world and the AIDS epidemic (to which Copi would fall victim, dying in 1987). As Aira says, the gay pantheon "can save itself simply by passing to the 'theatre of the world,' where they will logically be performed by transvestites" (108).

55. Rosenzvaig writes: "Evita, performed by a transvestite, makes it possible for us to gain some distance and think about what is it to be a woman. There are no more givens; it places 'woman' under suspicion. Being a woman, for Copi, is only this . . . dressing like a woman" (144).

56. Rosenzvaig provides a reasonable interpretation of the other roles in Copi's play: the nurse represents the popular classes, especially women, who supported Eva and sought her protection; Ibiza stands in for Evita's conniving confidants (among them her brother, Juan, who is often identified as the source for Copi's enigmatically named character); her mother here cares only about her own future (and tellingly is not in on the conspiracy, so that she, as Rosenzvaig states, can be manipulated in the subsequent mythologizing); and finally Perón is "a kind of ghost" (146), des-

perately aware that Evita's inevitable death can undo his power unless it is carefully orchestrated. With both husband and mother ineffectively self-involved, Ibiza kills the nurse (with Evita's help) in his role as, to paraphrase Rosenzvaig, the chief engineer of everything, the power behind the throne who knows that "Evita is more useful dead than alive" (149). It is fitting that Copi's Evita exits alone, going off to join her friend Fanny and leaving behind her two surrogates—the dead nurse and the living Ibiza—to construct her afterlife, physically, politically, and mythically. See Rosenzvaig, 144–49.

57. Maricarmen Arnó is credited with directing the first Buenos Aires productions of Copi's plays: in 1991 she staged *La noche de la rata* in the independent Payró Theatre, followed a year later by Copi's last play, *Una visita inoportuna*, at the General San Martín Municipal Theatre. The next fifteen years saw important local productions of many if not all of Copi's texts: fellow expats and longtime Copi collaborators Marilú Marini and Alfredo Rodríguez Arias brought their one-woman stage version of Copi's famous cartoon character, *La mujer sentada* (starring Marini), to the San Martín in 1998; *Cachafaz* (directed by Miguel Pittier) premiered in 2001 at the Belisario Club de Cultura; *Le frigo (la heladera o un trozo de carne)* premiered in 2004 at the Abasto Social Club under the direction of Javier Albornoz and Juan Andrés Ferrara; and *El homosexual (o la dificultad para expresarse)* was staged in 2005 at Teatro El Cubo under the direction of Guillermo Ghio. Over the past fifteen years, several of these plays, like *Eva Perón*, have received multiple productions.

58. I am by no means the first to make this connection. See, for example, José Amícola's study, *Camp y posvanguardia: manifestaciones culturales de un siglo fenecido* (Buenos Aires: Paidós, 2000), which devotes an entire chapter to Copi and Perlongher as "camp champions." Plotnik, in her study of Eva Perón as "literary character," separates the two authors, analyzing "Evita vive" in her chapter on "resurrection and reincarnation" while reserving her analysis of *Eva Perón* for a later chapter on the "phallic" Evita.

59. For a recounting of the 1989 republication in *El Porteño* and "el caso Evita," see Ben Bollig, *Néstor Perlongher: The Poetic Search for an Argentine Marginal Voice* (Cardiff: University of Wales Press, 2008), 18–20. I return to Perlongher's work in a later portion of this chapter when I examine six of his poems in performance.

60. Néstor Perlongher, "Evita vive," in *Prosa plebeya: ensayos 1980–1992*, ed. Christian Ferrer and Osvaldo Baigorria (Buenos Aires: Ediciones Colihue, 1997), 191–95, 192. Various foreign publications preceded the 1987 Argentine publication, including its English translation in the collection *My deep dark pain is love*, ed. Winston Leyland, trans. E. A. Lacey (San Francisco: Gay Sunshine Press, 1983). The quoted translation is Lacey, 54. As Weyland explains, the title comes from the still-popular slogan, "Evita vive," to which additions are made in keeping with a particular situation: "Evita lives in popular demonstrations, Evita lives in the proletarian slums, Evita lives in every hotel or apartment organised (the war-cry of the of Movement of Peronist Tenants), and so on" (53).

61. Ferrer and Baigorria, "Prólogo: Perlongher prosaico," in *Prosa plebeya*, 7–12, 10.

62. The other three texts are the poems "El cadáver" [The Cadaver/Corpse] (1980) and "El cadáver de la nación" [The Nation's Cadaver/Corpse] (1989), and the

brief commentary "Joyas Macabras" [Macabre Jewels] (1983), first published respectively in *Austria-Hungría* (Buenos Aires: Editorial Tierra Baldía, 1980), *Hule* (Buenos Aires: Ediciones Ultimo Reino, 1989), and *Leia Livros* 55 (April 1983). All four "Evita" texts are collected under the section titled "Eva Perón" in Perlongher, *Prosa plebeya*.

63. Ben Bollig, "Néstor Perlongher and the Avant-Garde: Privileged Interlocutors and Inherited Techniques," *Hispanic Review* 73, no. 2 (Spring 2005): 157–84, 176.

64. Bollig, *Néstor Perlongher*, 104.

65. As Bollig explains, the Argentine term *travesti* (often translated as transvestite) not only conjoins cross-dressing, drag, and transvestism but is also "a figure closely related not only to local sexual practices and identity politics, but also to economic necessity and class issues" in addition to legal and social persecution. Ibid., 125.

66. Ibid., 130. See especially the chapter "Perlongher and the *Travesti*." As Bollig points out, Perlongher would later question his earlier portrayal of the *travesti* as subversive, coming to believe that any potential for provocation by then had been absorbed into the marketing of popular culture (144). Though Bollig does not state so explicitly, I suspect he would agree with me that the imagery employed in Perlongher's final "Evita" text ("El cadáver de la nación") reflects that shift.

67. Amícola, 87.

68. Ferrer and Baigorria, "Prólogo," 10, emphasis in the original.

69. *des/Enlace* premiered the year before in the municipally run Recoleta Cultural Center before moving to the downtown independent theatre Andamio 90, where I saw it.

70. In this analysis I draw upon my own spectator's experience, Viñao's unpublished dialogue script, and a videotaped performance.

71. Mónica Viñao (b. 1948) studied visual arts in Buenos Aires, Rome (Accademia di Belle Arti), and London (Central St. Martins School). She has studied playwriting (with Mauricio Kartun and Dieter Welke), narrative writing (with Guillermo Saccomano), literary analysis (with Santiago Kovadloff), and direction (with Eugenio Barba).

72. A 1989 version of Mishima's Noh play *Hanjo* brought Viñao's work to Suzuki's attention, and the production was invited to the Toga Festival. Since then, Viñao has participated in actor-training programs in Toga, Shizuoka, and Saratoga. She was a member of Suzuki's working group at Delphi's 1995 Theatre Olympics and presented several of her own productions at Toga's annual festival.

73. Catherine Madden notes that the "Suzuki form involves a wide variety of physical and vocal challenges, from fast walking to marching, to extreme slow motion, to speech and singing while moving in challenging physical shapes." "The Language of Teaching Coordination: Suzuki Training Meets the Alexander Technique," *Theatre Topics* 12, no. 1 (March 2002): 49–61, 50. Viñao's connection to Suzuki is evident in the following description of her workshop: "Technically the training consists of learning to speak with clarity and strength and making the entire body express itself even in silence. Through rigorous and intense physical and vocal practice, the actor comes into contact with his own energy flow, trains his concentration, controls his breath, explores the potential of his voice and develops the possibility of expressing his inner self." Viñao's professional website http://www.autores.org.ar/mvinao/ (accessed 13

June 2012). I thank Zvika Serper for his observations regarding Suzuki's influence on Viñao's acting exercises.

74. Tadashi Suzuki, *The Way of Acting*, trans. J. Thomas Rimer (New York: Theatre Communications Group, 1985), 19.

75. Mabel Itzcovich, "Fantasmas de ayer, en clave oriental," *Clarín*, 8 June 1998; and Alejandro Cruz, "El espectáculo, desplazado por la técnica," *La Nación*, 10 July 1998.

76. Conversely, Cecilia Hopkins's review focuses exclusively on reading the production through Walsh's short story about Moori-Koenig, "Esa mujer," and thus ignores the play's references to the desaparecidos. "Alrededor de 'Esa mujer,'" *Página/12*, 6 May 1998 http://www.pagina12.com.ar/1998/98-06/98-06-05/pag31.htm (accessed 20 June 2013).

77. Indeed, Moori-Koenig's obsession with Evita was Viñao's initial inspiration for her play. The complete e-mail reads as follows:

> . . . when I wrote it, I had in mind that strange relationship of the 'milico' who fell in love with 'that WOMAN' all women Eva and who had that strange obsession with her even after her death as if he wanted to possess her and discovered that he had been possessed by her, but when rehearsals began, Perón appeared, unexpectedly just like one more man who could and couldn't stand her. . . . With respect to the *desaparecidos* the subject is emblematic and unavoidable a cadaver without a tomb . . . something too obvious to leave out . . . I wrote thinking about this tremendous love story, a kind of 'Night Porter' . . . at the same time a story that like a metaphor goes beyond the names in history . . . something also representative of our culture even though we might not like it so much . . . something still very deeply rooted (Mónica Viñao, e-mail message to the author, 26 February 2000).

78. In the unpublished dialogue text, the actor's physical shift accompanies a character shift, which is left unnoted in both the program notes and the performance. Initially identified in the script as Ella [She], the woman is disheveled and wears a torn, bloodstained white dress. A second character appears at this moment in the written text—Sombra, the character named in the production's program. Ella's lines are spoken by Sombra in performance, but, as seen in the above-described transformation, traces of the character remain in the actor's performance.

79. One might be able to read into *des/Enlace*'s individual "countering" the influence of Suzuki's well-known upper/lower body division.

80. In Spanish, verbs in the third person singular are generally conjugated the same as the second person singular. Therefore, unless a pronoun is provided (and rarely so in *des/Enlace*'s script), it is difficult to know if the performer is speaking of or to another. Only infrequently and inconsistently (and much later in the performance) is the familiar second-person "tú" form used in the script.

81. Although Perón rose to the rank of general, he was a colonel when he and Eva met.

82. About halfway through the performance, Mariela Viñao eloquently captures Moori-Koenig's internal conflict. Joven begins to fall apart physically and verbally, as

"No insista" [Don't push it] is gradually reduced to a hiss with the actor's body bent over as a rag doll gone limp. The performer then slowly rebuilds language and body until fully erect, and states, "You belong to me."

83. Translator's note in Jacques Derrida, *Specters of Marx. The State of the Debt, the Work of Mourning, & the New International,* trans. Peggy Kamuf (New York: Routledge, 1994), 177.

84. Olga Cosentino, "El teatro no perdió la memoria," *Clarín,* 17 June 1998.

85. Viñao, *des/Enlace* (unpublished manuscript, 1998).

86. Suzuki, 14.

87. Ibid.

88. Izcovitch.

89. Viñao's website http://www.autores.org.ar/mvinao/modo.htm (accessed 20 June 2013).

90. Cruz, "El espectáculo."

91. Qtd. in Cecilia Hopkins, "Escenas de la crisis" (interview with Viñao), *Página/12,* 1 November 2001.

92. Qtd. in Taylor, *Disappearing Acts,* 30. Viñao herself has stated: "If you analyze the present situation, you arrive at the conclusion that [the dictatorship] was successful: before people physically disappeared and now they're disappearing economically. One way or another, we continue to be desaparecidos." Qtd. in Hopkins, "Escenas."

93. The six poems, in the order they were performed, are: "El cadáver" [The Cadaver], "La murga, los polacos" [The Parade, the Poles], "Érase un animal" [There was once an animal], "Cadáveres" [Cadavers/Corpses], "Canción de amor para los Nazis en Baviera" [Love Song for the Nazis in Bavaria], and "Por qué seremos tan hermosas" [Why must we be so beautiful]. All poems except for "Cadáveres" were first published in Néstor Perlongher, *Austria-Hungría.*

94. My citations come from Perlongher's complete, posthumously released, poetry collection. *Poemas completos (1980–1992),* ed. and prol. Roberto Echavarren (Buenos Aires: Seix Barral, 1997).

95. Perlongher made this position clear in a 1991 interview given not too long before his death: "I've always considered Peronism to be a hallway, . . . a quick route for getting somewhere but with horrible consequences." Interview, Guillermo Saavedra, "Privilegio las situaciones del deseo," *Clarín* [*Cultura y nación*] 26 (1991): 2–3. Also qtd. in Bollig, *Néstor Perlongher,* 102.

96. Perlongher, "Cadáveres," *Poemas completos,* 109–23, 111. The poem was first published in *Revista de (poesía)* 1 (April 1984). An audiotape of Perlongher reciting "Cadáveres" was released by Último Reino in 1991. A partial translation is included in *The Argentina Reader,* ed. Gabriela Nouzeilles and Graciela Montaldo (Durham, NC: Duke University Press, 2002). (Any reader seeking Argentine plays or performance texts in translation should know that not one play or performance script appears excerpted in this 580-page "essential introduction to Argentina's history, culture, and society," and only one play, Gambaro's *La malasangre,* is included in the list of suggestions for further reading.) A snippet of Pista 4's performance may be heard at http://www.datamarkets.com.ar/experimenta/ssl5.mp3 (accessed 14 June 2013).

97. I quote from the translation by David William Foster and Daniel Altamiranda,

"Corpses," *torre de papel* 7, no. 2 (1997): 87–113, 87. The Spanish original also appears reprinted in this issue.

98. For another account of the production, see Cecilia Hopkins, "Las más terribles palabras," *Página/12*, 28 July 1998. *Murgas* are (neighborhood as well as professional) music groups that participate in parades, community events, and concert performances; they are extremely popular throughout the entire River Plate region.

99. Qtd. in Claudio Zeiger. "El oído atento," *Radar* weekly cultural supplement, *Página/12*, 5 July 1998 http://www.pagina12.com.ar/1998/suple/radar/julio/98-07-05/nota3.htm (accessed 24 January 2008). I find it telling that Zeiger's preopening note leads off with the warning "hardcore lovers of poetry and playwriting, stay away."

100. Production handbill.

101. Pista 4 built its reputation on only a handful of productions, of which the most cited are *Esperes* (1988) and *Nada lentamente* (1993). The group performed in Brazil, Chile, Colombia, Cuba, France, Spain, Uruguay, Venezuela, and the United States.

102. The group's name is at once an homage and an alternative to the circus tradition and its three rings.

103. In his various histories of the 1980s–1990s "new" theatre, critic Jorge Dubatti consistently mentions Pista 4 as one of the period's important groups. An early example would be *Teatro '90*, where several production photos of the group are prominently displayed but no discussion of the specific productions is included. See Dubatti, *Teatro '90: el nuevo teatro en Buenos Aires* (Buenos Aires: Libros del Quinquincho, 1992).

104. As Bollig explains, the early Argentine avant-garde poets, like Jorge Luis Borges, were not nearly as politicized as their European counterparts. The combination of politics and poetic experimentation came with the next generation of "social poets" such as Juan Gelman and Uruguayan Mario Benedetti. Perlongher belonged to a later third generation of Argentine poets, often referred to as post–post-avant-garde. Bollig, "Néstor Perlongher and the Avant-Garde," esp. 178–82.

105. Perlongher, "Introducción a la poesía neobarroca cubana y rioplatense," prologue to *Caribe transplatino, Poesía neobarroca cubana y rioplatense* (São Paulo: Illuminiras, 1991); repr. in Perlongher, *Prosa plebeya*, 93–102, 101.

106. Perlongher names Góngora, Lezama Lima, and Artaud (in that order) as his answer to the tenth question ("Who is your favorite poet?") in "69 preguntas a Néstor Perlongher," published first in 1989 in the magazine *Babel*. Repr. in *Prosa plebeya*, 13–21, 14.

107. Bollig, "Néstor Perlongher and the Avant-Garde," 157.

108. Ibid., 182.

109. Jorge Monteleone, "Una mirada corroída: sobre la poesía argentina de los años ochenta," in *Poéticas argentinas del siglo XX (literatura y teatro)*, ed. Jorge Dubatti (Buenos Aires: Editorial de Belgrano, 1998), 220–21. An earlier version of this essay appeared in *Culturas del Río de la Plata (1973–1995): transgresión e intercambio*, ed. Roland Spiller (Frankfurt am Main: Vervuert, 1995), 203–15.

110. Perlongher, "Cadáveres," trans. Foster and Altamiranda, 113.

111. I refer to, respectively, Somigliana's *Oficial primero*, staged in the last year of

dictatorship (in *Teatro Abierto 1982*, ed. Nora Mazziotti [Buenos Aires: Puntosur Editores, 1989], 105–16); Aída Bortnik's 1983 *De a uno* (*Hispamérica* 15, no. 43 [1986]: 57–72); Griselda Gambaro's 1986 *Antígona furiosa* (in *Teatro 3* [Buenos Aires: Ediciones de la Flor, 1989], 195–217); Gambaro's 1992 chamber-opera, *La casa sin sosiego* (in *Teatro 6* [Buenos Aires: Ediciones de la Flor, 1996], 27–58); and Eduardo Pavlovsky's 1990 *Paso de dos* (Buenos Aires: Ediciones Ayllu, 1989). As others, perhaps most extensively Diana Taylor in *Disappearing Acts*, have pointed out, the disappeared body on the Argentine (sociocultural) stage has almost always been female. Only rarely since re-democratization have the disappeared been represented other than corporeally; one additional exception would be Ricardo Bartís's 1992 version of *Hamlet* and Gertrude's shoe collection.

112. A noted shift in representation and topic occurred with the increasing focus on the children of the disappeared (most notably through the annual HIJOS- and Madres-sponsored festival Teatroxlaidentidad), but I would argue that the prevailing aesthetic remains mimetic.

113. Argentine FM stations largely followed the Italian Free Radio model. See Carlos Ulanovsky and others, *Días de Radio: Historia de la radio argentina* (Buenos Aires: Espasa Calpe, 1995), especially chapter 12, for an overview of the FM phenomenon in Argentina. While many of these local FM stations still operate, they no longer exert the influence they did well into the 1990s.

114. In 1966 Minujín staged what Michael Kirby calls "probably the first performance piece in history to make use of several coordinated mass media." Kirby, "Marta Minujín's 'Simultaneity in Simultaneity,'" *TDR* 12, no.3 (Spring 1968): 148–52, 148. Minujín conceived the happening as an "intercontinental" presentation with Allan Kaprow in the United States and Wolf Vostell in Germany. While the project was never fully realized, Minujín did make effective use of live performance, television, and radio in her event. See Kirby's article for a detailed description of the Buenos Aires performance.

115. See, for example, Michael Kirby and Victoria Nes Kirby, *Futurist Performance* (New York: PAJ Publications, 1986). A sound-clip of Marinetti performing "Sintesi musicali futuriste" is available at http://media.sas.upenn.edu/pennsound/authors/ Marinetti/Marinetti-Filippo_Sintesi-Musicali-Futuriste_1931.mp3 (accessed 20 June 2013).

116. See, for example, Allen S. Weiss, *Phantasmic Radio* (Durham, NC: Duke University Press, 1995).

117. Joe Milutis, "Radiophonic Ontologies and the Avant-Garde," *TDR* 40, no.3 (Fall 1996): 63–79, 70.

118. Ibid., 65.

119. Ibid.

120. See also Allen S. Weiss, "Radio, Death, and the Devil," in *The Wireless Imagination: Sound, Radio and the Avant Garde*, ed. Douglas Kahn and Gregory Whitehead (Cambridge: MIT Press, 1992), 269–308; Antonin Artaud, "To Have Done with the Judgment of God" in *Selected Writings*, ed. Susan Sontag, trans. Helen Weaver (Berkeley: University of California Press, 1988). Another translation, by Clayton Eshleman—first published in Antonin Artaud, *Four Texts*, trans. Eshleman and Norman Glass (Los Angeles: Panjandrum Books, 1982)—is included in Kahn and Whitehead, 309–27.

121. David Graver, "Antonin Artaud and the Authority of Text, Spectacle, and Performance," in *Contours of the Theatrical Avant-Garde: Performance and Textuality*, ed. James M. Harding (Ann Arbor: University of Michigan Press, 2000), 43–57, 51. Artaud deemed the recording of his radio-play "a model in miniature of what I want to do with my Theatre of Cruelty." Qtd. in Tony Gardner, "Antonin Artaud," in *Censorship: A World Encyclopedia* (Chicago: Fitzroy Dearborn, 2001), I:114.

122. Qtd. in Milutis, 66.

123. Ibid.

124. Ibid., 70.

125. Qtd. in Zeiger. The only other explanation cited is "technical reasons."

126. Milutis, 63.

127. Ibid., 67.

128. *Eva Perón* was the final production of the university season. It opened on 16 December 2000 and was directed by María G.González and Sergio Sansosti. I have located only one account of the production. See Federico Irazábal, "El regreso travestido de un mito: *Eva Perón*. Sobre el estreno de la obra de Copi en la Universidad de Tandil," *Revista Picadero* 3 (no year) http://www.inteatro.gov.ar/editorial/picadero03.php (accessed 29 February 2012).

129. Misemer mentions another "example of how Evita's iconicity has crossed national borders": *Güevita*, Luis Usabiaga's 1997 adaptation of Copi's play, staged by Mexico City-based performance artists Jesusa Rodríguez, Liliana Felipe, and Tito Vasconcelos as a "cabaret-style production" at the Teatro Experimental de Jalisco (Guadalajara, Mexico). The version satirized local and national politics. See Misemer, 113–14, n. 10.

130. Marcial Di Fonzo Bo (b. 1968, Buenos Aires) is a stage, film, and television figure based in France, where he moved in 1987. Di Fonzo Bo studied at the National Theatre of Brittany's School and founded the Théâtre des Lucioles with fellow classmates. He first drew attention for his work with Swiss-German *regisseur* Matthias Langhoff, under whose direction he played many roles, including the title character in *Richard III* (1995). Di Fonzo Bo continues to act and direct for the stage, often creating French-language productions of contemporary Argentine plays. He has staged many Copi texts, among them, *Copi, un portrait d'après Loretta Strong, Eva Perón, La nuit de Madame Lucienne, Rio de la Plata,* and *La Tour de la Défense*. His extensive film career includes an appearance as Pablo Picasso in Woody Allen's 2011 *Midnight in Paris*. Loren Ringer reviewed the Franco-Chilean production of *Eva Perón* in *Latin American Theatre Review* 35, no. 2 (Spring 2002): 149. I thank Di Fonzo Bo for the production photo included here.

131. The 1970 and 2001 productions exhibit another bond when we recall that Di Fonzo Bo worked as Alfredo Rodríguez Arias's assistant when he first arrived to Paris in 1987.

132. Prior to directing *Eva Perón*, Pista 4 member and stage, television, and film actor Gabriel Correa had performed in two local productions of Copi plays: *Las viejas putas* [The Old Whores] and *Cachafaz*, both directed by Miguel Pittier. The 2004 production premiered at the downtown Centro Cultural de la Cooperación, with set and costume design by painter Daniel Santoro, lighting by Santoro and Correa, music by María Eva Albistur, and starring Alejandra Flechner, María Inés Aldaburu, Fabián

Arenillas, Horacio Acosta, and Laura Pons Vida. I thank Correa for sharing the production photo as well as his recollections. Di Fonzo Bo's *Eva Perón* was performed at the President Alvear Municipal Theatre.

133. Flechner also performed in the 1992 Buenos Aires premiere of *Una visita inoportuna* [An inopportune visit], Copi's final play.

134. Rómulo Berruti, "Copi, entre la desmesura y la cautela" (no date) http://www.mundoteatral.com.ar/comentario-teatral/copi-entre-la-desmesura-y-la-cautela. See also "El mito de Evita revisado por Copi," *La Prensa,* 24 November 2004 http://www.laprensa.com.ar/300598-El-mito-de-Evita-revisado-por-Copi.note.aspx; Susana Freire, "'Eva Perón', con la mirada paródica de Copi," *La Nación,* 25 November 2004 http://www.lanacion.com.ar/657023-eva-peron-con-la-mirada-parodica-de-copi (all accessed 20 June 2013).

135. See "Flechner en versión local," *Página/12,* 27 November 2004 http://www.pagina12.com.ar/diario/espectaculos/subnotas/44109-15079-2004-11-27.html (accessed 1 June 2010).

136. The censorship and self-censorship surrounding Copi's play is one of the multiple examples I study in an extended essay: "'Common-sense catchword': The Applications of *Censura* to Argentinean Theatre and Performance," *Theatre Research International* 36, no. 2 (2011): 102–16.

137. Obviously, this is a project in which both Perón and Eva participated. In his study of Peronism as a cultural formation and its relationship to Manuel Puig's fiction, John Kraniauskas claims that, even during her own lifetime, Eva came to be a "political fetish." Kraniauskas, "Political Puig: Eva Perón and the Populist Negotiation of Modernity," *New Formations* 28 (Spring 1996): 121–31. To the concept of political fetishizing can be added state fetishizing; see, for example, Taylor, *Disappearing Acts*; and Michael Taussig, *The Magic of the State* (New York: Routledge, 1997).

138. Ott's language reflects his own Caribbean-inflected Venezuelan dialect. In *porteño* Spanish, the title would have been *Momia en el placard.* The subtitle, "The Return of Eva Perón" (which does not appear in Ott's online text http://www.gustavoott.com.ar/obras/es/momia_en_el_closet.pdf [accessed 20 June 2013]), suggests a response to V.S. Naipaul's dismissive essay of the same title, *The Return of Eva Perón with The Killings in Trinidad* (New York: Vintage, 1981). *Momia en el clóset,* commissioned by Washington, D.C.'s Teatro Hispano Gala, premiered on 4 June 2009 at Gala, with book by Gustavo Ott, music by Mariano Vales (who also conducted), and lyrics by Ott and Vales.

139. "Notas del director/Director's Notes," production handbill.

CHAPTER 4

1. Ricardo Monti, *The Obscurity of Reason,* in *Reason Obscured: Nine Plays by Ricardo Monti,* trans. and ed. Jean Graham-Jones (Lewisburg, PA: Bucknell University Press, 2004), 365. All subsequent quotations will be from the published English translation.

2. Buenos Aires's Yiddish Folk Theatre (IFT) was founded in 1932 as the *Prolet Bine,* or Proletarian Stage. The collective staged Yiddish versions of plays by Brecht and Miller, in addition to the works of Yiddish authors. By 1957, IFT was staging plays in Spanish and operating within Buenos Aires's "independent theatre" system. Kogan

(1937–1996) entered IFT's acting school in 1954 and joined the permanent company, first as a performer in supporting roles while working as assistant director and later as a director (Brecht's *Fears and Miseries of the Third Reich* marked his 1960 directorial debut). In 1967, Kogan left IFT, directing at the experimental Di Tella Institute before taking over the independent cooperative Payró Theatre to form his own Equipo de Teatro Payró, where he remained as artistic director until his death. Kogan was known for his remarkable use of space and light—what Argentine critic Gerardo Fernández has called a "scenic rewriting" of the dramatic text. Kogan's skill as a designer is reflected in his longtime design partner Tito Egurza's tribute to him as one of his five masters, along with Appia, Craig, Svoboda, and Brecht. See Egurza's website, which also has detailed descriptions and designs of several Kogan productions http://www.titoegurza.com.ar/TITO_EGURZA.htm (accessed 29 October 2011). In the postdictatorship years, Kogan began to work in the "official" theatre, mounting productions for the General San Martín Municipal Theatre and the Colón Theatre in addition to other venues around the city. For more information on Yiddish theatre in Buenos Aires, see Nora Glickman and Gloria F. Waldman's introduction to their critical anthology *Argentine Jewish Theatre* (Lewisburg, PA: Bucknell University Press, 1996), 9–18. For information on Kogan and the Payró Theatre, see Celia Dosio, *El Payró: cincuenta años de teatro independiente* (Buenos Aires: Emecé Editores, 2003).

3. *La oscuridad de la razón* premiered at the Payró Theatre on 8 September 1993. That year the production (and playtext) received nearly every Buenos Aires award accorded a dramatic play, including a municipal award for outstanding contribution to the theatre; the Association of Theatre Critics awards for best production, director, music, and dramatic play; and the Pepino 88 award for best set design.

Kogan's death in 1996 ended a twenty-five-year collaboration with compatriot playwright Ricardo Monti that has often been cited by critics as the ideal pairing of playwright and director. See, for example, Horacio C. Morando, "La conjunción de vanguardia y taquilla," *La Opinión Cultural,* 27 July 1980, 2. The duo premiered four of Monti's eleven plays, staged operatic versions of two Monti texts, and created a stage adaptation of Julio Cortázar's novel *Hopscotch.*

4. The only time a "Pietà-like" image is created onstage is when Mariano is first reunited with his mother, María. The Woman stands to one side, looking on.

5. In the Payró production, as in Monti's text, Mariano still spoke Jesus's scriptural lines, and the Men's Chorus continued to paraphrase *Revelation* as they insisted on avenging Dalmacio's murder.

6. The Woman appears first in the prologue, responding in *porteño* Spanish to Mariano's questions in French; in act one, she hands the bandage to Alma and witnesses María and Mariano's reunion; in act two, she reappears, immediately following Dalmacio's murder; and in act three, she makes her final appearance to "save" Mariano. It's interesting to note that the number of accompanying bell peals varies with each appearance.

7. Among the earliest examples of Evita veneration were the poems presented at the 1950 meetings of the Peña Eva Perón, organized by then undersecretary of culture, the poet José Castiñeira de Dios, with the writers meeting in the canteen of one of the Eva Perón Foundation's hostels for working women. Fifteen of these poems were published that same year in a limited edition. See Marysa Navarro, *Evita* (Bue-

nos Aires: Planeta, 1994), 274–76, 298 n. 9. Angela Rina Rodríguez's *Eva de América. Madona de los humildes* (Buenos Aires: Editorial Mayo, 1949) is another early example; Rodríguez states that she followed Evita's activities for four years before writing the book, intended not as biography but as an "impression of [Perón's] daily work" (6). The popular devotional practices that proliferated after her death were also satirized, perhaps most notoriously in Jorge Luis Borges's 1960 short story, "El simulacro" (The Simulacrum).

8. Julian Kreimer emphasizes the artist's use of "vernacular imagery": "Santoro has, in using the 'inferior['] local language to describe a specific story, created art of enormous power and complexity." "Portrait of a Country," *Modern Painters* 15, no. 1 (Spring 2002): 72–75, 72. For an insightful article on artistic imagery and historical Peronism, see Anahí Ballent, "La traición de las imágenes: Recuperación del peronismo histórico," *Punto de vista* 30, no. 87 (April 2007): 6–12.

9. Santoro is the author/illustrator of a "three-dimensional" guide to Buenos Aires (many of whose illustrations are posted around the city as "self-guides"), as well as the illustrator of a "for-beginners" graphic text on Evita's life. See Daniel Santoro and Liliana Cascales, *Guía tridimensional de Buenos Aires* (Buenos Aires: Secretaría de Turismo del Gobierno de la Ciudad de Buenos Aires, 2007 [2003]); Nerio Tello and Daniel Santoro, *Eva Perón para principiantes* (Buenos Aires: Era Naciente, 2002). On his professional website, Santoro lists two other theatrical productions (in addition to the 2004 production of *Eva Perón*) in which he participated as set designer (and as costumer though that information is not included): *Las mucamas*, a 2003 adaptation of Genet's *Maids*, directed by Román Podolsky and adapted by Podolsky and Patricia Espinosa, Teatro del Abasto; and *Orejitas perfumadas*, a 2006 production based on texts by Roberto Arlt and music by Juan Cedrón, directed by Roberto Saiz, President Alvear Municipal Theatre. http://www.danielsantoro.com.ar/biografia. php?menu=biografia (accessed 25 June 2011). Santoro is also credited with light, set, and costume designs for Juan Carlos Fontana's 2009 production of Alejandro Tantanian's *Muñequita ó Juremos con gloria morir*, Teatro del Abasto. http://www.alterna-tivateatral.com/obra14010-munequita-o-juremos-con-gloria-morir (accessed 25 June 2011). In 2005 he created, with former metalworker and Colón set designer Miguel Biancuzzo, a model of "el Pulqui," the jet fighter plane designed at Juan Perón's request and at one time called the fastest plane in the world. The creation of the model, reduced to the scale of Eva Perón's "Children's City," and its brief flight are documented in Alejandro Fernández Moujan's 2007 film, *Pulqui: Un instante en la patria de la felicidad* [Pulqui: One Instant in the Homeland of Happiness].

10. http://es.wikipedia.org/wiki/Daniel_Santoro (accessed 24 June 2011).

11. Latin American *retablos* are popular devotional paintings and sculptures (often in combination) that typically utilize a traditional Catholic iconography. The term originally referred to the altar-pieces found in Spanish churches from the late Middle Ages into the Renaissance and then introduced to Latin America.

12. Catalog from exhibit "Santoro: civilización y barbarie-el gabinete justicialista" at Palatina Gallery, 5–25 November 2008, 4.

13. Guillermo Saccomanno, "Verdades del justicialismo," *Radar* (Supplement), *Página/12*, 9 November 2008 http://www.pagina12.com.ar/diario/suplementos/radar/9-4924-2008-11-10.html (accessed 24 October 2011).

14. Mercedes Urquiza, "Mitos y centauros en el bosque justicialista," *Perfil*, 9 November 2008 http://www.diarioperfil.com.ar/edimp/0311/articulo.php?art=10914 &ed=0311 (accessed 17 October 2011).

15. I discuss these two murals in this book's conclusion.

16. Qualifying Evita's "divine" role as "Marian" has been subjected to debate. In an unpublished study, Laura Linford (Williams) provides a discursive analysis of *La razón de mi vida*, concluding that while Perón certainly appears in the text as a Messianic or Christlike figure, Evita is represented far more frequently as his apostle rather than as the evangelist, prophet, or Madonna so frequently invoked. Linford finds that among the various parallels—some sixty-seven in total—only fourteen refer to the Gospels and ten to the Old Testament's prophets; of the thirty-three apostolic references encountered, thirty come from Saint Paul's epistles, suggesting that Eva's transformation into Evita bears parallels to Saul's transformation into Paul. Linford thus concludes that *La rázon* provides the reader with a Paul-like Evita-Peronist apostle: Eva comes across as a strong, influential and even masculinized spokesperson, who—despite a superficially presented submission—plays the lead in the "discourse of power," creating "a mimetic hierarchy that, by situating itself within a religious hierarchy, gives the power she possesses the illusion of 'nature.' Behind the disguise of love, self-sacrifice, and egalitarianism, she promotes a uniform society governed by her and by Perón, who rise above all others." Laura Linford, "Eva, Evita; Saúl, San Pablo: transformaciones discursivas" unpublished manuscript, 24.

17. Qtd. in Norberto Griffa, "La lejana patria de la felicidad" http://www.danielsantoro.com.ar/mundoperonista.php?menu=mundo&mp=6 (accessed 21 October 2011).

18. My analysis has greatly benefitted from two extended personal conversations with Daniel Santoro, Buenos Aires, in July 2011 and June 2013. I thank Norma Quarrato, of Buenos Aires's Palatina Gallery, for arranging our initial meeting.

19. Daniel Santoro, "La construcción imaginaria de un mundo," in *Perón mediante: gráfica peronista del período clásico*, ed. Guido Indij (Buenos Aires: La Marca Editora, 2006), 21–23, 21.

20. I refer, respectively, to "La tempestad en Chapadmalal" (2008), "Cabeza de playa" (2009), "Eva Perón como una selva oscura" (2008), "Eva Perón como un jardín cultivado" (2008), "Hallazgo" (2006), and "Plan de vivienda" (2011).

21. Alberto Ciria, "Flesh and Fantasy: The Many Faces of Evita (and Juan Perón)," review essay in *Latin American Research Review* 18, no. 2 (1983): 150–65, 158–59.

22. Here I follow the lead of Latin American cultural scholars, like Néstor García Canclini, who argue that there is no single popular culture.

23. Indeed, the debates over the appointment of the country's former Archbishop Jorge Mario Bergoglio as Pope Francis (the first Latin American and Jesuit to attain the papacy) have underscored many of these tensions.

24. As the Madres de la Plaza de Mayo have been the worthy subject of many other related analyses, I will not detail their performance practices here. Instead, I recommend, among other studies, Diana Taylor's *Disappearing Acts: Spectacles of Gender and Nationalism in Argentina's "Dirty War"* (Durham, NC: Duke University Press, 1997); and "Making a Spectacle: The Mothers of the Plaza de Mayo," in *The Politics*

of Motherhood: Activist Voices from Left to Right, ed. Alexis Jetter, Annelise Orleck, and Diana Taylor (Hanover, NH: University Press of New England, 1997).

25. Following Ngũgĩ Wa Thiong'o, I consider performance to be "the central feature of orature." The term comes from Ugandan linguist Pio Zirimu and denotes "an oral system of aesthetics" not requiring literature's validation. See "Notes Towards a Performance Theory of Orature," *Performance Research* 12, no. 3 (September 2007): 4–7. In this same essay, he calls for an exploration of "cyber-orature."

26. I borrow the categorization from a special issue of *e-misférica,* the electronic journal of the Hemispheric Institute of Politics and Performance, dedicated to the Americas' *vírgenes viajeras.* In their editorial remarks, Alyshia Gálvez and José Carlos Luque Brazán remark upon the Virgin Mary's apparent "special powers of *desdoblamiento,* or self-duplication, enabling her to 'be in more than one place at once' and 'go and stay at the same time.'" (Self) duplication is an intrinsic element of the virtual. *e-misférica* 5, no. 1 (April 2008) http://hemi.nyu.edu/journal/5.1/eng/en51_pg_galvez_brazan.html (accessed 29 October 2011).

27. See María Celeste Lores, *De Luján a Sumampa por el camino real* (Buenos Aires: Ediciones Lohlé-Lumen, 1998), which the author calls "a kind of: travel log, collection of stories [*anecdotario*], registry of emotions . . ." (19). See also Lores's professional website in which she promotes—for religious and cultural venues—her "historical musical" performance piece that includes "historical account, songs, dances, and video projections." http://mariacelestelores.com.ar/MILAGRO%20VIRGEN%20DE%20LUJAN%20Espectaculo .html (accessed 23 May 2013).

28. The lyrics and part of the musical annotation are reproduced in Lores, 28. The composer's own version of the song can be heard at Lores's website.

29. Linda B. Hall, *Mary, Mother and Warrior: The Virgin in Spain and the Americas* (Austin: University of Texas Press, 2004), 198. María Gisela Hadad and María Pía Venturiello discuss the Virgin of Luján's appearance as part of a larger foundational myth. "La Virgen de Luján como símbolo de identidad popular," in *Símbolos y fetiches religiosos en la construcción de la identidad popular,* vol. 2, ed. Rubén Dri (Buenos Aires: Editorial Biblos, 2007), 27–44, 37–39.

30. As Hall reminds us, "Mary is not God but the Mother of God. She is fully human, the vehicle through which Christ became flesh, but not herself a deity." Each of her many advocations is typically associated with one of the "four dogmas that distinguish her from other humans: her divine motherhood; her virginity; her immaculate conception . . . ; and her bodily assumption into heaven at her death" (7).

31. From various sources, Father Juan Antonio Presas deduces that a chapel was constructed within the year following the first chaplain's arrival. Pedro Montalbo is said to have arrived in 1684 and, attributing to the Virgin recovery from a near fatal illness, devoted himself to her. Juan Antonio Presas, *Anales de Nuestra Señora de Luján: trabajo histórico-documental,1630–2002* 4th ed. (Buenos Aires: Editorial Dunken, 2002), 45–46. The figure then passed among several private homes before settling in the Pueblo de Nuestra Señora de Luján. See Hadad and Venturiello, 29.

32. Arguably the most complete source for Luján's tale is Presas's *Anales,* the product of significant archival research. Presas notes that the original Rosendo *estancia* was located about thirty kilometers from today's basilica (23).

33. My other sources are historical as well as theological, and they include, among many: Presas; Hall; Lores; Pablo Bajo García, *María: Reina y madre de los argentinos: breve reseña de historia mariana argentina* 3rd ed. (Buenos Aires: Gram Editora [Hermanos Maristas], 1991); P. Eduardo Ramos, *Historia y novena de la Virgen de Luján* (Gualeguaychú, Argentina: Ediciones Pan y Trabajo, 1981); Jorge Juan Cortabarría, *El santuario de Luján 1753–1904* (Luján, Argentina: Librería de Mayo, 1994); Emilio Rodríguez, *La virgen María y todas las advocaciones de la República Argentina: nombres y fechas de conmemoración* (Buenos Aires: San Pablo, 2008); Ham Deimiles, *Historia popular de la Virgen de Luján: patrona jurada de Argentina, Uruguay y Paraguay* (Buenos Aires: Talleres Gráficos San Pablo, 1944); and Luis V. Varela, *Breve historia de la Virgen de Luján: su santuario y su culto desde 1630 hasta 1897* (Buenos Aires: Nicolás Avellaneda, 1897). There are far too many websites about and dedicated to the Virgin of Luján to note here.

34. Félix Coluccio, *Devociones populares argentinas y americanas* (Buenos Aires: Corregidor, 2001), 13. Frank Graziano calls these figures "folk saints": "Folk saints, known variously in Spanish America as santos populares, santos paganos, santones, and almas milagrosas, are deceased individuals (some of entirely constructed identity) who are popularly regarded as miraculous and receive the devotion of a substantial cult, but who are not canonized or officially recognized by the Catholic Church. Tragic death and fame as curanderos (healers) are the principal catalysts of folk devotions." http://www.culturesofdevotion.com/ (accessed 19 June 2011). Unlike Graziano, I prefer the adjective "popular" to what I consider to be the quainter "folk."

35. Floreal H. Forni, rather than considering popular Catholicism to be a "degeneration" of official Catholicism, more productively regards religiosity as a series of concentric circles moving away from an "orthodox center." Individuals can thus move in and out of various circles. Forni, "Reflexión sociológica sobre el tema de la religiosidad popular," *Sociedad y Religión* 3 (1986): 17.

36. Hadad and Venturiello cite Gilberto Giménez, who describes Latin American "popular religiosity" along three axes: one counterpoised to ecclesiastic-institutional sects, another pertaining to marginalized social sectors, and a third reflecting a history of religious syncretism (31). The authors refer to Gilberto Giménez's *Cultura popular y religión en el Anáhuac* (México, D.F.: Centro de Estudios Ecuménicos, 1978). Though noting that this final religious-syncretic coordinate has not played a major role in the popular religious practices of the particular region under consideration here, Hadad and Venturiello suggest that the first two are complicated and even contradicted in the Luján devotional practitioners, who span the socioeconomic spectrum and include practicing Catholics and non-churchgoers. Such contradictions are rendered even more complex in metropolitan Buenos Aires's massive religious manifestations that attract the urban middle classes as well as rural middle and working classes, and in the tourist trade that has sprung up to support and encourage pilgrimages. Hadad and Venturiello, 32. The authors build this final argument on Forni's essay. For an example of how the Virgin of Luján and the basilica have been interpolated into contemporary touristic practices, see the city's website http://www.lujanargentina.com/ciudaddelujan_provinciadebuenosaires.htm (accessed 20 June 2011), whose "tourism" page welcomes the visitor to "tourism, history, and religion in the city of Luján." I will return to the role of tourism in devotional performance practices with the Difunta Correa.

37. On 8 May 2013, Pope Francis brought flowers to the Virgin of Luján during the effigy's feast-day visit to Vatican City.

38. Hadad and Venturiello, 38.

39. San Cayetano is a principal Catholic saint in Argentina, where he is considered the "patron of bread and work" (whereas elsewhere in the Catholic world he is more frequently identified with gamblers and good fortune). Each year on August 7 hundreds of thousands go to the sanctuary in working-class Liniers; with the post-2001 crisis the numbers went up significantly. For information on San Cayetano devotional practices in contemporary Argentina, see Carla Wainsztok and Felipe Derqui, "La religión como una forma de racionalidad: el caso de San Cayetano," in *Símbolos y fetiches religiosos en la construcción de la identidad popular*, ed. Rubén Dri (Buenos Aires: Editorial Biblos, 2003), 35–52.

40. The calendar for these and other events can be found at the City of Luján's website http://www.lujanargentina.com/turismo_calendariodefestividades_provin ciadebuenosaires_eventosyfechasespeciales.htm (accessed 20 June 2011).

41. Hadad and Venturiello, 40–41.

42. Osvaldo Guglielmino, "Noticia histórico-cultural," *Oratorio a la Virgen de Luján* (Buenos Aires: Corregidor, 1991), 7.

43. Guglielmino, *Oratorio*, 45.

44. Presas, 26.

45. Néstor D'Alessandro, *La historia de la Virgen de Luján, contada y cantada por su fiel esclavo el Negro Manuel* (Buenos Aires: Editorial Claretiana, 1994).

46. For the price of 250 pesos, according to Presas, citing public records, 40.

47. Hall, 198.

48. Ibid., 198–99.

49. Eloísa Martín, "La virgen en dos países: apariciones marianas en la Argentina y el Brasil" http://www.dios.com.ar/notas1/creencias/cultos/la_virgen/nota_la_vir gen.htm (accessed 7 June 2011).

50. Hall, 203.

51. Martín, "La virgen."

52. Ibid. Hall credits much of her discussion of the twentieth-century Argentine church-state consolidation project to two unpublished essays by Martín.

53. The rightwing connection is still very present, as attested in a couple of e-mails I recently received from an Argentine playwright when he learned of this book chapter: "I was born in Luján and of course had to tolerate the devotion and hypocrisies of that 'Catholic' city . . . the Virgin now has very little left of the divine."

54. See Hall for details, 204–5.

55. Martín, "La virgen."

56. Ibid.

57. Qtd. in Lores, 89–90.

58. Qtd. in Ibid., 92.

59. Guglielmino, "Noticia histórico-cultural," 7.

60. Lores, 97.

61. Hadad and Venturiello, 41.

62. Ibid., 41–42.

63. Frank Graziano suggests that Difunta Correa's now-iconographic image was likely based on one of the figures in Uruguayan artist Juan Manuel Blanes's well-known 1871 painting *Un episodio de la fiebre amarilla en Buenos Aires* [An Episode of Yellow Fever in Buenos Aires] (housed in the Museo Nacional de Artes Visuales, Montevideo). Graziano makes a persuasive argument for attribution. Graziano, *Cultures of Devotion: Folk Saints of Spanish America* (Oxford: Oxford University Press, 2007), 180.

64. According to Barbara Calamari and Sandra DiPasqua, holy cards "[o]riginally developed as a way for Catholics to carry images of their patrons as one would carry a family photograph." *Patron Saints: A Feast of Holy Cards* (New York: Harry N. Abrams, 2007), 9. Bibiana Apolonia del Brutto notes that *estampitas* like my Buenos Aires card are ubiquitous throughout the San Juan province—in "cars, trucks [camiones], bicycles, houses, hotels." del Brutto, "La Difunta Correa," in *Símbolos y fetiches religiosos*, vol. 2 (2007), 128.

65. Indeed, on Good Friday (2011) alone, some thirty thousand people visited her sanctuary. See Emilio Ruchansky, "El pueblo que nació de los promesantes," *Página/12* 23 April 2011 http://www.pagina12.com.ar/diario/sociedad/3-166845-2011-04-23.html (accessed 15 June 2011).

66. See Graziano's website supporting his 2007 book http://www.culturesofdevotion.com/ (accessed 19 June 2011).

67. Such emphasis on "religious tourism" prompted Graziano to write: "Perhaps Difunta Correa's most outstanding miracle is the transformation of an inhospitable, waterless, practically useless patch of desert into new promise for San Juan's economic development" (188).

68. Ruchansky.

69. In their 1978 study, investigators Susana Chertudi and Sara Josefina Newbery present forty-nine different versions of the devotional figure's life and miracles. See *La Difunta Correa* (Buenos Aires: Editorial Huemul, 1978).

70. Coluccio, *Devociones populares argentinas y americanas*, 21. Tellingly, Coluccio ranks Difunta Correa first out of thirty "principal devotions." Gilda occupies the final slot, a further argument for her inclusion in the national pantheon of popular saints.

71. Again, some versions have the child dying a day later, while others claim he died in old age; similar variations are seen regarding her husband's fate. See del Brutto, 119. Graziano claims that, in the earliest versions of Correa's legend, "the breast-feeding miracle is entirely absent" and that it was only by the 1940s that the story "began to enter the myth." In such a version, he notes, Difunta Correa's devotion is brought on by her "tragic death" (179). Graziano devotes an entire chapter to Difunta Correa, 167–90.

72. As Graziano points out, there are earlier miracles on record (168).

73. Among these various artistic productions, several bear noting here: 1) *La Difunta Correa* [or *El hijo de la Difunta Correa*], a historical play by Manuel de la Vega [Manuel Menéndez], premiered by the author's company on 1 June 1950 in San Juan, Argentina (Beatriz Seibel, *Historia del teatro argentino II, 1930–1956: Crisis y cambios* [Buenos Aires: Corregidor, 2010], 340); 2) *Difunta Correa*, a 1975 film directed by Hugo Reynaldo Mattar, with soundtrack by Miguel Loubet; 3) Félix A. Blanco's 1958 vocal and piano text; 4) José Rafael "El Chacho" Arancibia and Pedro Castro Har-

doy's 1974 folkloric music album (of Arancibia performing with Los Chilicotes), "La Difunta Correa, el Milagro de San Juan"; and 5) Agustín Pérez Pardella's novel, *La difunta Correa* (Buenos Aires: Plus Ultra, 1975).

74. Graziano traces the tradition back to the Paleolithic Era (and possibly resonant with Isis, Hera, and Charity). For a genealogy of "the miraculous breast," see Graziano, 173–81.

75. Graziano mentions a local, colonial-era indigenous myth of a father sustaining his infant child's life through his own breast milk (176).

76. del Brutto, 135.

77. A first attempt was made during the 1976 (precoup) campaign to counter the more tolerant Vatican II and then again in 1982. A local priest (Father Ricardo Baez Laspiur, who "regarded folk saint devotion as an authentic expression of faith," Graziano, 172) was instrumental in developing the shrine from 1963 on, until his displacement in 1976. See Graziano, 172–73.

78. The designation *promesante* has been translated as promise-maker or pledger. In light of the very particular devotional practices surrounding Difunta Correa, I'm tempted to translate the term as promise-keeper, despite its recent usage in the United States by an evangelical Christian men's organization http://www.promise keepers.org/ (accessed 16 August 2011).

79. This particular quotation, made by San Juan's provincial governor José Luis Gioja, comes from Sonia Renison, "Cuestión de fe," *El Federal* (1 May 2008): 22–30, 24.

80. Ex-votos, from the Latin *ex voto suscepto* [in pursuance of a vow or simply a promise kept], are offerings made to a divinity in gratitude or devotion for a favor received though they may also be commemorative. They typically take the form of plaques, paintings, or objects left in sanctuaries or other sacred spaces. Ex-votos might have inscriptions (usually of thanks but also sometimes including a narrative of the devoted's experience); they may represent the illness of which the devoted has been cured (e.g., a crutch no longer needed or a small metal leg); and they may reflect some element with which the saint is identified (e.g., Difunta's filled water bottles). The practice is believed to predate Christianity.

81. One amateur documentary provides a bilingual (Spanish and English) tour of the various chapels http://www.youtube.com/watch?v=3zJANUNjDUU&feature=r elated (accessed 24 June 2011).

82. See Difunta Correa's "official website": http://www.visitedifuntacorrea.com. ar/ (accessed 26 June 2013). For a 2011 description of expansion plans, as well as statistics regarding resource usage, see Ruchansky.

83. For an illustrative collection of images of the Vallecito shrine, see the photo "gallery" at Graziano's website http://www.culturesofdevotion.com/.

84. J. Esquivel, qtd. in Coluccio, *Devociones populares argentinas y americanas*, 182.

85. Coluccio, *Devociones populares argentinas y americanas*, 177.

86. http://www.youtube.com/watch?v=LwYkMsKJ0Jw (accessed 23 June 2011). Montaño herself uploaded the promotional trailer to YouTube, with the following production information: "'Promesantes' dir. Dolores Montaño (Nanika Cine), 2011. Dirección y Producción: Dolores Montaño/Guión: Dolores Montaño y Mariano Juárez/Fotografía y Cámara: Alejandro Gatti/Sonido: Franco Gregoris/Montaje:

Mariano Juárez/Música original: Pablo Borghi-Octavio Gómez/Participación especial: Antonio Tarragó Ros-Pacho O'Donell/69min/HDV color—© Derechos Reservados 2011 // ARGENTINA." I thank Montaño for providing me with a DVD of her documentary.

87. Montaño concluded her prescreening reflections as follows: "How to measure the Faith of these Promesantes? How to know the correct way to act so the miracle is fulfilled? Not all the Promesantes who go to the sanctuary have received their miracle, but they nevertheless keep doing it because they believe in it . . . . There's no Church that can justify this phenomenon: the thousands of people believing in a legend, in a story that some consider only a 'narration of traditional or marvelous, rather than historical or real, events,' but that nevertheless mobilizes masses. It has to do with the simple need to believe in someone who gives [you] the strength to take on the most difficult moments. Its materialization in water bottles, candles, and personal sacrifice is sufficient proof of this need to believe." Publicity material http://www. laseptimadigital.com.ar/8.6.8/app/?mod=portal&ver=noticia&id=20245 (accessed 23 June 2011).

88. Forty-five years earlier (1966), Argentine director Néstor Paternostro's documentary displayed many of the more standard pilgrimage practices (e.g., people walking with sticks, crawling on their knees, riding bicycles, and traveling in carts), but the site was much less developed then. A brief clip from the 8'27" black-and-white documentary short can be accessed at http://www.youtube.com/watch?v=0x6qB3cJAPA. *La Difunta Correa* (1966), dir. Néstor Paternostro; cinematography: Carlos Parera; text: Luis Puenzo; stories: Miguel Saravia; and music: Marina Ambrosia.

89. There are relatively few YouTube uploads on Difunta, and most focus either on her story, such as an animated documentary history of the Difunta Correa, which was originally transmitted on the television program "Coronados de Gloria," with a script by Diego Arandojo, research by Daniel Balmaceda, and artwork by Paula Gigliotti: http://www.youtube.com/watch?v=D9Km_aUoRfc (accessed 22 June 2011); or on the remarkable ex-voto chapels that one YouTube narrator could describe only as "impresionantes." http://www.youtube.com/watch?v=3zJANUNjDUU&feature=re lated (accessed 24 June 2011); or on documentation of the physical sacrifice of the pilgrimage itself.

90. The 2008 statistics come from http://www.canal-ar.com.ar/noticias/noti ciamuestra.asp?Id=6788; http://www.argentina.ar/_es/pais/C1862-Internet-se-suma ran-3-millones-de-usuarios.php (accessed 9 June 2011).

91. Recent statistics can be found at such business and national online sites as http://www.newmediatrendwatch.com/markets-by-country/11-long-haul/35-argen tina and http://www.Internetworldstats.com/stats2.htm (accessed 17 June 2013). Two programs were created to provide every public-school student with a laptop by 2012: Programa Conectar Igualdad [Equality Connect Program] and Plan S@rmiento BA [Buenos Aires S@rmiento Plan], part of a three-year government initiative to distribute some three million computers. Similar "One Laptop Per Child" [OLPC] programs have been undertaken in neighboring Peru, Uruguay, and Paraguay. Among the many articles, see http://www.argentinaindependent.com/currentaffairs/news fromargentina/wireless-education-free-laptops-for-public-schools-/ (accessed 16 August 2011).

Internet usage throughout Latin America has grown at an astounding rate in the past decade. In 2008 alone, usage increased by 900 percent (cf. U.S. growth of 137 percent). While Brazil and Mexico have the largest numbers of users, Argentina, Uruguay, and Chile often lead in percentage of the population surfing the Internet. One study positions Argentina as the third top "Facebook country" in the world, with 63.5 percent participating in social media. As a comparison, similar data shows that 78.1 per cent of the U.S. population accesses the Internet, with 59.1 percent on Facebook http://www.newmediatrendwatch.com/markets-by-country/11-long-haul/35-argentina (accessed 18 June 2013).

92. There is a growing body of scholarship on the role of the Internet in contemporary devotional practices. See, for example, George Edward Brandon, "From Oral to Digital: Rethinking the Transmission of Tradition in Yorùbá Religion," in *Òrìṣà Devotion as World Religion: The Globalization of Yorùbá Religious Culture*, ed. Jacob K. Olupona and Terry Rey (Madison: University of Wisconsin Press, 2008), 448–69; and Mark W. MacWilliams, "Virtual Pilgrimages on the Internet," *Religion* 32 (2002): 315–35.

93. In Argentina, *cosa de negros* ["black people's thing"] is a phrase employed to degrade popular cultural products. It is important to note that while *negro* can refer to a person of indigenous or African ancestry, it is a tag used to include just about anyone of the "lower" socioeconomic sectors (as in the marginalized *cabecitas negras* [little black heads] who supported Juan and Eva Perón).

94. It is therefore not particularly surprising that when, in her last televised interview, Gilda was asked to name her favorite Argentine artist, she unhesitatingly answered "Gardel." Marcelo Gopar, "El último reportaje a Gilda" http://www.homenajeagilda.com.ar/inicio2.htm and available on YouTube (last accessed 5 October 2009).

95. Indeed, and as Daniel Míguez and Pablo Semán point out in their introduction to an essay collection on contemporary Argentine popular cultures, most popular cultural studies projects tend toward limited "case studies" of an isolated social sector and rarely reflect upon a larger reality. See "Introducción: Diversidad y recurrencia en las culturas populares actuales," in *Entre santos, cumbias y piquetes: las culturas populares en la Argentina reciente*, ed. Míguez and Semán (Buenos Aires: Editorial Biblos, 2006), 11–32, 11.

96. Miriam's mother wanted to name her daughter Gilda, but Argentina has an official (albeit always changing) registry that prescribes which names may be lawfully used. At that time "Gilda" was not on the official registry. It now is.

97. Miriam/Gilda's father, Omar, suffered a stroke when she was ten; her mother, Tita, worked at home, giving piano lessons. I've yet to find concrete information about her father's profession, but the family's socioeconomic status is usually described as lower middle class. On her mother's side, Gilda was the second cousin of Daniel Scioli, onetime auto racer, governor of the Province of Buenos Aires, and potentially future Peronist presidential candidate.

98. Gladys, "La Bomba Tucumana," is best known for her Cumbia hit "La pollera amarilla" [the yellow skirt].

99. Ricky Maravilla [Marvel] is the stage name of Ricardo Aguirre, born in the northwestern Argentine province of Salta and one of the stars of the 1980s and 1990s Cumbia movement. For more information and clips, see Ricky's official website http://www.rickymaravilla.com/home.htm (accessed 1 October 2009).

100. My biographical sketch is culled from multiple sources, most of which follow a traditional hagiographic model in telling the same story and emphasizing the same key details of Gilda's life. See, for example, Pablo Francisco Di Leo, "El culto a Gilda: religiosidad, arte e instituciones populares," in *Símbolos y fetiches religiosos* (2003), 121–44. A biographical note signed by Analía Balbi reads practically verbatim http://cer0.tripod.com/gilda.html (accessed 1 October 2009).

101. The album included the singer's original songs along with covers such as "Jesus Christ" from the Lloyd Webber-Rice rock opera. Gilda's official discography consists of *Gilda, la única* (1993); *Pasito a pasito* (1994, with her first hit, "No me arrepiento de este amor" [I Don't Regret this Love]); *Corazón Valiente* (1995), whose first track, "Fuiste" [You Left], was made into a music video [uploaded to YouTube http://www.youtube.com/watch?v=axWsEHe0xC8 (accessed 24 May 2013)]; and the posthumous *Entre el cielo y la tierra*. See also the comprehensive Gilda YouTube channel (http://www.youtube.com/user/GildaPasionOficial [accessed 24 May 2013]) and her Facebook page (https://www.facebook.com/GildaOficial).

102. By 1998, Cumbia artists were selling six million records a year, and there were approximately three hundred dance clubs [*bailantas*] in Greater Buenos Aires, each attracting on average fifteen hundred patrons on any given weekend. Gabriela Almi, "La bailanta, un negocio que produce millones," *Clarín*, 8 February 1999, qtd. in Di Leo, 129.

103. The Cumbia itself is considered to have originated in Colombia. See Héctor Fernández L'Hoeste, "All Cumbias, the Cumbia: The Latin Americanization of a Tropical Genre," in *Imagining Our Americas: Toward a Transnational Frame*, ed. Sandhya Rajendra Shukla and Heidi Tinsman (Durham, NC: Duke University Press, 2007), 338–64, for a discussion of Cumbia's Colombian origins and various fluidly heterogeneous forms, including the Argentine variant of the *cumbia villera*, which sprang up in the late 1990s in Buenos Aires's slums or *villas miseria*.

104. Buenos Aires working-class and often marginalized *suburbios* should not be confused with the U.S. middle-class and typically privileged suburbs.

105. Eloísa Martín, "'No me arrepiento de este amor. Fans y devotos de Gilda, una cantante argentina," *Ciencias Sociales y Religión/Ciências Sociais e Religião* 6, no. 6 (October 2004): 101–15, 102. Between March 2002 and September 2003, Martín conducted fieldwork, interviewing members of Gilda's fan clubs and visitors to her tomb in Chacarita.

106. Ibid., 102–3. Soccer club San Lorenzo adopted "Fuiste," and Diego Maradona's former club, Boca Juniors, chose "No me arrepiento de este amor."

107. According to Martín, only one of the clubs founded before Gilda's death is still in existence. Ibid., 108. Their names are typically well-known song titles or modifications of the singer's name (e.g., "No me arrepiento de este amor," "Las Gilderas," "Noches vacías").

108. Ibid.

109. 7 September and 11 October, her respective death and birth days.

110. The number 7—together with the number 17—is considered particularly powerful. See Eloísa Martín, "La doble de Gilda, o cómo, cantando cumbias, se hace una santa popular," in *Entre santos, cumbias y piquetes*, 75–96, 83.

111. One prayer card reads, "Gilda, do not abandon me at any moment, because I need your infinite kindness to protect me from all evil." Qtd. in Martín Hugo Córdova

Quero, "Building up Ancestors in Argentinian Popular Culture: The Cases of Santa Gilda and el Angel Rodrigo," *Studies in World Christianity* 9, no. 1 (2003): 5–29, 14.

112. See Martín, "No me arrepiento," 110–11.

113. Particular mention is typically made of Gilda's feet, which suffered from some condition that left them bloody and caused her great pain even when standing.

114. http://www.youtube.com/watch?v=N5DfxWpZKI0&feature=related América Noticias, 7 September 2009 (accessed 2 October 2009, no longer available). See also http://www.youtube.com/watch?v=z2qMKn6mRZY (accessed 14 June 2013).

115. http://www.cumbiadelapura.com.ar/2010/12/una-tarde-de-fe.html (accessed 24 October 2011).

116. As the reporter notes, the formal portrait of vice president Julio Cobos was most likely hung in response to his defense of the "country" during the rural landowners' (and their workers') struggles with president Cristina Fernández de Kirchner, who until recently was noticeably absent from the devotional (and rurally identified) pantheon.

117. http://www.youtube.com/watch?v=N5DfxWpZKI0&feature=related América Noticias, 7 September 2009 (accessed 2 October 2009, no longer available).

118. http://www.myspace.com/celeste25h/photos/613450#%7B%22ImageId%2 2%3A613450%7D (accessed 2 August 2011).

119. Such impersonation crosses devotional lines. Martín dedicates an essay to discussing Silvia Corazón Valiente, a Cumbia singer from a Buenos Aires suburb who claims to be Gilda's double and direct successor. See Martín, "La doble."

120. Gopar, "El último reportaje."

121. As Martín points out, the media often use Gilda's death as a sort of matrix for understanding other tragic deaths, most frequently of celebrities. See Martín, "No me arrepiento," 103.

122. "Santa Gilda" in *Radar* supplement to *Página/12*, 24 May 1998 http://www.pagina12.com.ar/1998/suple/radar/mayo/98-05-24/vale.htm (accessed 5 October 2009).

123. See chapter three for an overview of the crisis.

124. Cucurto is also the founder of a publishing collective, Eloísa Cartonera, which creates artisanal editions from recycled cardboard collected by the *cartoneros*, Buenos Aires's independent recyclers.

125. Córdova Quero goes so far as to assert, "At the base of popular religiosity is the critique of rationalist modernism" (19).

126. Brandon, 466.

127. Joseph M. Murphy, "Òrìṣà Traditions and the Internet Diaspora," in *Òrìṣà Devotion*, 470–84, 472 passim.

128. Ibid., 475.

129. Although I do not dispute the claim that religions function as memeplexes, my focus here is on individual and limited collective devotional Internet practices. Likewise, a consideration of Internet memes—the circulating elements—would divert this chapter's focus from the practices and practitioners themselves. For an early application of Richard Dawkins's influential theory of memetics, see Susan Blackmore, *The Meme Machine* (Oxford: Oxford University Press, 1999).

130. An example is the actor Orlando Bloom, at one time a saint apparent of online devotional fandom. See P.J. Huffstutter, "'Rings' Role Vaults Actor to Hot Status," *Los Angeles Times*, 10 January 2002 http://articles.latimes.com/2002/jan/10/news/tt-tip10.2 (accessed 1 October 2009).

131. In the case of Gilda fan practices (and I suspect this holds for most others), social networking technologies seem to be replacing the "depository" website model.

132. *Muñeca brava*'s Uruguayan-born star, Natalia Oreiro, who appears in the clip as the red-cap-wearing Cholito, was slated to play Gilda in a biopic that has not yet been made. The clip's Romanian subtitles also give us an idea of just how far Argentine soap operas travel.

133. As MacWilliams points out, Christianity has long experienced slippage between the virtual and the real, the bread and the wine of the Eucharist being one historically debated example.

134. Philip Carr-Gomm, "Armchair Travel," *Resurgence & Ecologist* 255 (July/August 2009) http://www.resurgence.org/magazine/article2864-Armchair-Travel.html (accessed 1 October 2009).

135. Martín Kohan, at the 2009 Buenos Aires Book Fair, qtd. in Tucumán's *La Gaceta*, 10 May 2009 http://www.lagaceta.com.ar/nota/325577/LGACETLiteraria/Sarcasmo_garrotazos_durante_Feria_Libro_Buenos_Aires.html (accessed 1 October 2009).

136. *Soi Cumbio*, dir. Andrea Yannino, premiered September 2011.

137. See Alexei Barrionuevo's profile, "In Argentina, a Camera and a Blog Make a Star," *New York Times*, 14 March 2009, A7. This article's existence speaks to Cumbio's then-growing international fame.

138. On 15 July 2010, Argentina legalized same-sex marriage, including full adoption rights. In 2012, a "gender identity law" went into effect: public and private healthcare plans are required to include sex-reassignment surgery and hormone therapy, and Argentines over the age of eighteen may now legally change their official identities without a doctor or judge's approval. As Michael Warren wrote at the law's passage, "No other country in the world allows people to change their official identities based merely on how they feel." "Argentina's Gender Identity Law Takes Effect," *Huffington Post*, 4 June 2012 http://www.huffingtonpost.com/2012/06/05/argentina-gender-identity-law-takes-effect_n_1570830.html (accessed 30 March 2013).

139. Cumbio [Agustina Vivero], *Yo Cumbio: La vida según la flogger más famosa del país* (Buenos Aires: Planeta, 2008), 72.

140. Ibid., 158.

141. Both remain points of debate, with experts and statistics in support and opposition. Journalist, television producer, and monologist Gonzalo Otálora's book, *¡Feo!* [Ugly!] (Buenos Aires: Martínez Roca, 2007), called for a tax on the good-looking. Otálora's self-identification as *feosexual* [uglysexual] suggests that Argentina's cult of beauty is by no means exclusively female.

142. Graziano, 69.

143. Cumbio, 174.

144. Ibid., 107.

145. Ibid., 109.

146. P. David Marshall, "New Media–New Self: The Changing Power of Celebrity," in *The Celebrity Culture Reader*, ed. Marshall (New York: Routledge, 2006), 634–44, 637, 644.

147. Pappo, qtd. in Fernández L'Hoeste, 338.

CONCLUSION

1. Interview in *El País* (Spain), reprinted in *Clarín* (Argentina) 27 July 2007. http://www.clarin.com/diario/2007/07/27/elpais/p-00803.htm (accessed 3 August 2009).

2. I study these three Argentine femicons and their involvement in that country's recent politico-cultural scene in "Eva / Nacha / Cristina and the Argentine Trinity of Local, National, and Global Urban Politics," in *Performance and the Global City*, ed. D.J. Hopkins and Kim Solga (London: Palgrave Macmillan, 2013), 61–77.

3. Kirchner's economic and human rights victories have also been accompanied by criticisms of an excessive exertion of executive powers, as well as ongoing accusations, from the couple's years in Santa Cruz, of misuse of public funds and exploitation of public resources.

4. Cristina was first elected as national senator from Santa Cruz (1995–1997), then served as the province's national *diputada* [congresswoman] (1997–2001), and was reelected as its national senator (2001–2005) before being elected as national senator from Buenos Aires (2005–2007) during her husband's presidency.

5. *Diarquía* has been the term used most frequently to question the motives informing the Kirchners' joined forces. See, for example, one particularly critical op-ed note published shortly after Néstor's death by Martín Santiváñez Vivanco, "Kirchner, sic transit gloria mundi," *La Nación*, 31 October 2010 repr. http://www.elmundo.es/america/2010/10/29/argentina/1288378440.html (accessed 25 June 2013).

6. Argentina is not alone; Brazil and Chile, among other countries, have joined their neighbor in stopping Falklands-flagged ships from docking at their ports.

7. Robb Young, *Power Dressing: First Ladies, Women Politicians & Fashion* (London: Merrell, 2011), 77.

8. The accusation has been attributed to Elisa Carrió, who herself has undergone an Evita-style transformation from brunette to blonde, as well as the Kirchners' most visible media adversaries, the *Clarín* newspaper conglomerate.

9. "I have painted myself like I was a door since I was 14" is another often-cited quote. See Uki Goñi, "Cristina Kirchner: she's not just another Evita," *The Observer*, 4 February 2012 http://www.guardian.co.uk/theobserver/2012/feb/05/observer-profile-cristina-kirchner-argentina (accessed 5 June 2012).

10. "El extraño luto de Cristina Kirchner," *Perfil.com*, 15 March 2011 http://wap.perfil.com/contenidos/2011/03/15/noticia_0025.html (accessed 5 June 2012).

11. A recent musical based on Camila O'Gorman's brief life gets an easy laugh when Camila's mother states that one day "a woman will govern us," to which Camila's father responds, after a beat: "That would be a *disparate* [absurdity, folly]."

12. http://www.forbes.com/profile/cristina-fernandez/ (accessed 4 June 2012). At the time of this writing, she is listed nineteenth.

13. Goñi.

14. An Internet search of "Cristina-Evita" provides millions of hits, including: Philip Sherwell, "Argentina's New Evita has a clear run to office," *Daily Telegraph,* 21 October 2007 http://telegraph.co.uk/news/worldnews/1566878/argentinas-new-evita-has-a-clear-run-to-office.html; "Is Argentina's Cristina Fernández de Kirchner the next Evita?," *The Week,* 19 April 2012 http://theweek.com/article/index/226951/is-argentinas-cristina-fernandez-de-kirchner-the-next-evita; Goñi; Rachel Nolan, "Well-Coiffed World Leaders," *New York Times* Sunday *Magazine*'s "One-Page Magazine," 15 January 2012, 11; "She's sexier than Evita, as tough as Maggie . . . ," *The Sun,* 20 January 2012 http://www.thesun.co.uk/sol/homepage/features/4074118/Cristina-Fernandez-de-Kirchner-Shes-sexier-than-Evita-as-tough-as-Maggie-with-her-eyes-on-the-Falklands.html (all accessed 5 June 2012).

15. Qtd. in Martín Granovsky, "Las dos miradas de Evita," *Página/12,* 24 July 2011 http://www.pagina12.com.ar/diario/elpais/1-172939-2011-07-24.html (accessed 25 June 2013).

16. Ibid.

17. Two examples from the 2013 Buenos Aires theatre season should suffice: in the commercial hit musical, *Manzi, la vida en Orsai* (based on the life of tango lyricist, poet, and politician Homero Manzi), when the dying protagonist learns he is hospitalized down the hall from Evita, he asks his lover to deliver a religious medallion ("She needs it more than I do."); meanwhile, at a much smaller venue, the independent production *Piernas entrelazadas* [Intertwined Legs] takes its three working-class sisters through the early 1950s with, of course, radiophonic references to the Peróns.

18. Florencia Donovan, "El comercio no confía en el billete de Eva Perón," *La Nación,* 9 October 2012 http://www.lanacion.com.ar/1515606-el-comercio-no-confia-en-el-billete-de-eva-peron (accessed 25 June 2013).

19. Nicola Costantino states, in an interview, that she intended "to move away from biography" and "to analyze this icon in all her endless and paradoxical complexity." "All about Eva," *Drome Magazine* http://www.dromemagazine.com/nicola-costantino-all-about-eva/ (accessed 25 June 2013).

20. Lucian Comoy, "Evita, a sort of St. Margaret Thatcher at the Argentine Pavilion," *The Art Newspaper* http://www.theartnewspaper.com/articles/Evita,+a+sort+of+St+Margaret+Thatcher+at+the+Argentina+pavilion/29803 (accessed 25 June 2013).

21. Daniel Santoro, "Nadie sabe lo que puede un ícono," Unpublished manuscript. I thank Santoro for sharing it with me.

22. Martin Kemp, *Christ to Coke: How Image Becomes Icon* (Oxford: Oxford University Press, 2012), 181.

23. Ibid., 346.

24. Indeed, the President said she conceived the benevolent Evita while viewing a mural of Guevara at the Cuban Ministry of the Interior during a trip to Havana in 2009. Leonardo Míndez, "Con aires de campaña porteña, Cristina rindió homenaje a Evita," *Clarín,* 27 July 2011 http://www.clarin.com/politica/elecciones/campana-portena-Cristina-homenaje-Evita_0_524947548.html (accessed 11 June 2012).

25. Qtd. in Granovsky.

Index

Acosta, Clotilde. *See* Guevara, Nacha
Aira, César, 107
Aldaburu, María Inés, 119, 125
Alfonsín, Raúl, 38
"Altarcito" (Santoro), *134*, 135
Alvarado, Ana, 55. *See also pasión sudamericana, Una*; Periférico de Objetos
Amadori, Luis César
    amor nunca muere, El [Love Never Dies] (film), 33
Amalia (Mármol novel), 31
Amícola, José, 109
amor de la estanciera, El [The Love of the Rancher's Daughter] (anonymous play), 66
amor nunca muere, El [Love Never Dies] (Amadori film), 33
Anastasia querida [Dear Anastasia] (Guevara one-woman play, 1969), 66
Andrea, Miguel de, 145
Angelelli, Guillermo, 55
    pasión sudamericana, Una [A South American Passion Play] (Monti), in, 55
Apollinaire, Guillaume, 37
Ara, Pedro, 99
Aramburu, Eugenio, 100
Argentine Anticommunist Alliance (The Triple A), 67
Arias, Imanol, 48
Artaud, Antonin, 122, 124–25
    To Have Done with the Judgment of God (radio play), 125
Artime, Ignacio, 60
Ascasubi, Hilario, 28

Austria-Hungría (Perlongher poetry collection), 119–20
Auyero, Javier, 2
Avenida 9 de Julio (Buenos Aires), 137
Ayrinhac, Numa, *95*, 170
Azpilicueta, Jaime, 60, 61. *See also* Artime, Ignacio; *Evita* (Spanish-language version); "No llores por mi, Argentina"

Babilonia (Buenos Aires independent performance space), 119, 120
bailantas [dance clubs], 156, 158
Ballerini, Alberto, 31
    Camila O'Gorman: poema dramático en cinco actos, un epílogo y en verso [Camila O'Gorman: dramatic poem in five acts, an epilogue, and in verse] (with Rossi), 30–31
Banegas, Cristina, 91–92, 171
    El Excéntrico de la 18° (Buenos Aires independent performance space), founder of, 91
    Eva Perón (Desanzo film), as Juana Ibarguren (mother of Eva Perón) in, 93
    Eva Perón en la hoguera (Lamborghini poetry staging), in, 91–92
"Baptism of Camila O'Gorman's Unborn Child Before Going to Punishment" (Verazzi charcoal), 26
Barney Finn, Oscar, 89, 92
    Eva y Victoria (Ottino play), director, 89, 92
Barthes, Roland, 6–7
Bartís, Ricardo
    Hamlet: La guerra de los teatros (1991–92 staging), 101–2

Basi, Le [Feet] (Marinetti theatre piece), 124

Batlle Planas, Juan

   destino, El [Destiny/Fate] (film), 33

Bemberg, María Luisa, 43–50

   Camila (film), 11, 20, 31, 34, 43–50

      analysis, symbolic and visual, 45–46

      Argentine Catholic Church, conflicts with during filming, 45

      Arias, Imanol, in, 48

      Calvo, Leonor, researcher, 45

      characterizations, 45–50

      Foster, David William, on, 45, 49–50

      Gutiérrez, Uladislao, characterization in, 48–50

      King, John, on, 45, 47

      Latin American melodrama, as, 47–48

      malasangre, La (Gambaro play), comparison of father figures, 46

      Morris, Barbara, on, 47–48

      O'Gorman, Camila, characterization in, 47, 48–50

      Pecoraro, Susú, in, 48

      Perichon de Vandeuil y D'Abeille, Marie Anne ("Anita") (grandmother of Camila O'Gorman), characterization in, 48–49

      romantic drama, as, 46–47

      Schumann, Peter, on, 49–50

      Stantic, Lita, producer, 45

      success, commercial and artistic, 45

      Thompson, Currie K., on, 47

      tragedy, as, 48–50

      Williams, Bruce, on, 49–50

   De eso no se habla [I Don't Want to Talk About It] (film), 72

   Monti, Ricardo, comparison of Camila O'Gorman treatments, 56–57

   posthumous reputation, 44

Benjamin, Walter

   "Theses on the Philosophy of History" (essay), 73

Berruti, Rómulo, 128

Bianchi, Miriam Alejandra. *See* Gilda

Big Lebowski, The (Coen Brothers film), 6

Bilbao, Miguel, 26

Bishop, Karen, 73

Bo, Facundo, 106, *108*

   Di Fonzo Bo, Marcial, uncle of, 127

   Eva Perón (Copi play), portrayal of title role in original production (1970), 106, 107

Boal, Augusto, 32–33

Bollig, Ben, 109

Borges, Jorge Luis, 88, 159

   "simulacro, El" [The Simulacrum] (short story), 103

   Schwartz, Margaret, on, 103

Braidotti, Rosi, 71

Brando, Luisina, 90–91, 94

   Eva y Victoria (Ottino play), as Eva Perón in, 90–91, 94

Brandon, George Edward, 159

Brecht, Bertolt, 125

Buenos Aires (national capital and province), 15, 17, 18, 21, 22, 23, 24, 25, 26, 28, 30, 31, 51, 63, 71, 76, 85, 86, 87, 100, 104, 106, 109, 110, 125, 140, 145, 162, 168

Buenos Aires International Book Fair, 162

Cabildo Abierto, 80

café-concert, 66, 69, 176

Camila O'Gorman (Bemberg film), filming in churches, 45

estampita [prayer card] distribution, 148

Eva Perón (Copi play), 2004 restagings, 12, 105, 106, 110, 126–28, 176

Eva, el gran musical argentino (Guevara, Orgambide, Favero)

   original production (1986), 61, 67

   restaging (2008), 61, 96

Evita (Lloyd Webber-Rice musical), absence of professional staging, 61

Evita (Parker film version of Lloyd Webber-Rice musical), premiere (1997), 65

Evita tours, 3

Fernández de Kirchner, Cristina, provincial origins, 166, 167

geographical situation, 140, 143, 146

internal migration, 148

musical theatre tradition, 66

neighborhoods

   Constitución, 135

   La Boca, 2, 5

   Liniers, 143

   Palermo, 159

   San Cristóbal, 163

   Villa Devoto, 154

   working-class suburbs, 154

"No llores por mí, Argentina," local performances, 61

Perlongher, Néstor, departure, 120
Perón (Duarte), Eva
   move to, 77, 79, 84
   public iconography, *172, 173*
Primera plana (cultural magazine), 66
Rice, Tim, *Evita* research trips, 60
sites
   Abasto market, 163
   Avenida 9 de Julio, 137
   bailantas [dance clubs], 156, 158
   Chacarita Cemetery, 155, 160
   Constitución train station, 159
   Corrientes Street, 66
   Health and Social Development Min-
      istries Building, 169–70
   Kavanagh Building, 79
   National University of Buenos Aires, 3
   Perón (Duarte), Eva
      public iconography, 169–71
   Recoleta Cemetery, 3, 100
   San José Church, 164
theatre traditions, 111, 121, 122–23
theatres and performance venues
   Babilonia (independent performance
      space), 119, 120
   Cervantes National Theatre, 20, 50,
      55, 56, 81
   Colón Theatre, 135
   Di Tella Institute, 66
   El Excéntrico de la 18° (independent
      performance space), 91
   Gandhi (downtown bookstore), 91
   General San Martín Municipal The-
      atre, 50, 102
   La Trastienda (independent perfor-
      mance space), 53
   Maipo Theatre, 61
   Odeón Theatre, 38
   Olimpia Theatre, 39
   Payró Theatre, 132
   Recoleta Cultural Center, 91
   Yiddish Folk Theatre (IFT), 132
Tintas Frescas (theatre festival, 2004), 127
tourist industry, 5
Bustos, Clemente (Baudilio) (husband of
   Difunta Correa), 150
Byron, George Gordon Noel (Lord By-
   ron), 32

Cabildo Abierto, 80
Cabrera, Hilda, 128
"cadáver, El" [The Cadaver/Corpse] (Per-

longher poem), 120. *See also Cadáveres;*
   Pista 4
"Cadáveres" [Corpses] (Perlongher
   poem), 120, 122
Cadáveres [Corpses] (Pista 4 performance
   of Perlongher poems), 9, 12, 105,
   119–26, 130. *See also* FM radio theatre;
   Perlongher, Néstor
Basi, Le (Marinetti theatre piece), refer-
   enced, 124
Buenos Aires performances, 120–21
"cadáver, El" [The Cadaver/Corpse]
   (Perlongher poem), 120
"Cadáveres" [Corpses] (Perlongher
   poem), 120
Cardozo, Edgardo, sound track, 120
desaparecidos, theatrical representation
   of, 119–23
"Por qué seremos tan hermosas" [Why
   must we be so beautiful] (Perlong-
   her poem), 124
sound design, 119–21
café-concert, 66, 69, 176
Calegaris, Mariano, 131
Momia en el clóset [Mummy in the Closet]
   (Ott-Vales musical), director, 131
Calvo, Leonor, 45
Camila (Bemberg film), 11, 20, 31, 34,
   43–50
analysis, symbolic and visual, 45–46
Argentine Catholic Church, director's
   and producer's conflicts with dur-
   ing filming, 45
Arias, Imanol, in, 48
Calvo, Leonor, researcher, 45
characterizations, 45–50
Foster, David William, on, 45, 49–50
Gutiérrez, Uladislao, characterization
   in, 48–50
King, John, on, 45, 47
Latin American melodrama, as, 47–48
malasangre, La (Gambaro play), com-
   parison of father figures, 46
Morris, Barbara, on, 47–48
O'Gorman, Camila, characterization in,
   47, 48–50
Pecoraro, Susú, in, 48
Perichon de Vandeuil y D'Abeille, Marie
   Anne ("Anita") (grandmother of
   Camila O'Gorman), characteriza-
   tion in, 48–49
romantic drama, as, 46–47

Camila (Bemberg film) (*continued*)
  Schumann, Peter, on, 49–50
  *sombra donde sueña Camila O'Gorman,
    Una* [A Shadow Where Camila
    O'Gorman is Dreaming] (Molina
    novel), compared to, 45
  Stantic, Lita (producer), 45
  success, commercial and artistic, 45
  Thompson, Currie K., on, 47
  tragedy, as, 48–50
  Williams, Bruce, on, 49–50
Camila (Pérez Pardella musical), 33–34
Camila O'Gorman (Fajardo play), 28–29,
    30, 31, 43
  censorship at premiere, 29
  characterizations, 29
  Lázaro, character of, 29
  Míguez, Graciela, on, 29
  Seibel, Beatriz, on, 29
  Trigo, Abril, on, 29
Camila O'Gorman (Gallo lost silent film),
    30
Camila O'Gorman (Mendoza Ortiz verse
    drama), 30
  characterizations, 30
  Werth, Brenda, on, 30
Camila O'Gorman (Péllisot novel, translated
    into Spanish by Fajardo), 28
*Camila O'Gorman: poema dramático en cinco
    actos, un epílogo y en verso* [Camila
    O'Gorman: dramatic poem in five
    acts, an epilogue, and in verse] (Bal-
    lerini, Rossi), 30–31
Camila O'Gorman: una tragedia argentina
    [Camila O'Gorman: an Argentine
    tragedy] (Olivera play), 33
Camila, un misterio argentino (Monti). *See
    pasión sudamericana, Una* (Monti)
Cámpora, Héctor, 100
Capone, Stefania, 159
Capote, Truman, 104
Cardozo, Edgardo, 120, 125. *See also
    Cadáveres* (Pista 4 performance of
    Perlongher poems)
Carlson, Marvin, 5
Carnevale, Marcos
  Mercedes (short film), 21, 57
Carr-Gomm, Philip, 161
Casey, Michael, 7
Castellanos, Félix, 26
Castiñeira de Dios, José María, 85
Castro, Alfredo, 127

"cautiva, La" [The Captive Girl] (Echever-
    ría epic poem), 29
celebrity, 4, 6–9, 58–59, 65. *See also*
    femicons; icons; individual names;
    mythologization
  cults and religion, 132–65. *See also* Cor-
    rea, María Antonia Deolinda "Di-
    funta"; Cumbio (Vivero, Agustina);
    Fernández de Kirchner, Cristina;
    Gilda (Bianchi, Miriam Alejandra);
    Guevara, Nacha; icons; Perón (Du-
    arte), Eva as Santa Evita; Santoro,
    Daniel; Virgin of Luján
  cultural fabrication, as, 7
  Dyer, Richard, on, 6
  femicons in performance, 94–97
  globalized, 14
  Janes, Regina, on, 8
  Marshall, P. David, on, 8
  myth and, 6
  pre-figurative (Rojek), 58
  Quinn, Michael L., on, 6
  Roach, Joseph, on, 7–8
  Rojek, Chris, on, 6, 7, 58
  virtuality in, 14
Cervantes National Theatre (Buenos
    Aires), 20, 50, 55, 56, 81
Chacarita Cemetery (Buenos Aires), 155,
    160
Chamosa, Oscar, 10
Chávez, Hugo, 168
Che (Soderburgh film), 1
Chekhov, Anton, 32
Child, Jack, 103
Ciccone, Madonna Louise. *See* Madonna
Ciria, Alberto, 138
Clinton, Hillary, 75
Colón Theatre (Buenos Aires), 135
Coluccio, Félix, 142, 150, 152
Confederación General de Trabajo (CGT)
    [General Confederation of Work], 80
Constitución (Buenos Aires working-class
    neighborhood), 135
Constitución train station (Buenos Aires),
    159
Copi (Damonte Botana, Raúl Natalio)
  Amícola, José, on, 109
  Eva Perón (play), 9, 12, 105–8, 119, 126–
    28, 176
  Aira, César, on, 107
  Correa revival (Buenos Aires, 2004),
    127–28, *129*

des/Enlace (Viñao play), compared to, 111, 130
Di Fonzo Bo-Théâtre des Lucioles revival (Buenos Aires, 2004), 126–28, *129*
original production (1970), *108*
  Bo, Facundo, title role in, 106, 107, *108*
  Buenos Aires iconic images, use of, 107
  Moretti, Michelle, in, 107
  Platé, Roberto, set design, 107
  Rodríguez Arias, Alfredo, director, 106, 108
  violent response, 106
  Plotnik, Viviana Paula, on, 107
  Rosenzvaig, Marcos, on, 106, 108
  "tragic farce," as, 106
  transvestism, use of, 106–8
Lavelli, Jorge, collaborations, 105
Nouvel Observateur cartoon strips, 105
one-man drag performances, 105
Perrier television commercials, 105
readmission to Argentina (1984), 106
Corazón valiente [Brave Heart] (Gilda album), 158
Correa, Gabriel, 119. *See also* Pista 4
Eva Perón (Copi play), director of 2004 revival (Buenos Aires), 127–28, *129*, 135
Correa, María Antonia Deolinda "Difunta," 4, 13, 138–39, 148–54, 165, 176
  Coluccio, Félix, on, 150
  devotional practices, 149–54
  Difunta Correa Administration, 149
  economic status of followers, 151–54
  Facebook page, 153
  historiography and mythologization, 150–51
  Bustos, Clemente (Baudilio) (husband), 150
  Correa, Pedro (father), 150
  Quiroga, Facundo, 150
  Sarmiento, Domingo F., 150
  Zeballos, Don Pedro Flavio, 150
  pilgrimages, 150–54
  promesantes (followers), 151–53, 162
  Promesantes (Montaño film), 153
  Virgin of Luján, compared to, 149
  visual representations
    estampita [prayer card], 148, *149*

Correa, Pedro (father of Difunta Correa), 150
Cosín, Juan, 38
Costantino, Nicola, 171
Courtés, Joseph, 82
Covington, Julie, 68. *See also Evita* (Lloyd Webber-Rice musical)
Cucurto, Washington, 162–63
Cosa de negros (book), 159
cults and religion, 132–65. *See also* Correa, María Antonia Deolinda "Difunta"; Cumbio (Vivero, Agustina); Fernández de Kirchner, Cristina; Gilda (Bianchi, Miriam Alejandra); Guevara, Nacha; icons; Perón (Duarte), Eva as Santa Evita; Santoro, Daniel; Virgin of Luján
Cumbia, 13, 154, 155–59, 161. *See also* Cumbio (Vivero, Agustina); Gilda (Bianchi, Miriam Alejandra); Giménez, Carlos "Toti"; La Bomba Tucumana; Maravilla, Ricky
  bailantas [dance clubs], 156, 158
  class implications, 158–59
  cultural transformation, 154, 158–59
  definition, 156
  posthumous Gilda tributes, 155
Cumbio (Vivero, Agustina), 162–65, 176
  bisexuality, 163–64
  New York Times profile, 164
  Perón (Duarte), Eva, identification with, 164
  "queni" (do nothing) celebrity, as, 163
  Soi Cumbio (Yannino documentary film), 165
  Yo Cumbio (autobiography), 163–64

Dame aux camélias, La (Dumas *fils*), 32, 46
Damonte Botana, Raúl Natalio. *See* Copi
Davies, Lloyd Hughes, 104
De eso no se habla [I Don't Want to Talk About It] (Bemberg film), 72
de Grandis, Rita, 97
de la Rúa, Fernando, 102, 167
De Luján a Sumampa por el Camino Real [From Luján to Sumampa following the Camino Real] (Lores performance tour), 140, 146–48
de Luque, Paula
  Juan y Eva (film), 9
de San Martín, José, 9
del Brutto, Bibiana Apolonia, 151

Del sol naciente [From the Rising Sun]
(Gambaro play), 42
Silveyra, Soledad "Solita," in, 42
Yusem, Laura, director of, 42
Deleuze, Gilles, 121
Derrida, Jacques, 5, 116
des/Enlace [un/Link] (Viñao play), 12, 105,
111–19, 126, 130
critical response, 112, 118
desaparecidos, theatrical representation
of, 105, 110, 112–19
Dietrich, Silvia, in, 113, 116, 117
dramaturgical description, 112–16
Eva Perón (Copi), compared to, 111, 130
Rod, Jorge, in, 113
Viñao, Mariela, in, 113
Desanzo, Juan Carlos
Eva Perón (film), 12, 64, 83, 93–94
Banegas, Cristina, in, 93
critical assessment, 93–94
Feinmann, José Pablo, screenplay, 93
Goris, Ester, in, 93–94
perceived of as local counterversion to
Parker *Evita* film, 93
Peronism, portrayal of, 83, 93–94
desaparecidos (disappeared persons during
1976–83 dictatorship), 34
children born in captivity, 53
theatrical representations
Cadáveres (Pista 4 performance of
Perlongher poems), 119–23
des/Enlace (Viñao play), 12, 105, 110,
112–19
Oficial primero (Somigliana play), 123
Paso de dos (Pavlovsky play), 123
destino, El [Destiny/Fate] (Planas film), 33
Di Fonzo Bo, Marcial, 127–28, *129*
Bo, Facundo, nephew of, 127
Di Tella Institute (Buenos Aires), 66
Dietrich, Silvia, 113, 116, 117
"Don't Cry for Me Argentina" (*Evita*)
(Lloyd Webber-Rice), 61
analysis of lyrics, 68–69
comparison of English original lyrics
and Spanish version (Azpilicueta,
Artime), 68–69
iconic performances, 68–69
Duarte de Perón, María Eva. *See* Perón
(Duarte), Eva
Duarte, Juan (father of Eva Perón), 79
Duhalde, Eduardo, 167
Dujovne Ortiz, Alicia, 63

Eva Perón. La biografía, 74–76, 78–79,
81–82
Eva Perón: A Biography (translated
Fields), 74–75, 78–79, 81–82
Eva Perón: la madone des sans-chemise
(biography in French), 74–76
Dumas *fils*, Alexandre, 32
Dame aux camelias, La, 32, 46
Dyer, Richard, 6

Echeverría, (José) Esteban
"cautiva, La" [The Captive Girl] (epic
poem), 29
Ediciones Culturales Argentinas, 85
*El amor de la estanciera. See amor de la estan-
ciera, El*
*El amor nunca muere. See Amadori, Luis
César; amor nunca muere, El*
"El cadáver." *See* "cadáver, El"; Perlongher,
Néstor
El destino. See Batlle Planas, Juan; *destino, El*
El Excéntrico de la 18° (Buenos Aires inde-
pendent performance space), 91
"El simulacro." *See* Borges, Jorge Luis;
"simulacro, El"
Elortondo y Palacio, Felipe, 23, 24, 25
Entre el cielo y la tierra [Between Heaven
and Earth] (posthumous Gilda
album), 158
estampita [prayer card], 148, *149*
Eva de América [Eva of America] (Gug-
lielmino play), 12, 64, 83, 85–88, 128,
130
Evita; quien quiera oír que oiga (Mignogna
film), compared to, 88
linear chronology, 86
Misemer, Sarah M., on, 85–86, 87
Perón (Duarte), Eva
razón de mi vida, La (ghost-written
autobiography), 86
relegation to ancillary role, 85–88
spoken recordings, use of, 86
Peronism, portrayal of, 83, 85–88
Rovito, Oscar, on, 87
Eva de la Argentina [Eva of Argentina, or
Argentina's Eva] (Seoane animated
film), 9
Walsh, Rodolfo, use as framing narrator,
9
Eva la fuerza (Costantino installation),
171
Eva la lluvia (Costantino installation), 171

Eva los sueños (Costantino video installation), 171

Eva Perón (Copi play), 9, 12, 105–8, 119, 176
  Aira, César, on, 107
  Correa revival (Buenos Aires, 2004), 127–28, *129*
    Berruti, Rómulo, on, 128
    Cabrera, Hilda, on, 128
  des/Enlace (Viñao play), compared to, 111, 130
  Di Fonzo Bo-Théâtre des Lucioles revival (Buenos Aires, 2004), 126–28, *129*
    Castro, Alfredo, in, 127
  Eva y Victoria (Ottino play), compared to, 106
  original production (1970), *108*
    Bo, Facundo, title role in, 106, 107, *108*
    Buenos Aires iconic images, use of, 107
    Moretti, Michelle, in, 107
    Platé, Roberto, set design, 107
    Rodríguez Arias, Alfredo, director, 106, 108
    violent response, 106
  Plotnik, Viviana Paula, on, 107
  Rosenzvaig, Marcos, on, 106, 108
  "tragic farce," as, 106
  transvestism, use of, 106–8

Eva Perón (Desanzo film), 12, 64, 83, 93–94
  Banegas, Cristina, in, 93
  critical assessment, 93–94
  Feinmann, José Pablo, screenplay, 93
  Goris, Ester, in, 93–94
  perceived of as local counterversion to Parker *Evita* film, 93
  Peronism, portrayal of, 83, 93–94

Eva Perón en la hoguera [Eva Perón on the Bonfire] (Lamborghini poetry staging), 12, 64, 83, 91–92, 171. *See also razón de mi vida, La* (Perón ghost-written autobiography)
  alternative performances and versions, 91
  Banegas, Cristina, in, 91–92
  Eva y Victoria (Ottino play), compared to, 92
  Peronism, portrayal of, 83, 91–92
  razón de mi vida, La (Perón ghost-written autobiography), link to, 64, 83, 91–92
  Scaccheri, Iris, director of, 91

Eva Perón Foundation, 3, 73, 92, 99

Eva Perón. La biografía (Dujovne Ortiz), 74–76, 78–79, 81–82

Eva Perón: A Biography (Dujovne Ortiz, translated from French by Fields), 74–75, 78–79, 81–82

Eva Perón: la madone des sans-chemise (Dujovne Ortiz biography in French), 74–76

Eva y Victoria [Eva and Victoria] (Ottino play), 12, 64, 83, 88–91, 92, 130
  Barney Finn, Oscar, director, 89, 92
  critical success, 89
  differing acting styles of two leads, 90–91
  Eva Perón (Copi play), compared to, 106
  Eva Perón en la hoguera (Lamborghini poetry staging), compared to, 92
  extended national tours, 89
  Giardinelli, Mempo, on, 89
  Peronism, portrayal of, 83, 88–91
  Plotnik, Viviana Paula, on, 90
  reconciliatory gesture at end of play, 89
  revisionist national history, 89–90
  varied publicity campaigns, 91

Eva, el gran musical argentino [Eva, the Great Argentine Musical] (Guevara, Orgambide, Favero), 11, 61–70, *95*
  dramatic structure, 62–63
  Evita (Lloyd Webber-Rice musical), compared to, 62–63
  "No llores por mí, Argentina," insertion into touring production, 68
  original production (1986), 61–62
  Peronism, portrayal of, 63
  restaging (2008), 12, 61
    Fernández de Kirchner, Cristina, attendance at premiere, 96, 166
  "Si yo fuera como ellas" [If I were like (those women) . . .], 68
  transculturative affiliations, 66

Evita (Lloyd Webber-Rice musical), 11, 60–65, 72, 127, 130. *See also* Covington, Julie; "Don't Cry for Me Argentina;" Guevara, Nacha; LuPone, Patti; Lynch, Valeria; Madonna (Ciccone, Madonna Louise); "No llores por mí, Argentina"; Paige, Elaine; Parker, Alan; Prince, Harold; Roger, Elena; San Basilio, Paloma
  absence of professional Argentine production, 61
  British stereotypes surrounding Argentine culture, representative of, 64–65

Evita (*continued*)
Broadway revival (2012), 61, 176
dramatic structure, 62
Eva, el gran musical argentino (Guevara, Orgambide, Favero), compared to, 62–63
first US production (Los Angeles, 1979), 60
Guevara, Ernesto "Che," characterization, 62–63, 69, 137
influence on creation and circulation of recent Evita biographies, 75
London revival (2006), 61
original production (London, 1978), 60
Perón (Duarte), Eva
Guevara, Ernesto "Che," iconographic pairing, in, 62–63, 69
mythologization, 62
portrayal of, 64
Peronism, portrayal of, 62, 63
Spanish-language version (Azipilicueta-Artime)
premiere (Madrid, 1980), 60
Prince-directed staging (Mexico City, 1981), 60
studio concept album (1976), 60, 64, 68
Evita (Navarro biography in Spanish), 74, 75, 80
Evita (Parker film version of Lloyd Webber-Rice musical) (1996), 65, 83, 88, 92–93, 130
critical drubbing, 93
influence on creation and circulation of recent Evita biographies, 74
substitution of Budapest for Buenos Aires venues, 93
"You Must Love Me" (Lloyd Webber-Rice song), 60
Evita Museum, 3
Evita; quien quiera oír que oiga [Evita: listen if you want to] (Mignogna film), 12, 64, 83, 84–85
Eva de América (Guglielmino play), compared to, 88
Garré, Silvina, speaking and singing voice in, 84
Margulis, Paola Judith, on, 84
Nebbia, Lito, songs, 84–85
Palmiero, Flavia, in, 84
Perón (Duarte), Eva, archival footage of acting career, 84
Peronism, portrayal of, 83, 84–85

post-dictatorship premiere (April, 1984), 85
Evita: The Real Life of Eva Perón (Fraser-Navarro biography), 74–75, 77, 81–82
"Evita vive (en cada hotel organizado)" [Evita lives (in every organized hotel)] (Perlongher short story), 109–10, 119
Ezcurra y Arguibel, Encarnación (mother of Manuelita Rosas), 17

Facebook, 1, 13, 138, 164
Correa, Difunta page, 153
Santa Gilda fan pages, 160
Fajardo, Heraclio, 28
Camila O'Gorman (play), 28–29, 30, 31, 43
censorship at premiere, 29
characterizations, 29
Lázaro, character of, 29
Míguez, Graciela, on, 29
Seibel, Beatriz, on, 29
Trigo, Abril, on, 29
Camila O'Gorman (translation of Pélissot novel), 28
Falicov, Tamara, 101
Falklands War. *See* Malvinas/Falklands War
Fanego, Daniel, 55–56
Fanon, Frantz, 130
Favero, Alberto, 61, 66. *See also Eva, el gran musical argentino*
Feinmann, José Pablo, 93
Eva Perón (Desanzo film), screenplay, 93
femicons. *See also* Banegas, Cristina; Brando, Luisina; celebrity; Correa, María Antonia Deolinda "Difunta"; Cumbio (Vivero, Agustina); Fernández de Kirchner, Cristina; Gilda (Bianchi, Miriam Alejandra); Goris, Ester; Guevara, Nacha; icons; Legrand, Mirtha; LuPone, Patti; Madonna (Ciccone, Madonna Louise); mythologization; O'Gorman, Camila; Ocampo, Victoria; Perón (Duarte), Eva; Podestá, Blanca; Roger, Elena; Rosas, María Soledad; Silveyra, Soledad "Solita;" Virgin of Luján; Zorrilla, China
definition, 4–6
devotional and worship practices, 140–65
embodiment of one femicon by another, 33, 41–42, 48, 60–61, 94–96
Banegas, Cristina, as Eva Perón in *Eva*

Perón en la hoguera (Lamborghini poetry staging), 92
Brando, Luisina, as Eva Perón in *Eva y Victoria* (Ottino play), 90–91, 94
Eva Perón portrayals, 64–65, 94–97
Evita (Lloyd Webber-Rice musical), in, 60–61
Goris, Ester, as Eva Perón in *Eva Perón* (Desanzo film), 93–94, 94
Guevara, Nacha, as Eva Perón, 61, 65, 67–70, 94–96, 95
LuPone, Patti, as Eva Perón in *Evita* (Lloyd Webber-Rice musical), 94
Madonna (Ciccone, Madonna Louise), as herself in *Evita* (Parker film version of Lloyd Webber-Rice musical), 94
Moreno, Zully, as Camila O'Gorman, 33
Pecoraro, Susú, as Camila O'Gorman in *Camila* (Bemberg), 48
Podestá, Blanca, as Camila O'Gorman, 33
Roger, Elena, in title role of *Evita*, 61
Silveyra, Soledad "Solita," as Camila O'Gorman-like characters in works of Griselda Gambaro, 41–42
Zorrilla, China, as Victoria Ocampo in *Eva y Victoria* (Ottino play), 90–91, 94
examples, 3–4
Janes, Regina, on, 8
limits of representation, 27–28
pitfalls in portrayals, 94–97
theory, 4–9. *See also* Barthes, Roland; Casey, Michael; Gerassi-Navarro, Nina; Grove Hall, Susan; Hall, Dennis; Janes, Regina; Kemp, Martin; Marshall, P. David; Misemer, Sarah M.; Navarro (Aranguren), Marysa; Peirce, Charles Sanders; Quinn, Michael L.; Rojek, Chris; Rokem, Freddie; Rosano, Susana; Taylor, Julie M.
"Femicons" (Janes essay), 8
Fernández de Kirchner, Cristina, 14, 96–97, 102, 166–71, 174–76, *175*
appearance, critical assessment of, 169
Eva, el gran musical argentino, attendance at opening of 2008 restaging, 96, 166

"Operation Evita," 96–97
Perón (Duarte), Eva
comparison, 169–70, 174–76
identification with, 166
political career, history, 167
provincial Buenos Aires origins, 166, 167
Fevre, Fermín, 18
Fields, Shawn, 63. *See also* Dujovne Ortiz, Alicia
Eva Perón: A Biography (translation from French of Dujovne Ortiz), 74–75, 78–79, 81–82
Finlandia [Finland] (Monti play), 11, 20, 31, 50, 53–55
pasión sudamericana, Una, as radical revision of, 20, 53–54
structure and content, 53–55
Viñao, Mónica, production (2002), 53–55
Flechner, Alejandra, 128, *129*. *See also* Gambas al Ajillo (experimental cabaret group)
Flickr, 2, 5
FM radio theatre, 123–25. *See also Cadáveres*; Pista 4
Forbidden Broadway (parody revue), 94
Foster, David William, 45, 49–50
Foucault, Michel, 65, 69, 73
"Nietzsche, Genealogy, History" (Foucault essay), 65
Franco, Francisco, 99
Frank, Anne, 119
Fraser, Nicholas, 63. *See also* Navarro (Aranguren), Marysa
Evita: The Real Life of Eva Perón (biography, with Navarro), 74–75, 77, 81–82
Frente de Liberación Homosexual (FLH) [Homosexual Liberation Front], 109
"Fuiste" [You Left] (Gilda song), 161

Gaines, Boyd, 94
Galán, Graciela, 40. *See also malasangre, La* (Gambaro play)
Gall, Marsha, 91
Gallo, Mario
Camila O'Gorman (lost silent film), 30
Gallo, Marta, 35–36, 37
Gambaro, Griselda, 43
Del sol naciente [From the Rising Sun] (play), 42
Silveyra, Soledad "Solita," in, 42
Yusem, Laura, director, 42

Gambaro, Griselda (*continued*)
  Información para extranjeros [Information for Foreigners] (play), 34
  malasangre, La [Bad Blood] (play), 11, 20, 31, 34, 38–43
    author's denial of Camila O'Gorman similarities, 40
    Camila (Bemberg film), comparison of father figures, 46
    Galán, Graciela, set designer, 40
    Murúa, Lautaro, in, 41
    Nationalist Movement for Restoration [Movimiento Nacionalista de Restauración], mid-performance disruption by, 38–39
    Puga, Ana Elena, on, 40, 41–42
    Silveyra, Soledad "Solita," in, 41
    Werth, Brenda, on, 41
    Yusem, Laura, director, 39, 41
  Monti, Ricardo, comparison of Camila O'Gorman treatments, 57–58
  Real envido [Royal Gambit] (play), 38
    Cosín, Juan, director of, 38
Gambas al Ajillo (experimental cabaret group), 9, 102. *See also* Flechner, Alejandra
  Gambas gauchas (theatre piece), 9, 98, 128, 131
    Taylor, Diana, on, 98
Gambas gauchas (Gambas al Ajillo theatre piece), 9, 98, 128, 131
Gannon, Michael, 24, 31
  Camila (Bemberg film), characterization in, 46
  Camila O'Gorman (Fajardo play), renaming and characterization in, 29
  Camila O'Gorman (Mendoza Ortiz verse drama), renaming and characterization in, 30
García Márquez, Gabriel, 104
García, Charly, 68. *See also* "No llores por mí, Argentina"
García, Miguel, 24
Gardel, Carlos, 5, 7, 9, 138
Garré, Silvina, 84. *See also Evita; quien quiera oír que oiga* (Mignogna film)
  genealogy, 65–66, 73, 78
    "No llores por mí, Argentina" (Azpilicueta, Artime), transculturative associatons, 68–70
    Foucault, Michel, on, 65, 69, 73
General Confederation of Labor [Confed-

eración General del Trabajo (CGT)], 135, *136*
General San Martín Municipal Theatre (Buenos Aires), 50, 102
Gerassi-Navarro, Nina, 1–2, 6
Germanotta, Stefani. *See* Lady Gaga
ghosting (Carlson), 5, 96
Giardinelli, Mempo, 89
  Eva y Victoria (Ottino play), on, 89
Gilda (Bianchi, Miriam Alejandra), 4, 13, 138–39, 154–62, *163*, 176
  Corazón valiente [Brave Heart] (album), 158
  death, 155
  Entre el cielo y la tierra [Between Heaven and Earth] (posthumous album), 158
  "Fuiste [You Left]" (song), 161
  Internet-based devotion and fandom, 160–62
  Martín, Eloísa, on, 157
  miracles, attributed, 158
  pilgrimages by fans, 155–58, 162
  posthumous commemorations, 155
  posthumous fan worship, 157–62
  Santa Gilda, characterization and depiction as, 13, 138, 154, *156*, 157, 158, 160, 162, 165
  "Se me ha perdido un corazón" [I've Lost a Heart] (song), 160–61
  YouTube uploads, 160–61
Gilda (Rita Hayworth film), 154
Giménez, Carlos "Toti," 155
Gnazzo, Luisa Noemí. *See also* Brando, Luisina
Góngora, Luis de, 122
Goris, Ester, 93–94
  Eva Perón (Desanzo film), as title character, 93–94
  Madonna, comparison of Eva Perón portrayals, 94
Graver, David, 125
Greimas, A.J., 82
Grove Hall, Susan, 6
Guaquil, Juana, 79
Guattari, Félix, 121
Guevara, Ernesto "Che," 1–2
  Che (Soderburgh film), 1
  depoliticization, 2, 6
  Evita (Lloyd Webber-Rice musical), characterization in, 137
  iconic ubiquity, 2

Korda, Alberto, photograph, 4, 7, 174
Perón (Duarte), Eva, iconographic pairing, 2, 5, 171, 174
"piedad, La. Eva Perón devora las entrañas del Che Guevara" (Santoro painting), in, 135, *136*
Evita (Lloyd Webber-Rice musical), in, 62–63, 69
Plaza de la Revolución (Havana), silhouette at, 174
Guevara, Nacha, 61–63, 65, 66–70, 94–97, *95*, 98, 166. *See also Eva, el gran musical argentino*
Anastasia querida [Dear Anastasia] (one-woman play, 1969), 66
death threats and violence against, 67
Di Tella Institute (Buenos Aires), performing milieu, 66
election to congress and aborted political career, 97
Eva, el gran musical argentino [Eva, the Great Argentine Musical] (with Orgambide, Favero), 11, 61–70
dramatic structure, 62–63
"No llores por mí, Argentina," insertion into touring production, 68
original production (1986), 61–62
Peronism, portrayal of, 63
restaging (2008), 12
Fernández de Kirchner, Cristina, attendance at premiere, 96, 166
"Si yo fuera como ellas" [If I were like (those women) . . .], 68
transculturative affiliations, 66
mil y una Nachas, Las [1001 Nachas] (show), 67
Nacha de noche [Nacha by Night] (show, 1968), 66
"No llores por mí, Argentina" performances, 68–69
nueva canción movement, and, 66
reinvention, capacity for, 96
Guglielmino, Osvaldo
Ediciones Culturales Argentinas, director, 85
Eva de América [Eva of America] (play), 12, 64, 83, 85–88, 128, 130
Evita; quien quiera oír que oiga (Mignogna film), compared to, 88
linear chronology, 86
Misemer, Sarah M., on, 85–86, 87
Perón (Duarte), Eva

razón de mi vida, La (ghost-written autobiography), 86
relegation to ancillary role, 85–88
spoken recordings, use of, 86
Peronism, portrayal of, 83, 85–88
Rovito, Oscar, on, 87
Oratorio a la Virgen de Luján, 143–44, 147
undersecretary of culture in Perón 1973 government, 85
Gutiérrez, Uladislao, 11, 16, 23–25, 51. *See also* O'Gorman, Camila
Brandier, Máxime (pseudonym), 23
Camila (Bemberg film), renaming and characterization in, 46, 47, 48–50
Camila O'Gorman (Mendoza Ortiz verse drama), characterization in, 30
denial of iconic status, 25
execution, 16–17

Hadad, María Gisela, 142–43, 147
Hair (Ragni, MacDermott, Rado musical), 61
Hall, Dennis, 6
Hall, Linda B., 144–45, 146
Virgin of Luján, on, 140
Halperín Donghi, Tulio, 78
Hamlet: La guerra de los teatros [The War of the Theatres] (Bartís 1991–92 staging), 101–2
hantise (Derrida), 5, 116
Harvey, David, 102
Hayward, Susan, 6–7
Hayworth, Rita, 154
Herrera, Luis, 119. *See also* Pista 4
Historia de Nuestra Señora de Luján [History of Our Lady of Luján] (Salvaire, 1885), 142

Ibarguren, Juana (mother of Eva Perón), 77, 79
Ibarguren, María Eva (Eva María). *See* Perón (Duarte), Eva
Ibsen, Henrik, 32, 40
icons. *See also* celebrity; femicons; mythologization
contextualization, 5–6
critical engagement, 5
definitions, 5–6
evolution of terminology, 5
historiography and mythologization, 10–14
Misemer, Sarah M., on, 5

icons (*continued*)
religious, 132–65. *See also* Correa, María Antonia Deolinda "Difunta"; Cumbio (Vivero, Agustina); Gilda (Bianchi, Miriam Alejandra); Perón (Duarte), Eva as Santa Evita; Santoro, Daniel; Virgin of Luján surrogates, 5
theory, 1–8, 58. *See also* Barthes, Roland; Carlson, Marvin; Casey, Michael; Derrida, Jacques; Dyer, Richard; Gerassi-Navarro, Nina; Grove Hall, Susan; Hall, Dennis; Hayward, Susan; Janes, Regina; Kemp, Martin; Marshall, P. David; Misemer, Sarah M.; Navarro (Aranguren), Marysa; Peirce, Charles Sanders; Quinn, Michael L.; Roach, Joseph; Rojek, Chris
ubiquity, 1
Información para extranjeros [Information for Foreigners] (Gambaro play), 34
Izquierdo, Mirta, 91

Jaime, José, 146–47
Janes, Regina, 8
Jesus Christ Superstar (Lloyd Webber-Rice musical), 60, 61
Jiang Qing, 75
Johnson, Paul, 52
Juan y Eva (de Luque film), 9
Julianello, María Teresa, 22, 44

Kahlo, Frida, 5, 7, 9
Karush, Matthew B., 10
Kavanagh Building (Buenos Aires), 79
Kemp, Martin, 4–5, 7, 171, 174
King, John, 31, 45, 47
Kirchner, Néstor, 96–97, 102, 167–69
depictions, 171
Kirkpatrick, Gwen, 36
Kogan, Jaime, 9, 13, 132–33, 137
oscuridad de la razón, La (Monti), director of 1993 restaging, 9, 13, 132–33
Kohan, Martín, 162–63
Korda, Alberto, 4, 7, 174. *See also* Guevara, Ernesto "Che"

La Boca (Buenos Aires working-class neighborhood), 2, 5
La Bomba Tucumana (Cumbia singer), 155
"La cautiva." *See* "cautiva, La"

La guerra de los teatros. *See* Bartís, Ricardo; *Hamlet: La guerra de los teatros*
La malasangre. *See* Gambaro, Griselda; *malasangre, La*
La oscuridad de la razón. *See* Monti, Ricardo; *oscuridad de la razón, La*
La pasión según Eva. *See* pasión según Eva, *La*; Posse, Abel
"La piedad. Eva Perón devora las entrañas del Che Guevara." *See* "piedad, La. Eva Perón devora las entrañas del Che Guevara"; Santoro, Daniel
La razón de mi vida. *See* Perón (Duarte), Eva; *razón de mi vida, La*
La Trastienda (Buenos Aires independent performance space), 53
Lady Gaga (Germanotta, Stefani), 3
Lagos-Pope, María Inés, 71, 74, 82–83
Lamborghini, Leónidas
Eva Perón en la hoguera [Eva Perón on the Bonfire] (poetry staging), 12, 64, 83, 91–92, 171
alternative performances and versions, 91
Banegas, Cristina, in, 91–92
Eva y Victoria (Ottino play), compared to, 92
Peronism, portrayal of, 83, 91–92
razón de mi vida, La (Perón ghost-written autobiography), link to, 91–92
Scaccheri, Iris, director of, 91
Partitas (poetry collection), 91
Perón en Caracas (dramatic monologue), 92
Lanusse, Alejandro Agustín, 100
Las mil y una Nachas. *See* Guevara, Nacha; *mil y una Nachas, Las*
Lavelli, Jorge, 105. *See also* Copi (Damonte Botana, Raúl Natalio)
Le Basi. *See* Basi, *Le*; Marinetti, F.T.
Legrand, Mirtha, 163
Les mamelles de Tirésias. *See* Apollinaire, Guillaume; *mamelles de Tirésias, Les*
Lezama Lima, José, 122
Liniers (Buenos Aires working-class neighborhood), 143
Liniers, Viceroy Santiago de, 22–23, 46
Perichon de Vandeuil y D'Abeille, Marie Anne ("Anita") (grandmother of Camila O'Gorman), elopement with, 22

Lloyd Webber, Andrew
  Evita (musical, with Rice), 11, 60–65, 72,
    127, 130. *See also* Covington, Julie;
    "Don't Cry for Me Argentina"; Gue-
    vara, Nacha; LuPone, Patti; Lynch,
    Valeria; Madonna (Ciccone, Ma-
    donna Louise); "No llores por mí,
    Argentina"; Paige, Elaine; Parker,
    Alan; Prince, Harold; Rice, Tim;
    Roger, Elena; San Basilio, Paloma
  absence of professional Argentine
    production, 61
  British stereotypes surrounding
    Argentine culture, representative
    of, 64–65
  Broadway revival (2012), 61, 176
  dramatic structure, 62
  Eva, el gran musical argentino (Guevara,
    Orgambide, Favero), compared
    to, 62–63
  first US production (Los Angeles,
    1979), 60
  Guevara, Ernesto "Che," characteriza-
    tion, 62–63, 69, 137
  influence on creation and circulation
    of recent Evita biographies, 75
  London revival (2006), 61
  original production (London, 1978),
    60
  Parker film version (1996), 65, 74, 83,
    88, 92–93, 130
    "You Must Love Me" (song, with
      Rice), 60
  Perón (Duarte), Eva
    Guevara, Ernesto "Che," icono-
      graphic pairing, in, 62–93, 69
    mythologization, 62
    portrayal of, 64
  Peronism, portrayal of, 62, 63
  Spanish-language version
    (Azipilicueta-Artime)
    premiere (Madrid, 1980), 60
  Prince-directed staging (Mexico
    City, 1981), 60
  studio concept album (1976), 60, 64,
    68
  Jesus Christ Superstar (musical, with
    Rice), 60, 61
  "You Must Love Me" (song for *Evita*
    film, with Rice), 60
López Rega, José, 100
Loredo, María Salomé. *See* Madre María

Lores, María Celeste
  De Luján a Sumampa por el Camino Real
    [From Luján to Sumampa following
    the Camino Real] (performance
    tour), 140, 146–48
Luján, Virgin of. *See* Virgin of Luján
LuPone, Patti, 63, 68, 94, 95, 96. *See also*
  Evita (Lloyd Webber-Rice musical)
  Forbidden Broadway, parodied in, 94
Lynch, Valeria, 61. *See also Evita* (Lloyd
  Webber-Rice musical)

MacWilliams, Mark W., 161
Madonna (Ciccone, Madonna Louise),
  3, 60, 68, 74, 76, 88, 94. *See also Evita*
  (Parker film version of Lloyd Webber-
  Rice musical)
  Goris, Ester, comparison of Eva Perón
    portrayals, 94
  Menem, Carlos Saúl, command audi-
    ence during filming of *Evita* film,
    92–93
  reinvention, capacity for, 96
Madre María (Loredo, María Salomé), 138
Maggi de Magistris, María (pseudonym
  given to corpse of Eva Perón), 100
Main, Mary
  Woman with the Whip, The (Eva Perón
    biography), 64, 74
Maipo Theatre (Buenos Aires), 61
malasangre, La [Bad Blood] (Gambaro
  play), 11, 20, 31, 34, 38–43
  Camila (Bemberg film), comparison of
    father figures, 46
  critical analysis
    Puga, Ana Elena, 40, 41–42
    Werth, Brenda, 41
  Galán, Graciela, set designer, 40
  Murúa, Lautaro, in, 41
  Nationalist Movement for Restoration,
    mid-performance disruption by,
    38–39
  O'Gorman, Camila, resemblances, 41–43
  plot, 39–40
  Silveyra, Soledad "Solita," in, 41
  Yusem, Laura, director of, 39, 41
Malvinas/Falklands War, 39, 42, 68, 169
mamelles de Tirésias, Les (Apollinaire), 37
"Mantel de hule" [Plastic/Oilskin table-
  cloth] (Santoro painting), 137
Maravilla, Ricky, 155, 156–57
Margulis, Paola Judith, 84

Marinetti, F.T.
    Basi, Le [Feet] (theatre piece), 124
Marmo, Alejandro, 169. *See also* Santoro,
    Daniel
    Evita murals on the Health and Social
    Development Ministries Building,
    137, 169–70, *172*, *173*
Mármol, José
    Amalia (novel), 31
Marshall, P. David, 8, 165
Martín, Eloísa, 145, 146, 157
Martínez Cartas de Perón, María Estela. *See*
    Perón, Isabel "Isabelita"
Martínez, Tomás Eloy, 106, 119
    early career, 103
    Novela de Perón, 104
    Santa Evita (novel), 75, 103–4
    New Journalism, as inversion of, 104
Masiello, Francine, 37
Massari, Edoardo "Baleno," 15, 16, 18, 19
Maza, Carlos, 155
Medea (Viñao production, 1992), 111–12
Mendoza Ortiz, L., 30
    Camila O'Gorman (verse drama), 30
    characterizations, 30
    Werth, Brenda, on, 30
Menem, Carlos Saúl, 83, 101–2, 167
    Hamlet: La guerra de los teatros (Bartís
    1991–92 staging), portrayal in, 102
    Madonna, command audience during
    filming of *Evita* film, 92–93
    presidential pardon of military officers,
    105
    Rosas, Juan Manuel de, compared to,
    101
Mercedes (Carnevale short film), 21, 57
Mignogna, Eduardo
    Evita; quien quiera oír que oiga [Evita:
    listen if you want to] (film), 12, 64,
    83, 84–85
    Eva de América (Guglielmino play),
    compared to, 88
    Garré, Silvina, speaking and singing
    voice in, 84
    Margulis, Paola Judith, on, 84
    Nebbia, Lito, songs, 84–85
    Palmiero, Flavia, in, 84
    Perón (Duarte), Eva, archival footage
    of acting career, 84
    Peronism, portrayal of, 83, 84–85
    post-dictatorship premiere (April,
    1984), 85

Míguez, Graciela, 29
mil y una Nachas, Las [1001 Nachas] (Gue-
    vara show), 67
Milutis, Joe, 124–25
Minujín, Marta, 124
Misemer, Sarah M., 5, 7, 9, 85–86, 87, 99
    Eva de América (Guglielmino play), on,
    85–86, 87
Mitchell, W.J.T., 4–5
Molina, Enrique
    sombra donde sueña Camila O'Gorman,
    Una [A Shadow Where Camila
    O'Gorman is Dreaming] (novel),
    11, 20, 31, 34–38
    Camila (Bemberg film), compared
    to, 45
    critical analysis, 34–37
    sexism, critique of, 35–38
    surrealist elements, 34–38
Momia en el clóset [Mummy in the Closet]
    (Ott-Vales musical), 130–31
Mona Lisa (Da Vinci), 4
Monroe, Marilyn, 6, 107
Montaño, Dolores
    Promesantes (film), 153
Monteleone, Jorge, 122
Monti, Ricardo, 44, 50–57, 58, 137
    comparison of Camila O'Gorman treat-
    ments
    Bemberg, María Luisa, 56–57
    Gambaro, Griselda, 57–58
    failure of modernity and modernism,
    concern with, 50, 53
    Finlandia [Finland] (play), 11, 20, 31, 50,
    53–55
    pasión sudamericana, Una, as radical
    revision of, 20, 53–54
    structure and content, 53–54
    Viñao, Mónica, production (2002),
    53–55
    oscuridad de la razón, La [The Obscurity
    of Reason] (play), 9, 13, 132–33
    Perón (Duarte), Eva, portrayal as
    Woman, 132–33
    pasión sudamericana, Una [A South
    American Passion-Play], 11, 20, 31,
    43–44, 50–57
    Alvarado, Ana restaging (Cervantes
    National Theatre, 2005), 50, 55
    Angelelli, Guillermo, in, 55
    Fanego, Daniel, in, 55–56
    Camila, un misterio argentino [Camila,

an Argentine Mystery(-Play)]
(original title), 52
critical assessment, 43, 53
historical critique and artistic revision,
as union of, 50
melodrama and romantic tragedy,
subversion of, 53
Pellettieri, Osvaldo, on, 52
premiere (General San Martín Municipal Theatre, 1989), 43, 50
structure and content, 51–53
theatrical corpus, 56–57
Moori-Koenig, Carlos Eugenio de, 99, 112,
116
Morales, Evo, 168
Moreno, Zully, 33
Moretti, Michelle, 107
Morris, Barbara, 47–48
Movimiento Nacionalista de Restauración
[Nationalist Movement for Restora-
tion], 39
Muñeca Brava [Wild Doll] (Argentine
telenovela), 160–61
Murillo, Bartolomé Esteban, 141
Murphy, Joseph M., 159
Murúa, Lautaro, 41
mythologization, 3, 10–11, 11–13, 57–59, 61.
See also celebrity; femicons; icons
Barthes, Roland, on, 6–7
Casey, Michael, on, 7
celebrity and, 4, 6
depoliticizing power, 6
gender and, 8, 19
O'Gorman, Camila, 34–50
Perón (Duarte), Eva in portrayals of,
64–65
Hayward, Susan, on, 6–7
historiography and, 18, 20, 27–28, 53,
56, 72
Navarro (Aranguren), Marysa, on, 7
religious iconography
Correa, María Antonia Deolinda
"Difunta," 148–54
Gilda (Bianchi, Miriam Alejandra) as
Santa Gilda, 154, 156, 157–60, 162
Perón (Duarte), Eva, as Santa Evita,
132–38
Virgin of Luján, 140–48
transnational, 9, 10, 14

Nacha de noche [Nacha by Night] (Guevara
show, 1968), 66

Nación, La (newspaper), 39
National University (Tandil), 127
National University of Buenos Aires, 3
Nationalist Movement for Restoration
[Movimiento Nacionalista de Restau-
ración], 39
Navarro (Aranguren), Marysa, 7, 63, 74–76
Evita (biography in Spanish), 74, 75, 80
Evita: The Real Life of Eva Perón (biogra-
phy, with Fraser), 74–75, 77, 81–82
Nebbia, Lito, 84–85. *See also Evita; quien
quiera oír que oiga* (Mignogna film)
Nietzsche, Friedrich, 65
"Nietzsche, Genealogy, History" (Foucault
essay), 65
"No es mi despedida" [It's Not My Fare-
well] (Gilda song), 155
"No llores por mí, Argentina" (Azpilicueta,
Artime) [Spanish version of "Don't
Cry for Me Argentina" (*Evita*) (Lloyd
Webber-Rice)], 61, 127
Guevara, Nacha, performances, 68–70
insertion into *Eva, el gran musical argen-
tino* touring production, 68
Spanish and original English lyrics,
comparison, 68–69
transculturative associations, 68–70
Nouvel Observateur (news magazine), 105
Novela de Perón (Martínez), 104
Nuestra Señora de Luján. *See* Virgin of
Luján

O'Gorman, Adolfo (father of Camila
O'Gorman), 21, 24, 25, 31
Camila (Bemberg film), characterization
in, 46
Rosas, Juan Manuel de, supporter of, 23
O'Gorman, Camila, 4, 10, 11, 15–59, 101,
138, 176
ancestry, heritage and upbringing, 21–23
Julianello, María Teresa, on, 22
cinematic representations. *See amor
nunca muere, El* (Amadori); *Camila*
(Bemberg); *Camila O'Gorman*
(Gallo); *destino, El* (Battle Planas);
Mercedes (Carnevale)
Dessau, Valentina (pseudonym), 23
historiography, 10–11, 11, 16, 20, 21–28
Ascasubi, Hilario, 28
Bilbao, Miguel, 26
Castellanos, Félix, 26
Elortondo y Palacios, Felipe, 23, 24

O'Gorman, Camila (*continued*)
    Gannon, Michael, 24
    García, Miguel, 24
    Gutiérrez, Uladislao, 11, 16–17, 23–25,
       51
    pregnancy, purported, 16, 29, 31, 38,
       42, 57
    Reyes, Antonino, 25, 26
    Rivas, Pascual Alejandro, 26
    Rosas, Juan Manuel de, 11, 16–17
    Rosas y Ezcurra, Manuela Robustiana
       Ortiz de ("Manuelita"), 17–19
    Velarde, Manuel, 24
    Verazzi, Baldasarre (Baltasar), 26
    Virasoro, Benjamín, 24
    icon status, 19, 58–59
    literary representations, 11. *See also som-
       bra donde sueña Camila O'Gorman,
       Una* (Molina); *Camila O'Gorman*
       (Péllisot, translated Fajardo)
    malasangre, La (Gambaro play), historio-
       graphic resemblances, 41–43
    Perón (Duarte), Eva, mythologization
       comparison, 43, 59, 61
    pre-figurative celebrity, as, 58–59
    theatrical representations. *See Camila*
       (Pérez Pardella musical); *Camila*
       O'Gorman: poema dramático en cinco
       actos, un epílogo y en verso (Ballerini,
       Rossi); *Camila O'Gorman* (Fajardo);
       Camila O'Gorman (Mendoza Ortiz);
       Camila O'Gorman: una tragedia
       argentina (Olivera); *Del sol naciente*
       (Gambaro); *Finlandia* (Monti);
       malasangre, La (Gambaro); *pasión*
       sudamericana, Una (Monti)
    visual representations
       "Baptism of Camila O'Gorman's
          Unborn Child Before Going to
          Punishment" (Verazzi charcoal),
          26
       daguerreotype, purported, 21, 22
       Ximénez y Pinto, Joaquina (mother),
          21
O'Gorman, Eduardo (brother of Camila
    O'Gorman), 23
O'Gorman, Michael (ancestor of Camila
    O'Gorman), 22
O'Gorman, Thomas (grandfather of Ca-
    mila O'Gorman), 21–22
Ocampo, Orlando, 34, 35
Ocampo, Victoria, 12, 64, 83, 88–91

Eva y Victoria (Ottino play), portrayal
    in, 88–91
"Victoria Ocampo observa la vuelta del
    malón" [Victoria Ocampo Observes
    the Indian Raid's Return] (Santoro
    painting), 135
Odeón Theatre (Buenos Aires), 38
Oficial primero [Official Number One]
    (Somigliana play), 123
okupa movement, 15–16, 18
Olimpia Theatre (Buenos Aires), 39
Olivera, Miguel Alfredo
    Camila O'Gorman: una tragedia argentina
       [Camila O'Gorman: an Argentine
       tragedy] (play), 33
Oratorio a la Virgen de Luján (Guglielmino),
    143–44, 147
Orgambide, Pedro, 61, 68. *See also Eva, el*
    gran musical argentino
oscuridad de la razón, La [The Obscurity of
    Reason] (Monti play), 9, 13, 132–33.
    See also Kogan, Jaime
Ott, Gustavo
    Momia en el clóset [Mummy in the Closet]
       (musical, with Vales), 130–31
Ottino, Mónica
    Eva y Victoria [Eva and Victoria] (play),
       12, 64, 83, 88–91, 92, 130
    Barney Finn, Oscar, director of, 89, 92
    critical success, 89
    differing acting styles of two leads,
       90–91
    Eva Perón (Copi play), compared to,
       106
    Eva Perón en la hoguera (Lamborghini
       poetry staging), compared to, 92
    extended national tours, 89
    Giardinelli, Mempo, on, 89
    Peronism, portrayal of, 83, 88–91
    Plotnik, Viviana Paula, on, 90
    reconciliatory gesture at end of play,
       89
    revisionist national history, 89–90
    varied publicity campaigns, 91
Our Lady of Luján. *See* Virgin of Luján

Paige, Elaine, 68. *See also Evita* (Lloyd
    Webber-Rice musical)
Palermo (Buenos Aires neighborhood),
    159
Palmiero, Flavia, 84. *See also Evita; quien*
    quiera oír que oiga (Mignogna film)

Paper Tangos (Taylor memoir-cultural
  reflection), 3
Parker, Alan
  Evita (film version of Lloyd Webber-Rice
    musical) (1996), 74, 83, 88, 92–93,
    130
  Buenos Aires premiere, 65
  critical drubbing, 93
  influence on creation and circulation
    of recent Evita biographies, 74
  substitution of Budapest for Buenos
    Aires venues, 93
  "You Must Love Me" (Lloyd Webber-
    Rice song), 60
pasión según Eva, La [The Passion according to Eva] (Posse novel), 70
pasión sudamericana, Una [A South American Passion-Play] (Monti), 11, 20, 31,
  43–44, 50–56
  Alvarado, Ana, restaging (Cervantes
    National Theatre, 2005), 50, 55
  Angelelli, Guillermo, in, 55
  Fanego, Daniel, in, 55–56
  Camila, un misterio argentino [Camila, an
    Argentine Mystery(-Play)] (original
    title), 52
  critical assessment, 43, 53
  historical critique and artistic revision,
    as union of, 50
  María Guerrero award winner, 43
  melodrama and romantic tragedy, sub-
    version of, 53
  Pellettieri, Osvaldo, on, 52
  premiere (General San Martín Munici-
    pal Theatre, 1989), 43, 50
  structure and content, 51–53
Paso de dos [Pas de deux] (Pavlovsky play),
  123
Pavlovsky, Eduardo, 44
  Paso de dos [Pas de deux] (play), 123
Pecoraro, Susú, 48
Peirce, Charles Sanders, 8
Pelissero, Silvano, 15
Pellettieri, Osvaldo, 52
Péllisot, Felisberto
  Camila O'Gorman (novel), 28
Pérez Pardella, Agustín, 33–34
Perichon de Vandeuil y D'Abeille, Marie
  Anne ("Anita") (grandmother of
  Camila O'Gorman), 21–23, 25
  Camila (Bemberg film), characterization
    in, 45–46, 48

Periférico de Objetos (object-theatre
  troupe), 55
Perlongher, Néstor, 12, 105, 108–10, 119–22.
  See also Cadáveres; Pista 4
  Amícola, José on, 109
  Austria-Hungría (poetry collection),
    119–20
  Bollig, Ben, on, 109
  "cadáver, El" [The Cadaver/Corpse]
    (poem), 120
  "Cadáveres" [Corpses] (poem), 120, 122
  Cadáveres [Corpses] (Pista 4 perfor-
    mance of Perlongher poems), use
    of work in, 119–21
  emigration to São Paulo, 120
  "Evita vive (en cada hotel organizado)"
    [Evita lives (in every organized
    hotel)] (short story), 109–10, 119
  Frente de Liberación Homosexual
    (FLH) [Homosexual Liberation
    Front] membership, 109
  Monteleone, Jorge, on, 122
  Peronism, artistic response to, 109
  "Por qué seremos tan hermosas" [Why
    must we be so beautiful] (poem),
    124
  transvestism, use of, 108–10
Perón (Duarte), Eva, 1, 60–138, 166–77
  biographies. *See also Eva Perón. La
    biografía* (Dujovne Ortiz); *Eva Perón:
    A Biography* (Dujovne Ortiz, trans.
    Fields); *Eva Perón: la madone des
    sans-chemise* (Dujovne Ortiz); *Evita*
    (Navarro); *Evita: The Real Life of Eva
    Perón* (Fraser, Navarro); Halperín
    Donghi, Tulio; *razón de mi vida,
    La* (ghost-written autobiography);
    Savigliano, Marta; *Woman with the
    Whip, The* (Main)
  analysis, 71–83
  official website, on, 71–73
  cinematic representations. *See Eva de la
    Argentina* (Seoane); *Eva Perón* (De-
    sanzo); *Evita* (Parker); *Evita; quien
    quiera oír que oiga* (Mignogna); *Juan
    y Eva* (de Luque)
  corpse, 98–131
    historical displacement, 99–101
    preservation by means of paraffin, 99
    pseudonymous burial in Milan, 100
  cultural studies
    Chamosa, Oscar, 10

Perón (Duarte), Eva (*continued*)
  Karush, Matthew B., 10
  Rosano, Susana, 9
  depoliticization, 2
  Eva Perón Foundation, 3, 73, 92, 99
  Evita Museum, 3
  Fernández de Kirchner, Cristina, compared to, 166, 169–70, 174–76
  Guevara, Ernesto "Che," iconographic pairing, 2, 5, 171, 174
    Evita (Lloyd Webber-Rice musical), in, 62–63, 69
    "piedad, La. Eva Perón devora las entrañas del Che Guevara" (Santoro painting), in, 135–37, *136*
  historiography and mythologization, 3, 71–83
  iconic ubiquity, 2–3
  literary representations. *See Austria-Hungría* (Perlongher); *Cadáveres* (Perlongher); *Eva Perón en la hoguera* (Lamborghini); "Evita vive (en cada hotel organizado)" (Perlongher); *Novela de Perón* (Martínez); *pasión según Eva, La* (Posse); *Santa Evita* (Martínez); "simulacro, El" (Borges)
  musical theater representations. *See Eva, el gran musical argentino* (Guevara, Orgambide, Favero); *Evita* (Lloyd Webber, Rice); *Momia en el clóset* (Ott-Vales)
  names and designations, 70–71
  O'Gorman, Camila, mythologization comparison, 43, 59, 61
  politics of personal identification, 3
  razón de mi vida, La [My Mission in Life] (ghost-written autobiography), 12, 63, 64, 83, 88, 95, 135, 171, 174
    Eva de América (Guglielmino play), use in, 86
    Eva Perón en la hoguera (Lamborghini poetry staging), link to, 64, 83, 91–92
  Santa Evita, as, 10, 13, 27, 64, 106, 131, 132–38, 165
    "Altarcito" (Santoro), *134*
    Santoro, Daniel, in work of, 133–37
  theatrical representations. *See Cadáveres* (Pista 4, Perlongher); *des/Enlace* (Viñao); *Eva de América* (Guglielmino); *Eva Perón* (Copi); *Eva*

Perón en la hoguera (Lamborghini staged poetry reading); *Eva y Victoria* (Ottino); *Gambas gauchas* (Gambas al Ajillo); *Hamlet: La guerra de los teatros* (Bartís); *oscuridad de la razón, La* (Monti)
  transvestism, use of in portrayals of, 105–10
  visual representations, 2, 95, *134*, *136*, 169–71, *172*, *173*, 174–75, *175. See also* Costantino, Nicola; Marmo, Alejandro; Santoro, Daniel
  archival footage of acting career in *Evita; quien quiera oír que oiga* [Evita: listen if you want to] (Mignogna film), 84
  Ayrinhac, Numa, portrait, 95, 170
  Brazilian line of "woman warrior"-inspired nail polish, 104
  Buenos Aires public iconography, 170–71
  Health and Social Development Ministries Building murals, 169–70, *172*, *173*
  hundred-peso bill, on, 171
  postage stamps, 103
  Venice Biennale (2013), at, 171
Perón, Isabel "Isabelita," 100, 101
  Hamlet: La guerra de los teatros (Bartís 1991–92 staging), portrayal in, 102
Perón, Juan, 2, 62, 73, 77, 79, 99–102
  Eva, el gran musical argentino, near-absence in, 63
  Hamlet: La guerra de los teatros (Bartís 1991–92 staging), portrayal in, 102
Perón en Caracas (Lamborghini dramatic monologue), 92
Peronism, 10
  cultural history, 10
  Eva de América (Guglielmino play), portrayal of, 83
  Eva Perón (Desanzo film), portrayal of, 83, 93–94
  Eva Perón en la hoguera (Lamborghini poetry staging), portrayal of, 83, 91–92
  Eva y Victoria (Ottino play), portrayal of, 83, 88–91
  Eva, el gran musical argentino (Guevara, Orgambide, Favero), portrayal of, 63

Evita (Lloyd Webber-Rice musical),
portrayal of, 63
Evita; quien quiera oír que oiga (Mignogna
film), portrayal of, 83
gender performativity and, 2, 12
Perlongher, Néstor, artistic response to,
109
Santoro, Daniel, devotional portraiture,
13
"piedad, La. Eva Perón devora las entrañas
del Che Guevara" [Pietà: Eva Perón
devours Che Guevara's entrails] (Santoro painting), 135–37, *136*
Pista 4. *See also* Correa, Gabriel; Herrera,
Luis; Ziembroski, Luis
Cadáveres [Corpses] (performance of
Perlongher poems), 9, 12, 105, 119–
26, 130
Basi, Le (Marinetti theatre piece),
referenced, 124
desaparecidos, theatrical representation
of, 119–23
sound design, 119–21
Platé, Roberto, 107, *108*
Plaza de la Revolución (Havana), 174
Plotnik, Viviana Paula, 90, 107
Eva Perón (Copi play), on, 107
Eva y Victoria (Ottino play), on, 90
Podestá, Blanca, 30–31, 33
"Por qué seremos tan hermosas" [Why
must we be so beautiful] (Perlongher
poem), 124
Posse, Abel
pasión según Eva, La [The Passion according to Eva] (novel), 70
Presas, Juan Antonio, 144
Primera plana (Buenos Aires cultural maga-
zine), 66
Prince, Harold, 137
Evita (Lloyd Webber-Rice musical)
first US production (Los Angeles,
1979), 60
original production (London, 1978),
60
production of Spanish-language version (Mexico City, 1981), 60
Prince, Michael, 32
promesantes (followers of Difunta Correa),
151–54, 162
Promesantes (Montaño film), 153
Pueyrredón, Prilidiano, 18
Rosas y Ezcurra, Manuela Robustiana

Ortiz de ("Manuelita"), official
portrait, 18
Fevre, Fermín, on, 18
Puga, Ana Elena, 40, 41–42
malasangre, La (Gambaro play), on,
41–42

Quattrochi-Woisson, Diana, 44
Quinn, Michael L., 6
Quiroga, Facundo, 150

Rabinow, Paul, 69
razón de mi vida, La [My Mission in Life]
(Perón ghost-written autobiography),
12, 63, 83, 88, 95, 135, 171, 174
Eva de América (Guglielmino play)
use of Perón's own recording in, 86
Eva Perón en la hoguera (Lamborghini
poetry staging), link to, 64, 83,
91–92
Real envido [Royal Gambit] (Gambaro
play), 38
Cosín, Juan, director of, 38
Recoleta Cemetery (Buenos Aires), 3,
100
Recoleta Cultural Center (Buenos Aires),
91
Reyes, Antonino, 25, 26
Rice, Tim
Evita (musical, with Lloyd Webber),
11, 60–65, 72, 127, 130, Covington,
Julie; "Don't Cry for Me Argentina";
Guevara, Nacha; Lloyd Webber, An-
drew; LuPone, Patti; Lynch, Valeria;
Madonna (Ciccone, Madonna Lou-
ise); "No llores por mí, Argentina";
Paige, Elaine; Parker, Alan; Prince,
Harold; Roger, Elena; San Basilio,
Paloma
absence of professional Argentine
production, 61
BBC radio program as initial inspira-
tion, 60
British stereotypes surrounding
Argentine culture, representative
of, 64–65
Broadway revival (2012), 61, 176
Buenos Aires research trips, 60
dramatic structure, 62
Eva, el gran musical argentino (Guevara,
Orgambide, Favero), compared
to, 62–63

Rice, Tim (*continued*)
   first US production (Los Angeles, 1979), 60
   Guevara, Ernesto "Che," characterization, 62–63, 69, 64, 137
   influence on creation and circulation of recent Evita biographies, 75
   London revival (2006), 61
   original production (London, 1978), 60
   Parker film version (1996), 65, 74, 83, 88, 92–93, 130
      "You Must Love Me" (song, with Rice), 60
   Perón (Duarte), Eva
      Guevara, Ernesto "Che," iconographic pairing, in, 62–93, 69
      mythologization, 62
      portrayal of, 64
   Peronism, portrayal of, 62, 63
   Spanish-language version (Azipilicueta-Artime)
      premiere (Madrid, 1980), 60
      Prince-directed staging (Mexico City, 1981), 60
      studio concept album (1976), 60, 64, 68
Jesus Christ Superstar (musical, with Lloyd Webber), 60, 61
"You Must Love Me" (song for *Evita* film (1996), with Lloyd Webber), 60
Rivas, Pascual Alejandro, 26
Roach, Joseph, 4, 5, 7–8
Rod, Jorge, 113
Rodríguez Arias, Alfredo, 106, 107, 108
   Eva Perón (Copi play), director of original production (1970), 106, 107, 108
Rodríguez, Martín, 28–29
Roger, Elena, 61, 63, 97. *See also Evita* (Lloyd Webber-Rice musical)
Rojek, Chris, 6, 7, 58
Rokem, Freddie, 4
Rosano, Susana, 9
Rosas, Fénix, 17
Rosas, Juan Manuel de, 11, 16–19, 23
   account of Camila O'Gorman affair, 24
   Camila O'Gorman (Fajardo play), characterization in, 29
   lineage, 17
   malasangre, La [Bad Blood] (Gambaro play), characterization in, 39
   Menem, Carlos Saúl, compared to, 101

O'Gorman, Camila, execution order, 16–17
political motivation for Camila O'Gorman execution, 25
restorer of laws, as, 39
Rosas, María Soledad, direct ancestor of, 16–17
Rosas, María Soledad, 15–16, 18–19, 42, 58
   historiography, 18
   iconic photograph, 15, 18, 19
   suitability as icon, 18
Rosas, Juan Manuel de, direct descendant of, 16–17
Rosas, Pascual, 17
Rosas y Ezcurra, Juan de, 17
Rosas y Ezcurra, Manuela Robustiana Ortiz de ("Manuelita"), 17–20, 31, 42, 58
   Camila O'Gorman (Fajardo play), characterization in, 29
   Camila O'Gorman (Mendoza Ortiz verse drama), characterization in, 30
   eventual marriage, 17
   O'Gorman, Camila, friendship with, 18, 23, 25, 29, 31
   official portrait (1851), 17–18, 40
   Rosas, Juan Manuel de, influence over, 17–18, 29, 30, 31
   Saénz Quesada, María, on, 18–19
   Terrero, Máximo (fiancé and eventual husband), 17
Rosenzvaig, Marcos, 106, 108
Rossi, Eduardo R., 31
   Camila O'Gorman: poema dramático en cinco actos, un epílogo y en verso [Camila O'Gorman: dramatic poem in five acts, an epilogue, and in verse] (w/Ballerini), 30–31
Rovito, Oscar, 87
   Eva de América (Guglielmino play), on, 87
Running, Thorpe, 35–36

Saccomanno, Guillermo, 136
Saénz Quesada, María, 18–19
sainete criollo (popular musical spectacles), 66
Salvaire, Jorge María
   Historia de Nuestra Señora de Luján [History of Our Lady of Luján] (1885), 142
San Basilio, Paloma, 60. *See also Evita* (Lloyd Webber-Rice musical)

San Cayetano (patron saint of work and prosperity), 143, 147
San Cristóbal (Buenos Aires neighborhood), 163
San José Church (Buenos Aires), 164
Santa Evita (Martínez novel), 75, 103–4, 106
New Journalism, as inversion of, 104
Santoro, Daniel, 13, 133–37, 170, 171, 174.
  See also Marmo, Alejandro
  "Altarcito," *134*, 135
  Evita murals on the Health and Social Development Ministries Building, 137, 169–70, *172*, *173*
  "Mantel de hule" [Plastic/Oilskin tablecloth] (painting), 137
  "piedad, La. Eva Perón devora las entrañas del Che Guevara" [Pietà: Eva Perón devours Che Guevara's entrails] (painting), 135–37, *136*
  "Victoria Ocampo observa la vuelta del malón" [Victoria Ocampo Observes the Indian Raid's Return] (painting), 135
Sarmiento, Domingo F., 23, 150
Savigliano, Marta, 78
Scaccheri, Iris, 91, 92
  Eva Perón en la hoguera (Lamborghini poetry staging), director, 91
Schumann, Peter, 49
Schwartz, Margaret, 103
Scioli, Daniel, 96–97
Seibel, Beatriz, 9, 29
Selena, 5, 7, 9, 107–8
"Se me ha perdido un corazón" [I've Lost a Heart] (Gilda song), 160–61
Seoane, María
  Eva de la Argentina [Eva of Argentina, or Argentina's Eva] (animated film), 9
Servicio de Informaciones del Ejército (SIE) [Army Information Services], 99, 100
SIE. *See* Servicio de Informaciones del Ejército
Sierra, Francisco "Pancho," 138
"Si yo fuera como ellas" [If I were like (those women) . . .] (*Eva, el gran musical argentino*) (Guevara, Orgambide, Favero), 68
Silveyra, Soledad "Solita," 41, 42
Simpsons, The, 3

"simulacro, El" [The Simulacrum] (Borges short story), 103
  Schwartz, Margaret, on, 103
Sinfonía inconclusa [Unfinished Rhapsody] (Costantino installation), 171
Soderbergh, Steven
  Che (film), 1
Soi Cumbio (Yannino documentary film), 165
sombra donde sueña Camila O'Gorman, Una [A Shadow Where Camila O'Gorman is Dreaming] (Molina novel), 11, 20, 31, 34–38
  Camila (Bemberg film), compared to, 45
  critical analysis
    Gallo, Marta, 35–36, 37
    Kirkpatrick, Gwen, 36
    Masiello, Francine, 37
    Ocampo, Orlando, 34, 35
    Running, Thorpe, 35–36
    Vitor Bueno, Fernanda, 34, 36, 37
    Vogelius, Federico, 35
  sexism, critique of, 35–38
  surrealist elements, 34–38
Somigliana, Carlos
  Oficial primero [Official Number One] (play), 123
Stanislavski Method, 111
Stantic, Lita, 45
Stars (Dyer), 6
Sur (literary journal), 88
"surrogate," embodied and replaced (Roach), 5
Suzuki Tadashi, 54, 111–12, 117

Taylor, Diana, 37, 98, 100
Taylor, Julie M., 64
  Paper Tangos (memoir-cultural reflection), 3
Terrero, Máximo (fiancé and eventual husband of Manuelita Rosas), 17
"Theses on the Philosophy of History" (Benjamin essay), 73
Thompson, Currie K., 47
Tintas Frescas [Fresh Tints] (theatre festival, Buenos Aires, 2004), 127
To Have Done with the Judgment of God (Artaud radio play), 125
Todosjuntos (Buenos Aires performance group), 91

transculturalism
  affiliations
    Eva, el gran musical argentino (Guevara,
      Orgambide, Favero), 66
    "No llores por mí, Argentina" (Azpili-
      cueta, Artime), 68–69
  theory, 65, 73
transvestism, 105–10
Trigo, Abril, 29
Twitter, 1

Una pasión sudamericana. See Monti, Ri-
  cardo; *pasión sudamericana, Una*
Una sombra donde sueña Camila O'Gorman.
  See Molina, Enrique; *sombra donde*
  sueña Camila O'Gorman, Una
Unión Feminista Argentina [Argentine
  Feminist Union], 44

Vales, Mariano
  Momia en el clóset [Mummy in the Closet]
    (musical, with Ott), 130–31
Velarde, Manuel, 24
Venturiello, María Pía, 142–43, 147
Verazzi, Baldasarre (Baltasar), 26
  "Baptism of Camila O'Gorman's Un-
    born Child Before Going to Punish-
    ment" (charcoal), 26
"Victoria Ocampo observa la vuelta del
  malón" [Victoria Ocampo Observes
  the Indian Raid's Return] (Santoro
  painting), 135
Villa Devoto (middle-class Buenos Aires
  neighborhood), 154
Villarán, Ricardo, 31
Viñao, Mariela, 113
Viñao, Mónica, 53–55
  des/Enlace [un/Link] (play), 12, 105,
    111–19, 126, 130
  critical response, 112, 118
  desaparecidos, theatrical representation
    of, 105, 110, 112–19
  Dietrich, Silvia, in, 113, 116, 117
  dramaturgical description, 112–16
  Eva Perón (Copi play), compared to,
    111, 130
  Rod, Jorge, in, 113
  Viñao, Mariela, in, 113
  Medea (1992 production), 111–12
  Suzuki Tadashi, influence of, 111–12
Virasoro, Benjamín, 24
Virgin of Copacabana, 144

Virgin of Guadalupe, 144
Virgin of Luján, 4, 138–48, *141*
  appearance, 141–42
  artistic representations
    De Luján a Sumampa por el Camino Real
      (Lores performance tour), 140,
      146–48
    Oratorio a la Virgen de Luján (Gug-
      lielmino), 143–44, 147
  canonization, 142, 145
  class politics, implications, 145–48
  conservative Catholicism and, 145–46
  Correa, María Antonia Deolinda "Di-
    funta" compared to, 149
  foundational myth, 140–41
  Gilda and, 158
  Hadad, María Gisela, on, 142–43
  Hall, Linda B., on, 140–41
  historiography and mythologization,
    140–45
    Faría(s) de Sáa, Antonio, 140, 143
    Historia de Nuestra Señora de Luján
      (Salvaire) (1885), 142
    Juan, Andrea, 140, 143–44
    legend, 142–44
    Manuel (African slave), caretaker of
      icon, 144–45
    Matos, Ana de, 144
    Oramas, Rosendo de, 140–41, *141*,
      144
  Martín, Eloísa, on, 145, 146
  Mexican counterparts, 144
  patroness of Argentina, as, 13, 138, 145,
    146
  pilgrimages, 142–43, 146–48, 149–50
  Presas, Juan Antonio, on, 144
  racial politics, 143–45
  right-wing nationalism, associations with,
    146–47
  San Cayetano [Cajetan], patron saint of
    work and prosperity, linked pilgrim-
    ages, 143, 147
  Venturiello, María Pía, on, 142–43
Vitor Bueno, Fernanda, 34, 36, 37
Vivero, Agustina. *See* Cumbio
Vogelius, Federico, 35

Wallace, Jennifer, 32
Walsh, Rodolfo, 9. *See also Eva de la Argen-*
  tina (Seoane animated film)
Wayne, John, 6
Weiss, Allen, 124–25

Werth, Brenda, 30, 39
malasangre, La (Gambaro play), on, 41
White, Hayden, 27, 31–32
historiography, caveats on, 27
Whitehead, Gregory, 124
Williams, Bruce, 50, 56
Woman with the Whip, The (Perón biography, Main), 64, 74

Ximénez y Pinto, Joaquina (mother of Camila O'Gorman), 21

Yannino, Andrea
Soi Cumbio (documentary film), 165
Yeni, Felisa, 132–33
oscuridad de la razón, La (Monti), as Eva-Perón-like figure, 132–33
Yiddish Folk Theatre (Buenos Aires), 132
Yo Cumbio (Cumbio autobiography), 163–64

Yoma, Zulema
Hamlet: La guerra de los teatros (Bartís 1991–92 staging), portrayal in, 102
Yorùbá religion, 159
"You Must Love Me" (Lloyd Webber-Rice song for *Evita* film (1996)), 60
YouTube, 13, 138, 176
Gilda-related uploads, 160–61, 162
Yusem, Laura, 39, 41, 42

Zeballos, Don Pedro Flavio, 150
Ziembroski, Luis, 119, 121. *See also* Pista 4
Cadáveres (Pista 4 performance of Perlongher poems), on, 121
Zorrilla, China, 21, 90–91, 94
Eva y Victoria (Ottino play), as Victoria Ocampo in, 90—91, 94
Mercedes (Carnevale short film), in, 21
Zurbarán, Francisco de, 141